Scotching the Myths

AN ALTERNATIVE ROUTE MAP
TO SCOTTISH HISTORY

Jim Hewitson

MAINSTREAM
PUBLISHING

EDINBURGH AND LONDON

First published in Great Britain in 1995 by
MAINSTREAM PUBLISHING COMPANY (EDINBURGH) LTD
7 Albany Street
Edinburgh EH1 3UG

ISBN 1 85158 701 2

A catalogue record for this book is available from the British Library

Typeset in Times New Roman by Vector Graphics Limited, Newcastle
upon Tyne
Printed and bound in Great Britain by BPC Wheatons

CONTENTS WEEK BY WEEK

	ACKNOWLEDGMENTS	7
	INTRODUCTION	8
1	BEWARE THE HAIR OF THE DOG!	9
2	WE WERE THE PEOPLE	14
3	MAKING A SAUSAGE OUT OF THE BUTCHER	20
4	STRUT THAT FUNKY SALMON	25
5	SIEGE MENTALITY AT STIRLING	30
6	NEXT STOP, NEWFOUNDLAND	35
7	SKULL-SKITING FOR BEGINNERS	40
8	SATURDAY MORNING HEEBIE-JEEBIES	45
9	SCOTS JOIN THE BIG, BAD LEAGUE	51
10	EMILY'S RIOTOUS EVENING	56
11	THE PIEDMONTESE PLUCKER	62
12	AN EYE FOR THE LASSIES	67
13	RAGGLE-TAGGLE TARTAN ARMY?	72
14	VISIT FROM A LEGENDARY CUDDY	77
15	ROCK ISLAND REBELS, YA BASS!	82
16	LADY HAMILTON'S MOLTEN EMBRACE	87
17	A LION AWAITING HIS LONDON ALLOWANCE	92
18	ATHOLE'S FAIRYTALE CASTLE	98
19	WHAT A PICTURE, WHAT A PHOTOGRAPH!	104
20	BUNNETS OFF FOR A CANTANKEROUS DUKE	109
21	FROGMARCHED INTO A CONTROVERSY	114
22	PAPAL LEGATE AMONGST THE BARK-EATERS	119
23	LOCUSTS OFF THE BEATEN TRACK	124
24	DRAWING THE BORDERLINE	130
25	BANNOCKBURN – AN ECONOMIC MIRACLE	136
26	THE MERRY DANCERS, OR WHAT?	141
27	WHEN GLASGOW'S BLUBBERING HAD TO STOP	147
28	GOWF – A ROMAN IMPORT?	152
29	WHO THREW THE PRAYER STOOL?	158
30	THE PIED PIPER OF HAMILTON	164

31	OLD FEARS EXORCISED, ANY WITCH WAY	169
32	HAUNTING OF A HAPLESS KING	174
33	KEEPING HIS HEAD IN THE CLOUDS	180
34	RAINING ON VICTORIA'S PARADE	185
35	FLIGHT OF FANCY TO A DUNG HEAP	191
36	AMBASSADORS ON THE MENU?	197
37	SOLVING THE RIDDLE OF THE LILY	203
38	THE DARK SHADOW OF HOMESTEAD	208
39	MIGHTY CROMWELL TAKES A NOSEDIVE	214
40	SPOTTING THE SINISTER CLERIC	219
41	SORRY JOHN, YOU'RE JUST NOT ON	224
42	SECRET OF THE SILVER DARLIN'S	229
43	REQUIEM FOR SCOTLAND'S LOST LEGION	235
44	LOCH SUNART'S FLOATING PULPIT	241
45	WALLACE – VICTIM OF THE PROPAGANDA MACHINE?	247
46	WIDE-EYED IN MUSSELBURGH	252
47	MORE A KICK THAN A PUNCH	257
48	LOST BENEATH THE SHIFTING SANDS	262
49	WHERE HAVE ALL THE AMAZONS GONE?	267
50	BAPTISM – WITH A STING IN THE TAIL	273
51	THE RESURRECTION OF RICHARD II	278
52	STARING INTO THE PIT OF DESPOND	284
	CHRONOLOGY	290
	INDEX	310

ACKNOWLEDGMENTS

Special thanks are due to the staff of Scottish libraries from Lerwick to Dumfries. To Ian Watson and Jim McNeish for their help in obtaining prize-winning *Herald* archive photographs from which all the studies in this book have been selected. To Harald Nicolson for penmanship above and beyond the call of duty. To Jackie McGlone, Drew Allan and Lesley Duncan in *Herald* features for their constant support and interest, but principally to Bill and his team at Mainstream for breathing life into this idea.

INTRODUCTION

History is bunk, so said Henry Ford and he's been quoted endlessly on this theme ever since. But what did old Henry know about it, he was too busy making fast cars and big bucks. I'd rather paraphrase the sage who suggested that life (therefore history) is just one damned interesting thing after another. Admittedly, history is at best an anthology of gossip, at worst an agreed set of lies. And maybe most significantly, it is generally the record of winners.

With all these provisos I still believe that Scottish history, the record of a small nation, holds an enduring fascination. And although, for nearly three hundred years, we've been part of a united kingdom, we've retained a strong sense of nationhood. I'm convinced there is much, much more Scottish history still to come (if you'll forgive the paradox).

This book has its roots in what was originally a pile of scribbled notes on Scottish dates, tittle-tattle and folklore, gleaned from a wide variety of sources while researching my weekly historical column in *The Herald* which is now into its eighth year.

This book is a 'dipper' rather than a comprehensive dates-directory and is driven very much by the index which, hopefully, will allow the reader to pinpoint areas of particular interest. We have amazing anecdotes, sad stories and historic anniversaries – and many more permutations.

Assembling this book – which I believe provides a series of entertaining snapshots of life in Scotland, particularly over the past five centuries – has been a highly subjective exercise. The daily dates can offer only a taster, a flavour of the available anniversaries and many, many dates important to special interest groups and individuals alike will be missing from the lists. For this I can only apologise, but your local library is a goldmine of such information. Make use of it.

My hope is that this book will provide you, the reader, with a previously unavailable framework and an easily accessed backdrop to Scottish history. If it proves a useful ideas source for all who love Scotland and makes you ponder, even for a moment, on some aspect of our wonderful heritage then the long harvest of obscure anniversaries, unlikely pieces of folklore and tartan trivia will not have been in vain. Enjoy *Scotching the Myths*.

Jim Hewitson,
Papa Westray,
January, 1995

BEWARE THE HAIR OF THE DOG!

The town of Gap in the French Alps, fringed by snow-covered peaks, was where I first encountered St Bernard dogs in their natural surroundings. Attracted to an iron gate in a back street by a frantic scraping and scrabbling, I peered over to see three or four puppies trying to dig their way out under the gate, watched by their mum who lay languidly observing the escape bid from a nearby verandah.

I remember being ever so slightly disappointed that the adult dog had discarded her traditional brandy barrel from around her neck. Mind you, it's been a good number of years since people thought that a wee dram was just the job when you were stuck up to yer oxters in a snowdrift. It must have seemed logical to get some firewater into a frozen body, but as we now know, it's completely the wrong procedure.

Over the centuries whisky has achieved a remarkable reputation for its restorative powers and, presumably, it was from purely medicinal motives that St Patrick brought the secret of distillation from Germany to Ireland. Whisky may have been in production on a small scale in Kintyre from as early as the fifth century.

By the late 1500s aqua vitae, usquebaugh, or the water of life, was widely acclaimed for its health-giving properties. Historian Raphael Holinshed certainly must have enjoyed a glass and may even have been in the middle of a wee session in 1577 when he penned this marvellous piece of PR for the Scotch whisky industry. He suggested, 'Beying moderately taken, it cutteth fleume, it lighteneth the mynd, it quickeneth the spirit, it cureth the hydropsie, it healeth the stranguary, it pounceth the stone, it repelleth gravel, it puffeth away ventositie, it keepeth the head from whirling . . . '. Not so many years ago, a distinguished Professor of Surgery in London told the British Medical Association that, in his opinion, 'the best drug for the relief of pain is alcohol, and I don't mean anything pharmaceutical, but whisky.'

But back to the more sinister properties of the spirit when taken in defence of severe cold. Alcohol thins the blood and combined with hypothermia, that malign, beguiling companion who stalks the chill places of this earth whispering seductively, 'You'll be fine – just close your eyes and have 40 winks,' they make a deadly duo.

We have tragic evidence of this effect during the bitterly cold winter of 1601-02 when the deep freeze lasted a full six months. In the early part of the New Year there was a ten-day snowfall. The Earl of Sutherland was travelling with his party from Golspie through the glen of Loth, ploughing through deep snow when a fresh storm burst upon them, driving thick snow full in their faces. Reports of the incident say, 'Some of the company being thirsty, drank aqua vitae, which by chance happened to be there. This made them afterwards so feeble that they were not able to endure against the storm.'

The Earl and the bulk of his party stuck together and made it to safety but some of the drinkers dispersed by the storm, including the Earl's harper, were found frozen to death in the morning. Several of the whisky drinkers were thought to have been saved by being carried home on the shoulders of their comrades.

So, if you're out this week, enjoying a whisky to celebrate the arrival of another New Year and there's snow around, don't be tempted to tie your carry out around the doggie's neck for sampling *en route*. Just let him lead you home. Come to think of it, if you're lucky enough to have a St Bernard you could always put a saddle on him . . .

January 1

1559   A critical year in the Scottish Reformation began with a Beggars' Summons posted on friars' houses calling on occupiers to take up honest work and leave their riches to the poor, widows, orphans and the sick.

1661   Swans, which had abandoned Linlithgow Loch on the departure from Scotland of Charles II, miraculously returned only a few months after the Restoration.

1850   New Year was ushered in at Glasgow Cross in the traditional style with the crowd showing 'not the slightest tendency to riot'.

1919   Over 200 naval ratings were drowned within sight of Stornoway harbour as the *Iolaire* sank.

1934   'Nessie' given new status as Prime Minister Ramsay MacDonald announced he was to visit the loch in the hope of seeing the monster.

Delicate Balance

Aristotle, admittedly a clever chap, harboured some odd ideas about strong drink. Those who got drunk on wine always fell flat on their faces, he declared, while whose who preferred our national drink, whisky, usually fell over backwards.

January 2

1387   Sir Thomas Erskine was granted grazing and hunting rights for the forest of Clackmannan.

1632   Self-appointed witch-finder, John Balfour of Corshouse, condemned by the authorities for abusing simple people for his private gain.

1793   Thomas Muir, Glasgow-born advocate of radical Parliamentary reform, arrested and charged with sedition.

1834   A Perthshire woman from Bankfoot, known as widow Graham, died, aged 100. She recalled having seen Bonnie Prince Charlie at Blair Atholl where her father joined the Jacobite army.

1946   An Italian prisoner-of-war was jailed for 21 days at Stonehaven for stealing and eating a sheep.

Eye of Frog, etc.

Amid the folk remedies popular in seventeenth-century Scotland were many devoted to the scourge of gout. Directions included the use of skin from the feet of a large vulture applied to the patient's heel, or the ubiquitous frog, boiled in olive oil and the resultant liquid applied to the 'paynd place'.

January 3

1603   Captain Thomas Crawford, who captured Dumbarton Castle for Mary Queen of Scots leading a daring climb up the rock face, died, aged 73, and was buried at Kilbirnie, Ayrshire.

1746   Jacobite army left Glasgow in two columns by Kilsyth and Cumbernauld taking with them a bailie and a merchant as hostages for the supplies that the city had been ordered to provide.

1833   Two New Year fatalities were reported in Glasgow; a first-footer tripped and smashed his bottle, fatally puncturing his abdomen, and a tipsy diner choked to death on a piece of tripe in a Calton eating-house.

1838   Trial opened in Glasgow of cotton-spinners accused of inspiring disturbances; the organising committee was transported for seven years.

1906   Prussian and French teachers were to be attached as modern language teachers in Scottish secondary and higher grade schools.

Voices from the Tomb

The famous accidental echo at Hamilton Mausoleum in Lanarkshire has attracted leading singers from the world over anxious to test their vocal range using the building's unique acoustics.

January 4

1364	Consideration was being given in Scotland to translating an existing truce with England into a permanent peace.
1757	Montgomery's Highlanders, who fought with distinction against the French in North America, were formed; many chose to remain on the other side of the Atlantic after being discharged.
1803	Fifty-eight-foot-long pioneering paddle-steamer *Charlotte Dundas*, designed by William Symington, arrived in Glasgow having travelled along the Forth and Clyde Canal.
1905	Last surviving minister from the 1843 Disruption which saw the creation of the Free Church of Scotland, the Revd James Yuill, died in Aberdeen, aged 90.
1923	Glasgow Corporation approved a plan for a French-style boulevard between Anniesland and Duntocher; the work was aimed at relieving unemployment.

Right of Reply

The editors of *The Scotsman* and *The Caledonian Mercury* resorted to a duel after a heated exchange in print. The contest took place in 1828 at Ravelston but the pair found the pen mightier than the pistol – both missed their shots and the seconds declared the affair closed.

January 5

1550	Four leading Scots Reformers, who were imprisoned in the famous fortress of Mont St Michel in Normandy, made a daring escape as the drunken garrison celebrated the traditional feast of King of the Bean.
1609	People were reported blown over bridges, trees uprooted and haystacks toppled by a 'boisterous' wind which battered Scotland and lasted until March.
1700	Moffat school-teacher Robert Carmichael was scourged through the streets of Edinburgh and banished for killing one of his pupils during punishment for misbehaviour.
1852	Poachers were using chloroform impregnated sponges to stun rabbits on the Perthshire hills.
1882	Two 14-year-old boys made an amazing 170-mile rail journey from Edinburgh to Darlington perched on the Westinghouse brake unit of the Scotch Mail.

Ayrshire Acolytes

Abraham Lincoln numbered the weavers of Newmilns amongst his staunchest supporters in the fight against slavery. After the Union victory in the Civil War he presented the village with the Stars and Stripes which was proudly displayed at functions and marches. One of Lincoln's favourite poems, *Oh, Why Should the Spirit of Mortal be Proud*, was written by William Knox, a little-known Roxburghshire-born poet.

January 6

1540   First performance of the controversial anti-establishment play by Sir David Lindsay – *Ane Satyre of the Thrie Estaitis*.

1692   At Inveraray in Argyll, McEion, the chief of the Glencoe MacDonalds, was six days late in signing allegiance to William of Orange; the scene was set for the Glencoe massacre of 13 February.

1790   A brewer's servant fell into a vessel of boiling liquor in Edinburgh's Canongate and was 'scalded in such a shocking manner' that he died before he could be got out.

1831   Despite the efforts of the Temperance Society, it was reported that there was 'no dearth of drunken people' on the streets of Scotland.

1974   Volunteers applied in their hundreds as Scottish ambulance crews staged a five-day strike.

The Train Now Floating

The West Highland Railway line crosses the boggy and treacherous Rannoch Moor in Argyllshire on a 'raft' of brush wood which prevents the track vanishing into the mire.

January 7

1451   The University of Glasgow was founded by a papal bull following lobbying from James II and Bishop William Turnbull.

1629   A national appeal was launched after 16 small farms, on the fertile land between Falkirk and Stirling, were destroyed when a huge area of moss slipped, turning the district into a six-foot-deep quagmire.

1836   The Western Isles were being promoted as an ideal holiday destination with low prices compared with the south. Stornoway distillery whisky was selling at 8s 6d per gallon.

1929   Glasgow was the venue for the first Scottish screening of a 'talkie': Al Jolson's *The Singing Fool*.

1982   Extremely cold weather throughout Scotland saw the sea freeze at Oban, and killed the two-centuries-old date-palms at Glasgow's Winter Garden.

In-Flight Entertainment

Air services in the Highlands and Islands once boasted some of the most colourful characters ever to wrestle with a joystick. One pilot's favourite jest was to put the plane on auto-pilot, emerge from the cabin trailing a length of string which he would hand to an astonished passenger saying, 'Look after the plane while I'm at the toilet!'

WE WERE THE PEOPLE

Now then, lads and lassies. High time you stopped chowin' on your tammies and watering your export with bitter tears of disappointment. Football, after all, is only a gemme. So we missed out on the World Cup, on another chance to stagger gloriously to defeat on soccer's biggest stage.

What we have to do, as we watch these dramas unfold without us, is to console ourselves in the knowledge that we taught the world how to play football. Take the United States, venue for the most recent World Cup. Despite English claims to the contrary, it was the Scots who popularised the game in America during the late 1800s, showing our Stateside cousins just how the beautiful game should be played.

Our ancestors' influence was felt not only in the growing industrial cities but also in the Wild West. Researching my recent book on the impact of the Scots in the United States, I came across an epic tale of a football match in 1912 near the Kansas State capital of Topeka. It speaks volumes about the impression made by Scots on sporting America.

In a graphic despatch the reporter from the *State Journal* describes an encounter between husky Highlanders (ranchers from Maple Hill) and a scratch team from Topeka made up of the 'inhabitants of the English shires' and a few other assorted Britons. The city slickers drove 26 miles past Silver City to Maple Hill and on a fine Sunday afternoon were 'smeared over a 40-acre lot' by the Highlanders. 'It's a great game, this soccer, from the spectator's point of view,' declares the reporter, who admits to never having seen a match before, 'when played by these earnest Scotchmen of single purpose'.

A large crowd had gathered for the two o'clock kick-off, arriving from ranches all over Wabsunsee County. They were big men, most of them florid of face, earnest of manner and speaking a deep, Gaelic tongue. They love soccer, says the scribe, as their fathers loved it before them and their fathers' fathers.

The physical contrast between the teams was marked – Topeka's players not having the 'tonnage' of the Highlanders. Particularly impressive for Maple Hill were 'Stonewall' Jackson, a formidable half-back, and his partner in defence, Reid, an employee of the Adams ranch who went 'blithely home' after his soccer exertions to feed 500 head of cattle. These Scots were made of stern stuff, and a kick on the knee, shin or shoulder (foul, ref!) did not count for a fly. Injured men were seen rising like panthers.

'The Topeka goalkeeper had more trouble in the game than a bear in a bee-yard. Three times a goal was kicked on him, the ball passing by in a twisting curve like a brown streak.' When he finally caught a shot, down came Stonewall Jackson and the rest of the

Inspirational forward line

'Glegfoot Maple Hill clan' to kick the unfortunate custodian, still clutching the ball, through his own goalposts.

The goal, of course, was given. The foolish custodian should have parted with the ball, shouldn't he? Now isn't that football the way we Scots like to see it played? None of this namby-pamby 'don't touch the goalie' stuff.

Ah yes, it would be nice to take our place with the soccer greats once again. However, maybe the likes of Nigeria or South Korea might fail to recognise Scotland's contribution to world soccer and turn us over. It's happened before, hasn't it?

January 8

1583   Elders were appointed in Perth to go through the town at the time of the Sunday service noting the names of those in taverns and baxter's booths; a fine of 20s was proposed for these slackers.

1661   *Mercurius Caledonius* – said to be Scotland's first genuine newspaper – appeared, but survived for only three months and nine editions.

1707   Death of the Earl of Stair, hated by many for his role in the Massacre of Glencoe and the Union of 1707, aged 59.

1846   *Inverness Courier* reported how a flock of pigeons flew over the house of a Lochcarron gent who managed to shoot one. It dropped down the chimney into a pot of soup simmering over the fire.

1930   Sir Thomas Lipton, the tea tycoon, gifted £10,000 to his native city of Glasgow for the relief of poor mothers and their children and in memory of his own mother.

Defending the Faith

When James VI published his *Book of Sport* in 1618 to make Presbyterianism less rigid, he didn't reckon on John Ross, minister at Blairgowrie and a staunch opponent of the proposals. Sports were ordered in kirkyards after Sunday services. When football was selected at Blairgowrie, Ross, a strong, athletic man, joined in with vigour, kicking everything above ground level. As parishioners hobbled home each week, opposition grew to the sports edict and it was eventually dropped, thanks in no small way to the awkward Revd Ross.

January 9

1568   Inquiry into bad blood between Dundee and Perth over which town should get precedence after Edinburgh in the annual Riding of the Three Estates.

1671   Steeple of St Magnus Cathedral in Orkney was badly damaged by fire after being struck by lightning.

1700   Ayr postmaster Alexander Mitchell, who had the task of halting illegal importation of Irish cattle and horses, was given a hundred pounds bonus to encourage him in a difficult job.

1853   A fine golden eagle – captured in the glens of Inverness-shire – was sent as a gift to the Emperor of France, with its own food supply, a batch of live rabbits.

1972   Clydebank-built liner *Queen Elizabeth* gutted by fire in Hong Kong.

One for the Road

Edinburgh's position of prominence as a centre for medical innovation in the seventeenth and eighteenth centuries also meant an unexpected boost for the distilling industry. Bodies for the anatomist's dissection table were stored in cheap whisky.

January 10

1295   Burgesses of Scotland's four most important trading centres, Berwick, Edinburgh, Roxburgh and Stirling, met at Holyrood Abbey in Edinburgh.

1597   Perth baker William Williamson was accused of baking and selling 'great loaves' at Christmas which was said by the Presbyterians to be cherishing superstition in the hearts of the ignorant.

1643   Four Scots gentlemen, including the Earl of Kelly and Lord Kerr, died within a short time after taking part in a 'debauch' or spectacular drinking session; popular rumour had it that the Devil's health had been drunk.

1822   Edinburgh's Princes Street was lit by gas-lamps for the first time.

1922   Marquess of Linlithgow, complaining of high levels of taxation, announced that he was closing his home, Hopetoun House, near Edinburgh.

How's That for a Hailstone

An irregular shaped mass of ice fell on a Ross-shire estate in August 1849 after an extraordinary peel of thunder. According to *The Times* of London, which took great care with the accuracy of its despatches, the hailstone was said to have been 20 feet in circumference!

January 11

1631   Plans announced for a bridge over the River Ericht at Craighall, in Perthshire; at least 18 people had drowned in recent winters at this important ford.

1672   The supreme criminal court in Scotland, the High Court of Justiciary was reconstituted.

1717   People read with amazement of Minister John Gardner who lived near Elgin and who was taken for dead and about to be buried when he woke up in a coffin and made a complete recovery.

1836   A football match between the Lord Provost and the 'Youth of Perth', and Lord Stormont and the 'Men of Scone' was abandoned due to the immense crowd of spectators who spilled on to the pitch.

1951   Block of ice from a passing aircraft crashed through the roof of a joiner's shop in Dumbarton Road, Glasgow.

Hard on the Char

The Arctic Char, a trout-like fish which has survived in Scottish lochs since being trapped by the retreating ice-sheet 10,000 years ago, is under threat at the end of the twentieth century from acid rain which is changing the composition of loch and reservoir water.

January 12

1565   Scarcity of wild-fowl reported in Fife; Presbyterians blamed the excessive junketing of Queen Mary and her court.

1659   A visiting camel caused a sensation in Edinburgh, the first to have been brought north of the Border; threepence was charged to view this ship of the desert.

1777   Hugh Mercer, an Aberdeen-born brigadier in the American army who was a surgeon for the Jacobite army at Culloden, was fatally wounded by a musket blow at Princeton during the War of Independence.

1866   Aeronautical Society of Great Britain established by the Duke of Argyll.

1909   Scottish Rugby Football Union cancelled an international with England planned for March because the English Union had approved money in addition to expenses for visiting New Zealand and Australian teams.

Queen Mary Stepped Here

A mansion house near Castlemilk in Glasgow was called Pedmyre because tradition had it that Mary Queen of Scots stopped there while fleeing from the Battle of Langside and stepped into a muddy pool while dismounting; Pedmyre is claimed to be a corruption of the French for 'dirty feet'.

January 13

1364   Scots Parliament agreed that in the event of England being invaded they would lend 60 archers for her defence.

1687   A couple who stole a little girl away from a showman in Edinburgh where, because she was double jointed, she had danced in 'all shapes for public amusement', were cleared of all guilt.

1796   John Anderson, Professor of Natural Philosophy at Glasgow University and founder of the Institution named after him, died, aged 69.

1831   Lambing had already begun on Islay – as early in the year as any islander could remember.

1908   Licence granted for 50 motor taxi-cabs by Glasgow magistrates – the first batch in the city. The fare was identical to horse-drawn cabs, 1s for the first mile and 6d for every additional mile.

Tracks of my Tears

The first railway in Scotland – the Tranent-Cockenzie wagonway on the eastern outskirts of Edinburgh – was opened in 1722. Jacobite and Government forces fought across its tracks during the Battle of Prestonpans (1745).

January 14

1255   Alexander III chaired an Assembly at Holyrood at which he settled a dispute between the sheriff of Perth and the Abbey of Dunfermline.

1754   James Durham of Largo in Fife was born. In a remarkable military career spanning 70 years he rose from rank of Cornet to that of General.

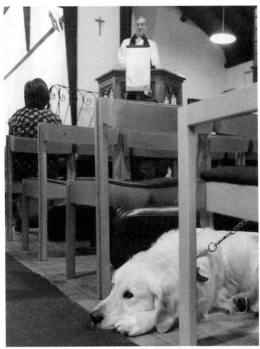

Snoozing between the pews

1872   Greyfriars Bobby, the faithful Skye terrier who watched by his master's grave in Edinburgh for 14 years, died.

1884   The first of the Cluthas – little steamers designed to run between Glasgow's Broomielaw and Partick – launched at Rutherglen.

1911   A plan for a 'garden city' to benefit golfers at Barassie in Ayrshire was suggested by the Duke of Portland.

Lots to Answer For

Sir John Clerk of Penicuik, who sent his son to Eton in 1715, is given the doubtful credit for starting this trend among the Scots nobility which created, some say, a remote anglicised aristocracy, speaking with the accents of the cultured south.

MAKING A SAUSAGE OUT OF THE BUTCHER

For three years after the defeat of the clans at Culloden there had been little for the Jacobites to smile about; that is, until news leaked out in mid-January 1749 of how the Haymarket Theatre hoaxer had made a dunderheid out of 'Butcher' Cumberland.

A real stir had been caused in London by adverts for a performance during which a spectacularly talented, but suspiciously anonymous, individual planned to play the music of every instrument on a common walking-cane, climb into a quart bottle and answer questions, identify masked members of the audience and arrange on-the-spot interviews with the dead.

Prices for this whopper of a show were: gallery 2s, pit 3s, boxes 5s and stage 7s 6d. For days before the event speculation was rife in the coffee shops and inns as to the identity of the performer, and on the appointed evening the theatre was packed. Many credulous society people attended, all anxious to witness the promised miracles. The most famous personage by far, however, was the 'hero' of Culloden, William Augustus, Duke of Cumberland, third son of George II.

Patiently they waited for the show to begin. After half an hour of handclapping the footstamping began, calmed only a little by the music of the orchestra. When the stage manager appeared and promised to return entrance money if the performer failed to appear, the crowd turned nasty, realising they had been duped.

Recklessly, a young man threw a lit candle on the stage and, after a military-style charge, a full-scale riot ensued. Most of the audience, foreseeing big trouble, scrambled for the exits. Wigs, hats, cloaks and swords were lost in the melee. One report says that the troublemakers who remained inside were joined by a mob from the street who tore up benches, destroyed the scenery, pulled down the boxes and carried debris into the street where it was piled into a bonfire, with the stage curtain on a pole serving as a fiery standard in the midst of the inferno. In short, says the witness, 'The theatre was dismantled entirely.'

But what of Cumberland? In a letter to a friend, a lady of Jacobite sympathies could scarcely disguise her glee at Cumberland's embarrassment over the hoax. She wrote: 'He was the first that flew in a rage and called to pull down the house – he drew his sword. He was in such a rage that somebody slipped in behind him and pulled the sword out of his hand, which was as much to say, "fools should not have chopping sticks".' Nothing was heard of the sword again.

The Bottle Hoax, as it became known, was obviously a godsend for the Jacobite satirists. In a newspaper called *Old England* great fun was had at Cumberland's expense when an advert appeared:

'Found entangled in a slit of a lady's demolished smock-petticoat – a gilt-handled sword of martial temper and length, not much the worse for wearing, with the Spey curiously engraven on one side, and the Scheld on the other. Supposed to be taken from the fat sides of a certain great General in his hasty retreat.'

January 15

1516   Alexander, Duke of Rothesay, infant brother of James V, died at Stirling Castle.

1624   Four Stirling gentlemen reported a strange phenomenon a couple of miles from the town – a phantom battle in the skies with the beating of drums and the firing of cannon.

1846   Mails to the Northern Isles were so badly affected by weather that news of political events in London were reaching New York before Kirkwall and Lerwick.

1931   President of the Gaelic Society of London pleads for £20,000 assistance from education authorities in Scotland to help with the teaching of Gaelic.

1968   Hurricane Low Q swept a path of devastation across Scotland with winds gusting up to 134 mph; 21 people were reported killed.

Under the Hammer

There are two interesting theories as to how King Edward I of England came by his nickname, as 'The Hammer of the Scots'. One school of thought suggests it was acquired because of the manner in which he battered the Scots into submission, while, alternatively, it is argued that through his oppressive overlordship he forged and hammered Scotland into a nation. On his death-bed Edward asked for his corpse to be boiled and the flesh stripped so that his bones could be carried on future campaigns against the Scots.

January 16

1524   Alexander, Third Earl of Huntly, who commanded the vanguard of the Scots army at Flodden, died at Perth.

1682   Hangman of Edinburgh, Alexander Cockburn, sentenced to death for murdering a beggar in his house.

1707   Scottish Parliament effectively put itself out of business by ratifying the Treaty of Union which brought the governing bodies of Scotland and England together later in the year.

1809   Glasgow-born Sir John Moore was killed by grapeshot during the Battle of Corunna as his forces defeated the French.

1926   A satirical broadcast from Edinburgh by Father Ronald Knox describing the blowing up of the Houses of Parliament caused alarm; thousands believed that the event was actually taking place.

Tarry Road to Health

One of Scotland's most unusual folk remedies of this century was the sniffing of fumes from tar-boilers out on road-repair duty. Mothers would encourage children out into the city streets believing the aroma was a cure for a variety of bronchial conditions.

January 17

1568   A play by Robert Semple was performed in Edinburgh before Regent Morton and the Scots nobility.

1781   Eight-foot-tall giant who had been appearing in Glasgow as a 'curiosity' thanked the citizens for turning out in such large numbers to see him.

1882   James Hogg, the Ettrick Shepherd, was visiting Edinburgh. Reports said he was a decent-looking man with a 'fair, fresh and rather ruddy complexion'.

1941   Envoy of United States President Franklin D. Roosevelt met Churchill in Glasgow's North British Hotel and pledged American support against Nazi Germany.

1982   Six families in Glencoe received their first 625-line colour television pictures thanks to a new mast.

Vestry Lounge Bar

Ministers of the Kirk in the mid-1570s were so poor that the General Assembly was told that many were compelled to eke out their stipend by selling ale to their flock. On the wild frontier of colonial America, Presbyterian ministers' salaries were often paid in whisky.

January 18

1348   Negotiations were underway in an attempt to have David II, who was made prisoner at Neville's Cross in August 1346, freed from the Tower of London.

1739	The Society for the Propagation of Christian Knowledge was maintaining 113 schools and 4,000 pupils in Scotland and had sent four missionaries to America.
1812	Trial trip of Henry Bell's *Comet* from Glasgow to Greenock. The 30-ton vessel effectively launched the Scottish steamship-building industry
1814	James Hedderwick, journalist and poet, who established the *Evening Citizen* in Glasgow in 1864 (one of the country's earliest halfpenny newspapers), was born.
1953	Plans to include an accordion class in the Perth Music Festival were opposed. One member warned that, if this 'instrument of torture' was allowed, boogie-woogie would be next.

And did those Feet?

Eccentric and patriotic journalist Comyns Beaumont tried to rewrite the history books in the 1940s with a detailed theory suggesting that most classical and biblical sites were located in the United Kingdom. Most startling was his argument that Jerusalem was, in fact, Edinburgh and that Christ made his journey to the cross along the High Street.

January 19

1595	A great 'tulzie' or street fight occurred between supporters of the Earl of Montrose and Sir James Sandilands at Edinburgh's Salt Tron. At least two men were killed and Sandilands was badly wounded.
1605	Gambler James Young, 'a player at cards and dice', was slain in St Giles Cathedral, Edinburgh, by a 16-year-old boy.
1671	William Head and John Fergusson given permission to stage a public lottery anywhere in Scotland; for several years they had operated a successful lottery in England.
1806	Notorious gang of seven Glasgow house-breakers who had plagued the city for months were captured by police.
1946	Touring New Zealand rugby team – weighing in at a ton and a quarter – stranded in a lift in their Edinburgh hotel for nearly an hour.

Time, Gentlemen, Please

The hard-drinking Earls of Strathmore are said to have kept a pageboy beneath the table at banquets to loosen the collars of diners as they slid, in a drunken stupor, from their chairs on to the floor.

January 20

1355	Ageing Edward Balliol appeared before Edward III at Berwick and in a humiliating ceremony had to concede all rights and claims to the Kingdom of Scotland.

1449	At a Parliament in Edinburgh called by James II, Alexander Seton was created Earl of Huntly and Lord Lesley, Earl of Rothes.
1564	A severe frost killed thousands of domestic animals and for 24 hours the 'sea neither ebbed nor flowed' around the Scottish coast.
1896	A carrier was fined £3 for infringing the exclusive rights of the post office by delivering a letter from Rothesay to a Glasgow merchant.
1908	Suffragettes demonstrated at several Scottish police courts protesting that women should not be tried using man-made laws.

Transport of Delight

Glasgow's beloved tramway system, closed in 1962, was a truly mammoth operation. The junction of Renfield Street and Jamaica Street in the city centre was said to be the busiest in the world with 516 'caurs' negotiating the crossroads hourly on a Saturday night, and in 1948 the system carried an incredible 595,673,261 passengers – everyone splendidly shoogled!

January 21

1264	A son was born to Alexander III, King of Scots, at Jedburgh.
1521	Scots Parliament resolved that if the Duke of Albany did not return from a prolonged stay in France, he should forfeit his Regency.
1750	Lord Thomas Erskine, advocate and Lord Chancellor, youngest son of the Tenth Earl of Buchan, born in Edinburgh.
1890	Strength of new Forth Rail Bridge tested by a 2,000-ton train.
1953	Glenbervie churchyard, where relatives of Robert Burns are buried, was closed on the orders of the sheriff because of overcrowding.

Rising Damp

The Duke of Lauderdale's coffin, interred at St Mary's in Haddington in 1682, was often found to have moved about the crypt. The much-hated Scots Secretary was getting no rest, even in death, for his sins against the Scottish people, it was whispered. The explanation was simpler – the nearby River Tyne often rose into the crypt floating the coffin across the chamber.

STRUT THAT FUNKY SALMON

As one of Clydeside's earliest exponents of the Watusi and the Mashed Potato, not to mention my much talked-about Gay Gordons, I find it really provoking the way younger folk sound off as if they'd just invented the jigging. If you're over 20 these days then, apparently, you're consigned to the veteran's section of *Come Dancing*, your last hope, the Zimmer formation team.

The Sonic-Mario generation seem to think if you take yourself off to a rave in some rural backwater (barn dance to you old timers), and stand around twitching for 15 hours, that then qualifies you as a dance-master *primus*. Half an hour of the Twist or the Hully-Gully would soon sort out the men from boys.

The fact is that all twentieth-century dancers in Scotland are heirs to a dance tradition which stretches back beyond the Middle Ages. Although the first detailed written records are of aristocratic functions around 1500, it's certain that the guid folk of Scotland enjoyed strutting their funky stuff, tripping the light fantastic, at every opportunity right back to the Dark Ages.

In the early 1400s, for example, regular fairs, market days, weddings and even funerals provided the chance for the loons and lassies to indulge in the most popular dance of all – the Salmon – which apparently consisted of 'active leaps like those of the fish from which it takes its name'. This conjures up a marvellous picture of our ancestors pogo-ing round the alehouse to a bagpipe accompaniment. Yes indeed, the more things change and all that.

There's a modern adage which suggests that dancing is nothing more than a perpendicular expression of a horizontal desire. Clearly, nothing much has altered in that respect either. We learn that after these energetic Salmon sessions, when the bagpiper had been paid and the Scots wound their way home, there was still a reserve of energy which allowed for 'abundant love-making along the way'.

Were the activities of the courtiers more refined? Not a bit of it. William Dunbar, court poet in the reign of James IV, in 'Dances in the Queen's Chalmer', pokes fun at the inelegant and stumbling dance-steps of the courtiers, and the noisy effects of over-indulgence in food and drink as they careered around the floor. Wind assisted and no mistake! In the background, according to Dunbar, 'licentious capering' took place. Indeed, one nineteenth-century commentator was moved to remark: 'Such a performance would scarcely be tolerated now in a gin cellar, among a bevy of fishermen.' Somehow, I can't see the Victorians excelling at the Salmon leap.

Strong Scottish connections with France during the reigns of James V and Mary Queen of Scots influenced the style of dancing in the mid-1500s; the principal toffs' dance being the Pavane or

Peacock, a stately dance of Spanish origin. Even the common folk were under the Peacock's spell and, after their national reels, would mimic the Pavane with more earthy versions such as the Plat-foot. Foreigners often came to the Scottish court to exhibit new dances and, according to the treasurer's accounts, were well recompensed for their efforts.

The fun, however, at least for a wee while, was nearly over. Dancing was considered ungodly and frivolous by the Reformed Kirk. Knox railed against the 'queen's dancing' and more and more men and women found guilty of 'promiscuous dancing' were forced to confess their fault in public. For a time the jiggin' went underground.

January 22

1567   Mary Queen of Scots arrived in Glasgow to visit her husband, Lord Darnley.

1691   Continuing anxiety over cattle raids by wild Highlanders in Moray, Angus and Strathearn.

1753   At Broomlands near Kelso, Jean, Countess of Roxburgh died. Her most tragic claim to fame was that she was 71 years a widow, her young husband having drowned in 1682.

1882   American evangelists Moody and Sankey packed Glasgow's St Andrews Halls.

1903   Glasgow magistrates decided to abolish family departments in the city's public houses and ordered a phasing-out in the use of barmaids.

Get to Freuchie!

The Fife village of Freuchie – notable in recent years for its exploits on the cricket field – is only one and a half miles from Falkland Palace. In former times, Freuchie was a place of temporary banishment for courtiers who had displeased the Crown. Hence, to order someone to 'Get to Freuchie' was a common regal command removing a nuisance from the royal presence.

January 23

1562   Lead-mining, probably begun in Scotland by the Romans, was officially licensed in Upper Clydesdale, including Wanlockhead.

1623   Plans were afoot for the re-establishment of the Garde Ecossaise. Lord Colville went to France to discuss details with the French King, Louis XIII. It had been originally formed during the Hundred Years' War.

1662   With the Restoration of Charles II, witch hunting resumed with renewed vigour in Scotland; on this day alone 13 commissions were issued for the trial of supposed witches and warlocks.

1836   A storm badly damaged the western harbour-wall at Portpatrick casting doubt on its future as a packet-station to Belfast and Larne.

1946   Brides of over 100 American soldiers were ready to sail for the States, confirmed Edinburgh GI Brides Association.

Drastic Measures

When the Stone of Scone was 'retrieved' from Westminster Abbey on Christmas Day, 1950, by a group of young Scots, a huge police operation was set up. Such was the constitutional alarm that, for the first time in over four centuries, the Border between Scotland and England was closed.

January 24

1502   Marriage treaty between James IV and Margaret, the 11-year-old daughter of the English King Henry, was signed in the Palace of Richmond after prolonged negotiations.

1657   A summer of trouble was predicted when thousands of cannon-shaped objects were found mysteriously carved in the snow of the Highland glens by the forces of wind and weather.

1721   Surgeons in Edinburgh inserted a clause into indentures, ordering apprentices not to violate graves in quest of dissecting-table candidates.

1754   Lord Grange, the Jacobite who banished his wife to St Kilda, telling friends she was dead and even staging a mock funeral, died.

1927   An earthquake – felt from Orkney to Fife – shook Scotland.

Educational Cock-up

In the 1700s boys were encouraged at Shrovetide in Scotland to bring fighting cocks to school for a day of 'sport'. The slain became the schoolmaster's property and formed an important part of his salary.

January 25

1462   Margaret of Anjou, who had taken refuge in Scotland with her imbecilic husband, Henry VI of England, sailed from Kirkcudbright to seek aid from the French in her campaign against Edward, Duke of York.

1544   Cardinal David Beaton's 'spiritual court', meeting in Perth, condemned four men and a woman to death for heretical offences which included eating a goose on Hallowe'en.

1759   Birthday of Robert Burns, at Alloway, Ayrshire. By co-incidence the birthday of another great Scots poet, James Hogg (1772).

| 1815 | Two highwaymen were executed beside Morningside Road in Edinburgh – scene of one of their crimes. |

| 1931 | Employers in the West of Scotland pressed for a reduction in wages of semi-skilled and unskilled municipal workers. |

Amazing Grace

James III, King of Scots, was reportedly so religious that he burst into tears every time he looked upon a representation of Christ or the Virgin Mary.

January 26

| 1602 | Efforts were being made to keep plague victims at Crail, in Fife, from wandering the countryside; they were banished to a neighbouring moor. |

| 1722 | Revd Alexander Carlyle, who watched the Battle of Prestonpans from the steeple of his kirk at Inveresk, and became prominent in literary circles in London and Edinburgh, was born. |

| 1861 | Edinburgh startled by the first lunchtime firing of the one o'clock gun from the Castle. |

| 1908 | First Glasgow Boy Scout Troop registered – the first in the country. |

| 1981 | Empty shell of 13-foot *Bass Conqueror*, used by East Lothian man Kenneth Kerr in a solo attempt to row the Atlantic, washed ashore in Norway. |

Origin of the 'Fair'

The original Glasgow Fair was held around a huge lump of volcanic rock in the grounds of the Greyfriars Monastery. The rock had to be broken up during the extensions to *The Scottish Daily Express* building in Albion Street in the 1950s. An old Glasgow tradition suggests that the distant Paps of Jura are always visible from the city's West End on Glasgow Fair Saturday.

January 27

| 1389 | Scots Parliament at Perth elected the Duke of Rothesay as the King's Lieutenant, discussed cash-raising schemes and the maintenance of peace with England. |

| 1616 | A great, fiery star, in the form of a dragon, appeared in the sky over south-west Scotland before disappearing with two 'mighty cracks'. |

| 1783 | *Glasgow Advertiser*, forerunner of *The Herald*, appeared for the first time. |

| 1911 | Opening the Scottish Motor Exhibition in Edinburgh, Sir John Macdonald predicted the car would cause the gradual disappearance of horses from our streets. |

| 1926 | Scots inventor John Logie Baird gave the first public demonstration of true television to members of the Royal Institution in his Soho workshop. |

Number 10 Dividend

Within a few hours of taking office as Britain's first Labour Prime Minister, Lossiemouth-born Ramsay MacDonald made his Socialist intentions clear. A Co-op van drew up in Downing Street bringing the first consignment of food to Number l0.

January 28

1664   Muggings were on the increase on the streets and closes of Edinburgh; 'sociologists' blamed the poverty of the land and the burdens on the people.

1669   Postal service established between Inverness and Edinburgh.

1729   Two women arrested for walking the streets of Edinburgh in men's apparel.

1884   Scotland defeated Ireland by 5–0 in the first football international between the sides in Belfast.

1908   Musician and bandleader Jimmy Shand was born at East Wemyss in Fife.

Name of the Beast

Popular names for the oxen which carried out most of the work in the fields of medieval Scotland included Brandie, Cromack, Hakey, Himby and Garie.

SIEGE MENTALITY AT STIRLING

War-Wolf, *All-the-World*, *Vicar*, *Parson*, *Gloucester*, and *Belfry* – what have all these in common? The clue is the Scottish War of Independence.

As far as I know, this question has never been put either on *Mastermind* or *Superscot.* But it's worthy of such a forum. They are, in fact, six of the mighty engines of war employed by the English King Edward I during the rather peculiar siege of Stirling Castle in the summer of 1304. This month marks the anniversary of the death of Sir William Oliphant (5 February, 1329), who commanded the garrison at Stirling on behalf of King John Balliol.

Edward had subdued the rest of Scotland and only the rock fortress of Stirling, with its small force of some 150 men, held out for three months against the encircling army with its ingenious weaponry. Only the eventual spectre of starvation forced them to seek terms.

Thousands watched the weeks of the siege, and the chroniclers tell us that a hole was knocked in the side of a house down in the town so that the English queen and her ladies could have a grandstand view of the proceedings.

Much effort had been put into bringing the siege engines, said to number a baker's dozen, north to Stirling, so when, early on, Oliphant asked permission to send a messenger to establish whether King John wished them to defend to the last or surrender, Edward refused permission. It seems the only reason for this was that he wanted to see the siege engines in action, hurling rocks at the fortress and threatening invasion from the tops of high, wooden towers.

Even when the garrison offered unconditional surrender, King Edward withheld his response until the arrival of the greatest siege engine in Europe, *War-Wolf*, in order that it could get a piece of the action and be properly assessed in combat by his military engineers.

The monastic houses of Brechin and St Andrews also have cause to remember this siege. The soldiers of the English king stripped the lead from the roofs of the church buildings to be made into weights for working the massive engines of war.

One engineer who was in Scotland around this time was the Fleming, John Crab, who designed a mobile crane capable of raising huge stones and dropping them with painful accuracy on the heads of the opposition. It was his pride and joy.

A clergyman who got in on the act was Robert Wishart, Bishop of Glasgow and a thorn in the side of Edward as Scotland moved towards independence. He was thrown into jail and one charge alleged that he had used timber intended for a new steeple to build siege weapons for use against English strongholds.

January 29

1591   'Gay doings' reported at the Holyrood court of the young James VI, with 'running at the ring', jousting and sailing about in boats and galleys at Leith.

1719   Vision of an army several thousand strong seen by dozens of people west of Aberdeen.

1852   Smugglers' caves and bothies on the Isle of Arran, numbering about a dozen, were discovered and demolished by revenue men.

1858   Town of Tobermory, on the Isle of Mull, lit for the first time by gas.

1917   Loss of the K13, a revolutionary steam-driven submarine in the Gareloch; 32 men died and almost 50 were rescued.

Blitz in the North

Surprisingly perhaps, Aberdeen was Scotland's most regularly bombed city during the Second World War – the *Luftwaffe* launched 34 raids on the city. During the Great War several little-known airship raids took place in the North. In 1916, children at Kingussie spotted a Zeppelin, although at first their parents thought it merely a fairy story.

January 30

1647   Scots agreed to hand over Charles I to a Parliamentary Commission in return for £400,000 army back-pay.

1729   Widespread vandalism by a group of 'night ramblers' reported in Edinburgh; windows were broken and seats overturned.

1834   A debate at Glasgow Police Board on overspending got so heated that 'the facetious Bailie Hood' suggested calling the fire-engines.

1936   Valuation Appeal Court in Edinburgh fixed the valuation for assessment purposes of Rangers Ibrox Stadium at £2,000.

1976   Muriel Naughton, riding her own horse, became the first woman to compete under National Hunt rules in a race at Ayr.

Angry Outburst

There was anger in 1680 when Mons Meg, the huge Flemish-built siege gun, which was the pride of Scotland, burst at Edinburgh Castle when fired in honour of a visit by the Duke of York. It was felt that the English cannoneer had applied too large a charge, jealous because there was no cannon of this size south of the Border.

January 31

1465   Commerce with France and Flanders was the main item on the agenda of a meeting of the Three Estates in Edinburgh.

1667   A regular horse-post – going north every Tuesday and Thursday – was established between Edinburgh and Aberdeen.

1761   Lachlan MacQuarie, an army officer who became Governor of New South Wales and was known as the 'Father of Australia' was born on the Isle of Mull.

1834   An active campaign against the use of threshing-machines spread to Forfarshire where stackyards were set alight.

1919   Striking Clydeside workers clashed with police during a demonstration at Glasgow's George Square.

No Through Road

Among the most startling evidence in Scotland of the Ice Age are the three parallel, 10-mile-long water-level terraces on the slopes of Glen Roy in Inverness-shire. Only within the past 100 years have the 'roads' been accepted as a natural phenomenon. Even the road and bridge-builder Thomas Telford was convinced they were man-made.

February 1

1316   The army of Edward Bruce, brother of King Robert, routed Edmund Butler, Lord Lieutenant of Ireland at the Battle of Skerries in Kildare, opening the road to Dublin.

1655   An exceptionally fierce storm cast up thousands of eels on to the banks of the Nor' Loch in Edinburgh.

1709   Largo-born adventurer Alexander Selkirk was found on the island of Juan Fernandez where he had been marooned for four years. The legend of Robinson Crusoe was born.

1865   Highland Railway formed by the amalgamation of Inverness and Perth Junction and Inverness and Aberdeen Junction Railways.

1953   On a night of storms with many lives lost the Orkney inter-island steamer *Earl Thorfinn* ended up in Aberdeen, 200 miles off course, having set out from Kirkwall for the short hop to Sanday.

Inflated Propaganda

Glasgow professor John Anderson was a staunch supporter of the French Revolution and, while visiting Paris, developed a novel means of spreading despatches beyond the encircling German lines. Small paper balloons, varnished with hot oil and filled with gas, had newspapers attached and were sent floating on the breeze over the frustrated enemy.

February 2

1194   Churches of St Andrews and Durham struck a deal signed and sealed in Edinburgh confirming their respective rights north and south of the Border.

1488   Young Prince James was handed over to rebel forces by the keeper of Stirling Castle while his father, James III, was in the North trying to drum up support.

1690   Scores of porpoises were beached near Cramond on the Forth along a half-mile stretch; local people sold them to a Leith soap-boiler.

1705   Three young Edinburgh men jailed for attacking the Governor of the Castle in his sedan chair as part of a drunken prank.

1906   Reassurances were given to the public after an outbreak of smallpox on a jute-laden ship which had docked at Dundee.

Lady Sings the News

Among the Highland clans, in what was decidedly a man's world, there were a surprising number of female bards. Among the most famous was Mairi Nighean Alasdair Ruadh, who died in 1674, at the age of 105.

February 3

1401   Earl of March and Henry 'Hotspur' Percy led 2,000 men into East Lothian, burning and looting; they were surprised in a night attack at East Linton and were driven back across the Border.

1504   Golf challenge match between James IV and the Earl of Bothwell; the result is unrecorded suggesting, say some experts, a royal defeat.

1700   A major fire, which made 400 families homeless, destroyed many buildings, some 14 storeys high, around Parliament Close in Edinburgh.

SIEGE MENTALITY AT STIRLING

1888	Sixteen crofters jailed for their part in protest riots over land-use in Stornoway the previous month.
1936	After dock trials of the Cunard liner *Queen Mary* at Clydebank five stones of fish, including herring, saith, cod, whiting and flounder, were found to have been sucked through a grating.

Bad Press

Macbeth – thanks to the Bard of Avon, William Shakespeare – is a name popularly associated with murder and mayhem, but it was also, ironically, the name of a series of physicians to the early Scottish monarchs, among them, Robert the Bruce.

February 4

1590	Clan Gregor were in trouble again having murdered one of the king's foresters at Glenartney in Perthshire; a commission was granted to pursue them with fire and sword.
1649	Charles II was proclaimed king at Edinburgh as news of his father's execution in London reached the Scots capital.
1779	Pioneering botanist Sir James Nasmyth, who planted his Peeblesshire estate with silver firs and birch, died.
1896	Town Council agreed that Edinburgh police-cells should have electric light; one councillor wanted to know if the next step would be 'cigars and turkey-carpets' for the prisoners.
1941	Freighter *Politician* foundered off Eriskay in the Western Isles with her cargo of whisky – the legend of *Whisky Galore* was born.

Eagle of the Ninth

Hadrian's Wall was begun in AD 122 on the orders of the Emperor, to shut out the troublesome Picts who were responsible, according to some sources, for the complete disappearance of the Ninth Legion, 6,000 men who had been sent north to rap the Pictish knuckles.

NEXT STOP, NEWFOUNDLAND

A circus clown, an Irish saint and an eccentric lone sailor are just three individuals who have shared an obsession for a 70-foot-high lump of rock out in the Atlantic, hardly big enough to make its mark on large-scale nautical charts.

Island fever is a well-enough known phenomenon – the urge to visit or, in more extreme cases, to settle on the wild and windswept corners of these British Isles, to share the unique flavour of remote community life and, with a bit of luck, find yourself closer to the greater realities.

In Western tradition the romantic escape to a Utopian island society has a long pedigree. The pursuit of this dream has inspired classic works such as *The Tempest*, *Robinson Crusoe* and *Swiss Family Robinson*. However, the fixation with Rockall is less easily explained.

This guano-stained lump of granite – the only visible reminder of a long-sunken landmass which separated the North Atlantic from the Arctic Basin – beloved principally by seals and seabirds, lies 191 miles west of St Kilda. This week, in 1972, the outcrop was formally incorporated into Scotland having been annexed by Britain in 1955 when naval commandos landed by helicopter, claimed it for the Queen, hoisted the Union Jack and cemented a plaque to the summit.

Since then, it has assumed strategic importance as a sea-mark in fishing disputes and oil exploration negotiations, and has attracted the adventurer, Tom McClean, to perch for a few days on its inhospitable ledges. And, of course, Rockall gives its name to the huge sea area forming part of the Meteorological Office's vital shipping forecast.

Widely held to be the first person to set eyes on Rockall is the intrepid Irish saint Brendan AD 484-577 who, with his team of 60 monks, roamed the Atlantic in search of a 'mysterious land amid the waves'.

And the clown? A French expedition which reached the rock in 1921 put ashore a nimble crew led by a merchant seaman who, in his civilian life, was a circus clown. This party spent an hour and a half on Rockall before departing, having left a sealed bottle with a commemorative record in a cleft.

One other intriguing possibility has been mentioned concerning Rockall. Could it be the last visible mountaintop of the lost and fabled continent of Atlantis?

February 5

1200   King William the Lion confirmed a land-grant to a gentleman called John Prat for the annual rental of a two-year-old sparrowhawk.

1284   Infant Margaret 'Maid of Norway', grand-daughter of Alexander III, was acknowledged as heir to the Scottish throne; she died in Orkney *en route* to Scotland six years later.

1720   Riot in Dundee over the export of grain which people believed was pushing up prices on the home market; two vessels were stormed by the mob.

1845   A five-foot-long cod, weighing 56lbs, was landed at Stornoway.

1907   La Milo, the 'statuesque goddess and exquisite *poseuse*', said to possess the most beautiful figure in the world, was appearing in Glasgow. Her show was 'unique, daring, yet chaste'.

What a Defence

In 1544, artillery belonging to the town of Aberdeen consisted of a falcon, a kilis-piece, a bollis-piece and three serpentines, supplemented a few years later by two ringed-dogs, two great-yeatlings, the Great Falcon of the Laird of Drum, and a set of English half-slungs and cut-throats.

February 6

859   Kenneth MacAlpin, the monarch who brought the Scots and Pictish nations together, died after a 16-year reign at the royal residence at Forteviot.

1619   John Davidson opened his business in Aberdeen as a manufacturer of virginals; the second such craftsman in the burgh.

1832   Cholera had caught hold in Scotland, having spread

through Russia and Germany from Bengal. Cases were reported in Edinburgh and Kirkintilloch.

1916   Marxist revolutionary and school-teacher John MacLean arrested for sedition and imprisoned in Edinburgh Castle.

1946   Bananas and oranges were to be made available to young people in Scotland through the ration books.

Secret of Ben Wyvis

Perhaps Scotland's strangest title-deed gave tenure of a forest to Sir Henry Munro of Foulis, on condition that he delivered a snowball to the Crown on any day of the year requested. Not such a difficult task as it seems, since snow lies all year round in the sheltered corries of nearby Ben Wyvis, north of Dingwall.

February 7

1568   Petty theft of lead from the roofs of Elgin and Aberdeen Cathedrals prompted Regent Moray to requisition all lead and sell it to support the army.

1633   Numbers of people smothered in their homes when a snowstorm of 'unmatched ferocity' overtook Scotland. The impressive ashlar crown on the steeple of King's College, Aberdeen, fell to the ground.

1756   Day of fast in Scotland in thanksgiving for the escape of the nation from the effects of the recent Lisbon earthquake which killed 35,000 people.

1850   World's first train-ferry, 417-ton *Leviathan*, began work on the Granton-Burntisland run for Edinburgh, Perth and Dundee railway.

1931   Plans for a university in the Scottish Highlands to serve as a world centre for Celtic culture announced by the American Iona Society.

Equine Appetites

In the late 1700s, the enormous number of horses in Scotland and their appetite for oats was often blamed for the recurrence of famine. More recently, seven Highland ponies – known for their healthy appetites – were leased to a nature reserve in Northern France to help keep down the vegetation.

February 8

1598   Six men were hanged at the Cross in Edinburgh for counterfeiting letters.

1836   Tenth-anniversary dinner of the 'Six-Foot' Club held in Edinburgh; plans announced for a specially large boat to be built to enable the tall men to take part in a regatta on the Forth.

1887   Two days of violent rioting by Lanarkshire miners led to 74 arrests.

1900   Lord Cameron, one of the most notable Scottish judges of the twentieth century, was born.

1928   Serious flooding around Blairgowrie when the River Tay burst its banks. Many had to be rescued.

Young Man's Death

The oldest recorded victim of a full-scale battle in Scottish history was William Maitland of Lethington, father of Sir Richard Maitland, the poet, lawyer and statesman. The old man was slain on the bloody field of Flodden in 1513 when he was in his 90th year.

February 9

1292   As the flame of independence begins to burn in Scotland John Balliol called a Great National Council at Scone.

1576   Madge Morison of Aberdeen was fined for dressing up in men's clothing at a funeral. Apparently it was a favourite pastime of young folk to swap clothes with members of the opposite sex and parade through the town.

1784   Tontine Tavern in Edinburgh was the venue for the formation of the Highland and Agricultural Society of Scotland.

1833   Plans completed by Glasgow's Merchants House to convert the Fir Park into the city's necropolis.

1934   The shooting of whooper swans (rare visitors to Scotland) was causing anxiety to the Royal Society for the Protection of Birds.

Green, Green Grass

In the warmer summers of medieval Scotland, cannabis was grown widely as hemp for rope-making to supply the nation's expanding merchant fleet.

February 10

1306   Robert the Bruce murdered the Red Comyn in Greyfriars monastery at Dumfries.

1495   Bull, or edict, from Pope Alexander VI confirmed the foundation of the University of Aberdeen.

1665   The growing threat of invasion by the Dutch saw night-watches stepped up in villages along the Fife coast.

1884   Anxiety was expressed that the Secretary of State for War was planning to abolish the Highland feather bonnet.

1953   Two soldiers fainted from the intense cold during the anniversary parade of Argyll and Sutherland Highlanders at Redford Barracks in Edinburgh.

Head of Steam (parts I and II)

Turkish baths were introduced to Britain after Black Isle scholar and adventurer David Urquhart wrote about them in a travel-book published in 1848. In the big league, James Watt is said to have hit on the idea of his reciprocating steam-engine while strolling on Glasgow Green. Arguably, the end product of this brainwave was the Industrial Revolution.

February 11

1483   Treaty signed at Westminster promising backing from Edward IV for the Duke of Albany, if he assumed the Crown of Scotland.

1682   Three men drowned after falling through ice on Edinburgh's Nor' Loch, now the site of Waverley Station.

1892   Dundee adopted the title of Lord Provost for its most prominent citizen.

1902   Steamer *Hurorian* left the Clyde at the start of a transatlantic crossing and was never seen again.

1924   Glasgow Chamber of Commerce urged the government to place orders for naval cruisers in the Clyde shipbuilding industry to help relieve unemployment.

Zoologist Puzzle

An alloy ring, last seen on the leg of a fulmar at Eynhallow, Orkney, was in 1969 returned to Aberdeen zoologists by Interpol, who discovered it adorning a china figurine which turned up in a Dutch garden.

SKULL-SKITING FOR BEGINNERS

Possibly you'll have the nicely bleached skull of a cuddy handy around the house somewhere, even an ox skull will do, and if so, we can get involved in what promises to be an exhilarating piece of experimental history.

In the early 1500s the pleasures of young Scots were surprisingly varied. When they weren't dancing, partaking of a wee drink or mingling with the opposite sex, the boys at least could be found at archery, leaping, running, shot-putt or wrestling.

One of the least dignified but nonetheless exciting, often dangerous, pastimes was summer sledging – the ancient sport of hurley-hacket – sliding down a grassy slope or 'incline plain' at breakneck speed on a piece of wood crafted for the purpose. Echoes here, for me at least, of sliding down the High Park in Clydebank on my schoolbag, remembering to brake before ending up under the ice-cream van. Similar success can be achieved by sliding downhill on a black plastic bag; a thrill that has to be experienced to be fully appreciated.

But what of hurley-hacket? The Heading Hill, in the shadow of Stirling Castle, was, it seems, Scotland's favourite venue for the sport and the place of execution had its name changed to mark its use for an altogether more civilised purpose.

However, Sir Walter Scott tells us this sport was also practised on Calton Hill, in Edinburgh, towards the end of the 1700s, when the boys of the capital used a horse's skull for a sledge. Sounds desperately uncomfortable, but Scott knew his local history. In another form, the pastime is called Hurly-Haaky, haaky being a cow. It would appear that any old skull of sufficient dimensions could be employed. It makes you wonder if some giant prehistoric skull had turned up in the Ochils, would Scotland have led the way in the introduction of the four-man bob?

James V gets the credit for this sporting development, just as he pioneered the 'egg wars' when the gay young blades of Stirling indulged themselves in mock sieges of the castle with a plentiful supply of eggs for ammunition.

Football and golf seem to have been favourite games of the time, perhaps all the more so because they were prohibited by Act of Parliament as an interference with the very necessary practise of the martial arts, such as archery.

Among the upper-classes we trace a sport called racket, which was presumably a form of tennis. Another court game of the period is variously described as ketche, kaiche, caiche, or cache, which may have been nothing more complex than good old-fashioned handball, or possibly just a game of hide-the-ball.

Hawking and hunting were extremely popular among the gentry, and during this period we also find reference to the introduction of organised horse-racing in Scotland. James IV seems to have been its chief patron, importing the best foreign breeds and his son was equally enthusiastic. The sport took on political undertones, however, as it was said to have been one of the pastimes employed by his faithless guardians to divert young James V's attention from serious matters of state.

But we digress; back to the experiment – hurly-haakers, are you ready? Skulls in position? Then, let skiting commence . . .

February 12

1562	Heavy snowfalls reported from all parts of Scotland with many cattle and deer frozen to death.
1624	George Heriot – 'Jinglin' Geordie' – founder of the Edinburgh school and hospital bearing his name, died aged 61.
1790	Grocer John Kennedy and a servant-girl were arrested in Glasgow for smuggling a saw into a prisoner in the town jail.
1911	A proposal to allow Sunday golf at Drumchapel Golf Club was defeated at the annual general meeting.
1972	Fraserburgh seine–fisher *Nautilus* lost in the North Sea with her crew of seven.

Not Tonight, Josephine

Such was the fame of James Macpherson's fraudulent 'translation' of the Ossianic legends that the famed German poet, Goethe, said he had abandoned Homer for Macpherson, and Napoleon Bonaparte confessed that his favoured bedtime reading were the adventures of Ossian. Despite being discredited, Macpherson managed to arrange – at his own cost – his burial in Westminster Abbey.

February 13

1624	Aberdeen town council expressed dismay at the amount of eating and drinking that went on at baptisms and limited such celebrations to 12 people.
1744	David Allan, painter of everyday Scottish scenes, was born at Alloa. A bump on the head when he fell from a basket, as he was carried on horseback through a snowdrift to a wet nurse, did not dent his talent.
1790	Fine weather saw many vessels leave the Forth for fishing in the Davis Strait.
1933	Two Bavarian pied pipers arrived in Perthshire to help exterminate muskrats currently infesting much of the countryside.
1957	Five stitches were inserted in a head-wound after Lord Inverclyde was thrown from his bunk on the Glasgow-Euston sleeper and struck his napper on an ashtray.

Time to Spare

The huge, four-faced clock on Edinburgh's Balmoral (formerly North British) Hotel is always set a couple of minutes fast in a tradition which has continued for a century. This is an attempt, so it is said, to ensure that rail travellers catch their trains.

February 14

1239   Pope Gregory XI confirmed a charter to the abbot and monks of Lindores allowing them to establish schools in the Dundee area.

1576   Scotland, blessed for once with a fine crop, agreed to send corn to France, Flanders and England, where food was scarce.

1602   James and George Vallam hanged in Edinburgh for the crime of 'stouthreif' – they had intercepted and spirited away a pack-train loaded with merchandise on its way to a fair at Brechin.

1746   Bonnie Prince Charlie's public-relations network had him 'hunting and hawking' daily at Blair Atholl, seemingly unconcerned about the activities of Government forces to the south.

1946   Picasso exhibition at Glasgow's Kelvingrove Art Gallery baffled many Scots. Dundee's Art Committee Convener William Lumsden said the paintings were 'fearsome, macabre, phantasmagorical: Disney on canvas'.

I Name This Child

Habbakuk Bisset, Writer to the Signet and author of a digest on Scots law, was the son of Mary Queen of Scots' caterer who begged the Queen to name the infant. Mary, in a hurry to Mass, opened her Bible and selected the first name she came across.

February 15

1489   Parliament of King James IV freed himself and his advisors from blame for the murder of his father, James III, after the Battle of Sauchieburn the previous year.

1564   John Knox reported remarkable meteorological happenings 'as if the joining of two armies'. It was probably an occurrence of the Northern Lights but Knox called it divine wrath over merrymaking at the Catholic Court.

1848   Caledonian Railway opened between Beattock and Glasgow.

1916   Twenty-year-old Black Watch private John Docherty was executed on the Western Front for desertion; he was the first Kitchener volunteer put to death.

1931   Glasgow Labour MP James Maxton told his constituents in Bridgeton that he would become 'revolutionary' if statesmen continued to tinker with the problem of poverty.

Bringing Home the Bacon

When pigs roamed the High Street in Edinburgh as dogs and cats do today, it was a common sight to meet Jane, daughter of Lady Maxwell and destined to become Duchess of Gordon, riding the family sow bareback down Hyndford's Close with her sister, Eglantine, thumping the poor creature with a stick to speed its progress.

February 16

1196   Lands at St Andrews confirmed to the leper hospital of St Nicholas by William I. The document was signed at Kinghorn.

1598   Habit of keeping long-murdered but unavenged Scots nobles unburied was deplored by the Privy Council which demanded that the Earl of Moray and Lord Maxwell be interred within 20 days.

1855   Emigration ship *Tornado* left Glasgow's Broomielaw with 500 settlers bound for Melbourne, Australia.

1883   Sheriff at Cupar refused to convict a labourer for neglecting to have his children – aged 7 and 10 – educated, saying that to begin education at 12 was quite sufficient.

1928   Glasgow education committee expressed concern that unfair discrimination in favour of rugby was being exercised in certain Glasgow schools.

Mary's Right on Cue

As well as being one of the most enthusiastic golfers of her generation, Mary Queen of Scots was also an accomplished billiards player who often challenged the gentlemen of the court to a quick frame.

February 17

1540   A writ in the name of James V recognised the gypsy kingdom of Little Egypt under its monarch, Johnnie Faw.

1725	Two soldiers whipped in Edinburgh for fighting a duel – a commonplace occurrence in the first half of the eighteenth century.
1818	Grave of the patriot king, Robert the Bruce, the exact location of which had been long forgotten, was uncovered by workmen at Dunfermline Abbey.
1822	Riot in Glasgow was broken up by a charge of dragoons. The mob had attacked a large house in Ruchill, thought to have been the home of a posse of grave-robbers.
1983	An incendiary device, sent by a protestor against a visit to Glasgow by the Princess of Wales, was received by the Lord Provost; no one was hurt.

Auld Reekie

The person credited with giving Edinburgh its nickname of Auld Reekie was a Fife laird, who regulated evening worship by watching over the Forth for the appearance of smoke above the city as fires were lit in preparation for supper.

February 18

1369	Burgesses and merchants were not to leave Scotland without the express permission of the king or chamberlain.
1485	Ferrymen throughout Scotland had been ordered by Parliament to cut fares which had doubled or trebled in recent years; severe penalties for non-compliance were threatened.
1621	Sir George Hay's glassworks – the first in Scotland – at the village of Wemyss in Fife, was reported to be operating efficiently.
1820	A census in Edinburgh was to reveal that the capital's population had reached just over 112,000.
1897	Kathleen Garscadden, Aunt Kathleen of BBC *Children's Hour* and a pioneer of early broadcasting, was born in Glasgow.

Remnants of Runrig

The last example in Central Scotland of the runrig system of agriculture – medieval strips of tenanted land – is to be found at Scotlandwell in Kinross-shire.

SATURDAY MORNING HEEBIE-JEEBIES

Smart Scots, in the year 1598, were convinced that the dark clouds of superstition had finally been chased away by the stern logic of the Reformation and the blind zeal of the witch-finders. But even the most educated and rational among the Scottish people reverted to a sort of pagan panic one Saturday morning in February, when the land was cast under an ominous, primeval shadow. Nothing could disguise the nation's palpitations as a total eclipse of the sun ran its spectacular course.

This particular eclipse is very well documented, being first observed between nine and ten in the morning and continuing for about two hours. Such darkness overtook the land that it was impossible to read a book without the aid of a candle, says chronicler David Calderwood. However, reading seems to have been the last thing on the minds of the Scots.

'Men and women were astonished, as if the day of judgment had been coming. Some women swooned. The streets of Edinburgh were full of cries, and some men ran from the streets to the kirk to pray.'

Work at the Court of Session was disrupted, stars could be clearly seen in the sky and the sea, land and air was uncannily still – 'stricken dead, as it were'. Disturbing, unprecedented scenes were witnessed. Ravens and fowls flocked together and 'mourned exceedingly'. Great multitudes of frogs ran together making an uncouth and hideous noise.

The religious scholar James Melville, a pillar of logic and 'not one particularly prone to superstition', relates how he knew from his studies the day, the hour and the cause of this sensational event and 'set myself to note the proceedings in a basin of water mixed with ink'. But when the darkness reached its greatest depth, even a cool customer like Melville got a touch of the heebie-jeebies. 'My sight lost all the sun. I was stricken with such heaviness and fear that I had no refuge but prostrate on my knees, commending myself to God and crying mercy.'

This 'fearful event' was remembered as Black Saturday, an omen of dark days soon to overtake the national church. Effects were indeed swift as a study of the annals of the Kirk reveals. Within a year, three luminaries of the church – Thomas Buchanan, Robert Rollock and David Ferguson – had gone to join the celestial majority, and disruption was soon to follow.

The significance that such awe-inspiring natural events had on the Scottish psyche is illustrated by a set of verses penned by Allan Ramsay after an eclipse of the sun on 22 April 1715.

The unlearned clowns, who don't our era know,
From this dark Friday will their ages shew,
As I have often heard old country men,
Talk of Dark Monday and their ages then.

The 'Dark Monday' to which Ramsay refers was another total eclipse on 29 March 1652, possibly better remembered as 'Mirk Monday'. Poetically, this particular eclipse was said to have caused a darkness which had not been matched since the Lord's Passion.

February 19

1315　Severe famine which had devastated England, was now being experienced in Scotland. The war with England, culminating at Bannockburn, was blamed for the shortages.

1519　Scots Parliament condemned Home of Wedderburn and his three brothers for the murder of a Frenchman who had been given the job of keeping the peace in the absence of Regent Albany.

1792　Sir Roderick Murchison, who travelled all over Europe in his study of geology, was born in Ross-shire.

1834　Carpenters on the Clyde were kept busy repairing vessels damaged during fierce Atlantic storms.

1908　Students disrupted a suffragette meeting at Corstorphine, Edinburgh; they allowed the ladies to speak providing they could have a sing-song afterwards.

Under Threat

Most of the population of Aberdeen anxiously set to work in December 1637 to clear the mouth of the Dee which had been blocked by a sandbar after a violent storm. It threatened the town's future as a port but all the digging was in vain, and it took another storm to clear the river-mouth.

February 20

1472　Orkney and Shetland were annexed to the Crown of Scotland having been offered, three years previously, as security for Princess Margaret of Denmark's dowry. Orkney was valued at 50,000 florins, Shetland at 8,000.

1594　Earl of Bothwell broke into open rebellion and King James was so terrified that he refused to live at Holyrood which had already been attacked twice by the Earl and his cronies.

1616　Three men condemned to death in the Borders for killing 40 sheep in an attempt to block the restocking of disputed lands.

1890　Proposal for Home Rule in Scotland was defeated in the House of Commons.

1973　MPs vote for Fife to remain an independent area under

local government reorganisation, thereby overturning a government plan to split the Kingdom between Tayside and Lothian.

Antarctica No More

Perhaps the most popular spot at Edinburgh Zoo is the penguin enclosure, but few visitors appreciate that the ancestors of some of the birds were brought to Scotland by whalers operating out of Leith. The Edinburgh penguin colony is the largest in Europe.

February 21

1301   Scots sought to refresh the Auld Alliance and agreed, at a Scone Assembly, to write to the French King Philip who seemed disinterested.

1592   John Pitscottie and his friends admitted that, on a Fast Sunday at preaching time, they had been playing football at Muirton, Perth. They were ordered to make repentance.

1681   'Sweet Singers' of Bo'ness, a group of religious zealots noted for their chanting of psalms, were thrown into jail in Edinburgh.

1882   A survey showed that in the previous week 8,500 books had been returned to Glasgow's Mitchell Library – most popular were religion and philosophy.

1975   Decision taken to close the city centre High School of Glasgow, which was relocated in the West End.

Road and the Miles

The standard mile – 1,760 yards – now recognised the world over, was calculated by a seventeenth-century Scot, John Ogilvie, from Kirriemuir, a member of the Royal Society. The distance was the average of the various miles in use at the time.

February 22

1452 Earl of Douglas was stabbed to death by King James II at his 'closet window' in Stirling Castle. Douglas had come for talks with a guarantee of safe conduct.

1603 Marriage of Moray's son to Huntly's daughter helped end a blood-feud between the families which had lasted over a decade.

1716 Jacobite Earl of Nithsdale escaped from the Tower of London on the eve of his execution having exchanged clothes with his wife, Winifred.

1854 Part of the old city wall in Edinburgh collapsed into Leith Wynd killing several people; an unsafe section was speedily demolished.

1981 Arbroath missionary Jean Waddell was freed from prison in Iran.

Natural Light

The beautiful countryside around Borthwick Castle in the Borders was noted in centuries past for its glow-worms. Travellers were said to have been astounded by the beautiful greenish light which fringed the evening footpaths.

February 23

664 St Boisil, prior of Melrose and a 'priest of great virtue', died.

1310 The church and people of Scotland declared in favour of Robert the Bruce from the church of the Friars Minor in Dundee.

1587 King James VI's secretary arrived in Edinburgh with final confirmation of the execution of his mother, Mary Queen of Scots; the king showed very 'great displeasure' and went to bed without supper.

1624 A severe frost which had gripped Scotland began to lift; at one point 11 carts carrying wine had travelled up the Tay from Dundee to Perth on the thick ice.

1950 When it emerged that King George VI had bought two tartan dinner-jackets, the editor of *Tailor and Cutter* was moved to comment that they were presumably meant 'for wearing in private only'.

Hollow Past?

The traditions which underpin the Scottish tourist heritage do not, alas, bear much examination. Haggis was a delicacy in Greece; golf was a popular Roman pastime; the Persians enjoyed the skirl of the bagpipes; and, horror of horrors, even the kilt, say some researchers, was introduced to Scotland . . . by an Englishman! At least we've got oor shortbread.

Piper's refreshment

February 24

1568   Fasting was reinstated at Lent because of a shortage of fresh meat; thus an economic measure replaced the religious practice of pre-Reformation days.

1594   Aberdeen became the latest Scots burgh to celebrate the birth of a son to James VI and much drinking was the order of the day.

1607   According to reports from London everyone at court was preoccupied with events on the continent. There was 'little curiosity' about what was going on in Scotland.

1846   Two hundred whales driven ashore at Basta Voe, North Yell, Shetland.

1921   Glasgow Dean of Guild Court approved two new housing-schemes for the city at Mosspark and Drumoyne, costing £2.5m.

The Scot at play

Penny for Your Thoughts

The niece of a Glasgow provost, Frances Stewart, who hailed from Dennistoun, was the sitter for the portrait of Britannia used on coins introduced in the last century.

February 25

1634   A Scot named Gordon was among a group of assassins who slew the awesome Czech Count Wallenstein. Wallenstein once had an officer put to death because his spurs clanked.

1746   Three Hessian hussars quartered in Edinburgh received 'upwards of 5,000 lashes' for attacking a constable; such a severe discipline, it was hoped, would prevent further disorder.

1755   Young David Allan, destined to become one of Scotland's greatest painters, entered the Foulis Painting Academy at Glasgow University, aged 11.

1907   New Scots comedian, George Melvin made his first London appearance. His 'quaint patter' and impersonation of a Highland postman made him an instant hit.

1941   First of the popular trolley-buses appeared on the streets of Glasgow.

Viking Legacy?

An unusual medical condition of webbing between the toes, found in the Western Isles, is traditionally thought to have been brought to Scotland by Viking settlers. On St Kilda this condition is said to have helped islanders clamber around the cliff faces in search of birds' eggs.

SCOTS JOIN THE BIG, BAD LEAGUE

The Italian Trick comes to Scotland – now, how's that for an enigmatic and intriguing index entry? Submerged beneath a pile of dusty tomes I hunted, on your behalf, for the story in question. What could this be all about, I wondered, as I leafed through the time-worn pages. Some sort of imported football skill; a deft heel-flick and a back heedie perhaps? A wee device to improve your pasta dishes, or maybe even a cute sexual peccadillo thunk up by Casanova?

As it happens, 350 years ago this 'trick' was enough to send a collective shiver down the spine of the Scottish nation and had folk diving for the most powerful purgatives they could find.

Over the centuries we Scots have fine-tuned all sorts of horrendous methods for disposing of compatriots who failed to toe the politically correct line, or simply failed to buy their round. Everything from starvation (the Duke of Rothesay, 1402), to multiple stabbings (David Riccio, 1566), and lots of sinister stuff in between – burning, explosives, hanging, disembowelling, beheading, drowning and the use of cart-horses to drag folk to bits.

But for the Scots, nothing held such terror as poisoning, the Italian trick of sending men 'to the otherworld in figs and possets' (an alcoholic cold remedy). This was the ultimate terror; a sudden, inexplicable choking death, or maybe worse, a creeping insidious end.

In the year 1676, in one of the most sensational cases of the century, two Edinburgh boys, Clark and Ramsay, reminded us of this peculiarly Scottish fear.

Merchant John Anderson, for whom Ramsay worked, had, according to the chronicler Sir John Lauder of Fountainhall, for many months been labouring under an 'enfeebling malady' which was likely, in time, to have brought him to his grave. During the sickness the two boys had started to steal jewellery and other valuable items from the invalid, trusting that he would eventually die and that their crimes would never come to light. However, Anderson, contrary to all expectation and medical opinion, began to pick up. The boys became terrified and took another lad called Kennedy into the plot. He was an apothecary's assistant and supplied a drug which, fed to Anderson in small doses, effected a successful relapse from which he eventually died.

Initially, there was no suspicion of foul play until one of the boys greedily tried to sell a gold chain which had formed part of their plunder. Sir John Clerk of Penicuik, a nephew of the murdered merchant, claimed that, while the crime was still undiscovered, he heard a voice in his sleep urging him to 'avenge the blood of his uncle'. Shortly afterwards, he came across Anderson's chain in a goldsmith's shop and it was easily traced back to the two apprentices.

The boys were hanged, and for months afterwards there was much anxious talk in the taverns and around the Mercat Cross that this 'Italian Trick' might have indeed come to stay in Scotland.

February 26

1589   The talk of the Holyrood Court was a five-hour debate in which the young King James VI had laid aside his crown and sceptre and disputed on religion as a 'private man' with the Jesuit, James Gordon.

1672   Philip van der Straten of Bruges was granted permission to set up at Kelso, the first Borders mill for dressing and refining wool.

1909   Duke of Montrose awarded £19,090 4s 5d as compensation for land lost raising water-levels to increase the supply from Loch Katrine.

1953   Health Service officials in Edinburgh were stunned by a doctor who had prescribed gin for a patient.

Gentlemen of the Soil

The importance of agriculture to sixteenth-century Scotland is illustrated by the annual dissolution of Parliament to allow the Commissioners to be on their farms at harvest-time. The year 1868 is widely regarded as Scotland's 'Year of the Short Corn'. In some districts the crop was so stunted that the scythe could not be used and the cutting was done with scissors.

February 27

1314   A Scots force, under Douglas, scored a notable success by storming Roxburgh Castle in a daring night-time escapade.

1545   A victory hailed all over Europe was achieved by the Earl of Angus when he defeated an English force at Ancrum Moor in the Borders.

1683   Soothsayers were in great alarm and consternation in Scotland over the conjunction of Saturn and Jupiter in the constellation of Leo. It was seen as an ominous portent for the year ahead.

1832   Parliamentary Reformers, seeking an extension of the franchise, hissed the Duke and Duchess of Buccleuch as they passed through Hawick.

1906   Paddle-steamer *St Peter* launched at Grangemouth for service on the Russian Lakes.

Too Close for Comfort

John Armstrong, the Roxburghshire-born poet and doctor of last century, got in a spot of bother by publishing two very different kinds of literary work back-to-back. First came a serious study called *A Synopsis of the History and Cure of Venereal Disease*. This was followed by a poem, *The Economy of Love*, which was condemned for 'inflaming the passions of youth'.

February 28

1536   Inverkeithing and Kinghorn asked for their tax contribution to be modified because of their poverty.

1592   Wizard Richard Graham, who had been accused of raising the devil in a backyard off Edinburgh's Canongate, was 'worried and burnt' at the Cross. He had been linked with the North Berwick witches.

1600   Hunting was banned in the vicinity of Perth, Dundee and Montrose because King James VI planned a visit and wanted to ensure good sport.

1831   A Paisley minister, in fear and trembling of a cholera outbreak, built a high paling around his home and communicated with the outside world using a bell and speaking trumpet.

1852   Committee of the Highland Society of Scotland saw a demonstration of a steam-plough in a field near Portobello.

Empty Flows the Don

Early one summer in 1750, the bed of the River Don, for three miles below Dyce, emptied itself, and locals were able to cross over and collect stranded fish. An earth tremor was felt around the time of this remarkable happening and half an hour later the channel refilled.

February 29

1528   Patrick Hamilton, the first Protestant Reformation martyr, was burned for heresy at St Andrews.

1739   Merchants in Scottish ports including Glasgow,

Edinburgh, Montrose, Dundee, Kinghorn and North Berwick petitioned Parliament asking that Scottish ships should be allowed to trade freely with the Colonies.

1836   United Labourers of Glasgow went on strike for increase in their wages from 10s to 12s weekly.

1848   William Thom, weaver poet of Inverurie, Aberdeenshire, died.

Ringing the Changes

When the bells of St Giles in Edinburgh rang out to signal the Union of the Scottish and English Parliaments in 1707 there was a dubious omen for the future. The first tune played was 'Why Should I be Sad on my Wedding Day?'.

March 1

1202   William Cumin abandoned a long-running lawsuit against Glasgow Cathedral over disputed ownership of land at Cadder, Lanarkshire.

1328   Freedom and independence of Scotland was confirmed by Treaty of Northampton following a devastating series of raids by the Scots into the North of England.

1621   Inquiry ordered into the price of coal in Scotland following pleas for help from Lothian pit-owners.

1728   Earthquake reported in various parts of Scotland. The Borders took the brunt and some people in Selkirk were said to have been tumbled out of bed.

1934   The 'New Road' linking Glasgow and Edinburgh via Harthill and Newhouse was completed at a cost of £2,330,000.

Prejudice and Pride

Scots anger at being lumped in under the general heading of 'English' dates back at least to the Union. One story is told of Trafalgar, when Nelson ran up his legendary 'England Expects' signal. There were Scots scattered throughout the fleet but on one warship two messmates from the same clachan saw the message and one remarked: 'No word for puir auld Scotland.' The other smiled: 'Man, Geordie, Scotland kens weel enough that her bairns will do their duty – that's just a hint to the Englishers tae do theirs!'

March 2

1539   Scotland and Antwerp began negotiations on a major trade deal which saw the Scots obtain many privileges in using the port.

1681   Three men were hanged in Edinburgh's Grassmarket for disowning the king's authority. When told they would be spared if they uttered 'God Save the King', they refused.

1801   Clackmannanshire-born Sir Ralph Abercromby led

military landing at Aboukir Bay in Egypt. It is regarded as one of the greatest exploits in British military history.

1881 Myers Hippodrome in Glasgow's Ingram Street was doing a roaring trade with 'lions, elephants, equestrianism and gymnastics'.

1940 Liner *Queen Elizabeth* began her epic five-day dash across the Atlantic to New York; within a week she was joined by another troopship – her sister *Queen Mary*.

Ye Gods!

Theatre-goers in Scotland in the early 1500s required stamina which would stagger a modern audience. Sir David Lindsay's *The Satire of the Three Estates*, a 'short narration', lasted nine hours.

March 3

1519 The French King Francis apologised through his ambassador for concluding a peace treaty with England and not taking Scots interests into account.

1790 Janet Baird was whipped through the streets of Glasgow for returning from banishment without permission.

1883 Three hundred inhabitants of Foula, off Shetland, were said to be on the point of starvation when the first supply-boat of the year reached the stormbound island.

1890 Prince of Wales hammered in the last of seven million rivets on the Forth Bridge (57 men died during its construction).

1970 Four Scots female bridge players claimed a once-in-a-lifetime experience: a complete suit dealt to each of the foursome.

Wee Arra Peepel

Flint arrow heads or 'elf-shots' were widely regarded in the Highlands as good-luck charms capable of warding off a whole variety of evils. It wasn't unusual to find gentlewomen sewing the flints into their petticoats.

EMILY'S RIOTOUS EVENING

Somewhere in the suburbs of Glasgow this March weekend in 1914, the legendary women's rights campaigner, Emily Pankhurst, was in hiding. She emerged at the start of the week to play the principal role in what was subsequently known as the St Andrew's Halls Riot.

The story of the sensational events of that Monday night has been told and retold by West of Scotland women to their daughters and to their granddaughters over the decades. At the peak of this suffragette frenzy in Glasgow that night, there were even threats of a women's rising.

Some 4,000 women attended the suffrage demonstration in the halls, and the city had never seen a gathering quite like it. The building had been bedecked in the suffragette colours of purple, white and green, and the gentle ladies, anticipating a police raid, had taken some extraordinary defensive measures. Lookouts were posted in the streets around the halls, barbed wire had been placed in front of the platform and female stewards stood in a formidable line below the stage, armed with Indian clubs.

What followed, according to one contemporary report, were scenes of violence 'unparalleled in the history of the city's principal meeting-place'. Emily Pankhurst rose to speak to tremendous applause, but during her address police burst into the halls and pushed their way towards the platform. Tumult ensued with suffragettes hurling potted plants at the advancing officers. As chairs were hurled, the ladies fought off the first rush of policemen.

There was momentary panic when a starting-pistol was fired at the back of the hall. Eventually, with batons drawn, the police-officers swept on to the platform and fights broke out all across the stage. The audience was in an uproar and, amid the mass of struggling men and women, several suffragettes and police-officers were injured.

The target of police interest, Mrs Pankhurst, was at last taken into custody with what her supporters termed 'unnecessary violence'. She was dragged off and taken away in a taxi. When a false rumour, that she had escaped the clutches of the police, reached the battlefield the women, some with tears streaming down their faces, sang the Marseillaise.

After her arrest, the action shifted to the city's central police-office in St Andrew's Square where there were open calls for insurrection and threats of a 'Women's Rising'. The situation only cooled when Mrs Pankhurst was taken off to London by car.

March 4

1363 David II, son of Robert the Bruce, astonished the Scots Parliament at Scone by suggesting that, if he died without issue, an English prince should be chosen as their sovereign.

1407 Burgh of Stirling accidentally burned to the ground; a common occurrence in the timber-built towns of fifteenth-century Scotland.

1578 A Dutchman was given a 19-year licence to search for gold and silver in Scotland; efforts were concentrated in Clydesdale and Nithsdale.

1619 Magistrates in Edinburgh ordered by the King to tidy up the streets of the town which he described as 'filthy and unclean'.

1946 Much opposition was being expressed in the Highlands to planned hydro-electric schemes. Locals questioned benefits of the upheavals and feared exploitation of the natural resources.

Come on, You Creeks!

Before the American War of Independence, Scots soldiers stationed in Georgia competed against Creek Indians in the first Highland Games to be staged in North America. Nowadays, there are upwards of 125 Scottish Highland Games held annually in the United States of America.

March 5

1406 Estates met at Stirling where Robert, Duke of Albany, was chosen Governor of Scotland until James I was released from English captivity.

1616 Edinburgh acted to rid itself of tribes of beggars who infested the town and passed their time in 'all kind of riot and filthy lechery'.

1725 Buchanan Charity Society, the oldest in Scotland, founded by a group of Glasgow merchants to help put poor boys of that surname through an education, and to support elderly folk by the name of Buchanan.

1884 Education officials ordered an end to the practice of administering castor-oil as a punishment in the school at Lochgoilhead, Argyll.

1979 A wind gust of 202 mph was recorded at the RAF base at Unst, Shetland.

Saved by a Psalm

When one of the Marquis of Montrose's chaplains was sentenced to death for his part in his master's exploits, he always believed he would be pardoned. Even at the gallows, when the ladder was brought, he remained confident and when he was asked (as was the custom) for a psalm, he chose the longest, Number 119. Before it was three-quarters complete, the reprieve came and he was spared the noose.

March 6

1368 Act of Parliament of David II appointed Lanark and Linlithgow to take the place of Berwick and Roxburgh as two of the four burghs of Scotland.

1621 Import of foreign glass to Scotland was banned in an effort to encourage local manufacture.

1734 John Dempster, an elderly, grey-haired man, was whipped through the streets of Edinburgh for horse-rustling. He was banished for life.

1855 Passenger-traffic on Clyde steamers increased dramatically with an early spell of fine weather.

1930 Several thousand people in Glasgow were expected to qualify for benefit under the new Unemployment Insurance Act.

Xanadu or Bust

When James Brown, the eighteenth-century Kelso-born traveller and scholar, became a representative in 1741 for 24 leading, London merchant-houses who wished to open trade in the East, one of his most important tasks was to carry a letter of greeting from George II to the legendary Khubla Khan.

March 7

1445 A pact of mutual protection was signed and sealed between the Earls of Douglas and Crawford and Donald, Lord of the Isles.

1592 King James VI wanted to 'break ministers' heads' over their failure to pursue the rebel Earl of Bothwell with utmost vigour.

1661 Saturday horse-racing on the sands at Leith was proving tremendously popular; another well-attended racing venue was Cupar in Fife.

1833 James Guthrie, who steered Admiral Freemantle's 98-gun ship *The Neptune* at Trafalgar, died at Newton-upon-Ayr, aged 65.

1852 Man fined a guinea for recklessly discharging a cannon near the Barclay Curle slip dock in Glasgow. One cannonball travelled half a mile.

Deadly Betrothal

The 11th Parliament of James II decreed that no Scotsman should marry an Englishwoman without royal approval, under pain of death.

March 8

1399   Earl of March, who was in dispute with Robert III over an arranged marriage between his daughter and the Duke of Rothesay which had fallen through, was forced to flee to England.

1568   Regent Moray held a 'justiciar', or touring court, in Glasgow where 28 people were hanged for a variety of crimes.

1702   William of Orange died in a riding accident when his horse stumbled in a molehill and Scots Jacobites toasted 'The wee gentleman in the velvet jacket'.

Marching makes thirsty work

1790   Gangs of armed horsemen had been terrorising residents and robbing houses on the South Side of Glasgow.

1955   Gypsy Agnes Morrison fined £5 at Dumfries under the Fraudulent Mediums Act for fortune-telling and threatening to cast a spell.

Strange Companions

Eighteenth-century Edinburgh surgeon Dr Alexander Wood was often seen in the city streets accompanied by his pets – a sheep called Willie and a sinister, black raven. In later years, Lord Gardenstone, one of the nation's top legal brains, kept pigs and trained one to follow him like a dog. As a piglet it shared his bed and as it grew he permitted the pig to stay in his room, his clothes providing a couch, and he was kept comfortably warm by the slumbering porker.

March 9

1696   Quartermaster's shopping-list for the garrison at Edinburgh Castle included 150 fathom of rope for hauling guns, and dozens of sledges for carrying soil to strengthen the castle defences.

1719   James Stuart, the 'Auld Pretender' arrived in Spain to give his support to a Jacobite invasion force equipping at Cadiz.

1828   Glasgow branch of the Greenock Bank was robbed of £28,350 in a raid by an English gang.

1833   An antique bedstead – a huge four-poster thought to have been several hundred years old – was removed from a house in Glasgow's Trongate.

1981   Four-year-old boy who squeezed his hand through fence at Edinburgh Zoo's polar-bear enclosure was bitten and slightly injured; first such incident in 60 years.

Stars in their Eyes

Astronomy in the Scotland of the 1600s was an undeveloped science. The tail of a comet was measured in yards, and discussions of its nature centred on the war and pestilence it might bring in its wake. In the early 1800s, astronomer Robert Blair showed a much more practical streak when he successfully argued for the use of lime-juice in the British Navy as a protection against scurvy.

March 10

1540   Parliament in Edinburgh focused their attention on laws relating to trade and merchandising.

1556   'Call' signed at Stirling bringing John Knox to Scotland from Geneva.

1719   Order issued for the arrest of Rob Roy MacGregor on charges of banditry.

1881   The 11th annual rugby match between Scotland and England, scheduled for Raeburn Place, Edinburgh, was postponed because the English couldn't get a team together.

1980   Image of Red Clydeside still hindered economic development, Scottish Development Agency officials told MPs in Glasgow.

End of the Road

One of the famous Roman distance slabs, which were found along the line of the Antonine Wall in Dunbartonshire, was sent on loan to the United States but was lost in the Great Fire of Chicago in 1871.

THE PIEDMONTESE PLUCKER

Davie Riccio, lute player and sharp operator around court, is said to have pleaded with Mary Queen of Scots, 'Sauvez ma vie, Madame,' as he was dragged from her apartments on 9 March 1566, and knifed to death by a heavy mob of Scots nobles.

This pitiful episode, combined with a remarkably fresh looking bloodstain on the floor of Holyrood Palace, where he is said to have been stabbed more than 50 times, has more or less guaranteed this 'stranger Italian' a place in the front-line of popular Scottish history.

But what do we really know about this enigmatic character who, for a brief period, occupied such a high political position through his influence over Mary? Remarkably little, it would seem. Gathering together what facts are available suggests an even more tantalising figure than at first glance.

Seigneur Davie was said to have been the son of a musician from Pancalieri in Piedmont. Riccio managed to secure a place on the staff of the Marchese Di Moretta, the Savoy ambassador to Scotland. Arriving in Scotland, Riccio made use of his excellent voice to insinuate himself into the choir of the Chapel Royal, where the queen might hear and notice him. This proved to be a successful ploy. According to Birrel's Diaries he was 'very skilfull in music and poetry' and soon made a conquest of the artistic queen who made him her French Secretary and began to heap favours on him.

From his position of power he assisted in organising the marriage to her 'worthless cousin' Lord Darnley. Ironically, Darnley was later to participate in the musician's murder. Gossip about Riccio, both before and after he was done to death, was juicy. Some said he was an agent of the Pope, a spy, and possibly a priest. The general impression in the early 1560s seems to have been that he was merely an intriguing Italian busybody, while the Reformers are certain to have considered him, at very least, a mischievous wee twerp.

One interesting piece of sideline speculation might detain us a little longer. Was Riccio a hunchback or a homosexual? Or even a hunchback homosexual? It has been suggested that one of the Queen's uncles recommended Riccio to Mary as her familiar because his 'deformity' would shield her from scandal. This has been taken to mean Riccio was slightly hunchbacked but, if 'deformity' is a metaphor, then it seems possible that Mary was protected from scandal because her boyfriend was overtly homosexual. We have little evidence about his physical attributes. However, Lord Herries, who knew him, simply describes Riccio as 'neither handsome or well-faced'.

Even Riccio's behaviour on that fatal night has caused confusion. At the tragic dinner-party at which he was surprised, he was seated in the queen's company wearing his cap. The Scots took this to be a sign of insolence, but it later transpired that this was the French style of the time.

Even in death Davie got no peace. He was buried in the Palace cemetery, according to Spanish State papers, but the Queen had him disinterred and placed in a 'fair tomb' in the Church of Holyrood. Popular discontent refused to leave him in peace, and tradition has it that his body was moved again to the Canongate Kirk.

Interestingly, Davie's brother, Joseph, succeeded him as French Secretary but, after Darnley's murder, chose to remain in France.

March 11

1415   Parliament at Perth decided that an urgent review of fire safety in Scots towns should be undertaken.

1503   Improvements in the judicial system in 'outlying areas' of Scotland were called for. Reports said that in the Highlands 'people are become almost savage'.

1601   John Napier, the younger, of Merchiston complained that people suffering from plague were being placed without permission in his yards and parks at Sciennes on Edinburgh's South Side.

1855   Two joiners were arrested by Glasgow police for 'thoughtlessly' dropping orange-peel on passers-by from their scaffold.

1953   House-breaking by girls in the Borders had reached epidemic proportions.

Hot Under the Collar

Among the questionable items taken by the ill-fated Darien expedition from Scotland to the oppressive heat of the Central American jungle in the late 1600s, were woollen stockings, tartan plaid and wigs.

March 12

1424   King James I appointed an advocate for the poor – an enlightened and far-seeing move.

1543   Largest-ever gathering of the Three Estates discussed a coming together with England, including the marriage of the infant Mary, later Queen of Scots, to the Prince of Wales, son of Henry VIII.

1790   Mail-coach from Edinburgh overturned near Musselburgh while attempting to overtake the Prestonpans stagecoach.

1853   Contracts signed for work on Queen Victoria's new mansion house at Balmoral.

1948   Professor J.R. Learmonth and his team from Edinburgh University operated on the King at Buckingham Palace to improve his circulation; an improvised operating theatre was set up in a room overlooking the Mall.

Stretching Tradition

The Covin Tree, on the Finhaven Estate in Angus, is said in local folklore to have grown from a chestnut dropped by a Roman soldier. In the 1400s, an estate-worker was hanged after cutting a walking-stick from its branches.

March 13

1188 Church in Scotland declared independent of the See of York by Pope Clement III.

1662 A young clerk, Thomas Hepburn, was murdered in his bed and dumped naked on a middenhead in Edinburgh's High Street. Five men who were drinking in a nearby lodging house were apprehended.

1873 Scottish Football Association was formed; its constituent clubs included Queen's Park, Clydesdale, Vale of Leven, Dumbreck, Third Lanark, Eastern and Granville Kilmarnock.

1886 New railway at Killin, Perthshire, declared open. Branching off the Callander and Oban railway at Ardchyle, it ran five and a half miles and cost £30,000.

1979 National Library of Scotland purchased a journal of Scots Nile explorer James Augustus Grant for £100,000.

Regime of Mercy

Barnhill Poorhouse in Glasgow's Springburn district demanded that able-bodied inmates make up 350 bundles of firewood or break up five hundredweights of stone, daily, for their keep. Failure to keep this nineteenth-century target meant a day in solitary on a bread-and-water diet.

March 14

1615 A secret trade in mutton developed after the government banned its sale in an attempt to preserve flocks hit hard by a severe winter.

1701 All illegal cargoes of grain brought into the West of Scotland from Ireland were ordered to be sunk.

1806 Lime trees planted beside the Clyde by residents of Carlton Place, Glasgow, destroyed by vandals; local folk were said to be furious.

1930 Rally attended by 6,000 in Perth calls for government action to save the farming industry from disaster.

1982 Forester Bob Taylor told of a close encounter with a UFO on Dechmont Law, near Livingston.

Miracle of the Fishes

A few hundred barrels of herring laid the foundation of Glasgow's reputation as one of the greatest trading cities in Europe. A merchant called Walter Gibson, using a hired Dutch boat in 1668, sent the fish to France and it returned laden with salt and brandy which was sold at great profit. Encouraged by this success, he bought the boat and began trade with Europe and Virginia.

March 15

1543   Permission was given for the production of a Scots translation of the Bible.

1832   Beggars were flocking into Glasgow from country districts causing great concern to magistrates.

1851   Sixty-one men died in an explosion at the Victoria Pit in Nitshill, Glasgow – a 'model pit' which at 1,050 feet was Scotland's deepest.

1921   Women jurors sat at Glasgow Sheriff Court for the first time.

1941   The Clydebank Blitz saw the town devastated by a series of Luftwaffe air-raids. Total fatalities were estimated at 500.

Short Recital

One of Scotland's most famous 'little people' – 38-inch-high Count Borulawski – earned his living in Glasgow and Edinburgh in the late 1700s by, among other things, performing studies on the guitar.

March 16

1602   Queensferry passage across the River Forth was stopped because of the danger of bringing plague from Edinburgh to Fife where the royal family were in residence at Dunfermline.

1712   Many people in south-west Scotland reported visions of land and sea battles; probably meteorological events, these phenomena were always regarded as ill omens.

1836   Whaler *Lady Jane* had arrived at Stromness, Orkney, having lost 20 men before leaving the ice. Three more men died while being carried ashore in blankets.

1848   Authorities in Glasgow warned about the amount of drunkenness in the city when many families were on the point of starvation.

1927   Scottish grocers decided by a majority against the stamping of imported eggs.

High-Speed Brush

In the 1600s a Dutch artist, Jacob de Witt, completed the 110 imaginary portraits of Scots monarchs to hang in Holyrood Palace in just two years – roughly one painting every week – for a fee of £2 3s 8d each. One of the most unusual artistic commissions made by Edinburgh District Council in recent years was a giant collage of Edinburgh Castle comprising passport photographs handed in by members of the public.

March 17

1441   Three suns were reported in the sky over Scotland at noon.

1565   Edinburgh-born Reformer Alexander Alesius, who studied at St Andrews and was a signatory to the Augsberg Confession, died in Leipzig, aged 64.

1883   Crofters Commission appointed to inquire into farming conditions in the Highlands and Islands.

1911   Queen Maria Christina of Spain refused to allow a crucifix worn by Mary Queen of Scots at her execution to be exhibited in Scotland because of its special sanctity.

1969   Eight-man crew of Orkney's *Longhope* lifeboat was lost during a rescue mission in the Pentland Firth.

Greek Tragedy

Glasgow solicitor John Crawford was fuming when he finished last in a Scottish heat of *Mastermind* even though programme planners admitted that at least six of his questions on the Pelopennesian War were from the wrong historical period.

AN EYE FOR THE LASSIES

No one at Scone would have been stunned if they had humphed 'Bleary Bob' along to his Coronation on a stretcher. This grandson of the freedom fighter Robert the Bruce and one of the nation's less well-kent monarchs, was crowned in March 1371, and the fact that he was able to walk to the ceremony must rank as a minor medieval miracle.

Certainly Robert II was past the first flush of princely youth; he was, at 55, much nearer pensionable age. But it was his lifestyle rather than his years which threatened to take its toll.

No contemporary king I can uncover better deserves the title of 'Sire'. According to the best genealogical estimates, he had 12 legitimate children – five sons and seven daughters. He had also surrounded himself with a team of bastard sons, eight in all, and those statistics, combined with Bob's impressive work-rate, would seem to suggest that a squad of illegitimate daughters must also have been lurking somewhere behind the arras.

His nickname, 'Bleary Bob', therefore, seems self-explanatory. Long, sleepless nights spent constructing a memorable dynasty left him little time for shut-eye. What dedication! What self-sacrifice! Hence the red-rimmed eyes which earned him his sobriquet? The explanation, alas, is less romantic.

Robert, had he lived today, would surely have been the 'shades' monarch. He suffered from an inflammation of the eyes to which, his biographers suggest, light and active exertion must have been painful. Froissart, who visited Robert's court, gives his usual colourful description of the king's affliction. One eye, says the chronicler, was turned up and red in colour like sandalwood. An eye for the lassies and no mistake.

The reign of Robert II – the first Stuart monarch – was characterised by struggles with economic difficulties at home and political problems on the international front. Unfortunately, Robert is reckoned to have been a peaceable sort of bloke at a time when the long struggle for freedom had made his people warlike, almost by nature.

Border battles persisted throughout his 19-year reign. Otterburn, where the Douglases squared up to the Percys of Northumberland in 1388, is seen by some historians as the rubber-stamp which confirmed Scottish independence. This battle is celebrated in song and ballad.

I suspect Robert II, as a lover more than a fighter, would have been drawn more to the ballad than the bloodshed. So, let's raise our glasses to Robert, hundredth successor to Fergus Mor mac Erc, 'Bleary Bob', the man who got creative kingsmanship down to a fine art.

March 18

1315   English vessels blockaded Scots ports in an attempt to halt imports of grain and cattle and make the effects of severe famine even more unbearable.

1689   King's Own Scottish Borderers raised as 'Leven's Regiment' to secure Edinburgh for William of Orange against the Jacobites.

1852   A 20,000 signature petition sent to Queen Victoria from the 'Protestant Women of Glasgow' demanding that convents be opened for public inspection.

1936   'Immoral behaviour', including nude bathing along the East Lothian coast, caused anxiety to the authorities and to local residents.

1974   Announcement of the closure of three Beaverbrook newspapers in Glasgow – *Scottish Daily Express*, *Sunday Express* and *Citizen* – with the loss of 1,700 jobs.

Undercover Effie

Lady Euphemia Lockhart, a staunch supporter of the Stuarts in exile, often dressed up as a man and toured the hostelries of Edinburgh in the quest for information. On one occasion she dressed her two grown sons in the finery of high-class hookers and caught the attention of a Whig gentleman. In a nearby inn they drank him under the table and stole important documents.

March 19

1661   Foot races amongst the brewster- and fish-wives of Musselburgh were advertised. One contest to the top of Arthur's Seat had a first prize of a 'groaning' hundred-pound cheese and a 'budgell of Dunkeld Aqua vitae'.

1674   After serving a long apprenticeship in Holland, Andrew McKairter of Dalmellington, Ayrshire, was given permission to set up as Leith's first tobacco-spinner.

1707   Official copy of the Treaty of Union was signed by the Scottish Chancellor.

1883   Statue of David Livingstone, the Blantyre-born missionary, was unveiled in Glasgow's George Square on the 70th anniversary of his birth.

1954   Pools fever gripped the remote parts of Scotland; Shetland postmen reported the pools coupon was often the only mail to lonely crofts.

Homing Instinct

During the World Cup of 1982 in Spain a harassed British Embassy official on his way home from work in Madrid found a tired Scots fan sleeping in an Underground-station platform wrapped in the Saltire. Shaking the voyager he asked him where he was going. 'Partick,' came the dazed and optimistic reply!

March 20

687   Death of St Cuthbert, Bishop of Lindisfarne, who joined the religious life after a vision in the Lammermuir Hills.

1596   A great shortage of ministers was reported in Scotland; of 900 kirks, only 500 had ministers or readers.

1756   An extraordinary whirlwind witnessed in Holyrood Park carried linen laid out to dry high on to Salisbury Crags.

1812   Three teenage boys were sentenced to death for being part of a riotous mob who murdered a policeman and a civilian in Edinburgh on New Year's Eve.

1928   Medical Research Council report condemned tenement living in Scotland as being particularly injurious to the health of young children.

It's a Dog's Life

A power-loom was used in the cotton industry in Glasgow as early as 1792 with Newfoundland dogs providing the motive power. In the same century, dogfights at Sunday services were so common in the Highlands that kirks employed a 'nipper' armed with long-handled forceps to pinch the tails, legs and ears of the mangy curs which scrapped in the church precincts.

March 21

1425   Murdoch, Duke of Albany, and his son Alexander Stewart along with some 30 members of the nobility, arrested on the orders of the Scots Parliament.

1780   Royal Highland regiment was raised at Perth and upwards of 12,500 men joined north of the Tay within eight months.

1853   Tomintoul woman who died at 104 had put her longevity down to a lack of luxuries such as tea.

1859   National Gallery of Scotland on the Mound in Edinburgh – begun nine years previously – was opened.

1955   Evangelist Billy Graham began a seven-week all-Scotland crusade at Glasgow's Kelvin Hall.

Another Young Pretender

A native of Fife, David Gillies, saw his main chance during the confusion of the 1745 Uprising and assumed the name of Charles Stuart, Prince of Wales. He gathered a mock court around him and went about accepting favours and bestowing honours, before being caught eventually at Selkirk.

March 22

1421   Scots and French troops, under the Earl of Buchan, defeated English forces at Baugé in Anjou.

1483   Longstanding bond of friendship and support between

France and Scotland was renewed.

1781   Glasgow magistrates warned parents about children playing 'tops and shinty indiscriminately in the street'.

1906   Four men injured at Clydebank when a portion of the bridge of the liner *Lusitania*, under construction at the yard, collapsed.

1912   Rioting around Kirkconnel, Dumfriesshire, where some miners had been working during a coal strike – a heavy team of several hundred Ayrshire pitmen descended on the town.

Revenge is Sweet

Visiting an English county town, Sir Walter Scott called the local doctor to see to one of his servants and was astonished to discover the physician was a former blacksmith and vet from the Borders who had set himself up in business. Scott, worried by this clandestine change of job asked, 'But John, do you never happen to kill any of your patients?' The 'doctor' explained that some died and some didn't, adding, 'Ony how, it will be lang afore it makes up for Flodden.'

Scotland in victory and defeat

March 23

1597   Edinburgh ordered to pay King James VI 30,000 merks following a disturbance in December when the King was besieged in the Tolbooth.

1846   A price war between steamers operating on the Kirkcaldy to Newhaven run meant a dramatic drop in fares – from one shilling to one penny in the cabin, and from ninepence to a halfpenny steerage.

848   Establishment of a Free Church of Scotland settlement at New Edinburgh, later Dunedin, New Zealand, under the Revd Thomas Burns, nephew of the poet.

943   Final Luftwaffe air-raid of the Second World War on Glasgow; little damage done.

Sanguine Outlook

The most famous nosebleed in Scots history has to be that of the extreme Presbyterian minister, James Guthrie, who preached at Lauder and Stirling. He suffered a violent nosebleed while delivering a powerful sermon on the Blood of the Martyrs and this was later seen as forewarning of his execution in 1661.

March 24

374   Walter Wardlaw, Bishop of Glasgow, was sent to France as an ambassador to renew ancient links between the kingdoms.

424   Parliament at Perth banned secret pacts between the king's subjects and ordered quarterly 'wappinschaws' or military musters in the burghs.

640   Covenanters got the blame for a shortage of peats in Aberdeenshire, having the previous spring chased away all the servants who would normally have done the cutting.

955   The biggest ever Russian trawling-fleet seen off the United Kingdom – some 80 vessels – was reported north of Shetland.

982   Despite protests from local residents, work began to remove 36 trees in Bellahouston Park, Glasgow, to provide a better view of the Pope during his summer visit.

Stamp of Approval

Sanquhar post office in Dumfriesshire – open for business before the first Jacobite Uprising in 1715 – is reckoned to be the world's longest, continuously operating post office, leaving its nearest rivals, Stockholm and Santiago, trailing in its wake.

RAGGLE-TAGGLE TARTAN ARMY?

Anxious whispering in the pews midway through Sunday-morning service and then a mad scramble to evacuate the church under the bemused gaze of the preacher, signalled news that Bonnie Prince Charlie was marching on Macclesfield.

Many accounts exist of the Highland army in Edinburgh, Manchester and Derby, but the most interesting chronicle of the little-known occupation of Macclesfield comes from the pen of a local lawyer, John Stafford, who admitted in correspondence to friends that his first reaction to the news had been to hide in the attic. However, when he finally steadied himself enough to keek out of the garret window he saw his wife and two sisters at the gate of the house and 'shame raised my courage and I ventured to stand by 'em'. What Mr Stafford was to witness over the next hour or two on that Sunday in December 1745, was history passing by his front door.

Following the outriders to the Cross he was told that 10,000 Scotsmen were expected and the lawyer retired home 'much dismayed'. A regiment on horseback commanded by the Duke of Perth, escorting a suspected spy called Sampson Salt, appeared. Close behind, and flying in the face of reports of a raggle-taggle tartan army, came 'ye foot in very regular order with bagpipes playing and everyone in Highland dress'.

Four of five regiments passed before the Prince, who, it was whispered, had walked all the way from Carlisle, arrived on the scene. Fortunately for the Staffords, a halt was called just opposite their door. The lawyer recalled: 'The Prince was in Highland dress with a blue wastcote trimed with silver, and a blue Highland cap, and was surrounded by 40 men who appeared as his guard. He is a very handsome person of a man, rather tall, exactly proportioned, and walks well.'

Macclesfield did not offer the ecstatic welcome of Manchester, the townspeople generally being 'amazed and horrified' at this unusual spectacle. The Prince's lodgings were thereafter mockingly known as 'Holly Rood House', and the mayor and aldermen were ordered to proclaim the Prince but, said Stafford, 'I believe not one Englishman joined in the huzza, except those picked up at Manchester.'

As the parade passed, the watchers noticed the elderly Glenbuckett who seemed to be at least 80 years old and bent double in the saddle. Many boys, aged about 12, were in the company, their task, it was said, was to go armed with knives among the enemy cavalry to cut and injure the horses' legs. Dangerous and dirty work.

With billets arranged, the town settled down for its first night of Jacobite occupation. Stafford, visiting a neighbour's house in the morning, found some 50 men, women and children 'lying promiscuously together like a kennel of hounds, and some stark naked'. It was discovered that the street 'in Edinburgh fashion, was beshit along both sides'. By the Tuesday morning word that the Scots were preparing to leave was greeted with joy and considerable relief.

However, a few days later, during the retreat from Derby, which was to lead eventually to the bloody field of Culloden, the folk of Macclesfield expected to be severely treated; they were not disappointed. The mayor fled, houses which had been locked were plundered, and money was demanded under threat of homes being burned. Our canny lawyer, Mr Stafford, for one, paid up 'rather than stand up to the fury of a refusal'.

March 25

1293 John Balliol, King of Scots, failed to respond to a summons from Edward I to attend a tribunal – defying the English king's efforts to assert his feudal authority.

1437 Coronation of six-year-old James II at Holyrood, 26 days after the murder of his father at Perth.

1886 Men acting on the orders of Lady Matheson of Lewis Castle, Stornoway, pulled down houses built by crofters on their hereditary lots. However, at Sheshader a hostile reception forced them to abandon their demolition plans.

1897 Foundation of the Scottish Trades Union Congress.

1975 Clydebank-built *QEII* became the largest liner to pass through the Panama Canal.

Airdrie's Shipyard

The first iron passenger-boat in regular service in Britain was the *Vulcan* built at Airdrie in Lanarkshire in 1819. She took fare-paying passengers on the Forth and Clyde Canal and ended her days there carrying coal.

March 26

1603 Sir Robert Carey arrived in Edinburgh after sixty hours on horseback, bringing news of the death of Queen Elizabeth in London and the succession of James VI to the English throne.

1707 Scottish regalia – crown, sceptre and sword – were locked away in an oak chest as the independent Scots Parliament disappeared under the Treaty of Union.

1831 'Sweeps, itinerant orators, ballad-mongers and a host of vagabonds' had disrupted a meeting of Glasgow University students called to debate the 'Triumph of Reform'.

1896 A new craze followed by female cyclists in Scotland was to have their wheels painted in colours to match their dresses.

1921   Gaelic classes in London had proved so successful that another winter session was planned.

Plague on Your House

Tradition, possibly originating in the Macdonald strongholds, has it that the three plagues of the Highlands are bracken, rabbits and Campbells.

March 27

1306   Robert Bruce was crowned King of Scots by the Countess of Buchan in a ceremony at Scone. The new king was 31.

1576   Privy Council acted to halt the slaying of deer with guns by Englishmen in the Borders. Some of these hunters were said to have been smuggled into Scotland by the Scots themselves.

1832   Twenty 'blooming damsels' were fleeced in Dunblane, Perthshire, by a female fortune-teller.

1943   British aircraft-carrier *Dasher* exploded in the Firth of Clyde off Arran; 358 lives were lost.

1963   Dr Richard Beeching's infamous rail-closure programme was unveiled; 435 of Scotland's 660 passenger-stations – from Ach-na-Cloich to Yoker Ferry – earmarked for closure.

Dress Sense

Great concern was expressed in the early 1700s about the fashion of steel-hooped skirts. Men were said to be in danger of breaking their shins in narrow places, and in Edinburgh a plea was made for alterations to staircases and enlargement of churches to accommodate these 'monstrous protuberances'.

March 28

1364   David II presented the burghs of Scotland with a charter outlining their privileges.

1583   French Catholic Ambassador, de Menainville, was causing chaos in Edinburgh by demanding the right to mass. On this day, in the popish manner he washed the feet of 13 beggars.

1612   Patent granted for chemical manufacture in Scotland.

1803   Demonstration of a 58-foot-long pioneering paddle-steamer *Charlotte Dundas* fails to convince owners of the Forth and Clyde Canal that steamships were the coming mode of transport.

1944   One hundred thousand volunteers were being sought by the Government to bring in the harvest in Scotland.

Root of the Problem

The Duke of Hamilton was considered a possible future King of Scots in the early 1700s by the anti-Unionist lobby but he let the side down when he failed to turn up at a crucial debate because of a toothache.

March 29

1298   Assembly at Torphichen saw Sir William Wallace, Guardian of Scotland, grant control of the Castle of Dundee to the standard-bearer Walter Skirmischur, for service in the Scots army.

1631   Major inquiry launched into the loss of packet of letters from the king; a Haddington postmaster was accused of carelessness.

1719   Storm dispersed a Jacobite invasion-fleet which had set out from Cadiz, Spain and only two vessels reached Scotland.

1742   A sedan chair which had been found abandoned with a corpse inside at Edinburgh's Netherbowport, was ordered by magistrates to be burned,

1834   A Kelso woman was placed in the stocks for stealing clothes from a hedge, and a big crowd watched possibly the last instance of such a punishment.

Family Fortunes

Serfs and their families were bought and sold in Scotland during the Middle Ages; the Prior of Coldingham is on record as having purchased the Hog family – father, sons and daughters – for £1.

March 30

1180   William the Lion oversaw an Assembly at Haddington at which a long-running dispute between the monks of Melrose and Richard de Moreuill was settled amicably.

1406   Future King James I captured by the English near Flamborough Head while on passage to France in the care of Henry Sinclair, Earl of Orkney.

1700   Ill-fated Scots colony of Darien finally surrendered to the Spanish in the jungles of Central America.

1888   Cupar prison finally closed with the remaining 25 inmates being transferred to Perth.

1941   Italian newspapers claimed that bombing raids on Scotland had been so intense that the Loch Ness monster had been killed by a direct hit.

Thanks to Bob

Aberdeen's Common Good fund, now worth £20m, originated in a grant of freedom-lands by Robert the Bruce in 1319.

March 31

1589   John Templeton and John Hair were appointed as cowherds to the city of Glasgow, one working above the Cross and the other below.

1652   Scottish regalia, saved from Cromwell, was hidden beneath the floorboards of Kinneff Parish Church south of Stonehaven by Revd James Granger.

1794   Andrew Gemmel, perhaps Scotland's most famous beggar, died in Roxburghshire. He was believed to be 105 years old.

1851   A robed procession of city magistrates took part in laying the foundation stone of Edinburgh's new slaughterhouse.

1928   Scotland's 'Wembley Wizards' scored a historic 5–1 victory over the Auld Enemy.

Quick Step for Geordie

George IV, on his famous 'tartan' visit to Edinburgh in 1822, had to retire early from a crowded dance at the Assembly Rooms when an over-enthusiastic Scot dropped his pistols on the king's big toe in the press to be officially presented.

VISIT FROM A LEGENDARY CUDDY

When the amazing 'chestain-coloured naig' called Marocco reached Edinburgh nearly 400 years ago, he took the Scots capital by storm. Never before had such a talented animal been seen north of the Border and this dancing horse was to find immortality when he rated a mention in Shakespeare's *Love's Labours Lost*.

For many years Marocco and his English master, a man called Banks, toured the cities of Europe, and witnesses who saw the remarkable performances in the Scots capital in April 1596, were treated to an exhibition of 'rare and uncouth tricks'. Marocco was able to select coins from a bag of 20 or 30 and return each coin to its owner in the crowd; he could indicate how much the money was worth with a tap of his hoof; he played dead in style that must have been worthy of his twentieth-century Hollywood successors when Banks theatrically threatened to sell him to a carter; he took a drink of water on command and could 'hackney, amble, ride a pace and trot' at the simplest commands.

At the name of the King of Scots he would bow nobly, while if the King of Spain (a contemporary bogey-man) was mentioned, he got really nasty, snapping and stamping.

For months after the visit, the horse was still the talk of the capital. Some time later came reports that Marocco had eaten his master thinking him to be 'spirit and naught else'. This information proved false but the actual fate of Banks and his clever cuddy is just as strange. While they were in Rome their performances so astonished the clergy and the superstitious local people that it was concluded that horse and man must be magicians – and they were burned at the stake.

Such a splendid animal must have attracted much attention in Edinburgh because only 35 years earlier Mary Queen of Scots is reported to have wept openly on her arrival at Leith to take the reins of government, when she saw the scrawny condition of the horses provided for her courtiers and family compared to the noble, high-bred steeds used by the French court.

It seems more likely, however, that the miserable Scots weather which greeted her that morning, and the fact that John Knox was already breathing down her neck, were the cause of her lamentations.

Hoofnotes

In 1247, Patrick, Earl of Dunbar, sold his stud in Lauderdale to the monks of Melrose for the considerable sum of a hundred merks, as part of his preparations for his departure to the Holy Land. Around the time of the Battle of Killiecrankie (July 1689), Highlanders held the strange belief that cavalry horses were trained to bite and kick out with their hooves in battle. A South Uist crofter was granted an increase in his fodder allowance in 1979 by the Western Isles education committee – he sent his children to school by pony because there were no roads. In the 1830s the mail-coach from London to Glasgow took an average of 44 hours; 180 horses were used, four in hand.

April 1

1565   A Roman Catholic priest was pelted with eggs by youths at the Mercat Cross in Edinburgh for officiating at mass.

1672   Archy Armstrong, jester to King James VI and an influential figure in court circles, was buried in Cumberland.

1847   Gorbals soup-kitchen in Glasgow opened for the first time in the yard behind the local police station.

1903   First order placed with Glasgow North British locomotive-works which was to build 28,000 locos and become the world's third largest manufacturer.

1944   Officials abandoned a relay-race round Dundee when confused competitors ran off in the wrong direction.

Accidental Regicide

A captain in the Scottish Guard of Henry II of France, a Montgomerie from Ayrshire, was responsible for the fatal injury sustained by the king in a friendly joust. Henry, who ensured that no blame should be attached to the Scot before he died, was Mary Queen of Scots' father-in-law.

April 2

1577   A spring of 'richt evil weather' was reported with no real sign of summer in Scotland until mid-June.

1690   John McGilter was jailed in Dumfries. While 'exceeding drunk', he struck the London post-horse causing it to fall upon the High Street.

1848	The historic Cardonald Mill in Glasgow was burned to the ground with a substantial quantity of grain lost.
1923	Striking Aberdeen fishermen pelted crews of three strike-breaking Russian boats with ice and fish before police made a baton charge.
1947	As large herds of deer were reported in the hills of Argyll, farmers complained of damage to crops.

Bare Bones

Universities place special importance on the regalia produced for occasions of pomp and ceremony; in its earliest days, however, Edinburgh University could only boast a modest mace and the skull of George Buchanan, tutor to James VI.

April 3

1058	Malcolm Canmore (Malcolm III) became King of Scots by defeating and killing Lulach in a battle at Strathbogie, in Aberdeenshire.
1573	Gipsies in Scotland ordered to settle in fixed habitations and 'take to honest industry', otherwise they faced imprisonment, scourging and banishment.
1666	Attendance at churches in Glasgow had fallen off dramatically since the introduction of episcopacy. The Archbishop threatened to bring in the militia and exact fines for non-attendance.
1882	Two Salvation Army officers from Dumfries jailed for leading a parade on the Sabbath, when men and women sang and shouted, carried a flag and gesticulated with hands and feet, causing a breach of the peace.
1933	Douglas Douglas-Hamilton MP, Marquis of Douglas and Clydesdale, piloted a Westland biplane on the first flight over Mount Everest.

Cool Reception

The wedding in Norway of James VI of Scotland and Anne of Denmark in 1589, was marred when four negroes, who had been specially commissioned by the king to dance artistically in the snow, died shortly afterwards from pneumonia. A Brazilian who played for Clydebank FC in the 1960s, did not adapt well to the Scottish climate. He was taken from the park suffering from exposure and hypothermia during a league match on a wild, winter's afternoon at Forfar.

April 4

| 1508 | The earliest known book to have been printed in Scotland – a work of Chaucer – became available. |
| 1603 | William Mayne, a Burgess of Edinburgh, was appointed official golf-club manufacturer to James VI. |

1835	Twenty-two male convicts – including four boys under the age of 12 – were embarked at Leith for prison hulks on the Thames.
1836	Phrenology, or the science of head bumps, seemed to have caught the imagination of the Glasgow public; audiences of several hundred people were common at lectures.
1952	Perth minister Joseph Shillinglaw told an RSPCC meeting that Scots had lost the 'fireside habit' and instead of enjoying their homes were dashing everywhere looking for excitement.

Shepherding a cinema queue, 1939

Dizzy Height of Fashion

The pullovers taken by Sir Edmund Hillary on his 1953 expedition which conquered Everest were knitted at Voe in Shetland.

April 5

1318	Thomas Randolph, Earl of Moray, took the town of Berwick from the English who had occupied it for the past 20 years.
1603	James VI left Scotland to take up the reins of government in England following the death of Queen Elizabeth I.
1693	Highway robbery had become so rife in southern Scotland that a 'Detector of Robberies' was granted £5 for every conviction.
1820	Skirmish at Bonnymuir near Falkirk saw a group of radical weavers routed by the Kilsyth Yeomanry and the Tenth Hussars.
1907	A giant who caused a stir in London by publicly declaring his love for a giantess, was the big attraction at Edinburgh's Empire Theatre.

Morocco-Bound

A tenement in Edinburgh's Canongate, with its unusual carved figure of a turbaned man, commemorates Andrew Gray who fled from justice in Scotland to North Africa. He returned in 1645 with a party of Barbary pirates, having made his fortune in the service of the Sultan of Morocco. Using Arabic techniques, he is said to have cured his cousin, the Provost's daughter, of plague, married her and settled again in his homeland.

April 6

1320   Declaration of Independence was sent by the Scottish Parliament meeting at Arbroath to Pope John XXII.

1599   Four Aberdeen fleshers were fined for contravening Acts of Parliament forbidding 'ony flesh to be slain or eaten from 1 March to 1 May'; the law attempted to ease food shortages.

1625   Paisley, at this time, was said to be a 'nest of Papists'. Robert Boyd, the new minister and a zealous Reformer, was chased off by the 'rascally women of the town'.

1832   Emigration had reached epidemic proportions in Elginshire, with 16 people from Rothes alone planning to sail for America.

Blowhard Bessie

The star turn among the numerous Orkney witches was a weird old woman called Bessie Miller who lived in Stromness and sold favourable winds to mariners. She charged a modest sixpence and many sailors refused to set sail until they had made their purchase.

April 7

1299   Negotiations on a prisoner exchange between Scotland and England were under way.

1565   Mary Queen of Scots ordered a Roman altar and bath-house, discovered at Inveresk near Musselburgh, to be protected.

1641   Sir Thomas Urquhart of Cromarty, poet, historian and humorist, was knighted by King Charles I at Whitehall.

1738   As a result of a butcher's dog going mad in Edinburgh, magistrates ordered the slaughter of all such vagrants. A shilling bounty was put on the head of each stray dog.

1968   Borders motor-racing driver, Jim Clark, victor in 25 Formula One Grand Prix, was killed in a crash at the Hockenheim Circuit in West Germany.

Literary Cover-Up

Prime Minister Gladstone's statue in Glasgow's George Square betrays some sensitive cosmetic work. The PM had lost his third finger on his right hand while cutting wood, and the sculptor, Thornycroft, decided to depict him holding a book in which his shortened finger is buried.

VISIT FROM A LEGENDARY CUDDY

ROCK ISLAND REBELS, YA BASS!

A hearty lunch of French wine and fine biscuits confirmed that Jacobite prisoners, who had seized and held the Bass Rock for three years, were just as skilled at crafty negotiation as they were at stout defence.

This month in 1694, when the garrison finally sought terms, government representatives sailed out to the awe-inspiring volcanic plug off North Berwick expecting to find a dispirited and starving little group ready to throw in the towel.

Instead, the comrades of the rock appeared well-off and in good heart and were able to offer the commissioners a fine meal, telling them to eat and drink freely as there was no scarcity of provisions. And on their departure the whole company, scores of men, lined the walls. Their apparent security and comfort in this formidable stronghold – the last place in Great Britain to hold out against William and Mary – weighed heavily in their favour in the final settlement. Eventually, they came ashore with life, liberty and property – even with payment arrears of aliment to which they were entitled as prisoners. Some chose to leave for France and the Government paid their passage.

The reality of their situation had been very different. The cutting off of supplies had reduced them to near starvation, and the extra-special lunch had been set aside specifically for the negotiations, while the garrison survived on rats and seabirds. The fine display of their military might had simply been a ruse – a series of old muskets, hats and coats set up along the battlements. In fact, there were never more than a handful of men on the rock at any one time.

For the duration of the siege, which began on 15 June 1691, the Government in Edinburgh was perplexed, embarrassed and indignant about the affair. As one chronicler explains, the Jacobites who had seized control during the unloading of a coal-boat led a merry life among the clouds of seabirds, intercepting passing ships to supplement their rations, cheering the occasional visits of French warships with supplies, and making plundering incursions into East Lothian and Fife.

The saddest moment came when one of their number was caught ashore and, after being convicted of treason, was ordered to be hanged on a cliff top opposite the Bass. However, a defiant shot from the fortress sent the execution party to a safer spot inland.

The ineffectiveness of the prolonged naval siege was indicated by the fact that the 'rebels' on the rock proudly showed off their collection of more than 500 cannonballs – inaccurately lobbed into the seabird colonies.

April 8

1602   Thomas Musgrave, captain of the Cumbrian border village of Bewcastle, was accused of allowing his charge to become a den of thieves and an open house for Scots.

1684   Most of Kelso was destroyed by fire which began in a malt-kiln, and 306 families lost their homes.

1724   Recruiting – with permission of King George – began in Edinburgh for Prussia's regiment of ultra-tall grenadiers. A good response from the city's big men was noted.

1882   Over 100 people in Inverness suffered food poisoning after eating hot cross buns (they included the baker and his family), and dodgy spices were suspected.

1973   Glasgow University appointed the first female professor in five centuries – Dr Delphine Parrot, a bacteriologist.

Fly as Get Out

Perhaps Scotland's oddest oracle was the immortal fly of St Michael's Well, in Banffshire. Every movement of the fly was recorded with 'silent awe' and, if he appeared spirited or dejected, a prediction was drawn correspondingly.

April 9

1139   Treaty of Durham was drawn between King Stephen of England and David I, King of Scots. David's son was to have Northumberland, except for the castles of Bamburgh and Newcastle.

1593   Shoemakers in Edinburgh were ready to chase ministers – seeking an end to the traditional Monday market – out of town. The clergy argued that the market meant folk travelling on a Sunday.

1662   Old John Kincaid, perhaps Scotland's most famous witch-pricker, was languishing in jail in Edinburgh, the most recent witch frenzy having spent its fury.

1788   Andrew Meikle from East Lothian patented his design for a threshing-mill, the first successful mill the world had seen.

Sad Decline

The gradual disappearance of Gaelic from Lowland Scotland is illustrated by the fact that the last native speaker in Carrick, Ayrshire, Margaret MacMurray, died when Robert Burns was still a baby.

April 10

1201   Rutherglen was commanded by William the Lion to double its three-merks annual contribution, to keep the deans and sub-deacons of Glasgow Cathedral in surplices and black copes.

ROCK ISLAND REBELS, YA BASS!

1593	Campsie adultress Margaret Steyne was ordered by local presbytery to make her repentance in sackcloth on the next several Sundays.
1631	Town Council of Edinburgh forbade wearing of plaids by women to cover their faces, because it was impossible to tell respectable ladies from 'loose-living' women.
1831	At Beattock Inn 21 guests helped one of their number celebrate his 21st birthday. One of the party was a 21-stone lady and this caused much 'badinage and mirth'.
1952	Scottish Temperance women's meeting in Aberdeen called for all drunk drivers to be jailed without the option of a fine.

In at the Shallow End

An English sub-aqua club spent months planning an expedition to Sutherland but, after driving hundreds of miles and humphing their heavy diving-equipment up the mountain, they were flabbergasted to discover that the loch was only six inches deep.

April 11

1574	A public suicide shocked Edinburgh when a convicted adulterer, Robert Drummond, stabbed himself four times in the chest during punishment at the Mercat Cross.
1689	The Scottish Claim of Right, placing significant legal and parliamentary limits on the Crown and marking the start of modern parliamentary democracy, was signed in Edinburgh.
1705	A huge throng gathered at Leith to watch the execution of three English mariners accused of attacking a Scots vessel off Malabar.
1885	Fishermen at Newhaven on the Forth agreed to form a protection association to secure the regulation of trawling

and arrange compensation for fishing-gear damaged by trawlers.

1948   The return of up to 50,000 people would make the difference between life and death to the Highlands, Robert Grieve (later Highlands Board chairman) told visiting planners.

Back Streets of Paris

A successful spy-ring operated in Paris during the Napoleonic War under the direction of a member of the Clan MacPherson.

April 12

1398   Robert III held a Great Council at Perth and raised his sons, David and Robert, to the rank of Duke, the first in Scotland.

1568   Aberdeen kirk session forbade ministers from attending contracts of marriage, the so-called handfastings; an attempt to encourage formal marriage and improve the moral climate.

1666   Harsh words exchanged at a horse-race meeting in Fife saw a duel between Lords Lithgow and Carnegie in which the former suffered a 'sore wound'.

1832   William Clark, who remembered seeing Cumberland's army cross the Spey *en route* for Culloden, died aged 108, at Newton of Cabrach.

1945   Doctor Robert McIntyre became the first Scottish Nationalist MP by winning the Motherwell by-election.

Rifleman Lee

James Paris Lee, co-inventor of the famous Lee Enfield rifle, of which more than two million were manufactured, mainly for American troops during the First World War, was born in Hawick.

April 13

1284   Guild members in Scotland were to be fined 12 pennies if they failed to be at their assembly places after the church bells were rung to signal an emergency.

1523   Scottish border towns and villages were being devastated by raids organised by the Earl of Surrey, whose plan was to create a 12-mile-deep 'desert', or sterile zone, inside the Scots Border.

1644   James Graham, First Marquis of Montrose, unfurled the Royal Standard prior to a brilliant campaign against the Covenanters.

1853   Glasgow gunsmith John Blaikie invented an ingenious device for slicing bread.

1951   Stone of Destiny, Scotland's famed Coronation Stone, which was taken the previous Christmas, returned to

Westminster Abbey, although some say that the real stone is still in Scotland.

Urquhart's Undoing

Seventeenth-century poet, historian and humorist Sir Thomas Urquhart of Cromarty, who translated Rabelais and planned a universal language, fought on the Royalist side in the Civil War and is reported to have died with laughter at news of the Restoration in 1660.

April 14

1578   To prevent hoarding, the government ordered all grain to be threshed by 12 June and only enough retained to serve a family for three months; the remainder had to be at market within 20 days.

1635   Smallpox was raging in Scotland and famine was widespread. A huge blazing crab-like star had been seen as a sign of great troubles.

1836   Plans were finalised for the demolition of Edinburgh's famous Assembly Rooms in the West Bow – a popular eighteenth-century dance-hall.

1947   A Government report said that of almost one million houses built in Scotland before 1914, 400,000 were without proper sanitary conditions.

1982   A student – accused at Portree in Skye of damaging a road sign – was refused permission for the case to be heard in Gaelic.

Royal Linguist

James IV, King of Scots, spoke eight languages – English, Gaelic, Latin, French, German, Flemish, Italian and Spanish. He was the last Scottish monarch to speak the Gaelic. Determined to discover whether Gaelic, Greek or Hebrew was the original world-language, he marooned a deaf and dumb nurse with two newly-born children on Inchkeith Island in the Forth to see which tongue developed. There is no record of the outcome of this eccentric experiment.

LADY HAMILTON'S MOLTEN EMBRACE

When Vestina, the voluptuous goddess of health, got together with an ageing Scots vulcanologist, it was always likely to be an explosive partnership. Emma Hart, better known to history as Lady Hamilton and girlfriend of Horatio Nelson, wed the part-time diplomat and patron of the arts, Sir William Hamilton, grandson of the Third Duke of Hamilton, in 1791. It was to be one of the most talked about marriages of the late eighteenth century.

Let's look at the career of the lady first. Emma was born in Cheshire on 26 April 1765. After what seems to have been a tranquil opening phase to her life, she went to London and the fun began. According to her biographers, within a few years she had borne children to a navy captain and a baronet. Of the several jobs she held down, the most notorious was at the Temple of Health in the Adelphi where, bare-breasted, she played the role of the health goddess in Edinburgh-born Dr James Graham's phoney health emporium.

She accepted the 'protection' of Sir William, a widower and 35 years her senior, who was ambassador at the Court of Naples, and she lived there for five years before their marriage took place. Within a short while she had become a close friend and confidante of Maria Caroline, Queen of Ferdinand I. Then she met the dashing Lord Nelson after his glorious victory at Aboukir Bay and, as one biographer so neatly put it, 'platonic friendship ripened to guilty passion'.

For his part, Sir William maintained that he had been condemned to make his way in the world with an illustrious name but little money. His diplomatic duties during 36 years in Naples (after a spell in the army) were minimal, but he took an active part in the excavation of Herculaneum and of Pompeii, and formed impressive collections of antiquities.

However, his consuming passion was for volcanoes. He repeatedly visited Etna and Vesuvius. The process by which volcanoes shaped the surrounding countryside fascinated him, if anything, a little more than the charms of his young bride. One of his most important discoveries was that the streets of Pompeii were paved with lava from explosions which took place years before the catastrophic eruption which destroyed the Roman town. He found even earlier strata beneath the town's foundations.

Imagine his excitement as he raced home of an evening to tell Emma about his latest geological or archaeological insight. Little wonder, some might say, that the passionate Lady Hamilton drifted into the arms (sorry, arm!) of the admiral.

April 15

1601 King James VI was created a Burgess of Perth during a ceremony at the Mercat Cross. He was given a banquet and signed the Guild Book.

1736 Porteous Riot in Edinburgh; 17 killed or wounded when the town's guard opened fire on the crowd during a public execution.

1831 A vessel from Scotland carrying 52 tons of potatoes, aid for the 'starving Irish peasantry', arrived at Newport, County Mayo.

1833 Three people – including two men confined for debt – died when Tain jail burned down. The saving of two portraits of local dignitaries was described as 'small compensation'.

1972 Thirty-two-year-old Armadale woman gave birth to quintuplets, four boys and a girl – the first in Scotland since 1858.

Milk of Kindness

A man who anticipated the problems of the fast-food age was Joseph Black, the famous chemist who, in 1754, presented his thesis for the degree of MD at the University of Edinburgh. It was entitled, *The Effect of Magnesia on Indigestion*.

April 16

1117 Earl Magnus, later St Magnus, was killed on the Orkney island of Egilsay; he was betrayed by his co-Earl Hakon.

1685 Equestrian statue of Charles II – which cost £1,000 – set up in Parliament Close, Edinburgh, 'much to the amazement of the vulgar people who had never seen the like'.

1746 Army of the Duke of Cumberland destroyed the Jacobites at Culloden; the last full-scale battle on British soil.

| 1803 | Glasgow magistrates sought a city executioner. They were anxious to get a 'sober, well-behaved man', the previous incumbent having brought a 'degree of disgrace' to the post. |
| 1981 | English judge refused to overturn a ban on the sale of tickets for the England-Scotland Wembley clash north of the Border. Such action was needed to curb drunken Scots in London, he said. |

Bay City Rollers

The ancient fraternity of porters of Leith had a division called the 'Rollers' whose task, in medieval times, was to roll barrels of newly-imported French wine from the docks up into the city of Edinburgh.

April 17

616	St Donan, a missionary active in northern and western Scotland, was killed along with 52 of his followers on the island of Eigg.
1497	Two fiddlers entertained James IV at Stirling with the famous old minstrel poem – *Greysteil*.
1852	Two Glasgow boys each received 12 lashes for chalking obscene words on walls in the East End of the city.
1909	Riot followed a drawn Scottish Cup final replay between Rangers and Celtic; 45 people were injured and the cup was retained by the SFA.
1946	Workers at Greenock began repainting the *Queen Elizabeth* from her wartime grey to the Cunard livery.

Flight Path

The Berwickshire village of Eyemouth developed architecturally with winding alleys and dark recesses to aid the thriving smuggling-trade, making escape from the revenue men easier. A noted eccentric of his day was Sir John Dinely who came to Stirling in 1768. His house was substantially altered to match his current tastes, creating a flat roof with a fish-pond at its centre, surrounded by gooseberry bushes and rare plants.

April 18

1586	Earl of Eglinton was murdered by Cunningham of Robertland as part of a bloody, centuries-old feud over titles to land in Ayrshire.
1690	Towns of Kirkcaldy and Dysart complained they were in serious debt having supported a regiment of troops quartered there on Government orders.
1930	Scottish Trades Union Congress voted to boycott cinemas where 'talkies' had been introduced and live orchestras replaced.

1955   Post-office speaking-clock 'Tim' became available to phone-subscribers in the Borders – 19 years after making its debut.

1979   Thirty-year-old Jim Watt became world lightweight boxing champion beating Colombian Alfredo Pitalua at Glasgow's Kelvin Hall.

Ruck and Maul

Two Kincardineshire schoolboys, Alexander and Francis Crombie, who studied at Durham in the mid-1800s before coming to Edinburgh Academy, are credited with introducing rugby-football to Scotland.

April 19

1550   The number of courses at meals was limited by law because of food shortages – archbishops were to have no more than eight dishes while burgesses had to make do with three.

1635   Ceremonial funeral of George, First Earl of Kinnoull, Chancellor of Scotland, to the parish church of Kinnoull, Perthshire.

1908   Death reported of 'Professor' Charlie Bell of Edinburgh, a famous prize-fighter of the mid-1800s who numbered Sir Arthur Conan Doyle among his pupils.

1947   Call for tobacco-rationing from Mrs Jean Mann, Labour MP for Coatbridge, because the high prices were having a serious effect on old folk.

1974   Scotland saw its first skiing streaker, a young man wearing only ski boots, who appeared at Carrbridge in warm sunshine.

Popular Thirstquenchers

So celebrated were the water-caddies of old Edinburgh who trailed casks from the public wells to the high tenements, that moves to pipe water into the buildings were delayed when it was realised it would mean the extinction of their trade.

April 20

1652   Countess of Wemyss, Eleanour Fleming, died after an unhappy two-year marriage. Her fondness for drink had led her to have a doorway built in her bedroom for easier access to the wine cellar.

1881   Hengler's Circus in Glasgow was doing a roaring trade with the 'Fairy's Garden Party' and a remarkably agile horse called 'Comet', who revelled in fire-leaping, being the star attractions.

1886   Greenock magistrates warned shopkeepers, with the exception of druggists, that they would be prosecuted if found trading on a Sunday.

1934   Scottish National Party formed by the amalgamation of the National Party of Scotland and the Scottish Party.

1952   Hull of the British Rail steamer *Countess of Breadalbane* carried 17 miles overland, from Loch Awe to Loch Fyne, prior to entering service on the Clyde estuary.

Vanishing Fish

The occasional disappearance of fish from waters around Scotland was often attributed to the spilling of fishermen's blood in the sea during disputes over catches. Probably the last sea battle in the River Forth took place near Leith Harbour in 1788, when oyster fishermen from Newhaven and Prestonpans fought for half an hour with oars and boat hooks over disputed oyster-beds. Victory, after 'much hurt', went to Newhaven.

April 21

1398   Sir David Lindsay, a famous Scots knight, who had many triumphs to his name, was created First Earl of Crawford.

1544   As the Earl of Hertford gathered his forces at Tynemouth, messengers were sent through Scotland warning of an imminent English invasion. It signalled the start of the 'Rough Wooing'.

1779   Report of mutiny at Leith by 50 Highland recruits who believed they were being forced to join a Glasgow regiment; troops were called in and 27 men, mostly Highlanders, died in the skirmish.

1923   Three hundred emigrants from the Western Isles embarked at Stornoway for Canada and each received a copy of the Scriptures in Gaelic.

1955   Two Edinburgh sewermen, who were past retirement age, were retained for an extra six months because they loved their job and were 'happy as bugs in a rug' down the sewers.

First of Spring

The Cuckoo patrol of Girl Scouts, founded in Glasgow in 1908 by schoolgirl Allison Cargill, is the earliest on record anywhere in the world. They used to join the Boy Scouts on Saturday-afternoon expeditions in Acre Wood, Maryhill.

A LION AWAITING HIS LONDON ALLOWANCE

Weighty matters occupied the attention of William the Lion, King of Scots, as the twelfth century drew to a close and the age of chivalry dawned. Not least of his concerns was whether he was going to get an increase in his travelling expenses and his London allowance. Was his leonine namesake, Richard Coeur de Lion, King of England, going to take into account inflation, the wages of a good dwarf and the spiralling cost of candles, when he looked at the traditional monies paid to the Scots king to make the long trek south to do homage for lands held in England?

Born in 1143, the grandson of David I, William may have had the bravery of the big cat which he adopted as his symbol of authority but, on occasion, he could show about as much sharpness as a punctured haggis.

In 1174, having failed yet again to persuade the English to hand over Northumberland (which he regarded as Scotland's by right), William launched an expedition across the Border exploiting a period of civil unrest in the South. On a foggy morning, near Alnwick, rushing forward to greet what he thought were reinforcements, he walked right into the arms of the Auld Enemy.

Ignominiously, he was tied to his horse and taken south, then across the Channel to Normandy and released only when he consented, under the terms of the Treaty of Falaise, to pay homage on behalf of the Scottish people to the King of England. The next 15 years was a period of utter humiliation for the Scots until William had the opportunity, in 1189, to purchase Scotland's independence for £6,666, which helped Richard fund his great crusade to the Holy Land.

Under the terms of this agreement the boundaries between the kingdoms were re-established and the castles of Roxburgh and Berwick were given up to William and his heirs forever. Like so many deals struck 'forever' between England and Scotland this one was hardly worth the parchment upon which it was scratched. However, Richard was keen to be on his way to Palestine and probably felt that getting shot of any commitment to Scotland would be a sensible move. We were, apparently, too poor to be taxed, and too turbulent to be coerced. What's new?

In 1194, a despatch reached William confirming details of the allowances he could expect in future when attending the English court. They provide an intriguing insight into the requirements of the Scots party during these trips to London.

For each day after the King of Scots crossed the Border he was to have 100 shillings sterling to support his entourage, both on the outward and return legs. The English king confirmed:

For every day from his arrival at our court until his departure for his own land – 30 shillings sterling and 12 loaves of finest flour; 12 casks of wine, four of top quality [such as was served to Richard himself]; four cakes of whey: 120 candles; 2lbs of pepper and 4lbs of the spice cummin.

Moreover, he shall have the escort which his antecedents used to have coming to our court and returning from it, namely, the Bishop of Durham and the sheriffs and barons of Northumberland shall meet him on the bounds of his kingdom . . . and shall escort him as far as the Tees.

There the Archbishop of York took over as far as Lincoln, where the Bishop escorted the Scots king on the remainder of his journey south.

April 22

1707   Parliament of Scotland met for the last time after sanctioning the Treaty of Union.

1778   John Paul Jones, Kirkcudbright-born founder of the United States Navy, anchored in the Solway Firth prior to a raid on Whitehaven and an attempt to kidnap the Earl of Selkirk.

1809   Glasgow weavers met and condemned Government rejection of their campaign for a scale of minimum prices.

1881   Glasgow police, who abandoned the chimneypot hat in the 1870s, now added a flat ornament to the top of their felt helmets.

1947   Demands for detailed plans of air-raid shelters prior to their demolition were described as 'absurd' by Stirlingshire county convener; most such plans, he argued, had been drawn on the back of envelopes.

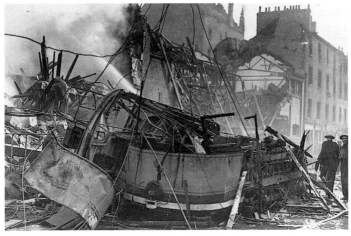

Tram bombed in Nelson Street, Glasgow, 1940

A LION AWAITING HIS LONDON ALLOWANCE

Risky Business

Before the Life Assurance Act of 1774 gamblers used to take out insurance on the lives of personalities with dangerous lifestyles in the hope of making a quick killing. One of the most popular targets for speculators was Bonnie Prince Charlie during the 1745 Uprising.

April 23

1124   David I, aged about 40, became King of Scots on the death of Alexander I.

1545   A plot by a group of Scots nobles, led by the Earl of Cassilis, to assassinate Cardinal Beaton, failed to receive the backing of the English King Henry VIII.

1644   A united army of Scots and Parliamentarian forces besieged York.

1888   Foxes were reported to be very numerous in the Banchory area – 17 were caught around this time within a radius of a few miles.

1935   Two young Scots bank-assistants were murdered during a raid by Chilean bandits on the Anglo-South American Bank at Santa Cruz, Patagonia.

Effluent Society

The Flooers o' Edinburgh, a popular fiddle-tune, recalls, not, as you might expect, the joys of the Royal Botanic Gardens, but was the popular nickname for the stench which emanated from the open sewers between the tenements in the days of 'Gardyloo!' – the warning shouted from the high windows as the sewage was hurled into the street.

April 24

1579   John Stewart, Earl of Athole, Chancellor of Scotland, died at Kincardine after a heavy drinking-session hosted by the Countess of Mar. Poisoning was suspected but never proved.

1601   Privy Council expressed concern about the activities of Jesuits and priests in Scotland, describing them as 'enemies of God's truth'.

1749   First mail-coach ran between Glasgow and Edinburgh – the fare was 6d per person.

1836   Some public alarm was expressed as warships were seen along the west coast of Scotland; it was simply a recruiting drive.

1974   Former Clyde steamer *Duchess of Montrose* left Greenock to be broken up for scrap at Troon.

End of a Sad Story

The last will and testament of Mary Queen of Scots was held for many years by the Scots College in Paris. Some of the words had been blotted out by the sad Queen's tears, claimed the romantics.

April 25

1525   Ambassadors returned from England with details of an Anglo-Scottish peace treaty designed to last three years and three months.

1707   An enormous school of whales arrived in the Forth and 35 ran ashore on the sands at Kirkcaldy.

1800   Famine prompted Edinburgh magistrates to urge the people to switch to wheat- and barley-meal due to the oatmeal shortage.

1832   A silver coin of the Emperor Hadrian was found in a field adjoining the Crown Inn at Clachan of Campsie, Stirlingshire.

1906   Paisley police-court dealt with over 50 cases of drunkenness among Glasgow visitors who were in Paisley for the spring holiday.

Tinderbox Townships

Research shows that 1244 was a remarkable year for accidental fires which consumed many of Scotland's timber-built towns. Haddington, Roxburgh, Lanark, Stirling, Perth, Forfar, Montrose and Aberdeen all suffered this fiery fate.

April 26

1315   In the aftermath of victory at Bannockburn, the Scots Parliament at Ayr agreed that Edward Bruce, King Robert Bruce's brother, should become heir to the throne and lead an invasion of Ulster.

1615   A scarcity of eggs in Scotland was blamed on the greed of exporters; heavy fines were threatened.

1836   Children from Glasgow's various charitable institutions made their annual march through the city in their new clothes to a service in St Andrew's Church.

1923   The Duke of York married Elizabeth Bowes-Lyon (the Queen Mother), daughter of the Earl and Countess of Strathmore, at Westminster Abbey; the bride was a descendant of the ancient kings of the Scots.

1931   On this day a census showed that the population of Ross and Cromarty was 62,799.

Interior Decorator

Albert the Prince Consort, although German-born, became fascinated, after his marriage to Victoria, with the romantic image of Scotland. He even went as far as to design tartan wallpaper and carpets for Balmoral Castle.

April 27

1124   Alexander I, King of Scots and fourth son of Malcolm Canmore, died at Stirling aged 46. His struggle had always been to assert the independence of Scotland.

1296   Battle of Dunbar saw defeat for the Scots by the forces of Edward I following Balliol's defiance of the English king.

1560   Third bond in support of the Protestant Revolution was signed by 50 high-ranking Scots at Leith.

1780   Half-a-guinea reward was offered in Glasgow for information on criminals who had been taking salmon fry from the Clyde.

1932   Gourock was launched as a tourist resort at a whist-drive attended by 1,000 people in the Pavilion.

Cut and Thrust

Up until the Second World War, prison officers at Peterhead – one of Britain's toughest jails – were armed with sabres to keep inmates in line.

April 28

1403   Bishop Henry Wardlaw, founder of St Andrews University, arrived from Europe, to take up his see which he held for 37 years.

1558   Last Protestant martyr in Scotland, Walter Mylne, burned at the stake for heresy.

1608   Lords of Council banned Peebles horse-racing because of bloodshed and drunken rowdiness between rival factions in previous years.

1720 A reconciliation meeting between George I and the Prince of Wales after a period of cool relations is said to have prompted jubilation and celebration in Glasgow and Edinburgh.

1917 Amazing scenes at a junior football match between Kirkintilloch and Baillieston; after a fight between two players, spectators chased the visitors from the field and across country for several miles.

Burning Passion

Blind Harry's *Life of Wallace* was one of the young Robert Burns's favourite books. He read and re-read it and is said to have been especially moved by the account of the patriot's execution in London. It was one act, he remarked, for which he could never forgive the English.

ATHOLE'S FAIRYTALE CASTLE

Fantastic tree kingdoms feature in the work of 'flight-of-fancy' writers from Tolkien to Stephen Donaldson, but they scarcely compare with the real-life fairy castle constructed in a Perthshire glen some 460 years ago.

Whether this wooden palace, news of which reached as far as St Peter's in Rome, provided the inspiration for those imaginary realms, is doubtful. Created by the Earl of Athole to impress young James V and his court, the story of the Perthshire pavilion is tucked away in the royal biographies. However, it's just possible that the Earl shared the same imaginative spark which has influenced the twentieth-century architects of fabulous, fictional domains.

Young James was certainly in need of a diversion. The previous summer (1529), he had spent traipsing around the Borders, ostensibly on a hunting expedition, but in reality his quarry was a regiment of rogues, marauders and plunderers who were strung up by the dozen.

Heading north this time, he was accompanied by the Queen Mother and the papal ambassador. The Earl of Athole, learning that his lands were the first to be honoured with a visit from the royal party, decided on a spectacular display of Highland hospitality and ingenuity. One record of the expedition tells us: 'On the arrival of the illustrious visitors they found a magnificent palace constructed of the boughs of trees and fitted with glass windows, standing in the middle of a level meadow.'

At each corner of this curious structure there was a tower or block-house, and the whole construction was joisted and floored to the height of three storeys. A large gate stood between the two towers and framed a formidable portcullis; a moat 30 feet wide and 16 feet deep had been stocked with an assortment of fish, and a wide drawbridge welcomed the visitors. Equal attention had been paid to the internal furnishings and design. Walls were hung with tapestries and the floors strewn with flowers like 'ane greine garden', according to Sir David Lindsay of the Mount.

There was great feasting with the choicest wines, fruits and confections, the entire beanfeast in fairyland setting the Earl of Athole back 'many thousand pounds', which in current conversion must have amounted to a small fortune.

The papal ambassador had been stunned and gratified by this show of opulence in what the rest of Europe considered, with some justification, a wild, uncivilised and occasionally barbaric country. But his surprise turned to astonishment at the moment of departure when he saw a party of Highlanders busily setting fire to the structure in which he had been so comfortably lodged.

When he expressed his disbelief to the king, James, still a teenager, is said to have smiled and replied, 'It is the custom of our

Highlandmen that, be they never so well lodged at night, they will burn the house in the morning.' The king clearly felt that this was a fitting end for a fantasy. The precise location of this fabulous building has never been properly established.

April 29

1294   John Balliol, King of Scots, finalised plans for a visit to London at which he was to hand over three years' revenue from his English estates.

1520   'Cleanse the Causeway' – a violent street-fight earlier in the month in Edinburgh between the Hamiltons and Douglases resulted in the town council appointing a bodyguard for the Provost.

Cavalry charge at Hampden

1669   Relief collections were being organised after the ancient burgh of Cupar in Fife was 'annihilated and turned to desolation' by a fire which left over 20 families homeless.

1833   Poor salmon-fishing reported on the Clyde; the only shot proving worthwhile being at Barns o' Clyde (now Clydebank).

1911   The population of Glasgow, according to census returns, was 783,401.

Sky at Night

Banffshire shepherd-boy, James Ferguson, taught himself astronomy while tending his flock in the field by night, mapping the stars on a stretched thread strung with beads.

April 30

1594   Steven Auldcorne of Rutherglen fined by Glasgow Presbytery for working on a Sunday.

1667   Dutch fleet appeared in the Forth with the intention of attacking the ports of Leith and Burntisland. During an exchange of fire a few chimneys were knocked down before a storm drove them off.

1717   Edinburgh tutor Robert Irvine, who murdered two boys in his charge, was sentenced to be hanged after having his hands chopped off.

1891   An Commun Gaidhealach, the Gaelic or Highland Association, formally instituted at Oban.

1901   Glasgow was reported free of smallpox after a 16-month outbreak which claimed 288 lives.

Explosive Outburst

Guy Fawkes, after his capture during the abortive attempt to blow up Parliament in 1605, was brought before King James VI & I. It was quickly apparent that much of his animosity was directed against those from north of the Border and he freely admitted that his intent had been to 'blow them back to Scotland'.

May 1

1438   Nine-year truce agreed between Scotland and England less than a year after the coronation of the infant James II.

1661	Charles II issued a warrant for the creation of a new regiment – The Scots Guards.
1707	Treaty of Union between Scotland and England came into force; this was the official date for the Union approved by the Scots Parliament in January.
1858	A sewing-maid was being sought by a well-to-do Argyllshire family, with a wage of £10 annually, tea and sugar included.
1943	New Solway Firth Road Bridge to be started immediately after the war and costing £4m, was under consideration.

Violent Heritage

An early victim of football hooliganism was Sir John Carmichael, warden of the Middle Marches, who was killed in 1600 by a rampaging band of Armstrongs on their way home from a football match.

May 2

1568	Mary Queen of Scots fled the Castle of Lochleven at her second attempt and headed west to gather support.
1580	Church condemned a 'merry procession' of young people to the so-called Dragon Hole on Kinnoull Hill near Perth. Those taking part in this 'superstitious ritual' were each ordered to pay 20s to the poor.
1858	Notorious umbrella thief, who had been plaguing the Royal Exchange in Glasgow, was finally arrested.
1870	New Caledonian Railway Station was opened at the west end of Edinburgh's Princes Street.
1959	Chapelcross nuclear power station, near Annan in Dumfriesshire, the first in Scotland, was opened.

Making Tracks

After the Napoleonic War, unemployment was a major problem in Scotland, particularly in Edinburgh, until someone hit on the idea of forming squads to build paths round Calton Hill, creating a new road through Holyrood Park and levelling Bruntsfield Links.

May 3

1587	General Assembly of the Church of Scotland announced that it was dismayed by the moral condition of the nation with 'sin lying in every nook' and the poor wandering the land in great tribes.
1620	Paisley town council agreed that an annual horse-race should be held in the town with a four oz, silver bell as the prize.
1709	Elspeth Rule became the last person in Scotland to be tried before the High Court for witchcraft; the judge at Dumfries ordered her to be burned on the cheek and

banished from Scotland for life.

1837   During quarrying at Buckhaven in Fife a six-inch-long fish was found in a cavity in the rock. It was alive and survived for a few hours.

1945   Senior officers in the Highland constabulary were concerned that constables were spending too much time chasing runaway sheep around the back streets of Stornoway.

Early to Bed

Magistrates in Edinburgh decided in the mid-1550s that lanterns should burn in the streets and closes to deter muggers, but felt it was appropriate that they should be extinguished at 9 p.m. – considering this a fitting time for all decent folk to be at their ain firesides.

May 4

1390   A famous victory in a tournament in London for Scots knight Sir David Lindsay over Lord Welles, the most noted English soldier of the period.

1544   English invasion force of 11,000 troops under the Earl of Hertford landed at Leith.

1654   Proclamation of the Protectorate and Union with England was read by General Monk at the Mercat Cross of Edinburgh.

1809   Vagrants and strolling beggars in Dumfries were causing increasing anxiety; licences were issued allowing them to beg in neighbouring parishes.

1944   Seventy-two-year-old Duke of Argyll appeared at Dunoon Sheriff Court and admitted striking the town clerk of Inveraray with a stick in a rammy over estates matters. The sheriff thought publicity enough punishment.

Roughly Justice

In 1640, when the Lord High Treasurer had an important lawsuit before the Court of Session, he gained the impression that Lord Durie, Lord President of the Court of Session, was against his argument. So, he arranged to have his lordship kidnapped while walking on Leith Sands and kept him a prisoner in Annandale Castle for three months until the lawsuit was settled to the Lord High Treasurer's satisfaction.

May 5

1570   Estimates suggested that most of the 'white kye and bulls' (thought to be remnants of the original cattle of the Caledonian Forest) had been slain in Lord Fleming's Forest of Cumbernauld.

1603   Public postal system in Scotland was launched with a link between Edinburgh and Berwick via Haddington and

Cockburnspath.

1656   The Quaker faith was gaining popularity in Scotland. Regular services of what critics called 'this damnable sect' were being well attended on the Castle Hill in Edinburgh.

1888   Ship *Roger Stewart* sailed from Greenock for New York with 100 mostly well-off emigrants planning to become 'Lords of the Soil' in the far west of America.

1941   Edinburgh's 'Victorian-like passion' for railings was described as 'unpatriotic' as calls were made by the Cockburn Association to hand them over as scrap iron to aid the war effort.

Yo, Ho, Ho

Rum was forbidden to be sold in Scotland in 1695 because it interfered with consumption of 'strong waters made of malt'. In addition, rum was said to be a drug rather than a liquor and 'highly prejudicial to the health of all who drink it'.

WHAT A PICTURE, WHAT A PHOTOGRAPH!

Disruption Day (18 May 1843), when the established church in Scotland split apart over the issue of church versus civil law represented, according to Lord Cockburn, the 'most honourable fea for Scotland that its whole history supplies'.

While there may be some argument over that claim, there can be no doubt that great deeds were enacted that spring day as hundreds of ministers filed from the General Assembly in St Andrew's Church, Edinburgh, to walk in procession to Tanfield Hall in Canonmills, where a new Free Church was born.

The rebels were determined that no ministers should be appointed over a congregation except by the consent of the heads of its families. Continuing patronage and the defence by some Highland ministers of the eviction laws had sickened them. The fact that their stance was in defiance of the law did not deter them.

All weighty and important stuff. But our investigation would be failing in its duty if we didn't take a wee keek in the back door at some of the curious fringe events attaching themselves to this momentous day. Surprisingly, one outcome of the day's action was the foundation of portrait photography as a popular art. Present at the Canonmills ceremony, when 474 ministers and professors signed the Deed of Demission, was the painter, David Octavius Hill.

He was determined that the proceedings should not be lost to history and planned a huge canvas to record the event. However, with so many faces to reproduce before they went their separate ways, Hill recruited a man called Adamson to photograph participants in groups of 25, allowing for faithful reproduction. Adamson's portraits were later put on display at the Royal Scottish Academy and the art of portrait photography was up and running.

Early on in the day's proceedings, the Marquis of Bute, the Royal Commissioner, was at Holyrood receiving distinguished folk when a portrait of William of Orange suddenly crashed to the floor. 'There goes the Revolution Settlement!' came a shout from the crowd.

This settlement, which had abolished patronage and on which the rebels based their case, had been ratified by William. The downfall of his portrait was read by many, wrongly as it turned out, to be an omen of coming victory for the establishment.

A few hours later at Tanfield Hall, as the devotional part of the proceedings of the breakaway church began with the 43rd psalm, a great thunder cloud cast a shadow over that part of Edinburgh. But as the line 'Oh, send out your light and truth' was reached, the sun burst through, flooding the hall in warm radiance. As the chronicler so nicely puts it, 'It was an animating coincidence to which even the most desponding could not be insensible.'

May 6

1471   Preparations for war and the need to re-equip and build more fishing-boats occupied the attention of Scots Parliament meeting in Edinburgh.

Waiting for a bite

1743   Ayr-born Andrew Ramsay, who supervised the education of the two sons of the Auld Pretender, died in France, aged 57.

1758   *Isabel* of Leith began the first regular packet-service between the Forth and Lerwick in Shetland.

1858   Singer Miss Blanche Cole appeared at Glasgow's Merchant Hall and her version of *The Hundred Pipers* had the audience 'carried almost beyond the bounds of concert-hall etiquette'.

1974   Fight began to keep the Warwick Vase – a huge Roman relic – in Scotland; it is now a principal feature of the Burrell Gallery in Glasgow.

Heavenly Ammunition

A landslip which exposed thousands of perfectly spherical stones from musket to cannonball size near Duns Law in Berwickshire, in 1639, was seen by the Covenanting Army camped nearby as a token of God's support for their cause.

May 7

1585   Year-long outbreak of plague began in Perth which eventually killed 1,400 people, about a sixth of the population.

1594   Mungo Craig, a popular Glasgow bagpiper, was warned by the kirk that if he played the pipes on a Sunday he would be excommunicated; the playing of 'profane games', probably football, was also frowned on.

1842   Two 'gentlemen' were fined £3 for smoking in a carriage of the Glasgow-Ayr railway and assaulting a guard in the execution of his duty.

1907   A highly successful season of cabbage growing was reported at Prestonpans, with millions of plants picked and sold.

1917   Bill to prohibit use of gaming machines in shops and other premises in Scotland was introduced in the Commons.

Edge of Eternity

The practical Scot of yesteryear was always conscious of his or her own mortality and the fragility of existence. A spinning-wheel was found in most households and the woman's first duty after her marriage was to prepare her own shroud.

May 8

1640   Young George Leslie, who was to have his hand severed at the Market Cross in Aberdeen for striking a laird, was reprieved at the last moment, literally as the axe was raised for the stroke.

1740   Town council of Glasgow agreed to an annual £10 grant to James Lochead, a teacher of cookery, who had set up business in the town.

1806   Satisfaction was expressed by the authorities that there were only 37 prisoners in Paisley jail when housing over 100 inmates was quite common.

1913   Despite its 'prosperous condition', Scotland still reported an increase in the number of paupers – 1,247 at the last count.

1934   First outing to the Campsie Hills by Glasgow Abstainers Union was disrupted by torrential rain.

Great Fire of Glasgow

Refugee camps to house thousands of Glaswegians were set up around the city after a dreadful fire in 1652 which raged for two days and destroyed timber buildings for a mile around the High Street. A thousand families were made homeless, and the rectangular grid of rebuilding in the city dates from this inferno.

May 9

1474   Parliament in Edinburgh took place two months later than planned because 'pestilence' or plague had been raging in Scotland.

1645   Battle of Auldearn near Nairn saw the army of the Marquis of Montrose defeat the Covenanters.

1726   Great concern in Edinburgh over so-called Hellfire Clubs or Sulphur Societies where men of 'atheistical opinions' met.

1844   Passers-by in Glasgow were astonished to find that a spider had flung its web from the north to the south side of Argyle Street.

1918   John MacLean, Glasgow schoolmaster, labour leader and the first Bolshevik consul in Britain, was tried for sedition at the High Court in Edinburgh.

Heavy Mob

In 1606 the Privy Council banned parties in lawsuits arriving at court backed by a team of friends or supporters 'with a view to exercising some influence over the course of justice'. A visit to any urban court in Scotland today would illustrate how that order was doomed to failure.

May 10

1307   Accepting a challenge from the Earl of Pembroke, Robert Bruce took the Scots army to Loudoun Hill, Ayrshire, and defeated an English force.

1611   James VI & I was said to be annoyed by the number of poor Scots wandering south to seek their fortune at court.

1692   Prisoners at Edinburgh's Tolbooth in the Canongate rioted and took possession of the prison, complaining about the quality of the food.

1941   Hitler's deputy Rudolf Hess landed by parachute at Eaglesham, Renfrewshire, in an apparent attempt to negotiate peace.

1945   Three tons of empty bottles were found in George Square as Glasgow tidied up after the joyous outpouring of VE Day.

Top of the Form

Clydebank High School pupil Sandra Townsley, studying for a sixth-year certificate in the 1980s, discovered a new chemical which was later called 'Sandrazol' in her honour.

May 11

1559   John Knox preached a rousing sermon at Perth against idolatry and launched the 'Protestant Revolution'.

1685   Two female Covenanters put to death by drowning in the narrow channel of the Bladenoch a mile from Wigtown. Margaret MacLauchlan and Margaret Wilson had refused to say 'God Save the King'.

1886   Annual meeting of the Scottish Football Association told that the balance in hand was £474.

1959   Edinburgh was preparing to draw up a parking-meter scheme for the city.

1984   Aberdeen beat Real Madrid 2–1 in the final of the European Cup Winners Cup in Gothenburg, Sweden.

A Good Read?

In the 1500s the Scottish public began to get the reading habit. Among the most popular of these early books were, *The Seeing of Urines*, *The Overthrow of Gout* and *Interpreting Dreams*. A survey has shown that Edinburgh has more booksellers per head of population than any other city in the United Kingdom.

May 12

1480   The Duke of Gloucester (later Richard III) was appointed Lieutenant-General of the North with a specific brief to make war against the Scots.

1790   A sailor in Edinburgh, who dressed up as a woman to avoid being press-ganged, was lifted when he forgot to shave off his bushy, black beard.

1859   Dentist in Glasgow advertised self-adhesive artificial teeth which did away with the need for extractions.

1913   Scottish squadron of the Royal Flying Corps, consisting of ten biplanes and ground support, was heading south from Montrose to Salisbury Plain.

1919   A major hoard of Roman silver was uncovered by archaeologists working on Traprain Law, East Lothian.

Back to the Caves

The Declaration of War on 3 September 1939 saw some remarkable preparations for the coming conflict; snakes were to be put down at Edinburgh Zoo and the bombing, some were convinced, would return mankind to a troglodyte existence.

BUNNETS OFF FOR A CANTANKEROUS DUKE

In the aftermath of Flodden there was one job in the sadly depleted Scottish court which always caused a headlong rush when it was pinned on the palace noticeboard.

What, pray, might you imagine this much sought-after position within the Renaissance court to be? Head cook and bottle-washer – with the occasional opportunity to purloin, half-inch, a tasty ox foot? Executioner's assistant – collecting loose change from the doomed nobility who were looking for a clean cut? Court musician – despite its dangers offering unlimited access to the house claret for a few tuneless pavanes?

No, all of these prime jobs with commensurate salary, pension plan and first-rate working conditions, paled compared to the post of court milliner. Hats, or to be more exact, bunnets, became big business when the French-born Duke of Albany accepted an invitation to govern Scotland during the minority of James V.

You see, John Stewart, Duke of Albany, when he reached Edinburgh on 26 May 1515, brought with him a volatile French temperament and, alas, a lack of sympathy for the Scottish situation. Despite this, he was to govern for nine years. He was greeted on his arrival in the capital by 'sundry farces' staged by the burgesses of the town in his honour, and these comic turns seem singularly appropriate when you learn of what was to follow.

Albany knew little of Scotland and showed no great desire to have his ignorance dispelled. He was depressed by the lack of little luxuries to which he had become accustomed in France, and he detested the sober, earnest style in which issues were debated. He regularly astonished the Scots nobles when, having been thwarted in an argument, he would hurl his bunnet into the fire.

How many hats were lost in this remarkable manner we can only surmise, but we do know that the court milliner was kept busy. Amazement among the nobility at Albany's strange antics inevitably turned to contempt.

Although it was to his credit that he did not try to supplant James V, his young cousin, the widely held view of his abilities was summarised by the Earl of Surrey, who called him a 'furious, wilful fool and a coward to boot'. Among the hat-makers, however, he is still a hero.

Hat-checks

Lady Wallace, a celebrated nineteenth-century Edinburgh beauty, set the fashion and dress style of the capital. Once, on her way to the races at Leith, she found her new bonnet had been torn. Undaunted, she wore the damaged hat and for days afterwards her milliner was besieged by ladies looking for bonnets in the same unusual style. The first conjurer ever to pull a rabbit from a hat is thought to have been John Henry Anderson, a farmer's son from Aberdeenshire, who became nationally known and staged a command performance for Queen Victoria in 1849. A popular Scottish punishment used by magistrates against gossips and scandalmongers was the Branks, a headpiece with an iron bar, which was jammed in the mouth, trapping the tongue and thus preventing speech. It was also used, more sinisterly, with spikes during the witch frenzies as an instrument of torture.

May 13

1424   Eight days before his Coronation, James I arrested three leading Scots nobles, including Walter Stewart, Earl of Fife.

1618   King James VI suggested that 'notorious and lewd' persons in the Borders should be sent to Virginia or other remote parts.

1809   A Bo'ness father of five drowned at a local brewery after falling into one of the tuns.

1888   Huge hailstones, some one and a half inches in diameter and weighing 3 ozs, fell during a thunderstorm in Central Scotland.

1943   Clyde goalkeeper Gilbert McKie was fined £18 at Stirling for failing to report for work as a miner because wet conditions gave him rheumatism.

Seat of Learning

Aberdeenshire's greatest educational era surely came in the 1590s when the district had three universities – the short-lived institution at Fraserburgh, and King's and Marischal Colleges in the town of Aberdeen itself; this at a time when England had only two universities, at Oxford and Cambridge.

May 14

1629   Jean Gordon, divorced by the Earl of Bothwell in 1567 to allow his alliance with Mary Queen of Scots, and the first person to work the famous Brora coal seam, died.

1690   Greenock saw the departure of a fleet of ships bound for the Western Highlands to construct Fort William as a bastion against rebellious clans.

1754   Society of Golfers of St Andrews was founded; this was the forerunner of the Royal and Ancient Club.

1859   Working classes allowed into Glasgow's Botanic Gardens for a penny; 800 took advantage of the offer and 'conducted themselves in a very orderly manner'.

1927   Sandy Hair's big day came when Partick Thistle thrashed Rangers 6-3 at Hampden to win the Charity Cup, and the Thistle striker netted five goals.

Bizarre Nickname

Engine No. 224, the locomotive which plunged to the bottom of the River Tay in 1879, with five coaches and 75 passengers, when the bridge collapsed, was recovered and put back into service with the nickname, *The Diver*.

May 15

1301   King Edward of England completed a document which outlined his claims to the overlordship of Scotland and which was to be presented to the Pope.

1568   Mary Queen of Scots spent her last night in Scotland at Dundrennan Abbey, near Kirkcudbright, before being taken to imprisonment and eventual execution in England.

1841   Three 'socialists' were charged with desecrating the Sabbath after sounds of a fiddle were heard at breakfast-time from a hall in Glasgow's Trongate.

1916   Glasgow's tramways department had collected 100,000 clay-pipes for despatch to troops at the front-line, along with 29,000 tins of thick, black tobacco.

1942   *Queen Mary* arrived at Gourock with nearly 10,000 United States troops on board.

Army of the Lord

Seventeenth-century conventicles are often pictured as small, family gatherings for worship in remote glens or on windswept hilltops. However, one held in Dumfriesshire brought together over 14,000 Covenanters.

May 16

1402   Duke of Albany called a council at which he and his cohorts sought to prove their innocence of involvement in the death of the Duke of Rothesay who had been imprisoned in the Castle of Falkland.

1617   James VI & I, against the wishes of his English advisors, returned to Edinburgh, for the only time, as ruler of the two kingdoms.

1763   Samuel Johnson and his Scots biographer, James Boswell, met for the first time – in the backshop of a Covent Garden bookseller.

1849   Packman poet William Nicholson, known as 'Wandering Willie', whose ballad, 'Aiken Drum', became popular, died, aged 67.

1938   Chief Constable of Glasgow proposed motor-cars for policemen on the extensive new beats around the city.

Early Doors

It was the nineteenth-century Scots antiquarian and archaeologist Daniel Wilson who coined the word 'prehistoric' to describe the story of mankind before the written record.

May 17

1532　The Court of Session, the highest civil tribunal in Scotland, was instituted by James V in an attempt to break the judicial stranglehold of the aristocracy.

1606　Edinburgh magistrates were ordered by the Privy Council to erect a stone pillar near the Mercat Cross where bankrupts were to be placed wearing a yellow bunnet.

1780　Glasgow, previously regarded only as a backwater up-river from Port Glasgow, became a port of entry in its own right.

1859　A sudden summer, after a wintry spring, burst upon Scotland with the sun 'radiating great heat', particularly in the south-west.

1909　'Unnecessary and objectionable' street noises were said to be making life in Glasgow unbearable.

Profit for All

The world's first Co-operative Society to pay a dividend on purchases was founded at Lennoxtown in Stirlingshire, in 1812.

May 18

1491　Scots Parliament confirmed the alliance and confederation with France.

1589　Kirk session of Perth ordered keepers of the town gates to exclude Spaniards (Armada refugees) and other idle vagabonds and beggars.

1803　Exhibition by Madame Marie Tussaud of 70 lifesize wax figures opened in Edinburgh, but attracted only a handful of people on its first day.

1840　A plague of stray dogs created much work for Glasgow's 'execution squad' – 36 'miserable curs' had been drowned in a barrel for a bounty of tuppence a head.

1913　A remarkable sandstorm enveloped Girvan harbour during a strong, westerly gale.

Sioux in the Slammer

Perhaps the most famous 'guest' at Glasgow's grim Barlinnie Prison was a Red Indian chief who got drunk on the local firewater while visiting the city as part of Buffalo Bill's famous Wild West Show.

May 19

1563   Sir John Arthur, a priest, was indicted for baptising and marrying several persons in the 'auld and abominable Papist manner'.

1784   Two Greenock merchants were ordered to be pilloried and banished from Scotland after trial, for boring holes and sinking ships with intent to claim the insurance money.

1809   Plans were unveiled for a common sewer along Glasgow's Trongate; contractors were sought by Richard Smellie, Superintendent of Labour.

1864   In a radical move, some large factories in Glasgow decided to stop work for the week at midday Saturday instead of 2 p.m.

1981   Plans for an alternative energy exhibition in empty cottages near the site of Torness nuclear power-station in East Lothian, were scuppered by the electricity board who demolished the buildings.

Scotland's Shame

Dornoch in Sutherland was the scene of Scotland's last witch-burning in June 1727, when Janet Horne was convicted of helping the devil put horseshoes on her lame daughter. Incredibly, that same year, a group of London gentlemen were formalising the rules of cricket!

FROGMARCHED INTO A CONTROVERSY

A squad of Ayrshire coalminers added fuel this week, in 1888, to what many contemporary scientists considered the biggest confidence trick of the nineteenth century – the marvellous 'toad-in-the-hole' mysteries.

Press reports of the incident are straightforward and to the point. A live frog was found embedded in a seam of coal 150-feet down in a Kilmarnock colliery. The miners were said to have been greatly astonished. However, this report was only the latest in a long series of similar, remarkable discoveries in the Victorian period, which really must have had folk wondering if the cosmic joker was at work.

Frogs and toads had been turning up inside blocks of coal all over the United Kingdom and the United States. When they were split open during mining, at the coalyard or even in the hearth, out would jump the frogs, having been encased, so it seems, in a carboniferous cocoon since the beginning of time. One live toad even turned up in a block of marble which was removed from the fireplace at Chillingham Castle because it was always damp and discoloured.

One writer on the mysterious and paranormal, Frank Smyth, has compared the great frog debate of the 1880s with the modern UFO enigma. Research in the seventeenth and eighteenth centuries seemed to indicate that crabs, snakes, lobsters, toads and frogs could indeed survive indefinitely without air, food, light or moisture. Shellfish of an exquisite flavour were found in stones used for paving Toulon harbour.

A story in the *Lancaster Guardian* of 1841 typifies these tales of discovery. A considerable sensation was caused in the town when a frog was freed from its dark tomb by Richard Tomlinson, 'a highly respected inhabitant', who was splitting coal when out popped the frog. Large numbers of people came to inspect the hollow in the coal and the report concluded that the recess had 'formed the house of the frog ever since the foundation of the seam'.

Now, the two sides in the debate would have stated their cases thus; the sceptics arguing that the frog had either arrived unnoticed at the scene just as the coal was split or, following through on the nationwide hoax theory, had been placed there. Following a series of experiments which saw creatures die in similar, but artificial environments they felt their case was proved.

However, the opposition would argue that it was widely known that frogs and toads spent the winter in a form of suspended animation deep in the muddy floors of ponds. If frogs could live for months in a solid casing of mud, why not for much, much longer? Annoyingly, there is no further word of the Kilmarnock frog. Such was the case in many of these supposed 'miracles'. Yet, tantalisingly, at the Brighton Museum you can still see a mummified toad in a flint nodule, uncovered by workmen at Lewes in Sussex.

The principal legacy of this almost forgotten debate is the sausage and batter belt-tightener, Toad in the Hole.

May 20

685   Egfrith, King of Northumbria, was defeated by the Picts in battle at Nechtansmere, near Forfar.

1594   A strange Scottish superstition demanding that a piece of land on every farm, known as 'the goodman's croft', should be left untilled in respect to the devil, was ordered to cease by the General Assembly.

1859   Corn-remover arrived in Glasgow offering his services. He claimed to be well versed in 'those venomous enemies to pedal comfort'.

1895   Britain's first female dentist, Lilian Murray, qualified LDS at Edinburgh.

1945   Thirty German U-boats had been brought in under escort to Kyle of Lochalsh and 1,100 crewmen were sent south by rail as prisoners.

Madame Fletcher

Demands for Parliamentary reform, including riots in Scotland's major towns, followed the French Revolution. In Edinburgh, Mrs Fletcher, a staunch advocate of social reform, is said to have practised guillotining chickens in the back garden of her house in Queen Street in preparation for the big day.

May 21

1150   The Cistercian Abbey of Kinloss was founded by David I. Its stones were later sold to help build the Cromwellian fort at Inverness.

1613   Lord Maxwell, who had been on the run for several years, was beheaded in Edinburgh; among his crimes was the murder of the Laird of Johnston.

1836   A huge herring – weighing 4lbs and measuring nearly two feet in length – had been landed at Irvine.

1863   'Dull demand' for servants at Paisley Whitsun feeing-market – wages for men ranged from £8 to £14 half-yearly, and between £3.10s and £5.10s for women.

1906   Scots sea-captains, arriving in the ports along the American eastern seaboard, reported that the Gulf Stream appeared to have changed course.

Turkish Delight

Eighteenth-century Scots soldier of fortune, Marshall Keith, had command of Austrian forces in a bloody and long-running combat on the Danube against the Turks. The sides eventually came together and, after talks, Keith was invited to meet the Grand Vizier privately. This distinguished person had arrived in Oriental splendour, mounted on a camel. When the men were alone, the Vizier threw down his turban, tore off his false beard and revealed himself as a former classmate of Keith's from the same parish school in Aberdeenshire, who had mysteriously disappeared 30 years previously. 'Ou, Johnnie, Foo's 'a wi' ye, man?' he greeted the astonished Keith.

May 22

1587   More reports of clashes between small merchant-vessels from the Fife ports and raiding English pirates.

1668   Kilmarnock badly damaged by a fire which made almost the entire population of 180 families homeless. Refugees were living in the fields in a condition of starvation.

1693   Fortrose minister David Angus, like other Episcopalian clergy, was brought before the Privy Council for not praying for William and Mary.

1784   Famous actress Sarah Siddons made her Scottish debut in Edinburgh.

1933   First civil aircraft to visit the Outer Hebrides landed on North Uist causing great excitement among the islanders, many of whom had never seen a plane.

Forbidden Territory

The centre of the Isle of Man is a dangerous place for Scots. A centuries-old law gives locals the right to slay any Scot who encroaches more than a mile inland.

May 23

1174   Election of Jocelin, Bishop of Glasgow, who was abbot of Melrose and who obtained Glasgow's charter as a burgh and began a new cathedral after a disastrous fire.

1579   Danish nobles who had accompanied James VI and his bride Anne from Scandinavia were entertained by the magistrates of Edinburgh with 'an abundance of beer, ale and wine'.

1764   Lord Prestongrange, Lord Advocate, who took a principal role in suppressing Highland garb after Culloden, died at Bath.

1808   Gipsies, who kidnapped a nine-year-old boy from his home at Auchtermuchty, were being sought.

1845   A display of archery took place in the grounds of Robert Knox's house at Kelvingrove, Glasgow, and the Royal Company of Archers from Edinburgh put in an appearance.

All Steamed Up

It's comforting to learn that even the great and good have their moments of despair. That pioneer of steam-navigation, Henry Bell, anxious to prove some new principle of construction, built a pier on the Clyde shore at Helensburgh, only to see it washed away by the first high tide.

May 24

1544   'Battle of the Butts': the forces of the Earl of Arran, Regent of Scotland who favoured an alliance with France, defeated the Earl of Lennox at Glasgow's Gallowmuir where archery targets stood.

1585   Kirk Session in Perth – in fear of the plague – ordered an end to banqueting at marriages or risk a fine of 40 pounds.

1809   Lanarkshire Militia urgently sought someone to teach the fyfe and 'a few stout boys' to act as drummers.

1883   Government commission inquiring into crofters' conditions finished taking evidence in Skye and moved on to Barra.

1972   Rangers became the first Scottish team to win the European Cup Winners Cup, defeating Moscow Dynamo 3–2 in Barcelona.

Fitting End

Perthshire-born botanist and explorer David Douglas, after whom the famous Rocky Mountain fir is named, travelled widely in North America's wilderness in the early 1800s, discovering new birds, plants and trees. Eventually, he met his death in the style of a true adventurer – he was killed in Hawaii, in the year 1834, by a wild bull.

May 25

1195   Paisley Priory was granted lands at Lochwinnoch, Renfrewshire, along with half a fishery at the mouth of the loch.

1579   Collections were taken throughout Scotland to help support Scots seamen captured by pirates and languishing in North African jails.

1601   Plans were finalised to 'plant' ministers in the homes of the Catholic nobles Huntly, Errol, Angus, Home and Herries, to convert them from their 'Papist ways'.

1888   Glasgow umbrella manufacturer, Wilson Mathieson of Glassford Street, had constructed the largest umbrella in the world – 21 feet in diameter – to allow an African king to entertain 30 guests.

1967   Celtic became the first British team to win the European Cup, beating Inter Milan 2–1 in Lisbon.

Ordeal by Water

As late as the mid-1600s, death by drowning for theft was still applied in Scotland.

May 26

1424   Football was banned. Gold and silver mines became Crown property under Acts passed at a Parliament at Perth – the first presided over by James I since his release from English captivity.

1563   Prices of foodstuffs in Scotland soared as famine swept the country. John Knox blamed the riotous feasting of Queen Mary's court.

1622   Edinburgh was buzzing with news of a sea battle in the Forth off Leith, between a ship belonging to the King of Spain and two Dutch vessels. Many were said to have been killed.

1809   Cows were brought in to supply warm milk for bathers at Willowbank washing-house in Glasgow's George Square.

1887   Unemployment in Paisley was on the increase with 2,500 out of work; the relief fund could only pay a few pence to one member of each family.

Not Salmon Again

Salmon was so plentiful in the West of Scotland in the late 1700s that it had almost become a monotonous meal. A farmer engaging a ploughman was bound to promise not to feed him salmon on more than four days a week.

PAPAL LEGATE AMONGST THE BARK-EATERS

Marie Antoinette's wee classic on hearing the poor had no bread, 'Let them eat cake,' would appear to have an equally stunning Scottish parallel. When Papal Legate Aenius Silvius Piccolomini, the future Pope Pius II, came to Scotland in 1435, he saw paupers begging for bread at the church doors being handed lumps of stone.

However, the seemingly heartless, even cruel gesture, Aenius was to learn, was in reality an act of great charity. These were no ordinary rocks. The 'sulphurous stones' which he had never before encountered were black in colour, and in a nation where wood was already becoming scarce, lumps of coal were treasured by the poor.

This was only one of a series of observations on the medieval Scottish scene noted by Aenius on his brief tour of Scotland (almost certainly only consisting of the Central Lowlands). His chronicle is a compact, but valuable, window on the lifestyles of our fifteenth-century ancestors. His arrival was dramatic, his ship being wrecked near Dunbar.

The burning-stones were not the only mystery he recorded. Mention is made of the remarkable legend of the seabirds which grew from barnacles; the embryonic shape could be clearly seen – to some eyes at least – in the flesh of the shellfish, although a hatching had never been witnessed. Over the centuries this odd tale resurfaced. It wasn't until the 1800s that the myth was finally exploded and even in the late 1600s, Sir Robert Murray, a founder of the Royal Society, wrote a serious treatise on the subject. At least we still have the barnacle geese to remind us of this controversy.

On the geographical front, Aenius tells us that Scotland 'is an island joined to England, stretching 200 miles to the north and about 50 broad'. After the fertile landscapes and hill-towns of Central Italy, old Scotia's grandeurs left Aenius distinctly under-whelmed. He reported that few sorts of grain were found and the place was generally devoid of trees. Towns were unwalled, houses were commonly built without lime, and in the villages they were roofed with turf, and cow-hides served as doors.

'The men are small in stature, but bold; the women fair and comely, and prone to the pleasures of love, kisses being there not more esteemed than pressing the hand in Italy.' Aenius knew a bit about this, having reputedly been a purveyor of pornography in his younger days.

Wine was imported, horses were mostly small, ambling nags, and large oysters could be found, and Scotland exported hides, wool, salt-fish and pearls. Wild Scots in the North ate the bark from trees, he tells us, and nothing gave them more pleasure than to hear the English dispraised.

On his way home through the north of England, an alarm was

raised when a raiding party of Scots appeared in the neighbourhood. Not everyone was dismayed. The men took to their heels but the women refused to fly, 'for they had no fear that the enemy would do them any evil – not reckoning violation any evil at all'.

May 27

1537   James V landed on Scottish soil with his new bride, Magdalen, daughter of Francis I of France. The sickly queen died within days.

1587   Guillaume Sallust, the French poet, visited Scotland at the invitation of James VI. It was a rarity for an eminent European literary figure to visit Scotland.

1600   William Watson, beadle at the kirk in Glasgow, was ordered to make repentance in his underclothes for being drunk on duty.

1808   Incorporation of the first railway company in Scotland, the Kilmarnock-Troon, opened in 1812 with horse-drawn coaches.

1991   Great Britain and Ireland won the Walker Cup at St Andrews; the first victory over the United States in this event since 1938.

Radio Ham

Ramsay MacDonald's mobile style of public speaking meant that Britain's first radio election broadcast from a meeting in Glasgow, in October 1924, was considered a failure, with the Labour leader wandering around the platform during his speech.

May 28

1333   Army of Edward III of England maintained a land blockade of Berwick despite success of Scots defenders in dispersing a seaborne attack.

1588   Alison Peirson, a healer of disease 'by magical powers', was tried for witchcraft and burned at St Andrews; titular Archbishop Adamson was said to be among her clients.

1650   Over a three-mile stretch of Lord Buccleuch's estate near the English border it 'rained blood' – sand blown from the Sahara was blamed in later years for this odd phenomenon.

1862   Jane Guthrie, a spirit-dealer in Glasgow's Gallowgate, was fined £5 for keeping her premises open at 2 a.m.; half the fine went to local orphans.

1911   Flittin' Day in Glasgow was quieter than usual because of a steady downpour.

Load of Bull

At the end of the century, an ox of quite enormous dimensions was sold by Colonel Hamilton of Pencaitland in East Lothian to an army butcher. The animal was reportedly 16 feet long from nose to tail, ten feet in girth, and stood over five foot, eight inches tall.

May 29

1223   An Assembly at Selkirk saw a long-running dispute between the abbeys of Holyrood and Newbattle amicably settled.

1570   Linlithgow, threatened with destruction by an English army under Sir William Drury, was reprieved at the last minute after much wailing and gnashing of teeth by the local populace.

1621   Reports were reaching the south of a great earthquake in the Montrose area. Many people had fled the town and several lives were lost.

1809   Overcrowding of coaches reached a crisis when 24 people were seen clinging to the outside of the Edinburgh-Haddington service; the Lord Provost intervened and an extra coach was put on the service.

1940   LNER paddle-steamer *Waverley* sank in the Channel during the evacuation of Dunkirk.

Great Balls Of . . .

Mysterious balls of fire, or in Gaelic *gealbhain*, have been reported in many parts of Scotland over the centuries. Lochs Tay and Rannoch seem to be favourite locations for this strange phenomenon which, some believe, is caused by unusual electrical activity.

May 30

1385	A French army of 2,000 men, including many nobles, had arrived at Leith; troops were being billeted around Scotland from Kelso to Dunfermline.
1574	A summer of 'evil' weather began which was to bring abundant rain and wind, resulting in a crop failure and great shortages of food in the following autumn and winter.
1787	Thomas Gentles was hanged in Glasgow, his offence – stealing a piece of cloth from a bleachfield.
1842	The right of doorkeepers at the General Assembly of the Church of Scotland to exact money from the public on entry was rejected in court.
1917	New figures showed that there were 6,621 public houses in Scotland – one for every 769 people.

Fireside Adventurer

Sir James Barrie, Kirriemuir-born creator of Peter Pan, was timid and sentimental by nature but seems to have admired courage and the spirit of adventure in others. This led him to become a sponsor of Captain Scott's Antarctic expeditions.

May 31

1608	Margaret Hertsyde, formerly a servant of Queen Anne, was declared 'infamous' and banished to Orkney for having taken jewellery belonging to her Royal mistress, wife of James VI & I.
1727	Royal Bank of Scotland was formed with a capital of £111,000.
1890	Masons in Dundee demanded an increase of ½d per hour in their wages.
1958	Peter Manuel was sentenced to death at the High Court in Glasgow for seven murders.
1982	Historic first meeting on Scottish soil between the Moderator of the General Assembly and the Pope took place at the Kirk's Assembly Hall in Edinburgh.

Golly Gosh

Legend has it that when Mary Queen of Scots felt unwell she would ask for her favourite fruit-preserve. Her French servants would declare, 'Ah, Marie malade', and so 'marmalade' came into the English language. Less romantic scholars suggest that 'marmalade' derives from two Greek words meaning honey-apple.

June 1

1250	Alexander III, at an Assembly in Edinburgh, gave the monks of Paisley the right to repair their fish-tank or pond on the River Leven.

1657   Glasgow matched Edinburgh by providing itself with a horse-drawn fire-engine 'for the occasion of sudden fire, in spouting out of water thereon'.

1697   St Kilda visited by a Kirk minister to clear up the population's 'confused notions' on religion that had been gained from a Roman priest who had stayed there decades before.

1708   The Earl of Ilay replaced his older brother, the Duke of Argyll, as an extra Lord of Session, even though he was only 24 years of age.

1894   Allan Line steamer *Pomeranian* sailed from the Clyde for Quebec and Montreal with a party of 120 girls from Quarriers Homes, Bridge of Weir.

Masticating English

An Ayrshire servant lass who spoke the broadest west country Doric returned from a visit to London with a pronounced English accent. Asked how she had learned this so easily, she reverted to Ayrshire dialect: 'Ou, it's easy eneuch. A' ye've got tae dae is just tae leave oot the Hs and the Rs and gie the words a bit chow in the middle.'

June 2

1291   Scots clergy and nobility gathered in a field opposite Norham Castle to put forward eight candidates from which Edward I of England was eventually to choose a King of Scots.

1508   Two scorpions were found in the garden of Craigmillar Castle on the outskirts of Edinburgh.

1590   James VI began to put the squeeze on his courtiers and richer nobles in an attempt to defray expenses incurred in entertaining his new bride Queen Anne and the Danish nobility.

1724   The largest woman in Scotland, wife of Captain Budd of Ford in Midlothian, was buried in Greyfriars Churchyard, Edinburgh, in a coffin two feet deep.

1944   Chief Constable of Fife insisted that women police-officers were quite unnecessary.

American Aristo

In the early 1700s, Scots gambler and financial wizard, John Law of Lauriston, who founded the Bank of France, was created Duc D'Arkansas for his work in developing the French colony of Louisiana.

LOCUSTS OFF THE BEATEN TRACK

Conditions seem just about right for an invasion. A steady east to south-easterly wind and thundery weather lasting over a period of weeks. Yes, indeed, this could be Scotland's year of the locust. The early signs are already there in the selection of exotic foreign bird species which are being blown into the Northern Isles this summer.

Similar meteorological conditions over the centuries have led to sightings and captures of *schistocerca gregaria*, the desert locust, the wee beasties made infamous by the biblical plague stories (before them, the Garden of Eden, behind them, utter devastation). Carried by prevailing summer breezes from North Africa and Southern Europe, they can end up way off their beaten track among the Highland glens and rocky loch shores.

Throughout the 1800s, solitary locusts turned up from time to time, but 1846 was a big year across the country on the locust front, and a particularly large flight of insects was seen passing over Sutherland; no captures were made.

Earlier in the century, in conditions of drought, insects of foreign origin, including locusts, are known to have reached as far north as Scotland. It seems likely that in previous ages they were not distinguished from the commonly found grasshopper.

With the correct set of weather features, a significant invasion was recorded in 1857. A nationwide locust-hunt was sparked off when a London cat caught an insect. The owner reckoned it was a locust and sent it to a newspaper. Soon reported sightings flooded the news-desk.

Particular interest centred on how far north the locusts had ventured. As late as 10 October 1857 the *Illustrated London News* carried a despatch from the far north, 'Several live locusts have been found in Orkney'. A locust was also said to have turned up on a farm in Northern Ireland after a thunderstorm.

It seems the locusts, whose capacity for multiplying quickly and migrating in enormous groups is simply staggering, were never treated as a potential pest – the numbers never justified those fears – but the insects were unquestionably a great Victorian curiosity.

Much more recently, in 1988, in fact, the amazing voyages of the locust were highlighted by a vast swarm of young insects which successfully migrated from West Africa to the Caribbean, completing the 5,000-kilometre crossing in six days and making the Scottish trip seem like a doddle. This was the first transatlantic flight on record, and twice as long as any previously noted. It immediately gave scientists the answer to the mysterious origins of the New World locusts.

Swarms can be almost unimaginably large, covering 1,000 square kilometres and containing up to 50,000 million insects. Such a formidable squad, we are told, can consume upwards of 80,000 tonnes of crop, daily.

Whether or not we see the locust in Scotland this summer remains problematical. But I wonder if any locusts, even a solitary specimen, from one of these previous invasions have been preserved, perhaps somewhere in the corner of a museum or mummified in a matchbox in grandad's attic. If anyone has such entymological treasures I'd be interested to hear.

June 3

1586   Privy Council banned a day of combat planned by Borderers with 'some English guests' in the Middle Marches because it might 'rekindle old feuds and serious evils would arise'.

Bunnet meets bowler on Wembley Way

1767   Architect James Craig presented with the Freedom of Edinburgh for his plan of the New Town.

1789   Stornoway-born explorer Alexander Mackenzie set out with 13 companions to survey the vast river-systems of north-west Canada.

1838   A suit of armour was uncovered by astonished workmen at Bothwell in Lanarkshire; there was no sign of the occupant.

1981   Renfrew councillors carrying out a ceremony to keep the burgh's fishing-rights alive, caught a salmon and two sea-trout in the Clyde near Dumbarton Castle; the first catch since 1951.

German for Beginners

A Glasgow sheriff was grateful when a member of the public offered to translate in a case involving four Germans who spoke no English. He said he had learned the language as a prisoner-of-war but when the sheriff asked the first German, 'What is your name?', the would-be interpreter translated, 'Vot iss your name?'. He was charged with contempt.

June 4

1563   Concern was expressed in the Scottish Parliament over the shortage of coal. Apparently, too much was being used for ballast in ships.

1674   Authorities were outraged by a demonstration involving a group of women in Parliament Close, Edinburgh, who were protesting about the 'starving congregations of Scotland'.

1695   Peterhead, whose harbour was often used as a refuge by vessels fleeing French privateers, was granted military aid after 22 'great balls' were fired at the town.

1818   The first recorded inter-club golf match, between Edinburgh Burgess Golfing Society and Bruntsfield Links Golf Club, took place.

1832   The Scottish Reform Bill, increasing the number of Scottish MPs from 45 to 53, and thus widening the vote, was passed at Westminster.

And so to bed

The famous North British Railway workshops at Cowlairs, Glasgow, produced Europe's first sleeping-carriage in 1873. Although passengers – all first-class – were expected to provide their own bedding, accommodation was made available for servants.

June 5

1598   The Laird of Johnston was denounced as a rebel for persistently lawless behaviour; a few days earlier his portrait had been hung upside down on the gibbet at the Cross in Edinburgh.

1762   Weekly newspaper, the *North Briton*, run by the novelist Tobias Smollett, was published for the first time.

1805   Edinburgh engraver David Scott and Hugh Adamson, a potter, were executed at Glasgow Cross for forging bank-notes.

1865   Dumfries-born polar explorer and naturalist, Sir John Richardson, who took part in the search for the missing Franklin expedition, died, aged 78.

1977   German rally-ace Walter Rohrl was disqualified from the Scottish International Rally and charged, after colliding with a police car near Huntly.

Deep Thinker

Dom Odo Blundell, a monk from the abbey at Fort Augustus on Loch Ness, pioneered underwater archaeology when, in 1902, he borrowed diving equipment to study the submerged crannogs or prehistoric loch houses of the Scottish Highlands.

June 6

1492   Fishing industry was becoming an increasingly important part of the Scottish economy, Parliament was told.

1597   Interest-rate for money-lending in Scotland was fixed at ten per cent; corporal punishment would result in failure to comply.

1612   An extraordinary drouth burned up and destroyed 'corns and fruits of the ground' throughout Scotland.

1789   Patrick Miller, steamship pioneer, ordered a new engine from the Carron Company at Falkirk.

1913   Glasgow magistrates decided to clamp down on the growing number of people professing to tell fortunes by palmistry.

Down at Heel

Up until the end of the eighteenth century shoe-heels in Lowland Scotland were made from birch; because they needed frequent repair, a supply of wood was kept in the wearer's house for these 'tree-clout shoon'.

June 7

1529   Forces of the Earl of Caithness routed by rebel Sinclairs at Summerdale, near Kirkwall in Orkney.

1594   Logan of Restalrig was condemned for ordering his servants to rob travellers on the road past his bleak, Berwickshire home of Fast Castle.

1637   Plague reported in the Borders and various orders were issued banning meetings in an attempt to confine the sickness.

1689   Seventy pounds was distributed among poor Irish and French Protestant refugees who had chosen Scotland for sanctuary.

1973   New tension in the 'Cod War' with Iceland as the Royal Navy reported the ramming of a frigate, and Scots complained of overfishing by Icelandic seine netters off Shetland.

What's in a Name?

Portobello was optimistically named in the mid-1700s by a retired sailor who built a cottage in an area much frequented by smugglers and thieves. The Royal Scots Greys, one of Scotland's most famous regiments, got their name after an incident in Flanders when they commandeered the white horses of the local gendarmerie. Forestry student Stephen Eagle perched in a tree for seven days in an Aberdeen park in 1985 to raise cash for the Third World.

June 8

1650   Scotland blighted by the 'Irish ague', a 'terrible sore pain in the head' cured, apparently, by a 'hard tying-up' of the head.

1778   Seaforth Highlanders, raised by the Earl of that name, were recruiting in Ross-shire and Sutherland for service against the 'rebel' American colonies.

1801   With daily rumours of an invasion by the forces of Napoleon, Edinburgh's Volunteer Brigade stepped up their exercises on Leith and Bruntsfield Links.

1838   78th Highlanders arrived in Glasgow from a tour of duty in India: their mascot, a young elephant, led the kilted warriors.

1928   Nineteen years after being convicted of murder, Oscar Slater was freed on appeal at the High Court in Edinburgh.

Level Crossing?

A skilful Kelso engineer, Sir James Brunlees, laid the first railway line across the Alps.

June 9

597   Death of St Columba of Iona, apostle of the Scottish Highlands; aged 76, he had been in Scotland for 34 years.

1455   The forfeiture of all land and property of the rebellious Douglas family was ordered in the aftermath of their rout at Arkinholm in the Borders.

1591   Three-day trial of Eupham M'Calvean, one of the so-called North Berwick witches, opened. She was condemned to be burned alive.

1655   Magistrates in Edinburgh were accused of negligence in preventing the sale of 'blown mutton, corrupted veal, fusty bread and light loaves'; greatly adulterated beer, wine and ale was also being sold.

1845   Mr Cowan, a well-known Glasgow distiller, was attacked and robbed of a large sum of money on Fintry Moor.

I Name this Cloth

An error by a clerk working for the London firm of James Locke who entered 'tweeds' by mistake in his records instead of 'tweels' is said to have led to the naming of Scotland's world-famous chequered cloth.

DRAWING THE BORDERLINE

Exhilaration, lightness of heart, sunshine on a rainy day – just a few of the unexpected sensations I recall on returning after my first trip out of the homeland. I think this was the moment when I realised I loved Scotland almost as much as I loved my mammy.

It wasn't that the summer camp with the Third Clydebank Cubs and Scouts in deepest Devon had been uneventful – on the contrary, I got my first sip of scrumpy and was bitten by a swarm of clegs – but something special happened on that steam-train during the climb to Beattock. It's a difficult phenomenon to explain, this inner smile of the Scot returning to the old country, even after a brief exile.

Outside on the high moors the sheep looked the same as they had done a few miles back, the sky was no different, nor was the wee, brown burn which bubbled along the trackside. And yet, there was something indefinable and familiar in the air. Everyone felt it and was happy. Spirits were raised and we didn't need a border sign to tell us we were home. Scotland, I suddenly realised, was a state of mind.

Since the days of electric skies and fierce long-necked beasties, when we fought over the rights to the most commodious cave, borderlines have occupied the attention of governments, kings and all those who foolishly believe they have some sort of claim to God's acres.

The River Tweed in its lower reaches has always been a natural boundary, just as Carlisle and Berwick have remained frontier towns right up to the present day. Just how silly this border business can become is illustrated by the story of a medieval meeting between Scottish and English knights – their task being to determine the boundary between the two nations.

In 1245, Hugh de Bolebec wrote to his master, the English King Henry III, giving him details of the bizarre congress at Redderburn, a tributary of the Tweed. Hugh, with the knights of Northumberland, met David de Lindesay, Justiciar of Scotland, Patrick, Earl of Dunbar and their team of Scots noblemen.

The idea was that a 'jury' of six English knights and six Scots should be chosen to make a 'true perambulation' between the kingdoms, between Carham and Howdean, near Jedburgh. However, it wasn't long before the traditional bickering began. The English knights were of one accord about the route which should be taken; the Scots, surprise, surprise, were equally unanimous in choosing another line. Dissent and contradiction were reported between the respective camps.

Somewhat naively, the leaders elected another half-dozen knights to the 'jury' from each side, to join the expedition, in the hope of achieving a compromise. However, almost as soon as the new batch were sworn in they predictably sided with the established position and the stalemate deepened.

By this time de Bolebec was beelin' and decided that with or without Scottish co-operation he would send 24 of his 'discreet and loyal' knights so that they might settle the ancient Marches between the kingdoms by riding 'from the Tweed, by the rivulet of Reddenburn, ascending south and on in a straight line through Hoperiglaw to Whitelaw'.

Word reached the Scots of this English plan and a scrap seemed likely as the Scots hindered the movement of the English knights, preventing them starting their tour with threats of violence. Eventually, the English retired, declaring that the boundaries they had been prevented from tracing were the 'true and ancient Marches'. The Scottish contingent agreed to differ.

June 10

1297   English army crossed into Annandale under Henry Percy intent on crushing an uprising led by Moray and Wallace against occupying English forces.

1578   Deadline set by Scots Parliament for all threshing of grain to be completed. This measure was designed to prevent hoarding; the grain had to be at market within 20 days.

1642   Arrival of shoals of pillaging dog-fish along the east coast of Scotland brought an acute shortage of white fish throughout the country.

1719   The Battle of Glenshiel saw the defeat of Jacobite and Spanish troops by Hanoverian forces. The castle of Eilean Donan surrendered after a lengthy bombardment.

1840   Plans were being considered with a view to connecting Aberdeen with Glasgow and Edinburgh by a railway linking up with the growing rail network to the south.

Made from Girders

Ironwork for the amazing opera house in the heart of the Amazonian rain forest, at the Brazilian town of Manaus, was manufactured in Glasgow.

June 11

1581   Young King James VI returned from church at Dalkeith with two pipers playing before him; he had been staying with the Duke of Lennox at Dalkeith.

1634   Walter, first Earl of Buccleuch, was finally buried at Hawick, after the ship carrying his body had been blown to Norway in a storm.

1665   News reached Edinburgh of a great naval victory over the Dutch off Lowestoft, bonfires were lit, bells rung and cannon fired, and 'loupin' for joy was reported in the streets.

1842   Owner of the first bicycle seen in Glasgow, a

Dumfriesshire blacksmith, Kirkpatrick MacMillan, was charged with riding along the pavement and knocking down a child.

1975   First oil came ashore from the North Sea, from the Argyll Field, 225 miles east of Edinburgh, a year behind schedule.

Continental Connection

Towns on both sides of the River Forth have characteristic red pantile roofs. The tiles were first brought back from Europe as ballast in times of steady international trade between East of Scotland ports and the continent.

June 12

1298   William Wallace attacked and routed an English invasion force under Aymer de Valence, the Earl of Pembroke, which had landed in Fife.

1597   Pack-trains passing through the uplands of Clydesdale, carrying lead from the Lanarkshire mines to Leith, were under attack from the 'broken men of the Borders'.

1625   Citizens of Aberdeen were learning to live with a remarkable order from the town council forbidding anyone from forcing drink on a neighbour. A penalty was fixed at 40 pounds.

1914   Calls for the return of the Stone of Destiny to Scotland followed a suffragette attack on the Coronation Chair at Westminster Abbey.

1974   Public appeal launched aiming to raise £175,000 to help Glasgow Corporation purchase a Van Gogh portrait of Alexander Reid, a Glasgow art dealer.

Body o' the Kirk

Churchgoing for the hangman of Edinburgh in the eighteenth century was a solitary penance. At the Tolbooth Church he always had a pew to himself and at the regular communions the clergyman was obliged to serve a separate table for the hangman after the rest of the congregation had left the kirk.

June 13

1496   An Act making education compulsory for eldest sons of barons and freeholders became law.

1799   Colliers were freed from servitude to coalmasters and the last vestige of medieval serfdom disappeared from Scotland.

1819   The notorious Strathnaver Clearances – moving people off the land to make way for sheep – began on the Sutherland estates.

1840   *Archimedes*, an experimental screw-propeller steamship

The future of mining in the 1930s

visited Glasgow's Broomielaw.

1914   Executive of the Scottish Miners Federation decided that they would push for a four-day week in the coalfields.

Locomotive Luddites

In 1842 railway workers at Perth destroyed an experimental electric locomotive, which had been tested on the Glasgow-Edinburgh route, fearing it would signal the loss of thousands of jobs on the steam-rail network.

June 14

1296   Army of King Edward I of England, having sacked Berwick, reached Edinburgh and, after a week of using three siege-engines, took the castle.

1508   An epidemic, named by the common people 'stoupe gallant' because it seemed only to affect the 'brave and able', raged in Scotland.

1623   An extraordinary tax was approved by the Privy Council to alleviate the suffering among thousands of Scots affected by a severe famine.

1693   To promote the making of linen in Scotland it was forbidden for corpses to be buried in anything but plain linen and relatives had to swear an oath to that effect.

| 1845 | The year's first basket of Scottish strawberries was sold in Princes Street; a fine, dry spell persisted. |

Peace in our Time

Berwick, a town which has often changed hands between Scotland and England over the centuries, ended a private war of its own with Russia as recently as 1966. At the end of the Crimean War in 1856 the town was omitted from the documents of settlement, and it was 113 years before a Soviet official made a goodwill visit and signed a peace treaty.

June 15

1567	Mary Queen of Scots was defeated at Carberry Hill near Musselburgh and surrendered to the Protestant lords.
1625	At breakfast-time the remarkable phenomenon of three suns appeared in the sky over Scotland and was, as usual, considered by many to be a sign of future calamities.
1798	For the first time the Welsh social reformer Robert Owen visited New Lanark which was to be the focus of his educational and social experiments over a period of 25 years.
1938	Veteran Dumbarton-built tea-clipper *Cutty Sark* arrived in the Thames on the completion of her final voyage.
1965	Twenty arrests were made at a Rolling Stones concert in the Odeon Cinema, Glasgow; 150 people were treated for hysteria.

Dear Green Place

When the impressive fossil trees, still seen in Glasgow's Victoria Park, flourished 300 million years ago, the West End of the city was a tropical jungle and Scotland was in the Southern Hemisphere.

June 16

1572	A shortage of ale in the besieged town of Edinburgh saw citizens resort to a substitute of vinegar and water.
1634	Licences were issued for the sale of tobacco in order that only a 'good and wholesome product' was available to the public; it was also hoped it might curb immoderate use of the weed.
1890	Caledonian Railway Station in Edinburgh was destroyed by fire.
1963	Prince Charles, aged 14, caused a rumpus by ordering a cherry brandy in a Stornoway pub during a school outing from Gordonstoun.
1981	Jury made Scots legal history when they were sent to an hotel for the night after failing to come to a verdict in a Glasgow High Court trial. This was the first occasion under the Criminal Justice (Scotland) Act.

Trouble Brewing

Duncan Forbes of Culloden, the eighteenth-century Lord President of the Court of Session, enjoyed a glass of whisky and was so concerned about the growing habit of tea-drinking that he campaigned to have its use restricted to the working classes. This gentleman wrote to friends during the 1745 Uprising complaining that he wasn't able to have his customary game of golf at Musselburgh because of the troubles.

BANNOCKBURN – AN ECONOMIC MIRACLE

In the Middle Ages win-bonuses were always on offer for victorious warriors, but following Bannockburn (24 June 1314) the 'Tartan Army' found themselves in possession of wealth beyond their wildest imaginings.

Every cut and thrust of our momentous victory is recorded in meticulous detail by contemporary chroniclers. What is less widely reported is the minutiae of the vast treasure-house of booty left by the fleeing English, and how it instantaneously transformed the Scottish economy.

Within an hour of the collapse of the English defence the Scots seized the 20-mile-long baggage-train and scores of important aristocratic hostages. One English war correspondent estimated the value of the abandoned spoils at £200,000, scarcely enough these days to buy you a roomy flat in Glasgow's West End. In 1341 it must have been the equivalent of a cash injection worth upwards of £100m for our poor and backward nation.

Before the battle, Bruce had generously promised that any spoils would be divided among the army at large. Even Bruce could hardly have predicted the wealth that was to come into their hands, so soon. According to one historical source it was 'Enough to rise the country at a single step from hunger to abundance and from poverty to wealth'. Thousands of cattle and sheep, vast stores of provisions, gold and silver vessels, money chests for the payment of troops, armour in heaps, hundreds of warhorses, tents and great stocks of wine and corn . . . the list goes on and on.

More money flowed into the Scottish coffers in the next few months as the company of noble hostages were returned to their families in the south, generally under fairly easy terms of ransom.

Contrast this remarkable story with the occupation of Edinburgh by the forces of Edward I after the Battle of Dunbar 18 years earlier. Edward could only find enough worthwhile booty to fill three chests and in the inventory the most intriguing item was a 'Griffin's Egg', broken and patched with silver, which the English king thought he might trundle out as a bit of a novelty at state occasions. This treasure was almost certainly an ostrich egg or a coconut. Tame fare, indeed, set alongside the riches of Bannockburn.

Battle Cries

The valour of the Scots regiments which changed the course of the Battle of Waterloo, and the remarkable effect of this on the French people, is shown by the fact that within weeks tartan had become a popular style among Parisian high society. Commander-in-Chief of the Swedish Army in the Second World War carried the name of

Douglas. He was a descendant of a Douglas who emigrated to Scandinavia in the seventeenth century. Five Scots were among 29 British soldiers killed fighting alongside Davy Crockett at the Siege of the Alamo in Texas. One of them, John McGregor, played the bagpipes to encourage the defenders facing the might of Santa Anna's Mexican Army. As many as seven native-born Scots died with General Custer and the Seventh Cavalry at Little Big Horn.

June 17

1390   Elgin Cathedral was burned by Alexander Stewart, Earl of Buchan and Ross, 'The Wolf of Badenoch'.

1597   King James VI was said to be 'crabbit' because so many foreign students were coming to study at St Andrews with Andrew Melville, the great advocate of church government.

1841   More than half of Glasgow's Irish population of 32,000 were said to be enrolled under the banner of teetotalism.

1867   Joseph Lister performed the first operation under antiseptic conditions on his sister Isabella at Glasgow Royal Infirmary.

1974   Foreign Office probed a visit to Glasgow of a Russian ship laden with complex electronic equipment which passed close to the United States nuclear submarine base at Holy Loch.

Dinner Invitation

Cutlery was virtually unknown in sixteenth-century Scotland, and merchants and burgesses were expected to bring their own spoons and knives when invited out to dinner; forks were unheard of.

June 18

1449   Mary of Gueldres, bride-to-be of James I, arrived in the Forth in a fleet of 13 ships and was accompanied by many noble lords and ladies.

1746   Flora MacDonald, who assisted Bonnie Prince Charlie to flee Scotland in the aftermath of Culloden, met the Young Pretender in Skye.

1846   North British Railway opened between Edinburgh and Berwick, two years after work commenced.

1895   Royal Family were present as the new church at Crathie near Balmoral was opened for public worship.

1941   'Radio Location', one of the best kept national defence secrets, was publicly revealed – credit for its development going to Brechin-born R.A.Watson-Watt.

Puff at the Top

A Scots soccer star of the late 1800s, who will never figure in national health education programmes, was 'stopper' Walter Arnott of Queen's Park. He always enjoyed a fag with his half-time tea and digestive biscuit.

June 19

1306   Robert Bruce was defeated by the English under the Earl of Pembroke at Methven in Perthshire. Bruce fled with a small band of followers into the Western Highlands.

1587   In a bizarre attempt to end civil unrest, James VI ordered bitter foes to march hand-in-hand in pairs from Holyrood up the Royal Mile.

1634   A terrible famine reported in Orkney and Caithness where, despite eating dogs and seaweed, many perished.

1861   Birth in Edinburgh of Earl Haig, who was commander-in-chief of the British Expeditionary Forces in France and Flanders (1915-19).

1980   Plans are announced to prevent drink being taken into Scottish football matches and rugby internationals.

Bonnie Fechters

When Bonnie Prince Charlie sought sanctuary in the Papal Territory he soon angered the authorities by trying to reintroduce boxing matches, banned by a previous Pope. During the First World War two special battalions of the Highland Light Infantry were formed, catering specially for small Glaswegians, averaging five foot in height. Called the Bantams, they were also known to the Germans as the fearless 'Demon Dwarves'.

June 20

1436   A Scottish fleet of 46 vessels under the Earl of Orkney prepared to sail for France with Margaret, daughter of James I and bride-to-be of the Dauphin Louis.

1623   A portrait of King James VI in the Hall of Linlithgow Palace fell and was smashed to pieces causing awe amongst the superstitious.

1843   Glasgow magistrates issued their annual proclamation against allowing dogs to wander the city unmuzzled during hot weather.

1939   Outrage in Argyllshire when a party of nudists was sighted sunbathing near the main Glencoe road.

1977   New figures showed a 20 per cent drop in drunkenness in Scotland after the extension of drinking hours from 10 pm to 11 pm.

Premier League

American historian Anthony Hart selected five Scots – Adam Smith, James Watt, James Clerk Maxwell, Alexander Graham Bell and Alexander Fleming – among the 50 individuals who had most influenced the lives of their fellow human beings. These Superscots joined Mohammed and Christ in the big league. In the long-life stakes Aberdeenshire has figured high on the world scale – four residents whose average age was 128 – were reported by the famous Doctor Webster in his world longevity top twenty.

June 21

1314   Forces of Edward II occupied Edinburgh – only three days before their defeat at Bannockburn.

1593   George Smollett, ancestor of the novelist and a burgess of Dumbarton, was denounced as a rebel for oppressing honest Highland folk who came to trade in Renfrew and Glasgow.

1633   Charles I, an 'able footman', decided to walk back to Holyrood Palace after attending a session of the Scots Parliament. He moved so swiftly down the Canongate that his footguard was 'thrown into a perspiration'.

1901   New supply-tunnel opened at Loch Katrine doubling Glasgow's water load.

1919   German High Seas Fleet, consisting of 74 vessels including 11 battleships and five battle-cruisers, scuttled by their crews at Scapa Flow in Orkney where they had been interned.

Yer Actual Swansong

Legend had it that when a black swan appeared among the MacFarlane flock on Loch Lomond the chief would lose everything. Such a swan did appear in 1785 just before the 23rd chief sold Arrochar and emigrated to the United States.

June 22

1402   At the Battle of Nesbit Moor, in the Merse near Duns, the Earl of March and Percy of Northumberland defeated a small Scots force under Sir Patrick Hepburn of Hailes.

1598   A patent was granted to Archibald Napier of Merchiston for a technique to manure land using common salt; nothing more was heard of the plan.

1635   A monster-like beast spent three days in the Water of Don at Aberdeen; the population stoned and shot at the creature which had a dog-like head and snorted. Was it a manatee which had strayed from warmer waters?

1895   Two parachutists, a man and a woman, who ascended in balloons from the Glasgow Industrial Exposition, were carried off by a gale, the man landing at Airdrie, the lady, a Miss Beaumont, at Haddington.

1959   Lewis small-boat fishermen were furious at the incursion of east-coast seine netters and are said to have fired shots at the 'poachers'.

Pity the Cuddy

The world-famous Mound in the heart of Edinburgh, an artificial hill begun in 1783, contains 1,501,000 cartloads of earth.

June 23

1585   The coining of gold, silver and alloy switched from Edinburgh to Dundee, the Exchequer to Falkland and the Court of Session to Stirling because of plague in the capital.

1624   Charles I gave £500 towards a relief appeal following the destruction of Dunfermline by fire; parishes throughout Scotland also contributed.

1726   Professional Irish sword-fighter Andrew Bryan was defeated in a public duel in Edinburgh by 62-year-old Killiecrankie veteran Donald Bane 'to the great joy of the Edinburgh citizenry'.

1915   Two German submarines practically wiped out the Lerwick fishing fleet when 17 vessels were reported sunk.

1928   Inaugural rally in King's Park, Stirling, of home-rule seeking National Party of Scotland, forerunner of the SNP.

Uganda No More

Scots Pipe-Major William Cochrane played 'Scotland the Brave' to attract rescuers when his party of tourists became lost in the African bush after their plane was forced down. The pipes are known as among the oldest of instruments, but in the last few centuries they have been particularly associated with Scotland. The first mention of bagpipes north of the border comes in the records of James IV (1473-1513), and the pipers were neither Highlanders nor Lowlanders – but Englishmen!

THE MERRY DANCERS, OR WHAT?

Now is the season for sky-gazing, the time to enjoy one of Scotland's hidden tourist resources, our heritage of mysterious airborne cities, battles and distant or surreal landscapes which have been reported on and off for a thousand years. Most of these phenomena, which make the Loch Ness Monster seem like a cheap, circus sideshow, are probably caused, according to the experts, by atmospheric curvature of light rays. High summer is the popular period for sightings.

It seems that the clear, unpolluted air from the north, combined with our impressive landscapes, make Scotland particularly suited to such odd occurrences. Various reports have been logged in the past century confirming that, in the right climatic conditions, folk in Scotland have been able to peer around the curve of the earth, seeing features normally lost below the horizon.

Extraordinary views, extending for example, from Argyll to Donegal or a panorama from Ben Ledi in Perthshire taking in the Forth Bridge to the east and Arran to the west, are not uncommon. People in Orkney, particularly favoured by clarity of atmosphere, will tell you how the rugged coast of Norway (hundreds of miles away to the east) appeared on the horizon one summer's afternoon during the Second World War.

Less easy to explain are mirages of strange cities and spectral armies which are sometimes seen. Again in Orkney, in 1840, a wonderful city of white buildings was seen away to the nor' west, identified by local legend as the crystal and pearl city of the Fin Folk. Stories are told of a fairy city in the sea, west of the Mull of Kintyre, and an apparition of Edinburgh is said to have appeared over Liverpool in September 1846.

May Island in the River Forth was the location of a series of spectacular visions in the early 1870s when the cliffs of the island seemed to shoot up to an estimated 1,000-feet with trees, columns, towers and arches observed. In years past phantom armies have been spotted in places as far apart as the Clyde Valley and Aberdeenshire. Over the centuries explanations have included the aforementioned bending of light, the effects of the Aurora Borealis, UFOs, religious frenzies or that old standby, delusion through drink.

Whatever the cause, keep your eye on the horizon this summer and you may catch a glimpse of these fleeting, insubstantial kingdoms. Statistically, you've a better chance of experiencing a long-distance refraction or seeing a mirage of some distant city than you have of spotting Nessie.

Mysterious Locations

One of Scotland's most intriguing streets is Mary King's Close by Edinburgh's High Street which was sealed off because of plague but still remains intact below more modern buildings. The Elephant and Castle District of London is said to have been so named after an inn which in turn was given its name by a soldier once stationed at Dumbarton. The coat-of-arms of the Royal Burgh features an elephant supporting a castle; some say the pachyderm represents the bulk of the castle rock by the Clyde. One legend about Holy Loch in Argyllshire is that it was named because a ship loaded with earth and sand from the Holy Land intended for a burying place at Kilmun, or for the foundations of Glasgow Cathedral, was lost near the mouth of the loch.

June 24

1314   The mighty army of Edward II of England was defeated by Robert Bruce and his pikemen at Bannockburn.

1693   Commission into the Glencoe Massacre presented its findings; the Master of Stair had caused a 'barbarous murder', it concluded, but Stair was to receive the support of the king.

1824   Five tenements destroyed in a major blaze in Edinburgh's High Street, which began in a spirit-dealer's back shop.

1932   Marquis of Linlithgow asked when the windows in the House of Lords had last been opened – fresh air might add 'pith' to the debates, he suggested.

1960   Lord Rudolf Russell, 16-year-old son of the Duke of Bedford, ran away from Gordonstoun School in Moray. His family said he was 'highly strung'.

Finger of Fate

Scots Doctor Henry Faulds, after conducting experiments in the early 1880s while working in a Japanese hospital, first suggested the use of fingerprints to aid criminal investigation.

June 25

1580   A 'vehement tempest' struck Scotland leaving behind a strange sickness called the 'kindness' which carried off old and corpulent people.

1601   Seven Flemings, who were brought to Scotland to introduce cloth manufacture, complained about a lack of organisation among the burghs.

1654   A group of Scots irregulars from the force of the Earl of Glencairn, who had opposed the Cromwellian Occupation, were deported from Leith to Barbados. They were described as 'Tories', a term first applied to Irish bandits.

1846   Pioneer of the travel trade, Thomas Cook, began his famous Scottish tours with 350 visitors being treated like royalty in Glasgow and Edinburgh.

1886   Crofters Act, which guaranteed security of tenure and set up the Crofters Commission, became law.

Over the Top

In the 1950s Glasgow's cut-throat image prompted film star Diana Dors to comment: 'I'm terrified every time I think of Glasgow.'

June 26

1559   Army of the Reformation took Perth from a French garrison.

1695   Formation of the company which undertook the ill-fated Darien scheme to establish a Scots colony in the jungles of Central America.

1763   Stagecoach service introduced between Glasgow and Greenock.

1888   Mrs and Mrs Andrew Carnegie and two friends left Edinburgh in a four-in-hand coach for Kingussie.

1970   Glasgow's £4.5m Kingston bridge, now groaning under the volume of late-twentieth-century traffic, was opened by the Queen Mother.

Canal Cuttings

A half-mile stretch of the bottom of the Caledonian Canal at Dochgarroch, five miles from Inverness, was so porous that during construction the canal bed was lined with woollen cloth and covered with clay and sand. A love of the sea remained with the famous Scots Admiral Sir Andrew Wood (b.1460) even when he was home at Largo in Fife. He had a canal constructed from his house to the vicinity of the church upon which he would sail in great pomp on his barge to the Sunday service. At Kirkliston, near Edinburgh, during the digging of the Union Canal in the early 1800s, a mammoth tusk nearly five feet long was uncovered beneath 25 feet of soil and rock.

June 27

1662   An 'uncommon abundance' of grain and fruit was reported in Scotland with the market stalls of Edinburgh filled with all sorts of cheap fruit.

1743   Scots Greys, Scots Guards and Scots Fusiliers took part in the Battle of Dettingen where George II became the last British monarch to personally command his troops.

1893   Alexander Howland Smith was jailed for 12 months at Edinburgh for forging the literary documents of Robert Burns and others.

1944   Several hundred wounded Scots soldiers arrived in Edinburgh with stories of the early days of the Normandy Invasion.

1965   Peat began to make a comeback as a fuel in the Highlands due to the cost of coal.

On the Piste

In the first years of this century, as skiing gained popularity in Scotland, skis were so scarce that Cairngorm distilleries were inundated with requests for whisky-barrel staves, an excellent substitute, apparently.

June 28

1606   English judges ruled that with James VI & I now on the throne in London, any Scot born after March 1603, was to be classified as a natural subject of the king of England.

1633   Charles I wrote to clan chieftains encouraging them to have their followers turn out in their 'country habit and best order' for his visit the following month to Perth.

1879   Geographer and explorer Alexander Johnston, son of the founder of the famous map-making firm, died from dysentery, aged 33.

1890   At least 60 lives were lost as severe gales battered the Scottish fishing fleet off the north and west coasts.

1965   The queen followed the example of her great-great-grandmother and sailed around the islands of Loch Lomond, which had so impressed Victoria.

Pain of Concealment

Normal penalty in the sixteenth century for concealing infectious illness was branding on the cheek and banishment.

Kilties at Gourock, 1990

June 29

1315   Scots army of Edward Bruce stormed into Dundalk after defeating the Anglo-Irish barons.

1654   A summer drought in Edinburgh saw wells in the city dry up requiring citizens to 'go a mile' before they could get clean water for brewing or cooking; washing seems to have been a low priority.

1759   William Roxburgh, botanist and doctor, who conducted early experiments in the rearing of silkworms, was born in Ayrshire.

1840   Lilac was the colour being favoured by Scottish society ladies this spring for dresses, bonnets and scarves.

1918   Bakery-workers in the West of Scotland planned a strike over a demand that the average minimum wage should be 80 shillings a week.

Cheery Bunch

In the early years of the Reformation the General Assembly of the Church of Scotland disapproved of 'fashion' and suggested that all clothes should be of 'grave colour, preferably black, russet, sad grey or sad brown'.

June 30

1582   Robert Montgomery, who had accepted the job of Archbishop of Glasgow, was hounded out of Edinburgh by 'lasses and rascals' who stoned him through the Kirk o' Field Port.

1817   An earthquake was reported in the vicinity of Inverness when hot water was said to have fallen from the sky.

1857   Trial of Madeleine Smith, the alleged Glasgow poisoner,

THE MERRY DANCERS, OR WHAT?

Burst water main delight

opened in Edinburgh with females clamouring for seats in the gallery. Some of them even brought along their knitting.

1859   The famous Symington hen, which had been habitually laying huge eggs, produced a whopper, said to be eight inches by seven inches.

1909   Glasgow's new tramway link between Pollokshaws West and Rouken Glen was approved by the Board of Trade, except for an 'exceedingly dangerous' corner at Spiers Bridge.

Crabbit Below Stairs

Servants' wages in parts of East Lothian in 1790 were remarked on in the Statistical Account. Their pay had doubled to over £15 annually, but these serving people were described as 'disobliging, perverse and obstinate'.

WHEN GLASGOW'S BLUBBERING HAD TO STOP

The next time you linger at the top of Glasgow's Candleriggs, in the shadow of the Ramshorn, clear your lungs and take a deep breath. Perhaps you'll sense it, too, a strange other worldly aroma, the scent of something with oil in it, I fancy.

This ghostly essence, now mingling with the exotic coffee blends of the Merchant City caffs, lingers on the location of what was, for more than 100 years, the site of Glasgow's Soaperie, one of the city's earliest and now forgotten industries based on the hunting of the whale.

The manufacture of soap seems to have been from early times a favourite area for the establishment of monopolies, certainly in Scotland. Up until the seventeenth century soap was imported into Scotland, principally from Flanders, but by the time of James VI, home-based manufacture was in place, tightly controlled by a network of exclusive grants.

In 1619, a patent was given to Nathaniel Udwart for making soap at his 'goodly work' at Leith; two years later he sought and achieved a protectionist measure banning all imported soap. The Privy Council decreed 'green soap' to be sold at £25 per barrel and white soap at £32; each barrel was to contain 16 stones. Such patents also gave the grantees the right to fish Greenland and home-seas to obtain the oils required for soap-making.

In 1667 an influential whale-fishing and soap-boiling company was formed, with its headquarters in Glasgow. Originally, there were nine partners who each subscribed £1,300. Its first efforts were directed towards whale-fishing and trade with Greenland, America and Russia. A ship of 700 tons, large for the late seventeenth century, was built at Belfast for the company and called *The Lyon*. Soon after, three more vessels were on the stocks.

Initially, catching proved very successful. The blubber was boiled down at Greenock in a large works known as 'Royal Close', but the main factory was in the heart of Glasgow. Universally known as 'the Soaperie' it was situated at the head of Candleriggs and consisted of a large square of buildings with houses for managers, stores, sheds and cellars.

Voyages began to be made less frequently, however, and after several company ships had been lost at sea the Committee of Trade opened business to all comers in 1695.

Sir John Shaw of Greenock took over the fishing side of the business and the Soaperie, freed from the albatross of costly and dangerous whaling expeditions, prospered. It's not clear if it remained in the hands of its original owners or was sold.

In 1700 soap manufacture is mentioned as an industry which had become well established in Glasgow, and in 1715 the manager was advertising 'good black or spreckled soaps at reasonable prices'. Apparently, the company continued a successful, if not spectacular, career until the 1770s when there were only half-a-dozen men employed 'in a very inactive manner', clomping about the workshops, according to one visitor, in their heavy, iron shoes.

Any enterprising young person out there thinking of setting up a perfumerie in the Merchant City could do worse than give it the historical title of the Soaperie. Copyright, however, remains with J. Hewitson.

July 1

1592   Two compatriots of the rebellious Earl of Bothwell, the lairds of Niddry and Samuelston, were captured while snatching 40 winks in the meadow of Lesmahagow.

1606   'Red Parliament' – so called because nobles wore red gowns and cloaks – was held in Perth; bishops reappeared for the first time in many years.

1703   A book which questioned Scotland's sovereignty and independence called *Historia Anglo-Scotica* was ordered to be burned by the public hangman of Edinburgh.

1859   Iona was fast becoming a tourist target with three steamers weekly from Oban; despite having 'no natural beauty' the ruins fascinated visitors.

1982   Anti-monarchist Labour MP Willie Hamilton claimed he was snubbed by the queen during a visit to Fife; he spoke of a 'frigid' handshake.

Slaves of Habit

When the Maharajah of Hyderabad visited the famous Atlas railway-works in Springburn, Glasgow, he was amazed to see thousands of workers streaming out of the yard at the lunchtime whistle. He is said to have leapt to his feet and shouted at company officials, 'Your slaves are escaping!'

July 2

1266   Treaty of Perth agreed between Scotland and Norway with the Norse-held districts, such as the Hebrides (not Orkney or Shetland), reverting back to Scottish control.

1296   King John Balliol forced to sign a humiliating document at Kincardine confessing his 'folly' in aligning himself with the enemies of King Edward of England.

1563   Henry Sinclair, Bishop of Ross and President of the Court of Session, left for Paris to have a gallstone removed.

1594   Burying corpses in other folk's lairs was becoming a macabre problem for kirk officers in and around Glasgow.

1939   Orders for 40,000 kilts had been placed by the War Office with West of Scotland firms; the orders were said to be worth £150,000.

Footing the Dinner Bill

The butcher's bill for Christmas meals at Holyrood in 1528 included £13.6s.8d for 1,000 ox feet and 1,340 sheep feet.

July 3

1307 King Edward I, Hammer of the Scots, seriously ill and with only a few days to live, led his army from Carlisle against the 'rebellious' Scots.

1582 James Crichton, the 'Admirable', tutor to King James VI, soldier, scholar, poet and athlete, died in a brawl in Mantua, Italy.

1610 Three Spaniards were allowed to live in Scotland and keep the nation supplied with mouse and rat-traps.

1702 Barrels of gunpowder exploded in Leith, killing eight people and damaging almost every house in the town.

1958 A watershed in Scottish society life: Holyrood Palace saw the final royal presentation party, with 200 debutantes from all over Scotland introduced to the queen in a traditional ceremony of obeisance.

Well-Turned Soil

Wooden plough-parts, which experts say may have been in use around the time of Christ, have been unearthed in south-west Scotland confirming the lengthy agricultural history of the area.

July 4

1195 Jocelin, Bishop of Glasgow, gifted a dozen churches within his diocese to Kelso Abbey, the deal being confirmed at Jedburgh.

1570 An earth tremor shook Glasgow and its surrounding area at 10 p.m. and 'causit the inhabitants to be in great terror and fear'.

1702 Perth apothecary George Robertson advertised a Turkish bath in the town which he claimed was 'of great use in curing several diseases'.

1836 Maybole farmer struck dead by lightning while tying his shoelaces, as severe thunderstorms battered Ayrshire.

1907 Rumours that the king was about to sell Balmoral were officially dismissed, the Royal Family said they were greatly attached to the district.

Trivial Pursuits

One of the most gifted men of his age, Thomas Chalmers, who led the breakaway from the Church of Scotland in 1843 to create the Free Church, was a preacher, moral philosopher, mathematician and economist but, above all, someone who was fascinated by life and living. In one piece of correspondence he writes with great pride of having invented a new technique for folding his coat which he thought would be of great value to the traveller.

July 5

1572   John, Fifth Lord Fleming, staunch supporter of Mary Queen of Scots, killed in Edinburgh in an accidental cannon discharge while he was arriving with French troops.

1790   Whaler *Findlay* reached Leith from Greenland with 106 butts of blubber – the produce of nine whales and 600 seals.

1813   Glasgow police advertised for a steady, active man for the force, 'certificates of sobriety' were essential.

1847   Mail-coach from Edinburgh to London made its final run; it was no longer able to compete with the railways.

1974   Scots football referee Bobby Davidson returned home 'sickened' after FIFA replaced him with an English referee for the West Germany-Holland World Cup final.

Square-Go Veto

Before the Battle of Flodden in 1513, James IV, perhaps the last of Europe's chivalrous medieval monarchs, challenged the aged Earl of Surrey to single combat to avoid massive loss of life. As well as the return of Berwick, James wanted the removal of a lucrative salmon-trap built by the English on the River Esk. The offer was rejected by the wily Surrey who said that a commoner could not cross swords with a king.

July 6

1436   Marriage at Tours of the Dauphin Louis to Margaret, daughter of James I King of Scots.

1608   Plague was rife in Dundee. One magistrate had already died and, with a second seriously ill, assistant law officers had to be appointed.

1747   John Paul Jones, founder of the United States Navy and who also served in the French and Russian navies, was born at Arbigland, Kirkcudbrightshire.

1862   Charles Mackenzie, scholar, soldier, journalist and aide-de-camp to Wellington, died in a fire at the Rainbow Hotel, New York, aged 74.

1919   Airship R34 completed the first crossing of the Atlantic after an 108-hour flight from East Lothian to New York.

Still in Force

Unrepealed laws on the Scottish statute books include the loss of the right hand for the third offence of shooting pigeons, and another against promiscuous sex or 'fornication', with the guilty party being 'thrice douket' in the deepest and foulest pool of water in the parish.

1575   Reidswire Raid was one of the last skirmishes between Scots and English Borderers. The outcome was a victory for the Scots under the Laird of Carmichael.

1788   The *London Mail* pulled up for the first time outside the Saracen's Head in Glasgow's Gallowgate. For over 60 years it was so regular that shopkeepers in the East End of the city set their watches by it.

1814   Sir Walter Scott's *Waverley* – recognised as the first historical novel set in the identifiable past – was published in Edinburgh.

1880   Launch at Govan on the Clyde of the ill-fated, saucer-shaped *Livadia*. Built for the seasick Tsar of Russia it was left to rust on a Crimean beach after he was assassinated.

1937   Earl of Moray left the Chamber of the House of Lords after being approached by attendants while rolling a cigarette during a debate on the Divorce Bill.

Top That

William Murdoch, the Ayrshire-born lad who developed gas-lighting, got his first job when a prospective employer noted that the enterprising boy had created an all-weather hat, fashioned from wood.

GOWF – A ROMAN IMPORT?

What sacrilege! What cheek! It's being whispered around the hospitality tents at the Open Championship that Scotland's claim to be the home of golf is false. To heap absurdity upon absurdity, the sneaky campaign would have us believe it was the invading Roman armies who brought the 'gowf' to the painted northern hordes.

The same spoilsports who found a selection of non-Scottish origins for the haggis, the bagpipes, and the kilt, now want to rob us of a central feature of our heritage, a pastime which holds together the very fabric of our society.

But they shan't get away with it, do you hear?

It's easy, right enough, to imagine a couple of noble Romans striding down the short fifteenth at the plush Via Flaminia Country Club after a hard day at the Senate, but the foot-soldiers on the rainswept Antonine front-line at Duntocher or Grangemouth reaching for their clubs on an off-duty afternoon? I don't think so.

The only clubs they were concerned with would be descending rapidly towards their heads attached to a strongly-muscled, woad-daubed Caledonian forearm.

No, when the final putt is sunk and the legions around the arena see the laurel wreath placed on the new champion's head, the Scottish nation can rest easy. The indisputable fact is that Scotland nurtured, developed and promoted the game as its own. Perhaps the Dutch played a part, and maybe the Romans did have a say in it, but whoever first put driver to ball in anger matters not a jot. It's Scotland's gemme.

Didn't Tom Morris score the first recorded hole-in-one at Prestwick's eighth during the 1868 Open Championship?

Didn't Mary Queen of Scots, fighting back the tears nae doot, turn out for a round of golf within a few hours of Darnley's murder?

Didn't the fishwives of Musselburgh organise the world's first tournament for women in 1811?

Didn't a succession of Scottish kings fret over their handicap?

And, more importantly, didn't Scotland's golfing pioneers introduce the element of imaginative eccentricity which gives the game its unique flavour?

Witness the amazing Andrew McKellar of Edinburgh who died in 1813. He loved the game with such passionate intensity that he even persuaded some of his friends to hold lanterns so that he could play the short holes at Bruntsfield Links by night. Then join the crowd, if you will, in the heart of Edinburgh one evening in 1798 as two city gents attempt to win a remarkable wager. Both successfully drove their golf balls from the south east corner of Parliament Square, over the weathercock atop St Giles, reaching Advocates Close on the north side of the High Street.

With such a pedigree wha daur meddle wi' our golfing inheritance.

July 8

1249   Alexander II, King of Scots, died at Kerrera near Oban while leading an expedition to the Western Isles. Alexander III became king, aged only seven.

1633   King Charles I visited Perth and was greeted regally, witnessing a sword-dance performed in his honour on a specially built timber island in the Tay.

1691   Kirkwall, Wick, Inveraray and Rothesay were exempted from a visit by a trade commission set up by the Convention of Royal Burghs because they were said to be too difficult to reach.

1857   As Madeleine Smith was freed in Edinburgh, a charge of poisoning her lover being found not proven, souvenir hunters were chipping bits of stonework from her house in Glasgow's Blythswood Square.

1907   Civil-list pensions of £100 each were granted to two granddaughters of Robert Burns because of their advanced age and inadequate means of support.

Forest of Fife

The construction of the *Great Michael* in the early 1500s was a mammoth shipbuilding operation. The vessel was some 240 feet long with a ten-foot-thick hull. Although much Norwegian timber was imported it is said all the forested areas of Fife, with the exception of the Royal Woods at Falkland, were cut down during the work. The *Michael* carried 120 gunners and 1,000 soldiers but went to France in 1513, two years after its launch, and eventually rotted away in the harbour of Brest.

July 9

1576   Gold prospectors in the Southern Uplands were cautioned against selling their finds for export and were ordered to bring them to the king's counting house for the benefit of the nation.

1676   A big crowd, gathered for a sermon on the Gargunnock Hills in Stirlingshire, was astonished to see a radiant star at midday when the sun was shining brightly.

1789   A 'neat' pleasure-boat called the *Duchess of Hamilton* was launched on Linlithgow Loch.

1867   Queen's Park, the first senior football club in Scotland, was formed.

1970   Three youths escaped from Polmont Borstal near Falkirk when the referee blew the whistle to end a football match. Closer supervision of future games was promised.

No Respecter of Persons

It was as recently as 1968 that a Danish expert, examining a cast of the skull of the patriot king, Robert the Bruce, was able to confirm medieval reports that the monarch had died of leprosy; his upper jaw was badly atrophied.

July 10

1308   English fleet ordered from Hartlepool to Aberdeen to help raise siege of the garrison there by 'rebel' Scots.

1469   Margaret of Denmark, the 15-year-old bride-to-be of James III, arrived at Leith.

1598   Edinburgh was taken by storm by an acrobat who performed tricks on a rope stretched between the top of St Giles Cathedral and a stair near the Mercat Cross.

1633   Charles I, crossing the Firth of Forth, could only watch as one of his escort boats sank, 33 people drowned and a royal treasure of gold, silver and jewels sank to the bottom.

1914   Suffragette Rhoda Fleming leapt on to the footboard of the king and queen's limousine at Perth and tried to smash the windows. Police saved her from an angry crowd who threatened her with a 'rough handling'.

Lochaber No More

The nineteenth-century population drift from the Highlands to Glasgow is well illustrated by the fact that in the 1830s there were said to be 5,336 children in the city under the age of ten who spoke Gaelic as their first and daily language.

July 11

1173 William the Lion, in the midst of an invasion of Northumberland, was captured by a group of Yorkshire knights who emerged unexpectedly from the fog near Alnwick.

1611 The habit among nobles and churchmen of wandering the streets of Edinburgh with their 'flocks of suitors' had been causing much unruly behaviour, so they were asked to ride on horseback or in coaches.

1826 Three hundred residents of Rhum were forced to give way to sheep and to emigrate to Nova Scotia, this Clearance was mirrored all over northern Scotland.

1843 Odd phenomenon reported at Leith where there was a sudden and mysterious inrush of water at low tide which retreated with equal swiftness.

1944 Staff sergeant Joe Louis, world heavyweight boxing champion, was in Glasgow for a 'meet the troops' visit. He boxed an exhibition match and played golf at Douglas Park.

The fighting Scot

Angling for Compliments

Former Duddingston minister Robert Menteith found himself mixing with church leaders and intellectuals after moving to Paris and adopting the Catholic faith in the early 1600s. He was often asked to detail his Scottish background and, ever anxious to impress, he cheekily styled himself a Menteith of Salmonet – his father had been a salmon-fisherman at Stirling.

July 12

1328　Amid great scenes of splendour at Berwick, Prince David, son of Robert the Bruce and aged only four, married Joanna, known as 'Makepeace', sister of Edward III.

1515　Lord Drummond was in serious trouble for 'striking' the Lord Lyon king-of-arms with his hand; he begged forgiveness of Parliament on his knees and escaped serious punishment.

1683　Edinburgh merchant Thomas Hamilton, who had been importing beaver and racoon skins from North America, set up Scotland's first beaver-hat factory.

1836　Glasgow cow thief William Kilpatrick was sentenced to 14 years transportation.

1965　Inquiry ordered into why confidential documents were delivered without envelopes to councillors' homes in Edinburgh.

Charming Maggie

Scottish queens often asked for good-luck charms during childbirth. Among the most macabre were relics of the saintly Margaret, her nightshirt and preserved head being much in demand.

July 13

1568　Envoy given permission to recruit 2,000 Scots for service in the army of the king of Denmark.

1790　Severe flooding in Kilmarnock after a deluge forced the townspeople on to their roofs; the town bridge was swept away.

1807　Death of Henry Benedict Stewart, Cardinal Bishop of Ostia, brother of Bonnie Prince Charlie and last of the Royal House of Stuart.

1845　First cargo of imported American ice unloaded at the Broomielaw from the brigantine *Acton* of New York.

1970　Five sailors charged with mutiny on board the minesweeper HMS *Ulveston* at Ullapool; it was the first such incident in over a decade.

Parkhead Puzzle

Police concluded that Rangers player Chris Morris, who thought he had been shot in the thigh with an air-rifle during an Old Firm reserve match at Celtic Park in 1978, had probably been stung by a bee.

July 14

1296   King Edward I, Hammer of the Scots, arrived in Aberdeen for a five-day stay and during a triumphal progress along the east coast, 'exacted homage' as he went.

1600   Slaughter of herons, which had been 'frequent and common' in Fife, Kinross and the Carse of Gowrie, was banned for three years as it was said that 'only a few or nane' were left.

1791   'Friends of Liberty', those who favoured a radical reform of the British political system, held a series of dinners in Scots towns to mark the second anniversary of the Storming of the Bastille.

1811   A notorious London gang robbed the Paisley Union Bank in Glasgow's Ingram Street of £20,000 and fled in a post-chaise and four.

1982   Two tourists, a German and a Belgian, were allowed to continue their Highland holiday after accidentally landing on the anthrax-contaminated island of Gruinard.

Proper Behaviour

Among the statutes ordered in the mid-1400s by Bishop Kennedy for St Salvator's College at St Andrews were that students should not keep concubines publicly or be common nightwalkers or robbers. What were the scholars studying? Why, divinity, of course!

WHO THREW THE PRAYER STOOL?

The story of how herbal-woman Jenny Geddes threw a stool at the Bishop of Edinburgh in St Giles for daring to allow Mass to be said 'in her lug' is, in newspaper parlance, a 'good tale'. Could it be, however, that in all the excitement of the Prayer Book Riot (23 July 1637), an even better story had been missed? I'd like you to try for size a rather startling proposition. Could Jenny Geddes, the lady held responsible for sparking off a religious war, have been a man?

No contemporary account of the event in St Giles and the attempt by Charles I to introduce the English liturgy mentions Jenny as even having been present. Indeed, it is 23 years before she emerges as an Edinburgh celebrity, burning her greengrocer's barrow in joy at news of the Restoration. An odd turnaround for such a devoted anti-papist.

Another authority on the period, Robert Wodrow, dismissed Jenny as 'a princess of the Tron adventurers', and named Mrs Mean, wife of an Edinburgh merchant, as she who cast the first stool.

So, was Jenny there at all? Did she get the credit simply because she was a colourful, romantic character? This leads us to a fascinating possibility.

It seems that many worshippers in St Giles that Sunday were waiting-maids who kept their stools for their masters and mistresses. But many of the gentry, either as a protest or anticipating trouble, had given the service a body-swerve. So to what purpose did the maids remain on station?

When the tumult began books and stools were pitched all over the shop. The stool which was directed at the Bishop of Edinburgh was flung with such force and accuracy that, had not the cleric ducked, he would surely have been smitten, floored even. One report in the city in the days after the riot explained its ferocity by claiming that many of the serving lassies were, in fact, craft apprentices in disguise.

Did Edinburgh at this period breed a particularly aggressive type of virago, or were the lassies, including Jenny Geddes, in their plaids and shawls, just Proddy liquor-loons in disguise? I wonder.

Riotous Times

Shakespeare's Scottish play, *Macbeth*, has always had a mysteriously chequered history. A riot in New York in 1849 caused by different interpretations of the title role, led to 22 deaths. Street riots were commonplace in sixteenth-century Edinburgh but the most spectacular of that period was in 1561 when magistrates banned the traditional Robin Hood pageant and general disorder ensued. The orchestra pit at Glasgow's Panopticon Theatre in the Trongate was said to be covered with wire mesh to prevent musicians being struck by rotten tomatoes, neeps or even the occasional rivet hurled by the pernickety audience. It was here that Stan Laurel made his stage debut.

July 15

1326   Parliament of Robert the Bruce introduced a tax to help suitably maintain the monarch 'as becomes his station'.

1563   Surgeon Robert Henderson collected 20 merks from Edinburgh town council for various wonderful cures. Apparently he had healed a man whose hands had been cut off and a woman who had been dead for two days.

1664   Young Earl of Leven died after a serious drinking bout with some noble friends in Edinburgh. He is said to have drunk large quantities of seawater while recrossing the Forth.

1839   Glasgow merchants were complaining about adulterated Irish butter, with the appearance of verdigris or dirty chalk, which was reaching the city.

1947   Royal train arrived 45 minutes late in Edinburgh owing to a delay while doctors attended to the queen's eye inflammation caused by a piece of grit.

Paying the Ferryman

When the royal tailor, Robert Spittal, was refused passage over the River Teith in Perthshire in 1535 because he had forgotten his loose change, he decided to fix the ferryman once and for all. Spittal had a bridge built over the river and put the ferryman out of business.

July 16

1563   Ships from the plague-ridden town of Danzig were ordered away from Scottish ports on pain of death.

1615   A group of gentlemen called 'whilliwas' were at work in East Lothian, ambushing travellers and demanding money with menaces.

1836   Brig *Mariner* left Loch Eriboll in Sutherland for Cape Breton and Quebec with 154 emigrants, mostly from the Reay district.

1859   Drunkenness at the Glasgow Fair was less prevalent with more citizens breathing 'fresh country air' rather than spending money in 'dram shops'.

A favourite Glasgow pastime

1965   A light aircraft was used for the first time in Scotland to control road-traffic flow when holiday traffic met racegoers around Hamilton.

Willie the Masochist

William Carstairs, a Cathcart-born diplomat who had been tortured in 1684, had the remarkable privilege, as King William's adviser in Scotland, of demonstrating the effect of thumbscrews on the royal digits. The king had been determined to test his courage but was eventually forced to cry for mercy.

July 17

1195   William I, King of Scots, agreed that the Prior of Coldingham should be permitted to move his tenants from the countryside into the town in order to boost the population.

1600   Stirling man Andrew Liddell was admonished by the town's kirk session who heard he had taken 'ouer great a surfet of wyne'. He was warned about his future conduct.

1699   More attacks on customs officers in Scotland's more remote areas were reported as the officials tried to track down undutied liquors; they were often 'bruised and bled to ane admirable height'.

1792   Glasgow advertised for a contractor to undertake lamp-lighting in the city, a round of about 800 lights was involved.

1895   East coast express train from London to Aberdeen set a new record covering the 540 miles in 10 hours 21 minutes.

Ghostly Gatekeepers

In rural Aberdeenshire, where tradition said that the ghost of the last person buried guarded the graveyard gate, scuffles occasionally broke out when two burials were scheduled for the same day. The respective parties exchanged blows to see which corpse should be buried first, freeing the deceased from the role of gatekeeper.

July 18

1594   Logan of Restalrig had entered into a contract with John Napier of Merchiston to search for a fabled hidden treasure at Logan's bleak Berwickshire home, Fast Castle.

1629   Supporters of the rival Earls of Cassilis and Wigton were ordered off the streets of Edinburgh where they had been parading in a 'tumultous manner', recalling disorders of the previous century.

1813   A thirty-foot whale was stranded on the shore at Irvine, Ayrshire.

1895   Fishery statistics showed that 647,454 cwts had been landed in Scotland in the previous month – an increase of over 20,000 cwts compared with June 1894.

1933   Glasgow got two-thirds of a £60,000 grant to depressed areas of Scotland.

All the Nice Girls

18 July 1792 saw the death of John Paul Jones, the Kirkcudbrightshire-born founder of the United States Navy. During the American War of Independence John Paul Jones carried out raids on the United Kingdom flying a national flag made from the petticoats of the young women of Portsmouth, New Hampshire, for whom he was a folk hero. The dance, 'The Paul Jones', named after this adventurer, features fresh partnerships and became popular when Jones and his fellow colonists were seeking independence from Britain.

July 19

1333   During the battle of Halidon Hill Edward III inflicted a crushing defeat on the Scots near Berwick; among the

14,000 Scots slain was the aged Malcolm, fifth Earl of Lennox, friend and companion of Robert the Bruce.

1600   Little children were reported to be dying in large numbers as famine gripped Scotland. Seven children died in Edinburgh on one day.

1641   Lord Kirkcudbright got leave of Parliament to take eight days to visit his sick wife. Fines were normally levied for non-attendance.

1838   Death reported at Ceres in Fife of James Friskin, a negro who was servant to Lord Lovat during the 1745 Uprising; he was 112.

1940   First daylight raid by the Luftwaffe on Glasgow brings few reports of damage.

Ness Built

By the mid-1200s Inverness had gained an international reputation as a centre of quality shipbuilding. When Louis IX set off for his crusade, one of the principal vessels in his fleet was built in the Highland capital.

July 20

1653   General Assembly of the Church of Scotland was broken up by Cromwell's officers who were ordered to drag the ministers out if necessary.

1779   Dougal Graham, storyteller and packman, who followed the Jacobite army throughout its campaign to Culloden and was later the official bell-ringer to the city of Glasgow, died aged 55.

1839   Bakers in Glasgow reduced the price of a 4lb loaf by a penny – a fine loaf was now sold at 9d.

1881   Ten fishing boats were sunk off Shetland with the loss of around 60 lives.

1913   Scots suffragettes, who travelled to London to put their case for reform, were snubbed by the Government but held a public meeting in Hyde Park.

Below the Dotted Line

One of the most stunning instances of over-optimism in Scots history must be the first Protestant Covenant of 1557. This document signed by five noblemen – the so-called Lords of the Congregation – had acres of space below the text for signatures which never materialised.

July 21

1403   Earl of Douglas and other Scots nobles were in captivity after the defeat of English rebels under Henry Percy and his Scots allies at Shrewsbury.

1622   In an effort to seek divine relief from a famine in the North of Scotland, a fast was ordered in Aberdeen.

1858   Stagecoaches which had been driven out of the south by mechanical substitutes appeared in Orkney. A regular service began operating on an improved road beween Kirkwall and Stromness.

1911   Crowd of 20,000 saw Samuel Franklin Cody, a cousin of Buffalo Bill, land his aircraft on Paisley Racecourse near the site of Glasgow Airport during the Great Air Race.

1934   Thousands of pens supplied for public use in Scots post-offices were being stolen; Glasgow was one of several places with none left.

Ecclesiastical Lawman

One of the jobs of the session officer at Perth in 1616 was to use his red staff to 'wauken sleepers and remove greetin' bairns furth of the kirk'.

THE PIED PIPER OF HAMILTON

Out of the houses the rats came running, big rats, small rats, fat rats, thin rats. Led to their doom in the River Weiser by the sound of the pipes of the man in the 'fantastical coat of sundry colours'. This was the week in July 1376 when the Pied Piper was said to have been about his tuneful business in the German town of Hamelin.

Whether the story, which, of course, ends with him taking away the children of the town to a kingdom beneath the hill, when the Burgomasters welched on the deal, is strictly factual or merely a metaphor for the Black Death, is open to argument. What is certain is, that around his time rat-catchers were out in force in the dingy alleys and insanitary closes of medieval Europe. There was plenty of custom for them.

But what of Scotland? Remarkably, at least away from the fetid towns, it seems to have been such a poor chomping ground for the rat population that I sometimes wonder if the historians have got a little confused and we're really talking about a bagpipe-playing rodent exterminator – a Pied Piper operating out of Hamilton.

For instance, the sometimes fanciful chronicler Hector Boece tells us that there were no rats to be found at all in Buchan, and a later author, Sir Robert Gordon, makes the same claim about Sutherland, asserting that if rats arrived from other parts of the country by ship they pegged out 'as soon as they do smell the air of Sutherlandshire'. This is all the more remarkable because, according to Sir Bob, neighbouring Caithness appears to have been overrun by the beasties.

In Morven rats had been introduced as an experiment but had failed to flourish, and on the Rosneath peninsula across the water from Helensburgh, the same situation prevailed. Just to add some extra spice to the problem the author of the 1790 Statistical Account says that it was widely believed that it was the soil of Rosneath which spelled death for the rats. So much so that in the mid-1700s a Jamaican planter took several barrels of Rosneath earth out to the West Indies with a view to killing rats which were attacking his sugar cane. A major export business failed to materialise because no improvement in the Caribbean infestation was reported.

The truth would seem to be that rats were just as common in Scotland as elsewhere in Europe, certainly in Edinburgh and the larger burghs. And in their wake came the bubonic plague. Little wonder that rats are still a group of God's creatures which most folk would happily live without.

July 22

1298   Scots army under William Wallace defeated at Falkirk by the forces of Edward of England.

1484   A peasant army, principally made up of market traders, defeated the rebellious Duke of Albany and the 'Black Douglas' at Lochmaben in Dumfriesshire, as they tried to rally support for an insurrection.

1688   Legal action began disputing the exclusive right of Culross in Fife to manufacture iron girdles for baking oatcakes.

1838   Whaler *Perseverance* reached Peterhead from Greenland with ten whales and 13 seamen from a Hull boat crushed in the pack-ice.

1931   Battle-cruiser *Tiger* and battleship *Iron Duke* arrived in the Firth of Forth to be disarmed under a recently signed international agreement.

Unwelcome Exports

Six young Confederate cavalry officers – all of Scottish descent – met in Tennessee around Christmas 1865, to form a club which took its trappings from the Brotherhood of Horse Whisperers whose roots were in Scotland. This organisation was to become the infamous Ku Klux Klan.

July 23

1430   Sir John Kennedy, nephew of James I languished in Stirling Castle dungeon for speaking 'against the king's government'.

1519   A man 'possessed with the diuell' ran amok in Dundee killing six people.

1597   North of Scotland shaken by a breakfast-time earthquake; it was seen by Reformers as God's displeasure with Papists and their supporters.

1609   Major street-rammy in Glasgow involving the parties of Sir George Elphinstone, the Provost and Sir Walter Stewart of Minto whose family objected to Elphinstone's changes in the electoral system.

1975   Three-month-old David Nicolle from Troon in Ayrshire became Scotland's youngest heart pacemaker patient.

You Fired, Sir?

Edinburgh advocate and writer Hugo Arnot kept poor health throughout his short life. He also had a short temper and, after moving into a house in the New Town in the late 1700s, began, much to the annoyance of the neighbours, summoning his servant by firing a pistol.

July 24

1593   Earl of Bothwell and his cronies, anxious to get back into favour with James VI, came in the back gate at Holyrood Palace early in the morning. In fear and 'with his breeks in hand' James gave them a hearing.

1630   A case of alleged demonic possession occupied the attention of the authorities in Duns – an 'illiterate, ignorant' woman called Margaret Lumsden was debating with officials in perfect Latin.

1689   John Blair, an Edinburgh apothecary, bought the general postmastership of Scotland at public auction, agreeing to pay the government £255 annually for seven years.

1841   Large bouquets of flowers giving off carbonic-acid gas were blamed for headaches and other pains and aches suffered by dancers after the grand society balls in Scotland.

1984   Historic first meeting of the new women's committee on Edinburgh District with Councillor Val Woodward saying she would like to be called chairperson, chair or convener – but never, ever chairman.

Barrel of Lard

Gluttony was a rare vice in medieval Scotland when starvation was a more common experience. However, one exception who proved the rule was the obese Douglas Earl James who, on his death in 1443, was found to have four stones of tallow in his stomach.

July 25

1622   Wine importation to the Western Isles was restricted as the arrival of a vessel carrying wine signalled 'excessive drinking and breaking of His Majesty's Peace'.

1745   Prince Charles Edward Stuart lands at Borrodale in Inverness-shire at the start of the Jacobite Uprising

1886	Resistance to crofter evictions reported on Tiree and marines were sent to assist local police.
1908	Record numbers of berry-pickers at Blairgowrie with large crowds begging and sleeping rough.
1982	West Highlands suffered an unprecedented four-month drought and many acres of the Loch Laggan foreshore which were exposed were described as a 'desert'.

Napoleon Breathing

The big attraction at the Assembly Rooms in Glasgow's Ingram Street in May 1835, was an astonishing mechanical figure representing Napoleon Bonaparte complete with uniform, hat and sword; the 'most perfect anatomical figure ever brought before the public'.

July 26

1298	Stirling in flames as Wallace and his army – defeated a few days before at Falkirk – fled the advancing English forces.
1599	Conference at St Andrews chaired by Andrew Melville discussed ghosts, witchcraft, demonic possession and out-of-body experiences.
1698	Ill-fated Darien Expedition, which attempted to set up a Scottish colony in the jungles of Central America, sailed from Leith.
1899	Memorial statue to the Highland heroine Flora MacDonald was unveiled on the Castle Hill, Inverness.
1941	Home-guard in Glasgow did themselves proud in beating off a mock attack by highly trained troops on rail centres in the city.

On Your Marks

The now familiar sprinter's crouch-start is said to have been introduced at athletics meetings in Scotland as early as 1884 by Maori runner Bobby MacDonald.

July 27

1610	Twenty-seven pirates who had plagued shipping around the coast of Scotland and were eventually captured in Orkney, were hanged at Leith.
1689	Highlanders under Graham of Claverhouse defeated General Mackay at the Battle of Killiecrankie. It was one of the first European battles in which the recently developed bayonet was employed.
1760	Scottish School of Design, later to become the Royal Scottish Academy, founded.
1841	A carter was badly injured in Greenock when he fell under the wheel of his cart and his head was crushed 'to an awful extent'.

1943   Comedian Will Fyfe told of a dramatic emergency-landing from a burning aircraft while he was in North Africa entertaining the troops.

Roll out the Barrow

Drinking in Scotland in the 1700s had achieved such an important social status that it was a point of honour among country gentlemen that no guest should leave the house sober; if they had to leave it was best that they were spirited away in a wheelbarrow.

July 28

1600   People of Dornoch reaped the benefit of an unusual harvest of the sea when 14 huge whales were stranded on nearby sands. Some of the creatures were 90 feet in length.

1636   Village of Denny in Stirlingshire sought help in rebuilding a bridge over the River Carron which had been swept away in an awesome flood.

1790   Forth and Clyde Canal opened to commercial traffic, having taken 22 years to complete.

1865   The last public hanging in Glasgow was watched by a crowd of 30,000. An Englishman, Dr Edward Pritchard, had been convicted of poisoning his wife and mother-in-law.

1915   An exhibition to launch a campaign against flies opened at the Scottish Zoological Park in Edinburgh, illustrating the fly's connection with disease.

Flagging at the Vital Moment

The aged Marquis of Tullibardine was so ill with gout when he ceremonially raised Bonnie Prince Charlie's standard at Glenfinnan in 1745, that he had to be supported by two companions.

OLD FEARS EXORCISED, ANY WITCH WAY

Blame it on oor Rabbie's vivid imagination, Stephen King, the Stepford Wives or even Jamie the Saxt. Actually you might as well blame it on the boogie because we're never likely to know for sure the source of the Scots fascination with witchcraft.

The fact is, that when market days are wearing late and folk begin to tak the gate we Scots still glance nervously sideways passing the kirkyard, still half-expecting to see shadowy figures in their semmits cavorting among the tombstones.

It's with personal reluctance, and only, as they say, as a result of popular demand, that I return to the topic of the witchcraft frenzy. My own feeling, for what it's worth, is that some deep-seated guilt relating to those troubled times still haunts the Scottish people. Perhaps we need to pay belated penance, hence the strange obsession.

I suspect that in every childhood there was a witch lurking along some leafy lane or down the nearest dark alley. In my Clydebank boyhood she lived in the gloomy and mysterious dunny below the adjacent church. For sure a witch lived there, cauldron and all, the older kids told us. You could hear her casting her spells by night. And there was the jet-black moggy which patrolled the church grounds. But why any self-respecting crone would choose to hole up among the sandstone canyons of Clydebank was never fully explained.

More than once as a dare, I clambered over the wall from our backcourt and dreeped into the rubble and dockens of the overgrown yard at the rear of the church. A dozen steps led down to the basement door. Once, I think I managed to edge down four or five steps, eyes fixed on the flaking paint of the green door, before a chorus of hoots from the wall sent me scrabbling back to safety. Aren't weans plain daft?

Mind you, I knew a boy whose friend's big brother's best pal actually entered that scary chamber. He didn't vanish for ever, end up in a stew, go mad or grow horns, but 40 years on he has a stunning mop of purest white hair. Coincidence? I think not.

Now that I'm old and cynical, I'm pretty sure that story was concocted by the church officer to keep the urchins from John Knox Street off the premises. But I still wonder. I suspect that kids from that corner of Clydebank, if television hasn't deadened the imagination completely, may still find fascination with such secret places. Perhaps, just perhaps, the legend of the witch of Bank Street lives on to this day.

Years later I went to live in North Berwick, the Scots burgh most often associated with the witch mania of the late 1500s. Now, this was more serious stuff. The old kirk by the harbour is a strange place, only a few forlorn stones now, so ruinous that it's difficult to visualise it as it was the night the devil is said to have appeared in the pulpit to 100 of his followers as they schemed to sink King James's ship in the Forth.

However, early (3 a.m. to be precise) one dark, autumn morning as I took the airs after a liquid night, I was staggered to be met by a big black dog, bounding down the slipway next to the kirk, eyes on fire, mouth lathered with foam. A favourite disguise for Auld Nick, I recalled. Only when the irate owner leaned unsteadily over the railings and hollered into the darkness, 'Get back here, Basil, ya bastard', was the spell broken.

July 29

1173   William the Lion, King of Scots, was brought before Henry II as a common thief, his legs bound beneath his horse. He had been captured at Alnwick earlier in the month.

1571   Government officials pondered the news that a messenger, sent to Jedburgh to declare the re-establishment of Queen Mary's rule, had been forced to eat his despatches.

1865   Glasgow angered by London writers who portrayed the city's double standard of 'sabbath keeping and toddy drinking'.

1913   Residents of St Kilda sent a message to the king to mark the establishment of a wireless station on the island.

1956   Edinburgh's Ecurie Ecosse sports-car racing-team, Ninian Sanderson and Ron Flockhart, shocked international racing by winning the Le Mans 24-hour classic.

Difficult to Swallow

It has been calculated that during the production process whisky evaporates from Scottish distilleries at the rate of over 150 million bottles annually.

July 30

1622   A fresh attempt was made to ban the importation of tobacco, 'the infectious weed', to Scotland; smuggling had made its use commonplace.

1696   Widespread food shortages brought fear of famine to north-east Scotland, where deaths had already been reported.

1790   A thunderstorm in Aberdeenshire was followed by an amazing fall of hailstones, the size of musketballs, which drifted to three feet.

1836   Ninety-two people enrolled as depositors on the opening day of the Savings Bank of Glasgow.

1971   Historic Upper Clyde Shipbuilders work-in began at Clydebank with employees occupying the yard.

Long Memories

It's said that the folk of Argyll, including Ayrshire immigrants, are less than enthusiastic about the national bard, Rabbie Burns, because of derogatory remarks he once made about the town of Inveraray.

July 31

1593   The citizens of Aberdeen were urged to arm themselves against raids by wild and lawless Highlanders who descended 'like a plague of locusts'.

1604   A brilliant star was noted in the skies 'aboon Edinburgh, hard by the sun', and many thought it signalled 'strange alterations' in the world.

1786   First edition of the poems of Robert Burns were published at Kilmarnock.

1819   Irish labourer was jailed for three months for 'streaking' down Glasgow's Union Street to the Broomielaw for a wager. In addition, on being caught he had been given a sound thrashing by some carters.

1979   Seventeen oilmen killed after a chartered aircraft failed to lift off and skidded into the sea at Sumburgh, Shetland; cabin staff were praised for their bravery.

Desert Islands, Not

So you thought that Shetland was sparsely populated? In fact, the most recent survey shows over a million residents: 30,000 gannets, 140,000 guillemots, 250,000 puffins, 300,000 fulmars, 330,000 sheep and, oh yes, 24,000 people.

August 1

1571   A piglet, one of a litter of 13, was born in Edinburgh with a face uncannily like that of a man. It was thought to be a bad omen for the city.

1606   Plague spread throughout Scotland with frightful rapidity, particularly in the densely populated areas. On this day Stirling and Perth were reported to be almost deserted.

1747   The wearing of tartan was prohibited in the wake of the Jacobite Uprising; six months jail for a first offence, transportation for a second.

1874   Rail construction work, which had been moving steadily north over several decades, finally reached Thurso on the Pentland Firth.

1965   Jim Clark, Borders-based Formula One driver, regained the world championship by winning the German Grand Prix.

Measure for Measure

Scots instrument designer Sir Keith Elphinstone who worked on naval instruments and gunfire control equipment also developed the modern speedometer in the early years of this century.

August 2

1440   Law and order was the main focus of debate for a meeting of the Scots Parliament at Stirling.

1588   First Spanish vessels from the Armada, routed in the Channel by Drake, appeared off the Scottish coast.

1621   A proliferation of bogus doctors 'including women and gardeners' led to a failed attempt by King James VI to create a Royal College of Physicians in Edinburgh.

1836   Dundee was reported to be in a healthy state with the number of funerals well down on the average of 35 per week.

1973   Rapid reform of Scottish drink laws urged by Clayson Committee after two years study. This eventually made Scotland's drink laws much more liberal than those of England.

The Big Time

Albion Rovers, whose little ground at Cliftonhill, Coatbridge, seldom held more than a few hundred spectators, played against Kilmarnock in the Scottish Cup Final of 1920 in front of 99,000 spectators. Alas, they lost 2–3.

August 3

1305   Patriot William Wallace was captured near Glasgow by Sir John Menteith. He was tried and executed with extreme barbarity in London on 23 August.

1460   King James II was killed by the accidental explosion of cannon during the siege of Roxburgh Castle.

1596   Englishman John Dickson hanged in Edinburgh for calling King James VI 'ane bastard king not worthy to be obeyed'. He had been asked to move his boat by royal officers.

1829   Start of the infamous Moray floods when the Spey and Findhorn rivers rose 50 feet above normal after torrential rain; many died despite a rescue operation.

1962   Dundee United and Scotland defender Maurice Malpas was born at Dunfermline.

Food for Thought

The Menteiths were never allowed to forget that one of their ancestors betrayed and handed over William Wallace to martyrdom. For centuries, whenever one of the family was being entertained to a meal the bannock was served face down to remind them of the treacherous act.

August 4

1244   Treaty of Newcastle was signed. Scotland agreed not to enter into alliances with the enemies of England who, for their part, promised not to attack Scotland.

1701   Cockfighting, the most popular sport of the day, banned from the streets of Edinburgh because of the disturbance it caused. The city was said to have some of the best 'cockers' in Britain.

1765   Thomas Muir, advocate of the Scots people and passionate believer in Parliamentary reform, was born in a flat above his parents' shop in Glasgow's High Street.

1914   Britain's Declaration of War on Germany was received quietly in Scotland although London was said to be seething with excitement.

1965   Specimen of vendace, among the rarest fish in the world, was caught by a Glasgow University zoologist at the Mill Loch, Lochmaben.

Wandering Clans

Scotland's tinker families, among them the MacPhees, Stewarts and MacDonalds, are considered by some scholars to be the wandering remnants of Highland families who were dispersed during the violence and confusion immediately after the Battle of Culloden.

HAUNTING OF A HAPLESS KING

If you are in search of the most public haunting in the annals of Scotland, I think you must steer your astral self back almost 500 years in the direction of St Michael's Church in Linlithgow.

In August 1513 James IV, against the wishes of his council, had called together a vast army and was in the West Lothian town preparing for a military campaign against England. He is said to have been in a sad and thoughtful mood, heavily involved in religious rites and observances, as was the custom for a commander at that time. He was probably reflecting not only on the coming conflict but on the murder of his father at nearby Sauchieburn, the anniversary of which had just passed.

A few days before the army was to move south, the king was in St Michael's at evensong, surrounded by his lords, when an elderly, grave-looking figure, clothed in a blue gown, wearing sandals and carrying a staff, made his way through the throng of nobles calling loudly for the king.

Without any sign of reverence or respect for the monarch, this apostolic figure with a bald forehead and long, straggling locks flowing to his shoulders, bent over and addressed the king.

The warning was this; 'Thou wilt not fare well in the journey, nor any that passeth with thee'. He was further cautioned about meddling with women or he would be 'confounded and brought to shame'. While the king pondered a reply this strange visitor vanished 'as if he had been a blink of sun or a whip of a whirlwind'.

The incident was confirmed by scores of witnesses, including Sir David Lindsay of the Mount and Sir James Inglis, who tried to collar the 'saint' but were defeated by his miraculous disappearance. Although Peter Underwood in his gazetteer of Scottish ghosts describes the Linlithgow affair as 'one of the best authenticated instances of a purposeful apparition', the general view of historians is that it was a 'solemn, admonitory masquerade'. Having failed by more orthodox means to persuade James against the adventure south, his queen is thought, with the aid of his closest nobles, to have engineered this bizarre incident. Of course, history tells us that James was not to be swayed.

It's worth noting, however, that after crossing the Tweed the Scots army took some small castles. At Ford the king found Lady Heron, a woman of remarkable beauty, whose husband at the time was a prisoner in Scotland. The king dallied awhile with Mrs Heron and, as a result, dispirited Scots soldiers started to drift away from the camp.

An army which had crossed into England, perhaps more than 60,000 strong, was reduced by half. His meddling with women had indeed 'confounded' him and most assuredly he and his fellow

Scots were not to 'fare well' on the bloody field of Flodden.

August 5

1320 William Lord Soulis and the Countess of Strathearn was sentenced to life imprisonment for conspiring against Robert the Bruce. Other minor characters in the plot were executed.

1423 A fierce blaze virtually destroyed the town of Aberdeen.

1600 The Gowrie Conspiracy, an attempt by Lord Ruthven and the Earl of Gowrie to murder or kidnap James VI, failed.

1707 'Equivalent Money', or £398,085.10s intended to create equality of trade under the Treaty of Union arrived in Edinburgh in 12 horse-drawn wagons guarded by dragoons.

1845 Estuary of the River Clyde was reported to be 'alive' with shoals of herring.

Flodden Facts

Scotland abounds with tales of the supernatural but one of the most chilling was the appearance prior to the carnage of Flodden of a ghostly herald in Edinburgh's High Street who read a list of the noble houses of Scotland. Only after the battle did it become apparent he had been naming those about to die, including the king and most of his nobles.

A pair of gloves was the wager made by her brother Gilbert which inspired Miss Jean Eliot to write a ballad on Flodden which later became the famous *Flowers of the Forest*. For centuries after the battle, Caithness folk were reluctant to cross the Ord on a Monday or dressed in green as the brave Earl and his men had done in 1513 *en route* to their deaths on the bloody, English field.

August 6

1332 Supporters of Edward, son of John Balliol, formerly King of Scots, landed at Kinghorn, Fife, prior to the Battle of Dupplin Moor near Perth.

1477 Scots were urged to 'honourably receive' foreign merchants and to encourage them in trade and commerce with Scotland.

1597 Plague or 'the Pest' was confirmed in Edinburgh and a fast ordered; Leith was identified as the point of entry of the disease.

1796 Death of Alloa-born painter David Allan who studied abroad and is noted for his Edinburgh street scenes.

1975 First ever theft reported on the Isle of Eigg; a Glasgow youth was fined £5 for stealing postal-orders from the sub-post-office.

Deep and Even

Thirty days after being buried in a snowdrift in 1978 in darkest Sutherland, a Cheviot sheep carrying a lamb emerged none the worse for the experience. Some sort of record, surely?

August 7

1400　Henry IV, the English king, resident at Newcastle, called upon Robert III and the Scottish nobility to pay homage to him at Edinburgh later in the month. The Scots ignored the order and prepared for invasion.

1548　Mary Queen of Scots, still a child, left Scotland for France as the intended wife for the Dauphin Francis, son of Henry II.

1783　American brigantine arrived in the Clyde from North Carolina with cargo of tobacco. It was the first vessel to arrive in Glasgow from North America since the War of Independence.

1807　Ship coming upriver fired her guns off Greenock as a salute, but a stray shot went through the roof of Laird's ropeworks and struck a house, narrowly missing the lady occupant.

1932　Council of the National Party of Scotland met to draw up a three-year plan in the belief that independence could be achieved in that period.

Light and Shade

In the 1970s a young lobster fisherman who was stranded on a deserted isle off Skye, attracted attention to his plight by *extinguishing* the automatic lighthouse.

August 8

1296   Scottish Coronation Stone (or a well-crafted substitute) was stolen by Edward I, Hammer of the Scots, from the Abbey of Scone, Perthshire.

1594   Witch-hunters in the Borders were being kept busy and on this day trials and burnings were reported as being underway in Duns, Eyemouth and Coldstream.

1634   Fears of famine as a result of a seven-week spring drought was thankfully not realised and a tolerable harvest began throughout Scotland.

1807   'Old Nelly', a Greenock worthy, died, aged almost 100, in the town's Poor House. She often occupied the police barrow when the worse for drink.

1963   Glasgow-London mail-train ambushed in Buckinghamshire in what became known as The Great Train Robbery. Two and a half million pounds was taken.

Letters from Home

Scots soldiers fighting in the Falklands War of 1982 had a bewildering variety of mail redirected to them in the foxholes. One Scots Guardsman, ducking the machine-gun fire, even received a final warning from his local authority about an unpaid parking-fine.

August 9

1176   In the presence of King William the Lion, the grassy slopes to the north of the Brothock stream in Angus were solemnly dedicated as the site of Arbroath Abbey.

1327   A Scots army which ravaged the North of England but successfully avoided a confrontation with English forces, crossed back into Scotland.

1703   Rum distillery in Leith got the go-ahead after a period in which drink was banned because of its effect on Scots consumption of whisky.

1843   A Newfoundland dog dived off the pier at Tarbert, Argyll, to rescue a toddler who had wandered away from his nurse and fallen into the sea.

1915   Advent of horse butchers in Glasgow was noted as a result of demand for horse meat from Belgian war refugees.

Flat on his Back

It is thought that the death of Alexander Runciman, the eighteenth-century historical painter who wanted to rival the Sistine Chapel with his ceiling paintings in Ossian's Hall at Penicuik, was hastened by lying for months in a recumbent position, à la Michaelangelo, with no physical exercise.

August 10

1377   Earl of March (or Dunbar) staged a raid on a fair at Roxburgh killing many English and carrying off plunder. The incident heightened tension yet again in the Borders.

1490   Scots Admiral Andrew Wood captured five English vessels in a sea-battle and returned in triumph to Leith in his warships *The Flower* and *Yellow Carvel*.

1506   A 'swift and violent' comet was seen in parts of Scotland moving across the sky from north to south.

1838   A wandering piper who claimed to have given away a fortune from his earnings in the United States, arrived in Glasgow.

1880   Three people were killed north of Berwick when the *Flying Scotsman* left the track and went down an embankment.

Solid Foundation

Archaen gneiss, the world's oldest rock, vintage 20,000 million years, is found at Torridon in Wester Ross.

August 11

590   Early Celtic missionary St Blane, who was active in Bute, Lennox and in the Dunblane area, died.

1419   Scotland was experiencing a severe drought, however, an abundant harvest was reported. Strangely, when the following year brought better weather, the harvest failed.

1600   James VI, after his escape from the Gowrie Conspiracy, arrived at Leith to a tumultuous reception with 'great joy, shooting of muskets and shaking of pikes'.

1789   A thatched house in Kirk Street, Gorbals, Glasgow, was destroyed by fire.

1965   Scottish Tourist Board embarrassed by an employee who told a visitor that the islands of Eigg, Rhum and Canna were uninhabited.

Chrome Dome No More

A popular remedy for baldness among the Scots gentry of the seventeenth century was the application of the burnt ashes of dove's dung. It seems the ashes of little frogs worked just as well.

KEEPING HIS HEAD IN THE CLOUDS

Were you a dreamer at school, finding that fabulous land beyond the classroom window, across the playing-fields where the hockey sticks clicked, over the chimney pots of the jannie's house, infinitely more exciting than Latin declensions?

If so, you must often have felt the crack of the dominie's ruler on your knuckles or the dull thud of a Latin grammar book making contact with the back of your head and the plaintive cry, 'You've got your head in the clouds, boy.' This admonition was not, I was subsequently to discover, a reason for despair . . . remarkably, a Nobel prize might still be yours.

The story of physicist Professor Charles Wilson, perhaps the most famous son of Glencorse, in Midlothian, shows that the outlook of the visionary must never be dismissed or pooh-poohed.

September 1894, saw Professor Wilson set out on a history-making expedition when he perched for several weeks in the rickety observatory which had been constructed atop Ben Nevis. Up there, with his head in the clouds, he made a series of observations which were to change the course of physics.

The professor described his experiences thus, 'The wonderful optical phenomena when the sun shone on the cloud surface on the hill greatly excited my interest and made me want to imitate the phenomenon in the laboratory.' Back at the Cavendish Laboratories in Cambridge the professor began to study the marvel of clouds in earnest and quickly made a significant discovery while observing the process of cloud formation.

Wilson had designed a cloud chamber in which the tracks of the single atoms were made visible as thin, water droplets – just like the vapour trail of aircraft which we often see arcing across the sky. The paths of the particles were visible for a moment as white streaks and were photographed for the first time, giving a convincing demonstration, in simple terms, that atoms, speculated on and theorised about since the days of ancient Greece, really did exist.

Later, the cloud chamber was to play an important role in the researches of Rutherford and his associates which established the foundations of nuclear science.

In 1925 Charles Wilson was appointed Jacksonian Professor of Natural Philosophy at Cambridge and two years later gained the Nobel Prize for Physics. Even in retirement, the old professor, who died in 1959, was still to be found tramping his beloved hills of Scotland, thankfully for the progress of science, with his head still fixed firmly in the clouds.

August 12

1595   Marion Martin, whose house was 'ane ressavear of huirs and harlottis', was ordered to make repentance in the kirk at Govan.

1627   A plan was unveiled to create a small troop of Highland bowmen; the weapon was still in use in the North of Scotland although it had been abandoned in most European countries.

1708   George Williamson of Edinburgh advertised his services as a swimming instructor; he could swim on his 'face, back or any posture, plum, dowk and perform other antics'.

1749   Highlander arrested in Edinburgh for wearing the philibeg, Highland dress having been prohibited after Culloden.

1974   Secretary of State for Scotland turned down a proposal for an oil-platform construction-yard at Drumbuie in Wester Ross because the sacrifice of a way of life was too great a price to pay, he said.

A Roman Vietnam

As many as 50,000 legionaires are thought to have been killed in three centuries of guerilla war with the Caledonian tribes as Rome struggled unsuccessfully to bring what is now Highland Scotland under her sway.

August 13

1614   Lord Walden, later the Earl of Suffolk, was touring Scotland, where he was entertained by noble families in Edinburgh, Stirling, Dunfermline and Falkland.

1692   One hundred pounds reward offered after the London-Edinburgh post was held up at Jock's Lodge.

1809   Forty people were drowned when the passenger boat *Frith* was wrecked in the Dornoch Firth.

1888   John Logie Baird, the inventor who developed the first workable television system, was born at Helensburgh.

1981   Scots jockey Willie Carson fractured his skull when his mount fell in the Yorkshire Oaks.

Horns an' A'!

The famous Glasgow glutton, Rab Ha', who died in 1843, and is buried in Gorbals Cemetery, is best remembered for eating an entire calf as a bet.

August 14

1040   King Duncan I killed by Macbeth in a battle near Elgin.

1615   Three Edinburgh citizens convicted of helping Catholics including John Ogilvie received a stay of execution at the gallows; their sentences were commuted to banishment.

1773   Dr Samuel Johnson arrived in Scotland to join James Boswell at the start of their famous journey to the Western Isles.

1808   Edinburgh Museum opened in the Trongate with the 'utmost value given for any rare bird, quadruped, armour or any uncommon article'.

1920   Duke of York arrived in the Highlands for a shooting holiday where he met up with Elizabeth Bowes-Lyon, his bride-to-be, the Queen Mother.

Boomps-a-Daisy

One of the oddest political gatherings of sixteenth-century Scotland was the so-called 'Creeping Parliament' of 1571 summoned by the Regent in Edinburgh's Canongate. Under fire from the Catholic guns in the castle, the members had to go about their business on their hands and knees.

August 15

1390   Festivities to mark the coronation of Robert III at Scone began, and his wife, Lady Annabel, was crowned.

1500   William Dunbar, formerly a priest in government service, was appointed court poet to James IV.

1645   During his brilliant campaign against the Covenanters the Marquis of Montrose routed a force under William Baillie at Kilsyth.

1822   George IV arrived in Scotland at the start of his famous 'Tartan Tour'. The two-week visit was the first by a British monarch in 171 years.

1920   A surrendered German torpedo-boat which broke from its moorings badly damaged the rail bridge over the Forth at Alloa.

Biting the Bullet

James IV, who saw himself as a patron of the medical profession, once paid a citizen 14s to allow the monarch to extract his teeth; whether they required pulling is not recorded.

August 16

1459   Army of James II had crossed the Border, its declared purpose was to punish repeated English incursions.

1569   St Andrews saw three executions on this day – a sorcerer was burned, a Frenchman implicated in Darnley's murder was hanged, as was William Stewart, Lord Lyon king-of-arms, for necromancy.

1628   Minister at Carstairs, Lanarkshire, was concerned about the insolent behaviour of men and women who were 'footballing, dancing and taking barley-breaks' on the Sabbath.

1829	German composer and conductor Felix Mendelssohn had arrived in Glasgow at the start of his Scottish tour.
1858	Glasgow-born Colin Campbell, a military hero who led British forces during the Indian Mutiny, was created Lord Clyde.

Mal de Mer

The beautiful Hebrides or Fingal's Cave Overture is a remarkable composition when you consider that on his visit to Staffa to see the famous sea-cave Felix Mendelssohn was violently seasick.

August 17

1424	French and Scots commanded by the Earls of Buchan and Douglas were defeated by English forces under the Duke of Bedford at Verneuil.
1579	Dunbar herring fleet of 60 boats was devastated by hurricane force winds in the Forth Estuary; some 300 men were said to have perished.
1661	Eminent English naturalist John Ray began a tour of Scotland. He was particularly unimpressed by Scottish womenfolk; he found them to be 'none of the handsomest'.
1944	Man fined £5 at Greenock Sheriff Court for writing a letter (from a ship lying in the Firth of Clyde) which may have been of use to the enemy.
1947	Opening of the first Edinburgh International Festival, now the biggest arts and music event in the world.

KEEPING HIS HEAD IN THE CLOUDS

Cats and Dogs Next?

There are several instances of mysterious fish falls in Scotland. One of the best documented was in Campbeltown in 1904 when a loud pattering on the roofs alerted the townsfolk to the fact that a shower of hundreds of small fish was falling. Waterspouts are usually held to be responsible for this odd phenomenon.

August 18

1662   A postal route was ordained by the Scots Parliament between Edinburgh and Portpatrick with immediate stations at Linlithgow, Kilsyth, Glasgow, Kilmarnock, Ayr, Drumbeg and Ballantrae.

1746   Jacobite Lords Kilmarnock and Balmerino were executed for high treason on Tower Hill, London.

1808   Bothwell School Board was accused by HM Inspector of Schools of neglecting the smaller morals – 'please' and 'thank you' – and soap.

1932   Scots aviator Jim Mollison made the first west-bound solo crossing of the Atlantic.

1957   Helensburgh man J. Norman Barclay became the first man to cross the Irish Sea on water-skis – the journey took an hour and 20 minutes.

Desirable Properties

Scotland's greatest con man – a title for which there are many contenders – was probably actor Arthur Fergusson who, in the 1920s, set himself up in the monument-selling business. He disposed of Nelson's Column, Big Ben and Buckingham Palace to gullible Americans. He was jailed after 'selling' the Statue of Liberty to a naïve Australian.

RAINING ON VICTORIA'S PARADE

Flick through that delightful book *Brewer's Dictionary of Phrase and Fable*, until you reach the entry 'Queen's Weather' and there you'll find an intriguing definition: 'Fine day for a fête, so-called because Queen Victoria was, for the most part, fortunate in having fine weather when she appeared in public.'

Fellow cyclists should particularly note the phrase 'for the most part' because this qualification points to one of the most famous ceremonial fiascos in British military history – the Wet Review – the day when more than Victoria reigned in Edinburgh.

The Review of Volunteers at Holyrood in August, 1881, had been one of the most keenly anticipated events of the century. Shops in Princes Street offered camp-chairs and even bedsteads for the comfort of the many thousands who were expected to view the event, and the whole city was bedecked with flags and bunting.

That fateful Thursday morning (25 August) was dull but brought no indication of the deluge which was in store. By the time the 41,000 Volunteers had mustered in the Queen's Park, the heavens had opened and onlookers reported that rain seemed to be falling by the bucketful.

Throughout the afternoon it poured, and by teatime a loch had formed in the middle of the park, thanks to a burst water main. Gradually the proceedings disintegrated into farce, with everyone, including the bedraggled military, drenched, disconsolate and seeking any available shelter.

High summer, Dunoon, 1954

Weather Words

During the first winter of the thirteenth century, historian Hector Boece claimed that Scotland was so cold that beer froze into lumps and was sold by the pound. Horatio McCulloch, a nineteenth-century Scottish landscape-painter famed for his mountain scenes, loved the outdoors but died from a chill brought on by sketching on a windswept hillside during bleak weather. In the late 1600s inventor David Gregory from Aberdeenshire was asked sternly by his local presbytery about his uncanny ability to predict changes in the weather. They were seriously considering charging him with witchcraft until he explained that he was the proud owner of the North of Scotland's first barometer. A study in 1983 into illness among visitors to Scotland, showed that many believed the weather was an important contributory factor.

Professor William Wilkie, a nineteenth-century St Andrews academic, had a classic case of thin blood and shivered constantly in the face of chill North Sea winds. To keep himself warm, he is said to have slept under a pile of 24 pairs of blankets. Mercedes, a polar bear brought from Canada's Hudson Bay as a mate for Edinburgh Zoo's Barney, was unable to join him for a first date when the sliding door linking their pens froze solid on one of the coldest days of the 1980s. In 1983, the mildest winter for decades saw wild birds in a state of utter confusion. Thrushes and blackbirds began building their nests in the middle of January.

August 19

1561   Mary Queen of Scots arrived at Leith from France to take over the reins of government.

1574   Janet Cadie was summoned before the kirk in Edinburgh accused of disguising herself in 'welvot breikis' and dancing in men's clothing.

1708   Six St Andrews boys swept out to sea in a rowing-boat finally made landfall near Aberdeen six days later; they were alive but exhausted.

1745   The royal standard was raised at Glenfinnan in Inverness-shire to signal the start of the Jacobite Uprising.

1914   A letter from Lord Kitchener was carried in the press appealing for volunteers for war service, and by the end of the month 20,000 had enlisted in Glasgow alone.

Pregnant Pause

During an expedition in Ireland led by King Robert the Bruce one of the camp followers of the Scots army, a laundress, went into labour. Bruce ordered the entire army to halt, a tent was pitched and the woman was safely delivered.

1158 Rognvald, Earl of Orkney, later canonised, was murdered on a hunting trip in Caithness.

1421 James I, King of Scots and a prisoner of England, was present at the capture by English forces of the town of Dreux in Northern France.

1673 Edinburgh's first taxi stance was set up on the High Street with 20 street-carriages operating the service; however, sedan chairs still predominated.

1807 A violent hailstorm pounded Glasgow, one piece of ice which fell in a Duke Street backcourt was five inches by four.

1841 Two giraffes – costing the enormous sum of £3,000 – had joined the Wombwell Menagerie in Paisley.

Strange Refuge

Jacobite engraver Robert Strange was a fugitive after Culloden and hid for a time in Edinburgh to be near his lover Isabella Lumsden. Once, when he was visiting her, Government troops appeared and searched the house from top to bottom. They left empty-handed and Strange emerged from beneath the hooped frame of Isabella's dress which had offered him sanctuary.

August 21

1591 Up to 20 people killed in Glen Isla, Angus, in an attack by a gang of Highlanders who were sent by the Earl of Argyll in reprisal for an earlier assault.

1598 Fierce winds 'blasted' wheatfields in Scotland which resulted in an extraordinary dearth towards the year's end.

1842	Theft of gas-pipes from staircases – even in broad daylight – had become commonplace in Glasgow.
1893	Statue unveiled in the Old Calton Cemetery in Edinburgh in memory of Scottish-American soldiers who took part in the American Civil War.
1950	Princess Margaret celebrated her twentieth birthday with a picnic on the moors above Balmoral Castle, complete with a pink-iced cake.

Sweet Victory

Robertson of Struan was given Sir John Cope's carriage as his share of the booty after the Jacobite victory at Prestonpans (1745). Among several items in the coach were rolls of a substance thought to be an application for wounds which was sold as Johnny Cope's salve. It transpired that the rolls were chocolate for the General's evening cuppa.

August 22

1138	In the Battle of the Standard the Scots, under David I, were routed by the English near Northallerton.
1282	Devorguilla, Countess of Galloway and mother of King John, founded Balliol College, Oxford.
1569	A dispute was in progress between Menteith of Westkerse and Bruce of Clackmannan over who should hold the traditional fair at Clackmannan.
1649	After a summer of extreme shortages, with unprecedented prices paid for grain, cheese, butter and meat, it was noted that a great number of 'creeping things' were being found in the crops.
1913	Two fires in Edinburgh, one at Fettes College and a second in a mansion house at Grange, were blamed on suffragettes.

What's the Rush?

On her long rail trips to and from Balmoral, Queen Victoria, who detested speed, never allowed the train to travel at more than 40 mph. Ironically, her last rail journey, on board her funeral train through the south of England, was completed at speeds of up to 80 mph because of late running.

August 23

1482	English army retook Berwick which had been in Scots hands for 21 years.
1504	Curry, King James IV's jester, being a plague suspect, was banished from the court.
1583	Fleming Eustachius Roche was contracted to search for gold in Scotland; to aid his mining operations he was given the right to use timber from the royal forests for 21 years.

1808	Greenock ship *Prince of Asturias* was taken by a French privateer off Barbados.
1956	Four million people were reported to have visited Scotland this summer but the Scottish Tourist Board was convinced it was only the 'fringe of a great potential traffic'.

We Arra Peepel (II)

The centuries-old Scottish aversion to pork, which Highlanders maintained until the mid-1700s, is said by some scholars to lend weight to the argument that the Scots were descended from the Lost Tribe of Israel.

August 24

1093	Malcolm Canmore, King of Scots, met William Rufus at Gloucester to discuss disputed territory in Cumberland. The meeting broke up in disarray and war followed.
1574	Glasgow bailie George Elphinstone of Blythswood was attacked in the council chambers by tailor Robert Pirry who, as a result, had his rights as a burgess withdrawn.
1637	The new service-book prepared by Archbishop Laud had received only poor and scattered support in Scotland following the St Giles disturbance the previous month.
1792	Riots in several Scottish towns to celebrate successes of the French Revolutionary armies caused considerable government anxiety.
1814	Captain James Burnett, the last commander of the ancient town-guards of Edinburgh, died.

Where is Thy Sting?

After hearing a death sentence passed on him for his role in the 1745 Uprising, Lord Balmerino stopped his coach on the return journey to the Tower of London at Charing Cross to buy a pound of gooseberries.

August 25

683	St Ebba, the abbess of Coldingham who is remembered in St Abb's Head, died.
1255	Henry of England threatened an invasion of Scotland as rumours spread that his daughter Margaret, married four years previously to Alexander III, was having a miserable, confined life.
1270	Louis IX, King of France, died in Tunis while leading a Crusade. His Scots contingent was led by the Earl of Atholl and Adam, Earl of Carrick.
1330	Sir James Douglas, warrior and friend of Robert the Bruce, died in battle in Andalusia, Spain, while taking the king's heart to the Holy Land.

1787   Robert Burns set out on a tour of historic Highland sites and battlefields, hoping also to get some aristocratic sponsorship.

Hosing down the bard

Dental Drawback

Medieval Scots ate no sugar and had fewer cavities than their twentieth-century counterparts, but they often suffered abscesses as a result of the technique of holding bowstrings in their teeth.

FLIGHT OF FANCY TO A DUNG HEAP

You may think it exquisitely appropriate that the most daring exploit of the Scotsman who penned the lyrics of 'The Muckin' o' Geordie's Byre' was an aeronautical adventure which ended on a dung heap.

If you've heard of James Tytler it's almost certainly in connection with his pioneering flights in the Montgolfier-style hydrogen balloon which caused much amazement and not a little hilarity.

The Forfarshire minister's son came to Edinburgh to study and then to work after two voyages as a ship's surgeon, on a Greenland whaler. According to his biographers, he was unable to apply himself and moved in and out of employment. Apparently, he had an immense fund of knowledge but no taste for 'anything superior', seemed to enjoy abject poverty and liked a dram.

After a couple of failed business ventures he fell into debt and took refuge in the Sanctuary at Holyrood. It was here that the great balloon experiment took place. He filled a 'huge, dingy bag' with hydrogen and the crowd cheered and then jeered as the balloon lifted off, carrying him over the garden wall before depositing Tytler gently on a dung hill.

Despite the laughter of onlookers he eventually went into the record books as having achieved the first free-flight balloon ascent in Britain (27 August 1784).

This intriguing character made a major contribution to the second and third editions of the *Encyclopaedia Britannica*, completing much of this memorable work on an upturned washing-tub which served as a writing desk in the mean, little family house in Duddingston.

In the 1790s Tytler embraced the cause of Parliamentary reform but was charged with publishing seditious material and fled to Ireland before the case fell due. He travelled on to the United States where he opened a newspaper at Salem, Massachusetts, which he operated until his death in 1803.

Tytler was a man careless of fame, content to live on the borders of starvation, a selfish, dissolute, mixed-up, yet enchanting individual. He was especially proud of a little pamphlet he produced after much research and personal sacrifice. It was entitled *A List of the Ladies of Pleasure in Edinburgh*.

Sniffing a Bargain

Auctions of dungheaps, valuable as field fertiliser, always pulled in the crowds and were regular events in the medieval burghs of Scotland. In the 1800s, Andrew Nicol of Kinross pursued a case at the Court of Session over a dunghill for more than 30 years. Known at Parliament House as 'Muck Andrew' he carried a detailed plan of the heap wherever he went and was always ready to discuss the strange affair with anyone prepared to listen.

August 26

1565	Twelve hundred Protestant lords and lairds taking part in the rebellion against Queen Mary, dubbed the 'Chaseabout Raid', entered Edinburgh.
1715	A gathering of leading Jacobites was summoned by the Earl of Mar at Braemar under the pretext of a hunting-party.
1838	To the amazement of farm workers in Dumfriesshire, a duckling had been born with an extra pair of feet.
1857	Two active boys, aged about 13, were sought to train as teachers at St George's Road School in Glasgow.
1916	A private in the Scottish Rifles who escaped from the Germans insisted that all enemy machine-gunners were wearing Red Cross armbands.

Sleep Tight

In the 1500s, Scots were told that the only way to get a good night's rest was to sleep with a cover over your head in a close-curtained bed. The same experts thought that combing hair in the evening was detrimental to health. A survey in 1986 showed that hospital wards in Dundee were ten times noisier than recommended.

August 27

1576	Three-year-old legislation aimed at forcing gipsies, or citizens of 'Little Egypt', to live a more settled life had failed and Scots authorities considered a further crackdown.
1652	Remarkably clear, dry, warm weather saw in the harvest all over Scotland. The warmth also brought on Scots chestnuts which were eaten in pasties at banquets.
1790	Smith, the notorious hen-thief, was whipped and banished from Edinburgh for life.
1860	So much snow filled the corries of Ben Wyvis in Ross-shire that a party of young men from Kiltearn were able to have a high-summer snowball fight.
1912	The tale of a Highlander pursued by the enemy after Killiecrankie leaping across the River Garry at the north end of the pass was proved possible when the jump was accomplished – by an English tourist!

I can't make head nor tail of this!

Hidden Talent

Scots character-actor James Robertson Justice was an expert falconer and taught Prince Charles the sport.

August 28

1400	Henry IV, having failed to take Edinburgh Castle, crossed back into England; a shortage of supplies for his army speeded his return.
1621	Proclamation published banning anyone with the name of Macgregor from carrying weapons, 'except for ane pointless knife to eat their meat', under pain of death.
1798	James Wilson, a lawyer born in Fife and a signatory to the American Declaration of Independence, died.
1845	A turtle, nearly six feet long, was gifted by a Troon fishing-boat skipper to the Earl of Eglinton.
1973	Increase in Glasgow bus and underground fares announced with the 4p ticket going up by 1p.

Henry's Hymn

Perhaps the most popular hymn ever written, and played most famously on the deck of the *Titanic* as she slipped beneath the Atlantic, is 'Abide with Me', penned by a native of Ednam, near Kelso, Henry F. Lyte.

August 29

1513	Norham Castle on the Tweed surrendered to James IV's army eleven days before the Battle of Flodden.
1618	Perth minister John Guthrie married the Master of Sanquhar to the daughter of an English knight 'and neither of the parties exceeded 13 years of age'.

1797	The so-called Battle of Tranent, a demonstration against conscription in the face of a threatened French invasion resulted in the deaths of 11 protesters.
1843	While in a fever, a young boy from Calton in Glasgow threw himself out of a tenement window three floors up but suffered only bruises.
1930	Final evacuation of St Kilda, the lonely Atlantic outpost, with the 36 inhabitants being taken by boat to the mainland.

Price of Knowledge

The *Encyclopaedia Britannica*, now requiring a second mortgage to purchase, was first published in Edinburgh in 1768 in 6d parts.

August 30

1624	The citizens of Danzig were dismayed by a persistent immigration of multitudes of 'miserable, debauched and weakly' Scots.
1790	Caithness herring-fishing industry had been so successful that there was a shortage of salt and casks.
1820	Strathaven weaver James Wilson, a mild-mannered man caught up in the Radical Revolt, was executed at Glasgow Green in front of a massive crowd.
1914	Three injured soldiers from the Black Watch were given a heroes' welcome on their return to London; unusually, one was wearing trousers under his kilt, having been 'singed by shrapnel'.
1965	Loganair announced an ambitious plan for inter-island air services in Orkney which were eventually to make the remote communities the most air-conscious in the world.

The Reel World

Radical weaver James Wilson (see above) was the inventor of the pearl-stitch in knitting. In the year of his execution J & J Clark of Paisley introduced cotton-reels for the first time – they were returnable with a ½d deposit.

August 31

651	Aidan, a monk of Iona and the first bishop of the holy isle of Lindisfarne, died.
1589	King James VI, anticipating the arrival of his bride-to-be, Anne of Denmark, wrote to his lords and nobles seeking money and supplies 'toward the proper outset of the court'.
1858	Montrose reported a big upturn in business at the docks with ten flax-laden vessels arriving from St Petersburg, Riga and Archangel.

1886   A disturbance took place at Snizort in Skye during the election of a new minister as supporters of the defeated candidate lifted their bibles and stamped their feet as a mark of protest.

1946   International festival of documentary films, the first film festival in the United Kingdom, was opened by Edinburgh Lord Provost at the Playhouse Cinema.

Wing and a Prayer

The battlements of Stirling Castle witnessed one of the first gliding experiments when, watched by James IV, an Italian clergyman launched himself into thin air paddling furiously with feathered, artificial wings. The sad abbot fractured his thigh and is not reported to have attempted a repeat performance.

September 1

1570   Gilbert, Earl of Cassilis and the self-styled 'King of Carrick', partially roasted a man called William Stewart over a spit in an attempt to extort cash.

1651   Over 1,000 men, women and children were killed after General Monk besieged and entered Dundee on behalf of the Cromwellian authorities.

1807   Heavy rains brought floods to the centre of Glasgow with the water advancing 'a considerable way' up Jamaica Street.

1939 Scotland's first genuine blackout of the war took place. The seriousness of the situation was reflected in the fact that many pubs closed two hours early.

1962 The last official tramcar ran in Glasgow between Dalmuir West and Auchenshuggle, followed by three days of 'souvenir' trips.

Steaming to Success

The first steamboat to cross the English Channel, the *Marjorie*, was built by Denny's at Dumbarton and the *Sirius* built at Leith was the first paddle-steamer to make the Atlantic crossing.

AMBASSADORS ON THE MENU?

Thrice auld Innes had hitched the king of beasts to the cart – fixing him in his golden harness – and three times the lion had thrown a bad turn, grinding his teeth, growling leonine obscenities, snapping at anyone who came within range and generally looking fierce and uncontrollable. What a contrast to the docile old lion who paced around his pen at Holyrood, stopping to casually chew a leg of lamb for the delectation of the dignitaries who visited the court of James VI. However, for the baptism festivities of young Prince Henry, scheduled for 30 August 1594, he was simply refusing to play ball.

The master of ceremonies had had enough. It was just too risky. With the lion in this mood he would step into the Great Hall at Stirling Castle and, instead of applause, there would be panic. Half the nations of Europe were to be represented at the splendid banquet and it would be a public relations disaster if any of the ambassadors ended up on the menu. He called the lion master to one side and conveyed his decision. Innes was stunned.

Having brought the lion all the way from Edinburgh and with hundreds of pounds being lavished on the animal and his attendants to prepare them for the big day, this was nothing short of a disaster. The king had wanted the proud symbol of Scotland – the lion rampant – to be seen in the flesh at Stirling. The trouble was that the old lion was currently too rampant for comfort.

The lion's journey to Stirling was pictured by Sir James Ferguson in his book of short stories *The White Hind,* 'the lion restless and snarling as the wagon bumped along the road . . . each relay of horses starting and shying at the sinister smell of the beast, the crowd running to stare at this extraordinary procession'. Of course, Innes guessed what was amiss. Since a cub the lion had never left Holyrood. So many unfamiliar sights and sounds, smells and sensations were worrying him.

In fact, the main attraction at the baptism feast was always going to be a huge mock-up of a ship of state weighing several tons and powered by a hidden crew, and which had been specially built for the occasion. The idea of the lion hauling in the dessert trolley was simply designed to add another talking point.

Even a few days respite caused by the late arrival of the English ambassador, the Earl of Sussex, had not been sufficient to get the lion calmed down, and the only ones who would remember him were the country folk who had seen his cage roll by on the way to Stirling.

From behind the screen at the end of the hall Innes, with a sad heart, watched the appearance of the dessert trolley. The chariot was propelled by men hidden beneath the drapes but hauled for theatrical purposes by a 'blackamoor'. This last-minute Arab substitute, secured in the harness where the lion should have been, was all rippling muscle and 'very richly attired', but Innes was not impressed.

News of this last-minute alteration in the stage management of the baptism reached a much wider audience and Shakespeare felt confident enough about the topicality of the event to make reference to it in *A Midsummer Night's Dream* – 'T' bring in (God shield us) a lion among ladies is a most dreadful thing.' This was guaranteed to raise a titter for years thereafter.

September 2

1536   James V set off from Kirkcaldy for France with a squadron of five ships – his mission, an official visit and to search for a bride.

1681   Edinburgh merchants were given permission to produce stamped and gilded leather, a popular wall-decoration in large houses of the seventeenth century.

1716   Eighty-nine Jacobite prisoners were to be moved from Edinburgh to Carlisle because it was thought they would not get a fair trial in Scotland.

1858   Seals were reported to be sunbathing at the mouth of the River Eden, near St Andrews.

1970   People of Scotland compared notes on sonic booms from Concorde making its first flight over Scotland; in Oban the noise was described as similar to the firing of the one o'clock gun at Edinburgh Castle.

Munro's Mermaid

Caithness schoolmaster William Munro had dismissed stories about the existence of a mermaid along the coast in the vicinity of Reay. That was until 1809 when, in a deserted bay, he watched 'an unclothed female' sitting combing her long, light-brown hair, on a dangerous offshore reef.

September 3

1574   Town council of Edinburgh agreed to a Frenchman's request to set up a school to teach French at an annual fee of 25 shillings per pupil.

1650   Cromwell routed the Scots covenanting army at Dunbar. Leslie, the Scots general, had been forced by his religious masters to give up the high ground.

1745   James Francis Stuart was proclaimed James VIII, King of Scots, by his son Bonnie Prince Charlie at Perth as the Uprising gained momentum.

1790   More miners arrived in Shetland from the south to work in the islands' copper and iron mines.

1939   Quarter of a million children from Glasgow had been evacuated to Aberdeenshire, Perthshire, Ayrshire, Stirlingshire and Lanarkshire as fear of German air-raids grew.

Children and a suitcase, Glasgow, 1941

First of the Coal Barons

The Abbot of Newbattle, near Dalkeith, granted a charter by the king in the early 1200s, is Scotland's first recorded coalmine operator.

September 4

1241   Alexander III was born at Roxburgh and was crowned eight years later when his father died on an expedition to the Western Isles.

1606   Dumbarton, plagued by flooding for centuries, got a new bulwark costing an amazing £30,000 and paid for by a special national tax.

1654   Musician Andrew Hill was convicted of using potions and abducting a young woman; in the 15 days before sentence was passed he was 'eaten of vermin' in jail 'and so died'.

1848   Inverness was experiencing a tourist boom with the Highland capital's four main hotels fully booked on a regular basis.

1964	Queen Elizabeth opened the Forth Road Bridge, at the time the fourth largest in the world, and the resident engineer paid the first toll of 2/6d.

Music Hall Crates

The interior of Dunfermline Opera House, which closed in 1955, its stage surrounds, boxes and ornamental plasterwork, was crated and shipped to America where today it can be found gracing a modern theatre at Sarasota, on Florida's Gulf of Mexico coast.

September 5

1673	Complaints heard that ship-owners licensed to carry off vagrants and criminals from Scotland to the American colonies were 'kidnapping free persons'.
1745	Army of Bonnie Prince Charlie was established in Perth as the Prince finalised plans to hold court at Holyrood.
1818	First gas-lighting in Glasgow turned on at a Trongate grocery store.
1860	Glasgow company of volunteers who were setting out to join Garibaldi were delayed when someone mixed up the steamer sailing timetables.
1944	Special train carrying Prime Minister Winston Churchill to Greenock *en route* to Quebec was stopped because the PM had left his glasses behind.

On the Borderline

The burn of Inch Ewan, near Dunkeld, was said in the eighteenth century to be a firm dividing-line between the Highlands and Lowlands, the people on either side of the stream having 'distinctive Celtic or Saxon characteristics'.

September 6

1544	Forty-four people were killed at the village of Eckford south of Kelso by an English Border raiding-party.
1791	Anatomist Robert Knox, whose need for corpses for dissection led him into dealings with the infamous Burke and Hare, and public abuse, was born.
1855	Sergeant J. Craig of the Scots Fusilier Guards was awarded the Victoria Cross for bravery at the storming of the Redan during the Crimean War; it was one of the first Victoria Crosses awarded.
1912	Suffragettes evaded police at Balmoral and replaced flags on the golf course with purple banners 'of a political nature'.
1942	To combat the growing problem of young girls loitering in Glasgow streets, the number of policewomen on duty was doubled to 40.

Add One Puffin

The traditional breakfast of the islanders on now abandoned St Kilda normally consisted of porridge, milk and a puffin boiled along with the oats for that added flavour.

September 7

1319   English army began a fierce onslaught against Berwick by land and sea. The strongly fortified town was under the command of Walter the Steward.

1570   Remarkable 18-mile chase on horseback from Bathgate to Edinburgh saw Roger Hepburn, a supporter of Mary Queen of Scots, riding an old nag, outstrip his pursuers to gain sanctuary in the Castle.

1736   Mob broke into Edinburgh prison and lynched Captain Porteous of the town-guard who had ordered his soldiers to fire on a crowd.

1912   Tramp piper, his wife and two children drowned when their cart drove into the Caledonian Canal.

1962   Traffic jams near Thurso as 100-foot masts were moved to the United States Navy radio station near the town.

Joust for Fun

As if real bloodshed wasn't sufficient, one of the favourite pastimes of the Scots nobility in the twelfth century was to sally off to France, to join knights from all over Europe competing in mock battles which could last for days.

September 8

1568   An outbreak of plague which carried off 2,500 people in six months began in Edinburgh. It was brought into the town, it was said, by merchant James Dalgleish.

1726	Adverts appeared outlining courses to be offered at the soon to be opened medical school in Edinburgh.
1843	Dingwall was abuzz at the trial of a woman on charges connected with the 'almost exploded belief' in witchcraft.
1916	Loss reported in combat of a famous set of bagpipes belonging to a Major Anderson. The pipes had been played on polar expeditions in the early 1900s.
1936	Hamilton Presbytery was concerned about low-lying aircraft disturbing Sunday services.

A Close-Run Thing

Edinburgh tailor David Duly should have been a victim of a serious outbreak of plague in 1585. He was hanged from a gibbet outside his house in the High Street for concealing his wife's illness from the authorities, but the rope broke. This was taken as a providential sign and it was decided to banish him from the city instead.

SOLVING THE RIDDLE OF THE LILY

When Aberdonian plant-collector Francis Masson went for a hike around Cape Town's Table Mountain in search of exotic plant specimens in the winter of 1772-73 he stumbled inadvertently upon the solution to the century-old mystery of the Jersey Lily. I don't suppose they'll name a plot in the Beechgrove Garden after him, or raise a statue in Duthie Park – after all, he doesn't even rate a mention in the *Encyclopaedia Britannica* – but his discovery took him into the horticultural histories and meant the rewriting of textbooks on the flora of the Channel Islands.

Francis Masson (1741-1805) has the distinction of being the first plant-collector ever sent out on a foreign expedition by the now world-famous Kew Gardens. His mission was to go to the Cape of Good Hope and his instructions were to gather as many new plants and bulbs as possible. This trip into the interior of Southern Africa began in December 1772, and Masson describes the region as being 'enamelled with the greatest number of flowers I ever saw'. He discovered a profusion of plant life and brought back specimens of heath, gladioli and irises – in all more than 400 new species. Many plants now common in our conservatories were first brought back to Britain by Masson, and the Swedish-born founder of modern botany, Linnaeus, named the genus Massonia after him.

But the most intriguing aspect of his expedition for wanderers along the margins of Scottish history concerns Narien Sarniensis, the Jersey Lily. It is the adopted flower of the Channel Islands but, despite its name (Sarniensis means belonging to the Channel Islands), it was thought to have come originally from Japan in a rather odd manner.

Tradition has it that in the seventeenth century a ship *en route* to Britain carrying bulbs of the plant was wrecked among the islands, the bulbs being washed ashore and on to the coastal dunes where they spontaneously flowered a few years later. Because the port of origin was in the Far East, it was always assumed that the beautiful flowers had their home in Japan.

The real story emerged, however, when 4,000 feet up on Table Mountain, the lily, with its 'marvellous pink or crimson flowers suffused with a radiance like a golden jewel', was found growing in profusion by Masson. It then became clear they had been taken on board when the ship berthed at Cape Town on its way to Europe.

Masson had an adventurous life even after he left the botanical splendours of South Africa behind. The wild flowers of North America attracted his interest and he set off for the New World. However, he reached New York only after a series of scrapes, one of which saw his ship attacked and sunk by pirates. He died in Montreal, Canada.

September 9

1574   Fornication and adultery were on the increase in Edinburgh; clergy warned of severe punishments for those indulging in such pastimes.

1630   Currie tailor Alexander Blair was condemned to death for marrying his first wife's half-brother's daughter – incest in the confused eyes of the law of Scotland.

1857   Queen Victoria, seeking fresh air, ordered windows of Crathie church opened because such a vast throng had gathered for Sunday service.

1916   Police visited tea and smoking-rooms in Glasgow and noted names of all men of military age who were wearing civilian garb.

1962   Work was to begin on 4,000 houses in the model suburb of Pollok in Glasgow, 'preserved in its natural surroundings'.

Verbal Abuse

Only a few years before the Reformation burst upon Scotland, our soldiers hurled abuse at the English army amidst the tumult of the Battle of Pinkie because the English had abandoned the Catholic faith.

September 10

1462   Poet Robert Henryson, formerly a schoolmaster at Dunfermline, was admitted to Glasgow University as licentiate in Arts and a Bachelor of Law.

1547   Battle of Pinkie near Musselburgh ended in a defeat for the Scots under the Earl of Arran, and up to 10,000 Scots were reported slain.

1583   Kate the Witch was secretly hired by the Earl of Arran 'for a new plaid and six pounds' to harangue Walsingham, the English ambassador, wherever he appeared publicly in Scotland.

1907   Glasgow United Free Church Presbytery heard of the evils for boys and girls of ice-cream shops where there existed 'endless opportunities for demoralisation'.

1985   Scotland football manager Jock Stein collapsed and died at Ninian Park, Cardiff, minutes after his team qualified for the World Cup finals.

Without Prejudice

Lord Braxfield was a very talented judge but occasionally he played fast and loose with judicial procedure. In the 1790s, during a political trial, he remarked to one of the jury as he headed for the jury box, 'Come awa', Maister Horner, come awa', and help us hang ane o' thae damned scoundrels.'

September 11

1297   English feelings of invincibility were shattered at Stirling Bridge when the Scots under Wallace achieved a brilliant tactical victory.

1600   A month after the Gowrie Conspiracy security was tightened around the Scottish court, and restrictions were placed on the numbers allowed into the king's presence.

1789   New steamboat service introduced on the Forth between Newhaven and Grangemouth.

1838   Annual influx of Irish sheep-shearers reported at East Linton in East Lothian with the local gentry paying a penny per day.

1911   Twenty-game draughts-match between James Wylie, 'The Herd Laddie', champion of the world, and William Bryden, West of Scotland champion, ended with a convincing win for Wylie – 4–0 and 16 drawn.

Wrecker's Prayer

The low-lying island of Sanday in Orkney has been the scene of numerous shipwrecks over the centuries. Tradition has it that local residents were not averse of a dark night to drawing hapless vessels on to the rocks. In stormy weather the minister is said to have prayed: 'Lord, send a vessel to the poor island of Sanday.'

September 12

1578   Common people of Glasgow and Edinburgh were said to be very upset by Government efforts to raise the value of the coin; refusal to accept the new rates was punishable by death.

1773   Dr Samuel Johnson and his biographer James Boswell were entertained at Kingsburgh by Flora MacDonald and her husband.

1858   A cow belonging to Mr Watson of Keillor was offered for sale at Aberdeen; she had reached the 'hoary age' of 34 and apparently looked every year.

1885   World-record victory was established by Arbroath FC when they edged out Bon Accord 36–0 in a Scottish cup-tie.

1937   Campaign to stamp out gambling schools in Edinburgh had a vigorous opening when a raid on a South Side housing scheme netted 30 arrests.

Fangs for the Memory

American comics and biblical traditions have both been cited to explain an odd affair in the 1950s when Gorbals children in Glasgow went in search of a child-eating vampire with metal teeth.

September 13

1645   Covenanters under David Leslie defeated Montrose and his Royalists at the Battle of Philiphaugh near Selkirk.

1746   Party of fugitives led by Bonnie Prince Charlie left Cluny's Cage on Ben Alder *en route* to Borrodale and France in the aftermath of Culloden.

1877   Freedom of Glasgow given to Civil War hero and ex-President of the United States, Ulysses Grant.

1937   Increasing number of crofters around Kingussie were letting their homes to summer visitors, a valuation appeal was told.

1978   Strathclyde Regional Council confirmed a decision to add fluoride to the area's water-supply.

Bogged Down

The world's most noted escapologist, Harry Houdini, once locked himself in a toilet in Glasgow's famous Empire Theatre in Sauchiehall Street and had to be freed by theatre staff.

September 14

1184   King William the Lion confirmed the lands of the monks of Newbattle Abbey following a site inspection by leading Scots civic officers including the Sheriff of Haddington.

1402   Battle of Homildon Hill in Northumberland. The Scots were defeated by the English and many of the Scots nobility were taken prisoner; as many as 1,500 of the fleeing foot-soldiers are said to have drowned in the Tweed.

1600   A party of 'rough Borderers' came to the fair at Jedburgh and slew Thomas Kerr, claiming they were acting on a sheriff's order.

1643   Foundation of the Scots Church in Rotterdam by exiled Covenanters.

1901   Memorial unveiled in Dundee to J.B. Lindsay, pioneer of wireless telegraphy.

Toil and Trouble

Some authorities suggest that James VI & I, a firm believer in sorcery, specifically requested that Shakespeare write the three witches into the plot of *Macbeth* because they would lend authenticity to the story.

September 15

1266   Birth in Berwickshire of the philosopher and theologian John Duns Scotus.

1595   Edinburgh High School pupils refused a holiday, rioted and took control of the school buildings. During the siege, a city bailie was shot dead but the young gentlemen were freed without punishment.

1620   Head of St Margaret, authenticated as genuine by the Bishop of Antwerp, was made available for public veneration.

1652   English justice established at Leith under Cromwell's occupying forces found favour with the Scots, one diarist acknowledging that the English were more indulgent to the Scots than the Scots were to themselves.

1889   An apprentice flesher was fined 20s for driving his horse and van furiously through Alloa and knocking down a pedestrian.

Ashes to Ashes

Fourteen standards, which were carried by the Jacobite army during the final defeat at Culloden, were brought to Edinburgh for ignominious public destruction. Chimney-sweeps carried the clan flags while the hangman was entrusted with Bonnie Prince Charlie's standard. At the Mercat Cross they were burned 'with every contempt'.

THE DARK SHADOW OF HOMESTEAD

The names of two famous Scots exiles are sadly linked in the violent and bloody end to a steelworks strike in Pennsylvania which stains the early industrial relations record of the United States.

When Andrew Carnegie, the great ironmaster, visited his hometown of Dunfermline in the autumn of 1912 it was as the greatest benefactor Scotland had ever known. In every sense he was a local hero.

After the family emigrated to Pittsburgh in 1848, Andrew worked to amass a staggering fortune. In his later years much of this was dispersed through a multitude of health and educational projects both in Britain and in the United States. It has been calculated that he literally gave away something in the region of £70m.

But if Andrew Carnegie (who as a child declared the overtly republican goal of 'killing a king') had a blank spot, it was surely in the field of labour relations. Despite his paternalistic outlook as an employer, he abhorred the idea of the ordinary workers 'getting organised'.

In 1892 his employees at the sprawling, smoke-shrouded Homestead Steelworks struck for higher pay while Carnegie was on holiday in Scotland and his partner, Henry C. Frick, was minding the store. The management were determined to end the dispute by whatever means and brought in a team from the Pinkerton Detective Agency founded by the late Allan Pinkerton, a Glasgow cooper, who had been head of the American secret service.

Ostensibly they were simply there to provide an escort for steelmen who wanted to work, but the Pinkerton men effectively provoked a battle in the shadow of the steel mills which left ten dead and up to 100 injured. Cowed, the workforce returned on half pay and the débâcle resulted in a life-long frostiness between Frick and Carnegie.

Some say, however, that Carnegie knew all the details of what was planned but the comment of a workers' leader on his return, 'It wouldn't have happened if you'd been here, Mr Carnegie' must have haunted the expatriate for the rest of his life. Strangely, it's possible to trace the start of Carnegie's philanthropic giving to the years after the Homestead Riot. A coincidence? We'll probably never know.

Sidelines

When Carnegie's parents were planning to emigrate they had to borrow £20 for their passage before they could sail for New York. Pinkerton honed his skills as a detective by hiding inside barrels and listening to criminal conversations. Carnegie spent £500,000 during his lifetime on church organs, because he believed their sound was 'the true Word of God'. Pinkerton was accused of prolonging the bloody American Civil War by up to three years by overestimating Confederate military strength.

September 16

1421   A cloudburst in East Lothian saw boats floating down the aisle of the Church of the Friars at Haddington, and a dozen mills on the nearby River Tyne were destroyed by floodwater.

1606   Reports from the Borders suggested that His Majesty's Commissioner George, Earl of Dunbar, had been busy rounding up and hanging thieves and troublemakers.

1873   Queen Victoria travelled on the steamer *Gondolier* on the Caledonian Canal and although she admired the engineering, she is said to have found the journey monotonous.

1907   Nearly 7,000 Kilmarnock schoolchildren were each supplied with half-a-pound of Victoria plums by the local MP Cameron Corbett.

1937   Ten young Irish 'tattie howkers' died in a fire in a blazing bothy at Kirkintilloch.

Kerr's Error

In London on business in 1792 Provost Kerr of Peebles attended a meeting of the Whig Club when the 'Majesty of the People' was toasted. The Provost, who had been struggling to make out the English accents, rose, to everyone's amazement, and made a long and pompous speech in reply. It transpired that Kerr thought the toast had been 'The Magistrates of Peebles'.

September 17

1830   The Northern Lights, the Aurora Borealis, were reported in Dumfriesshire as an amazing luminous arch.

1839   Glasgow weaver William Cuthbertson was sentenced to seven years transportation for stealing a pocket handkerchief.

1861   Mrs Mechin, wife of Stirling's ratcatcher, died after swallowing a quantity of arsenic from her husband's stock.

1923   Britain would be a 'dry' nation within ten years it was predicted at a Glasgow meeting of the Anti-Saloon League.

1942   Glasgow supplied almost 10,000 tons of metal railings for the war effort, the highest total of any city outside London.

Wily Windbreaker

One of the most famed 'wise' women of seventeenth-century Perthshire was Janet of Black Ruthven whose speciality was 'helpin' bairns who had gotten ane dint o' ill wind'.

September 18

1547   The Duke of Somerset, victor at the Battle of Pinkie, retreated with his Protestant army after a week of pillaging; their departure was marked by the burning of Leith.

1745   Audiences at the Drury Lane and Covent Garden theatres in London sang 'God Save the King', for the first time as news came of the advance of the Jacobite Army.

1841   Sutherland sheriff, procurator fiscal and sheriff's officers, were carrying out an eviction at Durness when they were attacked by a mob of 400, some of the lawmen 'narrowly escaping with their lives'.

1939   Tenement closes in Glasgow were reinforced to serve as air-raid shelters.

1959   Application by the Duke of Argyll seeking to have his wife banned from Inveraray pinned up at the Court of Session as one of the most sensational divorce actions of the century got under way.

Firm Footing

The hard-wearing and water-resistant flagstones of West Caithness were used in Victorian railway stations, markets, factories and public places from Bombay to Brazil, from London to Sydney. More recently the Royal Mile in Edinburgh has been reflagged using Caithness stone.

September 19

1698   Episcopacy (rule by bishops) was formally abolished in Scotland and their revenues confiscated.

1721   William Robertson, historian and principal of Edinburgh University and praised by Gibbon and Voltaire for his writings, was born in Midlothian.

1842   Edinburgh taxidermist Mr Carfine began work on a capercailzie, a blackcock, three red grouse and three hares shot by Prince Albert.

1906   James Robson, teacher of music at Hutcheson's Grammar School, began his retirement – at the age of 96.

1935   People from all over Islay gathered in the White Hart Hotel for the inauguration of their new telephone link with the mainland.

Some Like it Hot

This century's proliferation of Indian restaurants is not the first Scots skirmish with hot dishes. In the thirteenth century huge quantities of spice were used in cooking at the court of Alexander III. One chronicler describes the dishes as 'burning with wildfire'.

September 20

1580   Ship carrying Edinburgh merchants from Danzig forced to land crew and passengers on St Colm's Isle in the Forth after plague was discovered on board; at least 40 of the travellers died.

1789   Citizens of Aberdeen asked to pay 25 guineas towards annual board and lodgings for the council chambers cat which was brought in because of rat infestation.

1806   Plans unveiled for a tunnel under the River Forth between North and South Queensferry.

1944   Plagues of midges were a blight on Scots tourism said Secretary of State Tom Johnston, anti-mosquito techniques developed by the United States army might be used, he suggested.

1967   Last of the great Clyde-built liners, *Queen Elizabeth II*, launched at John Brown's yard in Clydebank.

Happy Holidays

Lanark-born William Lithgow, adventurer and travel-writer whose *Peregrinations* (published in the early 1600s) is considered the first travel-book written by a Scot, was once imprisoned and tortured by the hot metal merchants of the Spanish Inquisition on the Costa del Sol.

Awaiting the launch of the QEII

September 21

1513   King James V, aged one year, five months and ten days, crowned at Stirling following the death of his father at Flodden.

1675   A great storm which blew down centuries-old oaks in Central Scotland and flattened corn also wrecked the Earl of Argyll's expedition against the Macleans on Mull.

1745   Colonel James Gardiner was killed fighting for the Government side against the Jacobites at Prestonpans – only a few yards from his own front door.

1860   Self-supporting cooking-centres for working folk were set up in Glasgow by Thomas Corbett, providing the model for other successful depots in the urban areas of Britain.

1948   The Grangemouth librarian in his annual report said that cinema, dance-halls, and radio had made reading unfashionable.

Quack, Quack

One of the most famous phoney medical men of eighteenth-century Scotland was nicknamed Doctor Duds because of his dishevelled appearance. He was attacked so often by the disbelieving throng at his street stage that he always had a coach waiting to make his escape. The most ancient Scots patent approving quack medicine was granted in 1487 when James III confirmed the use of St Fillan's crosier, which had supposed healing properties, to a family in Strathfillan, Perthshire.

September 22

1483   New tax-roll for towns north of the Forth showed Aberdeen and Dundee each paying £26.13.4d while Inverbervie had to find 10s.

1631   Sir John Ogilvy of Craig, 'a known Papist', was ordered to be detained in St Andrews for preventing his servants and children going to the kirk.

1845   Britain's largest recorded school of pilot whales, 1,540 creatures, came into Quendale Bay, Shetland, the site of the l990s *Braer* disaster.

1935   Chancellor of the Exchequer Neville Chamberlain, speaking at Hawick, said Britain's low level of defensive readiness was unhelpful in efforts to secure peace.

1975   Scotland's first bomb-squad was set up by Strathclyde Police after a series of explosions in the West of Scotland.

Dicing with Death

McPherson of Cluny earned a remarkable first in the mid-1700s when he set up a casino in his Jacobite hideaway on the slopes of Ben Alder.

MIGHTY CROMWELL TAKES A NOSEDIVE

For days afterwards it was the talk of the taverns in the High Street, around the luckenbooths and along the Grassmarket. Oliver Cromwell, the future Lord Protector, had arrived in the city fresh from his victory at Preston. The day was 4 October 1648. He was to return to Edinburgh again two years later having defeated the Covenanters under David Leslie at Dunbar.

He came to the city as a mighty figure who held the future of Scotland in his grasp. His visits were occasions of historic import. Powerful figures in seventeenth-century Scotland sought an audience with him and, of course, the crowds turned out in force to catch a glimpse of this austere and hard-headed leader.

But from both visits, what was the abiding memory of the great man which remained with the ordinary folk of Scotland and immediately became the talk of the steamie? Was it his noble military bearing, his stern and resolute demeanour, his skilful diplomacy or perhaps his tactical genius? Indeed, no. What impressed the good citizens of Edinburgh so much was the size of the general's nose. The Cromwellian conk was, by all accounts, a notable landmark and the source of great hilarity and anatomical speculation for quite a time thereafter.

It would appear that the people of the capital in the 1600s were a rather pass-remarkable crowd and that Cromwell did not suffer alone. Witness the visit in 1611 of a certain John Stercovius who wore his colourful Polish national dress around town. The citizens, it is recorded, 'hooted him in the streets'. The Edinburgh Festival parade, of course, ended all that sort of prejudice but John didn't take this insulting behaviour lightly. In response he penned a *Legend of Reproaches against the Scottish Nation*. This so angered James VI that a legal action was initiated on the Continent seeking the beheading of the hapless Pole.

If the most memorable aspect of the Cromwellian occupation of Edinburgh was the Protector's nose, in Orkney the garrison got little credit for improving the islanders' lot. Tradition there says that the main 'achievement' of the soldiers was to introduce door-locks, cabbages and venereal disease.

The bold and popular commander of the Black Watch, Dickson of Kilbucko, was famed throughout Scotland for his bright, cherry nose – possibly accentuated by his liking for a drop of the hard stuff. During an audience with King George III, who knew him well, the monarch jokingly asked how much Dickson had paid to have his nose painted. Unabashed, the soldier is said to have replied, 'I cannot tell, Majesty, because it is not yet finished.'

September 23

704   St Adamnan of Iona, biographer of Columba, died.

1680   The king, the Duke of York and leading Scots politicians were digesting the news that they had been excommunicated by Donald Cargill, last remaining field-preacher of the Covenant.

1842   *John O' Groats Journal* apologised for suggesting that the nurse to the Prince of Wales had been dismissed because of her 'over-love of gin'.

1845   Highlander Donald Ross, who had been employed as a special messenger during the 1745 Uprising, died at Kiltearn, Ross-shire, aged 116.

1983   Glasgow's Labour administration looked into the possibility of taking over the Edinburgh Festival. The capital's Lord Provost would only comment, 'Do they want the Castle too?'

Sting in the Tail

A European pioneer of beekeeping was John Geddie, sheriff clerk of Fife who designed an eight-sided hive in 1650 which gained royal approval. Not so successful were the first experiments with beekeeping in Orkney in the early 1800s. The gentleman who imported the bees discovered the mouth of the hive stopped up with clay and the bees suffocated. An anxious servant had been afraid that the bees might not know the geography of Orkney and so get lost when he saw them flying off to hunt for pollen.

September 24

1332   Edward Balliol, son of King John Balliol, crowned King of Scots at Scone following his victory at Dupplin Moor.

1611   Sir James Lawson of Humbie, East Lothian, perished when his horse fell into quicksand at Balhelvie Sands. He was found the following morning but his horse was never seen again.

1712   Widespread flooding in West Central Scotland; hundreds of families were marooned in their homes in Glasgow city centre; boats sailed in the Briggate and many lives were lost.

1839   Eagle with a five-foot wingspan trapped in the dome of Girdleness Lighthouse in Kincardineshire during a storm.

1962   Scottish Interplanetary Society launched a space awareness project, but admitted it might be a year or two before the first Scots astronaut.

Occult Earl

Francis Stewart, Fifth Earl of Bothwell, who had been accused of dealing with witches in efforts to bring about the downfall of James VI, ended his days in Italy where he earned a meagre living telling fortunes.

September 25

1790   A major breakout attempt by inmates at the overcrowded Perth Prison was foiled.

1793   Last instance of a woman being whipped through the streets of Glasgow; Mary Douglas, convicted of housebreaking in Bridgeton, was also banished for life.

1856   A labourer was jailed for ten days for stealing two slices of bread (unbuttered) and four (buttered) from a Glasgow shipyard; his plea was one of hunger.

1886   Seven people, including two Glasgow councillors, were killed and many injured at Crarae Quarry on Loch Fyne while watching blasting operations.

1923   Forty men died when a pit at Redding near Falkirk was inundated by a flash flood.

Up the Wrong Tree

When a valuable cargo of cinnamon was wrecked on the East Lothian coast in 1528, the local people mistook it for common tree-bark and burned it as fuel on the cottage fires.

September 26

1290   Margaret, 'Maid of Norway' and granddaughter of Alexander III, and the acknowledged heir to the throne of Scotland, died in Orkney *en route* to her new home; she was only seven.

1653   The 'trembling exies' – an ague or fever – had Scotland in its grip and, along with smallpox, claimed many lives, young and old.

1858   Report that the Riot Act had been read in Rothesay as Free Church members protested an order for services to be preached in English at least once each Sunday as well as in Gaelic.

1861　First British Open Golf Championship was held at Prestwick and won by Tom Morris, a native of St Andrews.

1934　Passenger-liner *Queen Mary* launched from John Brown's shipyard in Clydebank; the 81,000-ton Cunarder was sent on her way with a bottle of Australian wine.

Kiltie Wilcox

In 1959 an Afrikaans-speaking comedian, Al Wilcox, agreed to wear the kilt in public for a year to qualify for £30,000 under the terms of his grandfather's will.

September 27

1588　Crew of a wrecked Spanish Armada galleon took refuge on remote Fair Isle, halfway between Orkney and Shetland.

1607　A priest was taken to the Mercat Cross in Edinburgh where his 'mass clothes and chalice' were publicly burned.

1848　Frederick Chopin gave a recital in Glasgow's Merchant Hall, but only a small audience turned out to see the great French pianist.

1938　*Queen Elizabeth* – the largest passenger-liner ever built – was launched at Clydebank, but officials were dismayed to see her slowly begin her slide into the Clyde before the launch speech.

1979　Clydebank guitarist Jimmy McCulloch, who played with Paul McCartney's band Wings, was found dead in his London home.

Keep up the Good Work

Andrew Barton, the sixteenth-century Scots scourge of North Sea pirates, anxious to prove he was doing a good job, despatched three barrels full to the brim with the heads of Flemish pirates for the king's inspection.

September 28

1396　Clan fight on the North Inch of Perth in the presence of Robert III saw Clan Chattan overcome Clan Kay with the loss of a total of 48 clansmen.

1598　Two Stirling men were put on bread and water for a day by the local kirk session for playing dice all night.

1660　Magistrates in Edinburgh licensed Willie Woodcock to set up a coach-run between Leith and Edinburgh, the hire 'up and down' was a shilling per person.

1760　Gilbert Burns, brother of the national bard, was born at Alloway, Ayrshire.

| 1836 | Ploughman Allan Stevenson died at Johnstone, aged 85. In the 1770s he caused a sensation as the first man to plough without a 'gaudsman' who prompted the horses into action. |

Voice of Experience

George Buchanan, tutor to young King James VI, was so worried about his royal pupil's weakness in complying with every request that one day he handed a document to the young monarch which James signed without question. Buchanan had transferred royal authority to himself for 15 days and insisted on the title of Majesty for the period. When young James, thinking his master had lost the place, asked for an explanation, Buchanan produced the document and gave him a lecture on rashness. Buchanan died on 28 September 1582, aged 76.

September 29

1589	The court of King James was stunned by the death of Jane Kennedy, Lady Melville, drowned when a ferry sank in the Forth; she had attended Queen Mary on the scaffold at Fotheringay Castle.
1621	Charter to colonise Nova Scotia was granted to Sir William Alexander of Menstrie.
1781	Pigs roaming the streets of Annan and desecrating kirkyards, forced magistrates to impose a five-shilling fine on the owner of any swine found wandering the burgh.
1891	Three painters were killed when scaffolding collapsed on the Forth Railway Bridge opened the previous year; 57 men died during construction.
1940	Lunde, the new propaganda minister in occupied Norway, declared that Orkney and Shetland formed a necessary part of Norway's living space.

Heading for Success

Experts consider that the first surgical operation on the brain was performed by Sir William McEwan at Glasgow Royal Infirmary in 1869 when he stopped a haemorrhage.

SPOTTING THE SINISTER CLERIC

In the annals of murder and mayhem the neat redstone village of Spott tucked away in the shadow of the Lammermuir Hills in East Lothian, commands an especially malignant chapter. Here, in 1570, a murder was committed, so cold and calculating that it still chills the blood in the retelling more than 400 years on.

As the church bells rang for Sunday devotion, the Revd John Kello slowly choked his wife to death with a blanket then faked her suicide by hanging. He then went out and calmly delivered what was widely regarded by the congregation as his best-ever sermon. On 4 October 1570, Kello, who had been regarded as a prime example of the parish preacher in the young Reformed church, was brought out into the autumn afternoon before a large crowd in Edinburgh's Grassmarket and hanged.

The motive for the killing appears to have been greed. He had impressed a number of the local ladies and the thought of a comfortable future not dependent on his stipend transformed him from concerned minister to cold-blooded murderer.

Kello's clever cover-up might have worked. He told his parishioners that his wife had been in low spirits and even suggested that she may have been under a spell cast by a local coven. East Lothian, of course, was notorious as a busy centre for diabolic practices around this time – witches and warlocks were everywhere. This theory began to gain credence and it did seem for a time that the evil Kello might be home and dry.

That was until the nightmares started. Kello dreamed of throwing himself into a river to escape the wrath of some dread judge. He was so concerned he consulted a colleague in Dunbar who sensed that something was tragically amiss.

Eventually, Kello confessed to the crime and after being hanged, his corpse was burned and his property confiscated. Spott remains a beautiful corner of Scotland. Well worth a visit on a summer afternoon. It might be advisable, however, to keep well clear on 4 October.

In the league table of cold and calculating crimes even John Kello must surely give way to an anonymous French soldier who fought with the victorious Scots at the Battle of Nesbit in 1355. This man was so bitter over the slaying of his father by the English that he purchased a group of prisoners, took them to a secluded spot and beheaded them, coldly and methodically, in an act of terrible vengeance.

Well Named

When William Wallace routed an English force on the north shore of the Clyde in what is now Glasgow city centre, the victorious Scots dumped the bodies of the enemy into a nearby spring. Wallace is said to have shouted, 'Stock it well! Stock it well!' Hence, Stockwell Street got its name. The bad quality of the water from that spring was consistently reported by local historians thereafter.

September 30

1426 Workmen's wages and the repair of castles were among the topics for a meeting of the Scots Parliament at Perth.

1652 Much to the delight and amazement of the Cromwellian garrison at Leith, a pilot whale was stranded in the harbour.

1839 A huge Cheviot tup, weighing over 20 stones and answering to the name of 'Jock', was on show in Glasgow.

1907 Animal lovers in Scotland were delighted by the arrival of the commercial motor vehicle, ending the daily grind for thousands of cart-horses.

1920 Lord Hamilton appeared before the Committee on Smoke and Noxious Vapours in Glasgow armed with his wife's blouse which had been ruined by smoke from works near his Lanarkshire home.

Post Haste

The determination of the early postal service in Scotland is illustrated by an advert for the new Edinburgh-Inverness service in 1669. It defiantly stated, 'A waggon will leave the Grassmarket for Inverness every Tuesday, God willing, but on Wednesday whether or no'!' Even into the early 1700s a mail delivery was such an event in Hawick that when letters arrived they were set out on a stall on market-day to be claimed. This attracted great interest particularly from those who never received correspondence.

October 1

1658 Town Council of Glasgow gave permission for Robert Marshall to set up business as a house-painter – a rare profession in those days.

1726 Summer road-building programme in the Highlands, by the troops of General Wade, was completed.

1851 A survey showed that there were 146 licensed brewers in Scotland.

1891 A football match in Glasgow was thrown into chaos when a herd of bullocks from an adjoining field was attracted by the colourful team strips. One goalie fled and the opposition scored.

1978 Glaswegian Ian McCaskill joined the BBC team as a weatherman.

Domain of the Brewster Wife

For centuries the task of producing fine ale in Scots wayside-inns was left to the woman of the house, and her skills in brewing and the quality of the ale determined the success of the business. The husband would meddle at his peril in the activities of the brewster-wife.

October 2

1263   Battle of Largs saw a historic and significant victory for the Scots over the Norsemen, whose fleet had been devastated by a storm of 'almost supernatural ferocity' on the eve of the battle.

1625   Scottish burghs were ordered to pay an annual tax totalling £40,000 to the Crown, ranging from £815.12s.6d for Glasgow to 100 merks (1 merk equals 13s.4d) for Hamilton.

1721   Government factors were ambushed in Kintail by Jacobite Mackenzies. This event confirmed the view in the South equating Jacobite clans with banditry and disorder.

1894   Motherwell police-commissioners agreed to a scheme to light the town by electricity.

1942   HMS *Curacao* accidentally sunk by the troopship *Queen Mary* in the Western Approaches; 331 officers and crew were lost.

Basic Rations

It is generally accepted that the Duke of Rothesay starved to death in 1402 while a prisoner at Falkland Palace in Fife. Less easy to verify is a suggestion that he was so hungry that he ate his own hands.

October 3

1357   Under the Treaty of Berwick, David II was freed after 11 years in English captivity; conditions for Scotland were very severe with a ransom of £100,000 agreed.

1570   Rumour rife throughout Scotland that John Knox, who had been ill, had become deformed, with his head twisted on his shoulders, and was unlikely ever to preach again.

1637   Almost a hundred soldiers drowned when four ships, lying at anchor in Aberdeen harbour, were driven ashore and wrecked during a gale.

1842   Severe drought had drastically reduced the level of water in the Monkland Canal in Glasgow; many mills were closed and up to 2,000 people faced unemployment.

1940   Scottish Southern League Management Committee fix admission prices for league games at 1/1d and for boys and soldiers, 7d.

Phlegmatic Reaction

The Heart of Midlothian is a section of paving stone laid in the shape of a heart outside St Giles Cathedral in Edinburgh's High Street. It was the popular name for the old Tolbooth which stood on the spot, and citizens still spit on the slabs as a mark of contempt for authority.

October 4

1588   Concern in Glasgow over the spread of plague, which had already reached Paisley, led to the town gates being guarded preventing the entry of people from infected areas.

1837   Third ship of the season left Tobermory for Australia with 300 emigrants; a piper played during emotional scenes at the quayside.

1883   Boys Brigade movement founded in Glasgow by Sir William Smith.

1911   Dr Joseph Bell, distinguished Edinburgh surgeon and the prototype for Conan Doyle's Sherlock Holmes, died, aged 74.

1982   Allan Wells (100 metres) and Meg Ritchie (discus) won gold medals for Scotland at the Brisbane Commonwealth Games.

Medium Rare, Madame

The wayward wife of a MacFarlane chief had been dallying with Sir Humphrey Colquhoun of Luss. When the knight was slain by the MacFarlanes in a skirmish, the poor woman had her boyfriend's genitals served up to her as sweetmeats.

October 5

1318   Edward Bruce, brother of Robert, the hero of Bannockburn, died in battle at Dundalk after being crowned King of Ireland and notching up 18 successive victories.

1451   Members of the powerful Douglas family were condemned as traitors and their land and property was confiscated.

1790   An Edinburgh businessman was looking for boys and girls of eight years and upwards to make pinheads, giving them the opportunity to earn their bread instead of being a burden on the community.

1840   A dredger working on the Clyde at Whiteinch brought up an ancient two-edged sword, four feet long with the letter 'S' engraved on the blade.

1974   Two young Scots Guards from Barrhead were among five people killed in the IRA Guildford pub-bombings.

Saucers in the Sky

Moffat's Lord Hugh Dowding, Commanding Officer of the Royal Air Force in the Second World War, was convinced that we were being visited by extra-terrestrials. In 1954 he said, 'Flying saucers are real – and they are interplanetary . . . the evidence for their existence is quite overwhelming.'

October 6

1508   James IV leased the Burgh Muir to citizens of Edinburgh allowing them to clear it of wood; timber-fronted houses began to appear in the town as a result of this concession.

1744   James McGill, who became a fur-trader after emigrating to Canada and founded the university in Montreal named after him, was born in Glasgow.

1843   Inspector of the Poor in Glasgow's Gorbals was fined £1.10s for assaulting a woman who applied to him for assistance.

1943   Roxy picture-house in Hamilton fined £25 for not showing their quota of British films.

1983   Outer Hebrides, unable to find a local bagpipe instructor to teach in island schools, gave the job to a pipe-major from the Lowlands.

Less than a Jailbreak

The 'open' nature of Scottish prisons in the early nineteenth century is illustrated by a court case in Inverness where a prisoner, scornful of security, admitted escaping. He told the bench that he had warned the gaoler that if the food didn't improve he would leave, which he promptly did!

SORRY JOHN, YOU'RE JUST NOT ON

Ah, that accursed handle! Nobody, but nobody, was going to allow the son of Robert II to take the throne of Scotland and remain a 'John'. Bitter memories of the last King of Scots to carry that dread name a century before – John Balliol, Toom Tabard (empty coat) – remained too fresh. He had sold out his kingdom under English pressure and he was never forgiven.

And yet the roots of the name were innocuous enough. From the Hebrew word meaning 'Grace of the Lord' it was popular in the Eastern Church and was brought back to England by the Crusaders in the twelfth century. Its earliest form seems to have been the Latin Johannes and today it is still one of the commonest boys' names in Britain.

Plans went ahead for the Coronation of John, Earl of Carrick, eldest son of Robert II at Scone in 1390. However, there was much whispering behind hands in the royal apartments and among the nobility about the most suitable new name for the monarch. How the debate was conducted we can only speculate but it would appear that any Scottish variant of John such as Jock, or the Gaelic forms, Ian and Iain, were ruled out straight away as being too lightweight.

Here we can see one of the great missed opportunities of Scottish history. With a wee bit of imagination a new sequence of impressive regal names might have begun. Out would go the solid old stand-bys such as David, Robert, Malcolm and Alexander and in would have come a zippy new dynasty of kings and queens whose names would have echoed down the centuries.

One of the first regulations should have been that the same name should never be used twice. Perhaps scholars trying to memorise the dates of the Stuart monarchs would disagree (what a bonus the Jameses were in that respect) but it would have made Scotland's royal genealogical tables a lot more interesting.

Now to my mind it's one of the great anomalies of Scottish history that this nation has never had a King Andrew. From the Greek word for 'manly' it seems to me to be everything Scottish and, of course, with the present construction of our royal family, Andrew may yet be king.

Gaelic should have its place and I would like to have seen Alasdair, King of Scots. That has a nice sturdy and secure ring about it. Our King Alasdair would have been the sort of bloke you could have trusted. King Archie would have been an earthy, man of the people. Although the roots of Archibald are Teutonic, it was adopted almost exclusively by the Scots after the Norman Conquest.

Brian is a Celtic name meaning 'hill' or 'strength' and surely would have been an appropriate name for a monarch of the land of hills and heather. King Cameron, I'm not so enthusiastic about.

Sounds very much like a triple-decker hamburger, brand of malt whisky or Texan rancher who should be running for President. King Colin has a nice, snappy feel and he'd be the sort of person to get things done. Dirk (a diminutive of Derek) has a military feel, and King Douglas would have been a stout, cheery old chap, much inclined to slapping the court jester on the back and loudly cheering his cunning stunts.

The more alert amongst you will see that I've only reached 'D' on this epic voyage. The possibilities are limitless. If you've any likely candidates, please let me know. Yes, I almost forgot. After all the lengthy deliberations, the powers that were in 1390, including the new king, we're led to believe, plumped for Robert III. Imaginative, or what?

October 7

1337   Edward III declared his claim to the throne of France but his pleas to the Scots for a lasting peace, which would have secured his northern flank, were rejected.

1780   Patrick Ferguson, Aberdeenshire-born inventor of the breech-loading rifle, was killed with other Loyalists at King's Mountain, South Carolina, during the American War of Independence.

1862   Teacher sought for Tighnabruaich school in Argyll, a married man with a knowledge of music was preferred, and the salary offered was £30.

1876   Bowl of Samian ware – dropped, it was thought, from a Roman vessel – was found in mudbeds at Flesher's Haugh in the centre of Glasgow.

1983   Scots walk more than their counterparts in the United Kingdom; during the summer of 1983 a survey showed they regularly walked two miles or more.

Bury 'em Deep

A major problem after funerals in the Highlands in the fifteenth century was to ensure that the recently deceased were not dug up by marauding wolves.

October 8

1593   Magistrates in Aberdeen ordered the town cleared of the host of 'idle persons not having land nor master, craft nor occupation'.

1630   Six people, including Lord Melcum, were burned to death when the castle of Frendraught near Huntly caught fire around midnight. Arson was suspected and John Meldrum was later tried, convicted and executed.

1807   Honest Bob, a bay, won the Dumfries Maiden Plate and the first prize of £50.

1907   Doctors called in to measure the strain faced by Glasgow postmen who had miles of tenement stairs to scale.

1960   Lady Redesdale, mother of the controversial Mitford sisters, was earning a crust delivering letters on the island of Inchkenneth off Mull to its 13 residents.

Dust a Minute

One of the most bizarre medical remedies offered up by physicians in Edinburgh during the 1800s was powdered Egyptian mummy – it was to be taken with a little milk, we're led to believe.

October 9

1571   Tillyangus in Aberdeenshire was the scene of a skirmish between the Gordon and Forbes factions; the latter were put to flight and about 120 men were killed.

1601   Cash award made to a company of theatre players who were visiting Aberdeen and may have included William Shakespeare.

1875   Queen's Park *v* Wanderers match at Hampden saw the earliest known football programme on offer to the fans.

1914   Magistrates and representatives of the licensed trade in Glasgow met to discuss ways of preventing soldiers being supplied with excessive amounts of alcohol.

1941   Lord Tyneham, a lieutenant-commander in the Royal Navy, was fined £1 at Campbeltown for poaching on the Duke of Argyll's estate at Inveraray.

Last of the Line

Colonel Alex MacDonnell was said to be the last genuine specimen of the Highland chieftain. Always attended by a retinue when travelling, he died in traditionally dramatic style – drowning while trying to escape from a grounded steamer in 1828.

October 10

1196   William the Lion commanded his bailies in Moray to ensure that all dues owed by parishioners to the local bishop should be promptly paid.

1689   Glassworks in Leith which had successfully produced green bottles and chemistry and apothecary jars was given the status of a factory, and import of foreign bottles was banned.

1733   Post due in Edinburgh on this day from London did not arrive because the post-boy, 'being in liquor', fell off his horse.

1889   Schoolboys in Hawick, Dundee, Aberdeen, Glasgow, Greenock and in Edinburgh staged an abortive 'strike' demanding shorter hours and fewer lessons.

1985   Four crewmen lost when the Macduff-based fishing boat *Ocean Harvest* sank in fierce gales east of Fraserburgh.

Ancient of Days

The little village of Fortingall in Perthshire has two quite remarkable claims to fame. It has the oldest piece of vegetation in Europe, the 3,000-year-old Fortingall Yew (56 feet in circumference when it was measured in 1796 before splitting in two). This tree may have been familiar to Pontius Pilate, the son of a Roman official, as he is said to have been born here, on the wild Caledonian frontier.

October 11

1297   One month after the momentous victory at Stirling Bridge, Wallace and Moray wrote to the mayors of Lubeck and Hamburg reporting the Scottish ports were open to foreign merchant ships.

1673   Glasgow's first coffee-house – run by Colonel Walter Whiteford – was given the go-ahead.

1852   Queen Victoria and Prince Albert watched the completion of a cairn at Balmoral to commemorate the purchase of the estate.

1886   Dornoch in Sutherland was the latest venue for a meeting of the Crofters Commission when 70 cases were heard.

1905   Five passengers were swept overboard when Clyde-built Cunard liner *Campania* was struck by a huge wave in the Atlantic, and 30 people were injured.

Ahead of the Pack

The famous physicist Lord Kelvin entered Glasgow University at the age of ten years and four months, while at the age of 14 our greatest historian Thomas Carlyle walked 100 miles to enrol at Edinburgh University.

October 12

1405   Four burghs (Edinburgh, Stirling, Lanark and Linlithgow) met at Stirling, local commerce was top of the agenda.

1467   Edinburgh Parliament raised the value of money 'not only the king's auen, bot forraine also'.

1621   Severe flooding in Perth swept away the town's beautiful new bridge across the Tay and people were rescued in large numbers from the rooftops.

1845   First sod was cut as work began on the Caledonian Railway's Glasgow-London line.

1947   Lord Boyd-Orr, a Scot who had directed his life's work towards feeding the world's poor long before it became a fashionable philosophy, learned that he had won the Nobel Peace Prize.

Name-dropping for Beginners

The first Scot to be known by name is said by some experts to be the first-century military leader, Calgacus, a thorn in the side of the occupying Romans. Also, there is a school of thought which suggests the name was invented by the Roman historian, Tacitus.

October 13

1563   Mary Queen of Scots, on her tour of the South-west, passed through Newton Stewart on her way to Kenmure near New Galloway.

1797   William Motherwell, poet and ballad-collector, was born in a tenement in Glasgow's High Street.

1861   A young Banffshire lady out walking in the parish of Logie-Coldstone in Aberdeenshire, and 'well-furnished with crinoline', was lifted off her feet by a gust and blown into a loch.

1892   For the first time ladies compete in examinations with male students at St Andrews University, and women were admitted as medical students to Edinburgh Royal Infirmary.

1906   *Forward*, Scotland's first Socialist weekly, was started.

Smoke Signals

The winter of 1803–04, with the threat of French invasion growing daily, saw perhaps the most sensational false alarm in Scottish history. Thousands of men took to arms and rushed to muster-points when a beacon at Hume Castle in Berwickshire was lit by mistake and other warning beacons through southern Scotland were set ablaze in response.

SECRET OF THE SILVER DARLIN'S

Tam Broon, the Fifer who couldn't wipe the fishy grin off his face, is noted in our alternative annals of Scottish history for perhaps the most audacious 'theft' on record. It was Tam who single-handedly pirated the River Forth herring fishery.

Shortly after the unsuccessful Jacobite rising of 1745–46 the herring began to disappear from the estuary of the Forth. Gloomy Stuart sympathisers and the more superstitious members of the community blamed the loss on the Prince's downfall. Whatever the explanation the neat fishing villages of Fife were in trouble.

Most fishermen, hauling in their empty nets, were convinced that the shoals of 'silver darlin's', one of the most abundant and long-lived species in the world (they can have a life-span of 20 years), were gone from the estuary, probably for ever. Although these beautifully streamlined fish with their metallic sheen had been taken from these waters for centuries, it did seem that the end had come.

No attempt was made to track them down – fatalism prevailed. Even in the 1770s when the mainsail of a fishing boat fell into the bay at Inverkeithing and was brought back to the surface, its folds brimming with herring, no action was taken. Local historians suggest that the crews were so set in their old ways, locked into their traditional fishing-rounds, that they refused to consider the possibility that the shoals had moved upstream.

Thomas Brown, a 'poor man who lived near Donibristle', is credited with the actual discovery of this marvellous migration. For years he had fished with hook and line for haddock but also took many herring this way. On occasion, confided Tam, the herring were so close to shore they could be taken up in buckets.

Smiling Tam, whose fishing expeditions always seemed to be blessed with success was, however, a greedy man and kept his secret for years. Eventually neighbours, as neighbours always do, got to know of his piscatorial triumphs and soon he was forced to share his spoils with his pals. Together they caught enough herring to sell in neighbouring counties.

When reports reached the villages further down the Forth that large shoals were being found upstream the fishermen, at first, still refused to budge. At last, in October 1793, when Queensferry fishermen set their nets in the new ground and met with immediate and astonishing success, the fishing industry gradually shook itself back into action and boats started to congregate, some coming from as far away as Ireland.

Burntisland became the new centre of activity with its wealth increasing dramatically. The town previously had been in a state of 'decay and wretchedness', but was to change dramatically as a result of this relocated harvest from the sea.

October 14

1574   Demand for Sunday services in Edinburgh saw the Kirk decide to designate the Tolbooth in the High Street as a place of worship.

1714   Declaration issued by James VIII in Lorraine was in circulation stating that, apart from himself, there were 57 descendants of James VI with a better claim to the British throne than George I.

1777   Glasgow town council agreed to employ a third man to clean streets: in winter they were to be paid a pound each weekly; in summer, ten shillings.

1836   A dinner given for the Earl of Minto at Hawick went unrecorded because the *Kelso Mail* reporter was refused admittance, his paper being Conservative.

1939   Royal Navy battleship *Royal Oak* torpedoed by a German submarine in Scapa Flow, Orkney, with the loss of 810 lives. The wreck is now a war grave.

Charlie's Tipple

Heavy drinking by Bonnie Prince Charlie in his later years is traced by some historians to the five months spent hiding in the Highlands after Culloden. He is said to have regularly enjoyed a dram which helped keep the cold, hunger and fatigue at bay. Tradition has it that the recipe for the famous Drambuie liqueur, still kept a closely guarded secret, was given to the MacKinnon clan by the Prince.

October 15

1632   James Grant of Carron, a Speyside bandit, joined a select band of those who have escaped from Edinburgh Castle, using a rope smuggled into the fortress by his wife.

1654   Hares had been sighted sprinting around the High Street and Parliament Close in Edinburgh – an unheard of occurrence put down to the exceptionally dry weather.

1662   Publication of an early post-mortem report: the young Earl of Balcarres had died suddenly, and Dr Martin, assisted by the apothecary Mr Gourlay, found a notched stone the size of a fist in his heart.

1837   The citizens of Glasgow were having their weekends disrupted as the fire-service tackled outbreaks with 'much drumming about'.

1985   Argyll girl Karen Matheson (22) was banned from the Annual Mod and branded a professional singer. The rules on amateur status were later clarified.

Coals to Westminster

James VI & I, who used to burn coal in the fireplace at Falkland Palace in Fife, is credited with introducing the fuel to the Palace of Westminster on his accession to the English throne in 1603. As soon as royal favour was seen to shine on coal, it was quickly adopted by fashionable society.

October 16

1430   King James II, considered to be a wise but impetuous ruler, and known as 'Fiery Face' because of an unusual birthmark, was born.

1511   Launch of the *Great Michael* at Newhaven on the Forth after five years construction; it was described as the largest vessel of its day.

1690   The General Assembly of the Church of Scotland met for the first time in nearly 40 years.

1774   Poet Robert Fergusson died in an Edinburgh madhouse at the age of 24; he is buried in Canongate churchyard.

1978   Orkney seal cull called off by Scots Secretary of State after large-scale international protest.

Landlocked Flagship

A shipwright who had worked on the construction of the *Great Michael* in the 1500s, planted a stand of hawthorn at Tullibardine in Perthshire which was exactly the dimensions of this impressive warship (240 feet by 36 feet).

October 17

1346   Scots army under David II was defeated by the English at Neville's Cross; 15,000 Scots were slain and the Black Rood, a piece of the True Cross set in an ebony crucifix, was taken as booty.

1637   Charles I, alarmed at the number of folk gathering in Edinburgh to protest about the new prayer book, ordered everyone not on official business to leave the city.

1858   Female poacher was apprehended on an estate at Fettercairn, in Kincardineshire; her presence 'astonished' the gamekeeper and constable.

1889   Parisians witnessed a spectacular meeting of Scots athletes and musicians, advertised as a 'Gathering of the Clans'. The event was staged in heavy rain in the grounds of Buffalo Bill's Wild West Show.

1939   German aircraft, in the first raid of the Second World War, attacked Rosyth and the Forth rail bridge; four aircraft were shot down and seven British sailors manning anti-aircraft guns were killed.

Jack High

The East Lothian market-town of Haddington is credited with having the first proper bowling green in Scotland. It was opened in 1662 in Lady Kitty's Garden.

Face of a caber-tosser

October 18

1620   A collection was made in the district on behalf of the young Earl of Sutherland whose family resources were 'much reduced'. It helped put his two brothers through university.

1836   Sensation at Banff as the circus arrived in town and a lioness burst into the buffalo cage, attacking the beast which later died.

1887   Excisemen uncovered an extensive whisky-making operation in Strath Oykell in Ross-shire.

1958   Denis Law became the youngest player to play for Scotland at the age of 18 years and seven months, the game was against Wales, in Cardiff.

1963   Earl of Home unexpectedly became Prime Minister after a controversial leadership election; renouncing his peerage he became Sir Alec Douglas-Home but was voted out of office a year later.

Change of Scene

The turnstiles at Kelso's Poinder Park rugby ground came originally from Celtic Park in Glasgow just after the Second World War, while an enclosure at Dumbarton FC's ground at Boghead, sheltered generations of Sons supporters after serving a previous existence providing cover for rail travellers at Turnberry station in Ayrshire.

October 19

1456   Parliament in Edinburgh planned for an attack on England to avenge the Border raids carried out by the exiled Earl of Douglas.

1616   Murmurings in Edinburgh forced bishops to abandon a plan to set up wooden sculptures of the 12 apostles in Holyrood for the king's visit; people feared 'a great change in religious practice'.

1810   The *Active Souter*, *en route* to America from Oban, had to turn back after being badly damaged in a storm; several emigrants died.

1844   A major dredging operation removed 11,000 cubic yards of mud from the bed of the Clyde in Glasgow's city centre.

1905   Self-made multi-millionaire, Andrew Carnegie, who made his fortune in the American steel industry, received the Freedom of Montrose.

Kill and Cure

Hangmen in Scotland in centuries past received payment in kind which took many bewildering forms – in Aberdeen he was entitled to a fish from every fishwife's creel. The Archbishop of St Andrews was, according to popular rumour, cured of a serious illness in the mid-1500s by being hung upside down by his heels for a week, and fed with the flesh of puppy dogs.

October 20

1579   An over-optimistic Act of Parliament urged the poor to seek sanctuary in the alms-houses of Scotland – unfortunately, in the 1570s there was none in existence.

1792   Birth in Glasgow of Colin Campbell, later Lord Clyde, who became a distinguished soldier, leading British forces during the Indian Mutiny.

1808   Blatant and audacious theft was rife in Edinburgh. One young man entered a High Street shop and made off with a tray of shortbread 'right before the proprietor's eyes'.

1874   A night of storms in the West of Scotland saw the loss of the clipper *Maju* off the Hebrides and the merchant ship *Chusan* off Ardrossan; up to 30 lives were lost in these incidents.

1941   The keel of HMS *Vanguard*, Britain's biggest and last battleship, was laid at Clydebank.

Knicker-Knocker

One of the great scandals of the Kirk in the late 1600s concerned the Revd John McQueen, an Edinburgh minister who was so besotted with local beauty, Mrs Euphame Scott, that he stole pieces of her undergarments. From these he made himself a waistcoat and drawers, believing this would magically and inexorably draw her to him.

REQUIEM FOR SCOTLAND'S LOST LEGION

The towering Cathedral of Durham is the glory of that northern city, yet it hides a dark secret – beneath its soaring arches 1,600 Scots prisoners, taken at the Battle of Dunbar, died while Cromwellian authorities decided what to do with them.

This little-known disaster, which cast a shadow over the autumn of 1650, transformed a place of worship into a hellish prison camp; the event is not commemorated at Durham. As an official at the Cathedral told me, 'This is not a period of British history that people particularly like to remember.'

The Battle of Dunbar (3 September), when the Covenanting army gave up the high ground and were routed by Cromwell's cavalry, was a catastrophe in which 3,000 Scots were killed. About 4,500 prisoners, destined for transportation, were marched south, but in a week-long nightmare trek 1,500 died, escaped or were killed. On 11 September, a remaining 3,000 were counted into the Cathedral.

Having fasted for eight days before the battle and then gorged themselves on raw cabbage, roots and plants at Morpeth, sickness was already widespread among the dispirited and filthy remnants of the Covenanting army. Around 30 prisoners per day died at the Cathedral, until the end of October, when the dysentery outbreak had run its course.

To be fair to Sir Arthur Haselrigge, who had overall charge of the prisoners, he did write to the Mayor of Durham asking that the men wanted for nothing 'fit for prisoners'. Despite the large number of deaths, Sir Arthur believed that 'never the like of care had been taken for any such number of prisoners in England'. To counteract the 'flux', milk was ordered from towns within a five-mile radius around Durham.

But with the cruel confinement and lack of any basic hygiene, disaster was inevitable. The wraith of dysentery stalked the transept and patrolled the aisles. In the cramped, fetid conditions prisoners jostled for a few square feet of floor on which to sleep. One by one the sick were removed to the nearby Bishop's Castle.

Bids were already being received from aristocratic entrepreneurs who wanted the prisoners for colonial or commercial projects, but Haselrigge was beginning to despair over the Scots: 'They are so unruly, sluttish and nasty that it is not to be believed; they act like beasts rather than men, killing each other for a half-decent shirt.' Hardly a surprise, bearing in mind their circumstances.

On 31 October Haselrigge had to tell the Council of War in London that he had only 600 healthy prisoners, '1,600 were dead and buried' from the Cathedral. The mass grave was discovered in 1946 when central-heating pipes were being put into the nearby music school.

A sad, broken group of men these Scots prisoners may have been, forgotten by their ain folk and an inconvenience to Cromwell's counsellors, but they surely deserve some sort of recognition, a simple memorial perhaps. Spectacular victories, glorious defeats are easily recalled but war is a messy business with many uncomfortable loose ends. The lost legion of Durham are entitled to haunt the Scottish nation for our forgetfulness.

October 21

1586 Plague reported in Dundee and so the coining of gold and silver, which had been transferred from Edinburgh to Tayside because of the outbreak, was moved again to Perth.

1669 Dundee was picking up the pieces after a fierce storm which damaged the harbour and several ships; help from outside the town was being sought for a rebuilding programme.

1746 Patrick Lindsey, who proclaimed Bonnie Prince Charlie at St Andrews and became a captain in the Jacobite army, was executed at Brampton.

1911 Twenty-six boys from Lochgelly in Fife were birched at Dunfermline Sheriff Court for malicious mischief at the pithead of the Jenny Gray mine.

1923 Ninety-one vessels, totalling 167,241 tons, had been launched on the Clyde in the first ten months of the year; the lowest total since 1887.

Andy Cameron and enigmatic friend

Light in the East

Before the First World War, the Saracen Foundry in Glasgow had a worldwide reputation for its splendid ornamental lamps which decorated public buildings all over the world, including one of the Tigris bridges in the middle of Baghdad, in Iraq.

October 22

1436   Parliament of Scotland meeting in Edinburgh ordered the closure of all public houses by 9 p.m., under pain of imprisonment.

1509   Action begun by the burgomasters of Bruges to recover a cargo of sugar said to have been taken illegally by a Scots vessel called *The Lion*.

1848   Clyde-caught eels were fetching big prices on the English market.

1877   Two-hundred-and-thirty miners were killed at Dixon's Pits at High Blantyre, Lanarkshire, by a fire-damp explosion.

1914   Private Henry May of Bridgeton, serving with the First Scottish Rifles, won the Victoria Cross for bravery at La Boutillerie.

The Hills are Alive

The Caprington horn is said to be Scotland's oldest musical instrument. The 2,000-year-old horn has a range described by one expert as 'three notes and a squeak'. One of the most intriguing archaeological finds this century was made by Melrose doctor Dan Jones who, while walking in the Eildon Hills, picked up a 6,000-year-old hunter's bow made from yew and which had been preserved in a peat-bog.

October 23

1295   The Auld Alliance came into being through a treaty signed by John Balliol and Philip of France; the Scots were soon making preparations for war with England.

1641   Irish rebellion and reports of massacres of the Protestant population led Scots Covenanting leaders to promise military aid.

1807   A 'money panic' in the West of Scotland saw large amounts of cash withdrawn from Glasgow banks.

1885   Court of Session decided that lecture-notes from university classes could be published but Professor Edward Caird of Glasgow thought that making notes available in this form would have an adverse effect.

1973   Scottish Local Government Act created nine regional and island authorities and 53 district councils.

The Viaduct Miracle

Broxburn, West Lothian, was the unlikely setting during the reign of Queen Victoria for a short-lived Eighth Wonder of the World; a sturdy, 100-foot-long icicle formed from a viaduct on the Union Canal and quickly became a tourist attraction. A picture-postcard was even produced to mark the phenomenon.

October 24

1574   A young Kirkcaldy woman was blamed for bringing the plague into Edinburgh; as usual the first precaution was the early closure of the Court of Session.

1694   Town council of Edinburgh gave permission for corpses from the city's Correction House to be dissected at anatomy lessons.

1769   Alexander, the Third Earl of Eglinton and an Ayrshire agricultural improver, was shot and killed in a scuffle with a poacher who later committed suicide.

1774   Astronomer Royal Neville Maskeleyne made a plumb-line from Schiehallion in Perthshire which enabled him to calculate the density of the earth.

1944   Two sheep, found wandering in Paisley Road, were among the items of lost property waiting to be claimed at Glasgow's Central police office.

Pineapple Surprise

The first pineapples grown in the Northern Hemisphere are said to have been cultivated in a greenhouse at Dunmore near Falkirk in 1761.

October 25

1514   Bishop William Elphinstone, founder of King's College, Aberdeen, died at Edinburgh, heartbroken, it is said, by the defeat at Flodden.

1611   Scottish universities were forbidden to receive fugitive students from foreign seats of learning because of the bad influence they were having on Scots students.

1716   London-Leith packet-ship set off on a journey which, because of 'great stress of weather', took three weeks to complete.

1942   President of the Scottish Vegetarian Society said that wars would continue as long as man was a beast of prey; he discounted suggestions that both Hitler and Mussolini were vegetarians.

1978   Two-year fight by a young Sikh forced Scots police authorities to change a rule banning turbans and beards.

Something Fishy Here?

In the Hebrides jellyfish were known by the Gaelic for congealed sea (*muir-teuchd*), an idea possibly relating to vague rumours and travellers' tales of the existence of polar ice.

October 26

1474 Betrothal ceremony of two-year-old Prince James, son of James III, and four-year-old Cecilia, youngest daughter of Edward IV, was performed at Low Greyfriars Church in Edinburgh.

1579 Money collected for relief of Scots prisoners in North African jails was transferred to help a Scots sea captain in custody in Bordeaux. It had been decided that the African captives were dead.

1788 Sir Samuel Greig, a Scots-born admiral who reorganised the Russian Navy, died, aged 53.

1803 Demolition began on the historic luckenbooths around St Giles Cathedral, opening up splendid new views of Edinburgh's High Street.

1962 St Andrews Halls in Glasgow were destroyed by fire; a major redevelopment plan was quickly under discussion.

Film '98

Balmoral Castle was the location of the first moving-picture show on record in Scotland in 1898. Queen Victoria saw a local enthusiast William Walker filming at the Braemar Gathering and he answered a royal summons to show his movies in the salon at Balmoral.

October 27

1625 Catholic noblemen were making hurried arrangements to bring their sons home from abroad where they were being secretly educated. A new edict of the Scots Parliament threatened severe penalties if caught.

1739 *The Scots Magazine*, said to be the world's oldest popular periodical, made its first appearance.

1836 Just before midnight an earthquake shook Renfrewshire and Dunbartonshire; people ran into the streets in fear of their lives.

1953 Arbroath lifeboat *Robert Lindsay* lost with six of her seven-man crew.

1980 An opinion poll showed that most Scots found the Sabbath too dull.

Civic Trust

Animosity towards local authority and its representatives is not confined to the twentieth century. In the 1600s, a certain Mr Erskine delivered a prayer in the capital's Tron Kirk saying, 'Lord have mercy on all fools and idiots, and particularly on the magistrates of Edinburgh.' In the North-east, folk take great pride in their towns and traditions. During a discussion one man proudly declared, 'We've got oor Provost and he wears a chain.' Says the other, 'Oh aye, we have a Provost tae, but we let him gang aboot lowse!'

LOCH SUNART'S FLOATING PULPIT

Ships, ships, ships. So many mighty and magnificent vessels have undergone their baptism rites along the banks of the Clyde, but surely none was more outlandish than the floating church of Loch Sunart. The last living link with the strange vessel was broken in November 1949, with the death, at the age of 88, of crofter Alexander Macphee.

After the Church of Scotland split apart in the Disruption of 1843, many landowners denied property or potential building-sites to those thousands who had opted for the breakaway church. This was the situation at Ardnamurchan in Argyll where Sir James Riddell refused to have anything to do with the Free Kirk. As a result, there were regular open-air gatherings – winter and summer – at Strontian with congregations of 500 and upwards, and in excess of 2,000 attendants for the summer Communion.

Eventually, the worshippers raised £1,400 and launched an incredibly imaginative plan. Shipbuilders in Port Glasgow were commissioned to build a vessel, a timber frame on an iron hull, complete with pulpit, vestry, gallery and packed mews. After construction it was towed around the Mull of Kintyre and headed north to Loch Sunart.

Ironically, the most suitable anchorage lay directly under the windows of Sir James's mansion, but tactfully, it was decided to use a mooring a couple of miles along the shore.

Inside the vessel there was seating for 750 worshippers, and for ten years rowing-boats conveyed the congregation to and from services. It was said that for every hundred worshippers the church sank an inch in the water so an accurate count of the churchgoers was always available.

It was finally blown ashore in a storm but remained in use for some time thereafter. It was on board the floating church of Loch Sunart that old Alexander Macphee had been baptised.

Among those who greeted Bonnie Prince Charlie on his arrival in Scotland at the start of the 1745 Uprising, was the Gaelic poet and Ardnamurchan school-teacher, Alasdair Macmhaighstir Alasdair. His employers at the Society for Propagating Christian Knowledge, which ran the Ardnamurchan school, didn't see his patriotism in favourable light and sacked him.

View from the Pew

When John McVicar, preacher at Inveraray in Argyll, found he was unable to persuade large numbers of his congregation to embrace the Reformed faith he struck on the neat idea of a double-bowled stone font. In one he baptised Presbyterian members of his flock, while the other contained holy water for those who had kept to the old faith.

Front pews were highly prized in the Dumbarton church of the Revd James Oliphant who was famed for his asides during scripture reading. His classic came during the reading of a passage on Peter who was declaring he had given up everything to follow Christ. Oliphant muttered, 'Aye boasting, Peter, aye bragging – what had ye to leave but a crazy boat and maybe three rotten nets?' Bishop Robert Leighton, an Edinburgh-born cleric, had often said he would like to die in a public house. Unlike most folk he got his wish pegging out in The Bell in London's Warwick Lane in 1684. So popular was the original version of *Dr Finlay's Casebook* in the 1960s, that the Church of Scotland considered rescheduling evening services to avoid a clash.

October 28

1562   Battle of Corrichie in Aberdeenshire saw the defeat and death of the Earl of Huntly who had taken up arms against Mary Queen of Scots.

1701   As many as a dozen people lost their lives when a tenement caught fire and collapsed in the centre of Edinburgh.

1748   Cameron of Lochiel, a stalwart supporter of the Stuarts, died in exile in France, aged 53.

1911   William Ewen of Lanark School of Aviation made a successful flight from Lanark to Edinburgh, 32 miles in 35 minutes.

1922   Birth of Glasgow writer and journalist, Cliff Hanley.

A Peel of Lochiel

When Cameron of Lochiel persuaded Bonnie Prince Charlie not to put Glasgow to the torch in his retreat to Culloden, the burgesses, in gratitude, agreed to ring the Tolbooth bells whenever the clan chief was in town. Although the tradition has been maintained into the present century, the chieftain is also said to make less noisy public visits to the city.

October 29

1263   Devastated fleet of King Hakon of Norway arrived in Orkney after defeat by the Scots at Largs; he died six week later.

1634   A spell of mild weather in late autumn – the 'go-summer' or 'go-hearst' – was reported. It was 'matchless fair' in Moray as garden herbs revived and roses and violets sprung at Martinmas.

1740   James Boswell, lawyer and biographer of Dr Samuel Johnson, was born in Edinburgh, the son of a judge.

1807   Brig *Rambler* of Leith was wrecked off Newfoundland after setting off from Thurso; 138 people were lost and only seven survived.

1980   After three years of sightings, a puma was captured by a Highland farmer near Cannich, Inverness-shire.

Showing at the Coliseum

Along with the wolf and the wild boar, one animal now extinct in Scotland, the Great Caledonian bear, used to be shipped to Rome in iron cages to provide 'sport' in the arenas.

October 30

1592   Edinburgh ministers urged city merchants to end trade with Spain because dealing with that Catholic country was a 'danger to their sauls'.

1792   Fire raged for four hours near Glasgow Cross destroying a tenement block – it was caused by a visitor to a house of 'bad fame' who threw a bottle of brandy into the fireplace.

1833   Reporters allowed to attend meetings of Edinburgh town council for the first time.

1932   Seven classifications of candidate announced in Glasgow municipal elections; Moderates, Labour, ILP, Communists, Scottish Protestant League, Scottish Nationalists and Independents.

Roy Jenkins fails to capture the Hillhead youth vote

LOCH SUNART'S FLOATING PULPIT

| 1940 | Deer-stalking season in the Great Glen had ended with reports of a reduction in shooting because of the war; many stags had 'gone to supplement the national larder'. |

Dance, You Devils

First mention of the Jew's Harp in Scottish history comes in the accounts of the North Berwick witch trials, during the reign of James VI. A young girl is said to have provided accompaniment for the coven as dancing took place on the kirk green.

October 31

1579	Beggars, minstrels, fortune-tellers, vagrants, idle people and the 'vagabond scholars' of Aberdeen, Glasgow and St Andrews were the target of legislation from the Scots Parliament.
1628	Janet Boyd, wife of a Dumbarton burgess, ordered to be tried for witchcraft having 'freely confessed' to making a pact with the Devil.
1882	Hallowe'en was celebrated at Balmoral in the traditional manner with a torchlight procession, bonfire and reels; the Queen was in attendance.
1914	London Scottish became the first Territorial Army regiment in full combat with 321 casualties in Flanders,
1952	English residents of Glasgow took over from the Irish as the single biggest 'foreign group' in the city; 37,032 of its residents had been born South of the Border.

Cunning Cockpen

When the Laird o' Cockpen, musician friend of Charles II, was denied an audience by court officials in connection with a disputed inheritance, he persuaded the organist at the Chapel Royal to let him play when the king came to worship. As the royal party left the chapel, Cockpen struck up one of the king's old favourites. The king was delighted, recognised the Scot, listened to his case and returned his inheritance.

November 1

1140	Abbey of Newbattle in Midlothian founded by King David I.
1624	King James VI wrote to the Earl of Mar asking him to procure four or five Argyllshire terriers. They were to be sent to France in separate vessels 'lest one should miscarry'.
1755	Effects of the Lisbon earthquake which killed 35,000 people were felt in Scotland – the level of Loch Lomond rose by almost three feet and the shock was felt by mineworkers at Leadhills, Lanarkshire.
1889	Twenty-nine women and girls were killed in Glasgow

when the partly constructed Templeton carpet-factory collapsed on a temporary weaving-shed in high winds.

1951   A new housewives' newspaper *Dundee Commonsense* made its first appearance.

Pigeon Post

The high tower in the Charles Rennie Mackintosh building – the former *Glasgow Herald* office in Mitchell Street – housed a pigeon-loft to which birds carried despatches from football matches in the days before phones were installed at grounds.

November 2

1585   Protestant party arrived in force at Stirling and drove the Earl of Arran, the last psuedo-Regent, from the court.

1665   Edinburgh merchants given permission to transport beggars and thieves, whom they had brought to justice, to the plantations in America and Barbados.

1803   Several cases of cholera were reported in Edinburgh and fatalities were to follow.

1841   Montrose-born traveller and diplomatist Sir Alexander Burns, who voyaged widely in Asia, was murdered during an uprising in Kabul.

1951   Two Lanarkshire girls were reported unwell after taking part in demonstrations of hypnotism.

Dignity, then the Big Drop

Right into the 1800s, during the frequent famines which plagued Scotland, a 'common coffin' was used in parts of the country to bury the poor with a little dignity. It had a hinged floor and spilled the body into the grave at the appropriate moment allowing the casket to be re-used whenever necessary.

November 3

1597   The marriage of the young Earl of Cassilis to the middle-aged Dame Jean Fleming was the subject of much mockery by the king and court, the monarch led the fun by composing suggestive sonnets.

1677   Hundreds were made homeless when a large section of Glasgow's Saltmarket was destroyed by a fire which was started in revenge by a smith's apprentice who had been beaten by his master.

1785   Two-headed, live heifer caused astonishment in Glasgow where it had been put on show as a curiosity.

1882   Riots at Linthouse in Glasgow as strike-breaking, English shipyard joiners were stoned and had their tools smashed.

1902   Whaler *Diana* arrived at Dundee with a catch of five whales, eighteen bears, three walrus and many seals.

Women of Substance

Many women in medieval Scotland earned a crust by acting as fordswomen, wading across swollen rivers with a gentleman or an equally heavy burden on their backs.

WALLACE – VICTIM OF THE PROPAGANDA MACHINE?

The St Albans Raid, a wild, rampaging sortie into the English heartland by an army under William Wallace, should have a prominent place in our history, you might think. Alas, this spectacular incursion, which would have taken the Scots almost to the gates of London, is pure fiction.

Blind Harry, writing his life of Wallace in the fifteenth century, mentions the episode, probably using sources such as William Rishanger, a St Albans monk who wrote a chronicle covering the years 1259–1307. In this he spoke of the Scots atrocities – of babies speared and children burned in schools and churches. However, there is little or no scope for this legendary invasion in the year historians have pinpointed it, 1298.

During the winter of 1297–98, Wallace had led his troops in a drive through the North of England before disappearing back across the Border. It is unlikely that they went very far south on the expedition. In the early part of 1298, Wallace is thought to have taken on the role of Guardian of the realm and was working to consolidate Scotland's defences and dealing with domestic matters. By July the Scots had been scattered at the disastrous Battle of Falkirk and Wallace is thought to have set off for France, possibly before the year's end.

There is no doubt that he had infuriated the English King Edward by styling himself William the Conqueror during that northern raid. The details of his subsequent betrayal, mockery of a trial and barbaric execution are well enough known.

Was the story of the St Albans Raid a piece of English propaganda designed to further blacken Wallace's name in retrospect? It's quite possible. It was, perhaps, felt that more evidence was needed to justify the 'rebel' leader's horrific end.

Certainly the descriptions of Scottish raids south of the Border during the twelfth and thirteenth centuries bear remarkable similarities of style, and it would have been quite simple to throw in an extra invasion with all the standard atrocities, just for effect.

Battle Cries

The MacGregor clan were led to the Battle of Sheriffmuir in 1715 by the legendary Rob Roy. Late in arriving, they are said to have waited until both sides had left the field then stepped in to lift the booty. The Borders castle of Roxburgh was taken by the Black Douglas in 1313 when his troops, disguised in cattle skins, were able to get to the foot of the battlements undetected, before launching a devastating surprise attack. The single biggest domestic tragedy of the Second World War surely came when 15 members of the Rock family died as over 200 bombers attacked Clydebank, one device scoring a direct hit on their home. In two nights of bombing 1,000 people died in the Glasgow area, and in Clydebank only seven houses were left undamaged. It was the custom in Scotland never to baptise the 'good right hand' because it would be used in later years for killing.

November 4

1551   Mary of Guise was received at Whitehall where Edward of England tried to persuade her to cancel her daughter Mary's engagement to the Dauphin of France.

1611   'Nightwalkers' – idle, debauched people who roamed the unlit streets of Edinburgh – forced magistrates to impose a ten o'clock curfew.

1854   Street-begging in Glasgow was very prevalent with 'stout, young idle women and girls' loitering in the main thoroughfares, with children in their arms.

1964   Exercise-book belonging to Prince Charles, which contained essays on the monarchy and which had vanished from his classroom at Gordonstoun, turned up after having been offered to continental publishers.

1976   Dame Flora MacLeod of McLeod, 28th chieftain of the Clan MacLeod and the first woman to succeed to the ancestral territory around Dunvegan in Skye, died, aged 98.

Merry Old Soul

Old King Cole of the nursery rhyme was probably a British chief of the pre-Christian era, slain in the district of Kyle by a Scots leader called Fergus.

November 5

1153   Somerled, Lord of Argyll and the Hebrides, invaded Scotland a few months after the death of David I and the succession of his 12-year-old grandson Malcolm.

1605   On the night of the gunpowder plot in London the North of Scotland was battered by ferocious winds which many took to be a sign of treason at hand.

1690   Mutiny by the depleted Government garrison at Fort William was averted by the arrival of supplies.

1931   Three members of a Glasgow gang called 'The Rajah Boys' from Calton were each fined 10/6d on charges of breach of the peace having gone to the South Side of the city looking for trouble.

1941   Commercial Bar in Fraserburgh received a direct hit from a German bomb. Its owner, Peter O'Hare, and his wife were killed along with over 30 of their customers.

Suffer the Poor

Fletcher of Saltoun, with a deep compassion for the vagrant poor in seventeenth-century Scotland, suggested offering hundreds of them to the State of Venice to serve in galleys against the enemies of Christendom.

November 6

1357   Parliament of David II ordered that ale and bread-merchants should not try to make a killing by overcharging visitors to Scotland.

1567   Borders custom of paying blackmail to avoid kidnapping was outlawed; locals were urged to hound extortionists from the district.

1616   Captain William Murray was granted a patent giving him the sole privilege of importing tobacco to Scotland for a period of 21 years.

1746   James Reid was hanged at York after a judge ruled – in the aftermath of Culloden – that bagpipes constituted an instrument of warfare.

1830   A common white turnip was pulled up on a farm near Dalkeith in Midlothian; it weighed 20lbs and was three feet, three inches in circumference.

King-Size Complaint

King James VI, a lifelong opponent of tobacco, who once described smoking as 'loathsome to the eye, hateful to the nose and harmful to the brain', was forced on one occasion to forget his aversion. While out hunting, a storm sent his party scurrying for shelter in a pig-sty. The stench was so overpowering that one of the group was given the royal assent to light up and mask the smell.

WALLACE – VICTIM OF THE PROPAGANDA MACHINE?

November 7

1581   Heavy fines and imprisonment faced Scots who undertook pilgrimages, used crosses, observed saints' days or sang carols, as Reformers tried to remove the last 'dregs of idolatry'.

1725   Margaret Gibbon, a convicted thief, was drummed through the streets of Edinburgh wearing a false face and festooned in bells.

1805   Two hundred pounds of potatoes were dug up on a farm at Bonawe in Argyll, the progeny of an enormous tattie weighing over 4lbs which had been planted in pieces the previous year.

1832   A plan to attract larger crowds to public executions in Glasgow by changing the time from morning to mid-afternoon, failed, with the 'usual crowd' watching the execution of wife-murderer George Doffy.

1974   Retired Scots surgeon George Mair caused a sensation by admitting that he carried out mercy-killings on patients.

Selkie Meat Taboo

The Hudson's Bay Company's expectation that seal meat would provide a basic diet for recruits had to be quickly forgotten when it was discovered that Orcadians – among their best and most numerous employees – refused to eat selkies because of the island's tradition about human links with the 'seal folk'.

November 8

1297   Monastery at Hexham was granted a charter by William Wallace giving them protection against rampaging Scots following complaints from the canons that their buildings had been 'sacriligeously plundered'.

1608   About 9 p.m. an earthquake shook Central Scotland; in Perth the Tolbooth was damaged and in Dumbarton people flocked to the kirk to pray for deliverance.

1884   Crofter agitation in Skye resulted in an armed police-unit being set up by Inverness-shire constabulary. They were drilled in the use of revolvers, but only for 'self-protection'.

1949   Sutherland County Council decided to approach the Duke of Sutherland to sell or lease a piece of land at Loch Laxford for a whaling-station.

1951   A double Bailey bridge was suggested for Glasgow city centre to ease traffic flow across the river.

Chewing over History

One of the most important early Scottish historical documents, *The Scotichronicon*, now held at Cambridge University and written in the 1400s, was saved from destruction by an Archbishop of

Canterbury while in storage. Rats had begun to make a meal of the priceless scripts.

November 9

1579   Reformer John Knox made his last public appearance at St Giles in Edinburgh at a ceremony to induct his successor. He died two weeks later.

1769   First Co-operative Society in Britain was formed by weavers at Fenwick in Ayrshire.

1885   Famous Hengler's Circus opened in Glasgow's Wellington Street; the star turns were the 'whimsical walker' and 'Bimbo' who, with his seal, had the audience roaring their approval.

1927   Liberal Party won one of the briefest annual 'Pease-meal' battles on record, it was a highlight of Aberdeen University Rectorial campaign.

1931   A major manhunt was under way for an 'elusive terrorist' who made four attempts, during one month, to wreck trains on the Dundee-Arbroath line.

Writer's Middleman

Aberdeen man, A.P. Watt, founded the world's first literary agency when he settled in London in the early 1870s.

November 10

1310   An English army after two months of fruitless marching around Central and Southern Scotland, and harassed all the way by the guerrilla forces of Robert Bruce, reached Berwick.

1579   Every relatively well-off Scot was ordered to have a copy of the recently produced Bible and Psalm book in the vulgar tongue, under threat of a penalty of ten pounds.

1636   A group of gipsies imprisoned at Haddington were ordered to be executed, men were hanged and women drowned, because they were a drain on the town's resources.

1871   Missionary and explorer David Livingstone met Henry Morton Stanley at Ujiji.

1946   Country-dancing could unite different social classes in Scotland who were frozen into their localities, Lord James Murray told the AGM of the Scottish Country-Dance Society at Dundee.

Whipping Boys

A rather drastic method of recording land boundaries was employed in the Western Isles in the 1600s. When the limits of a field had been decided, a group of young men were whipped at the location with leather thongs so that in later life they would remember the details if called to give evidence.

WIDE-EYED IN MUSSELBURGH

John Row, selected by the Pope as his emissary to lead the fight against the dawning Reformation in Scotland, suddenly, almost overnight, it seems, changed camps to become one of the staunchest advocates of the new faith. This switch of allegiance has always intrigued me.

Only by dusting down the histories do we come across the amazing, some might say implausible, explanation for this sudden conversion. It involves the sensational exposure, in 1558, of the fraudulent, blind beggar of Musselburgh.

The wonder-working chapel of Loretto in the Honest Toun had a marvellous reputation and was particularly favoured by women having, or anticipating, a difficult childbirth. Robert Colville of Cleish, a Fife squire, was an enthusiastic Protestant, and his pregnant wife was an equally devout Catholic. When Colville's wife heard of the miracles being performed by the Virgin of Loretto she sent her servant with her nightgown and an offering of gold in the hope of guaranteeing a safe delivery.

Colville, hearing of this, took off after the servant, arriving at Loretto just in time to see, at the climax of a session of prayers and praise, a blind boy being led out, groping his way, his eyes only showing a slit of white. After invocations and 'kneeling to the Virgin' the youth stood up – cured! It seems that Colville was the only man in that great company who remained doubtful. He spirited the boy away and at his lodgings threatened to strike off his head unless he confessed details of the hoax.

Not surprisingly, the boy told all. When priests discovered his ability to turn up his lids and show nothing but the whites of his eyes he was taken into care for several years, kept well fed and entertained in the vaults of a nunnery, before being released to wander as a beggar under oath to keep his secret and await the call for his big day.

Colville, by offering him employment and protection for life, persuaded the boy to go to the Mercat Cross in Edinburgh where, again at swordpoint, he re-enacted the fraud and urged the furious throng to embrace the Reformed faith. The pair then made a sharp exit down a close to the Cowgate, where saddled horses were awaiting them.

But back to John Row. He had been a house-guest of the Lady of Cleish. On his return from Edinburgh, Colville engaged him in a conversation on the nature of miracles before dramatically producing the 'blind' beggar who once again went through his routine.

Row was stunned. His history, as the chroniclers tell us, was 'thenceforth identified with that of the Scottish Reformation, in which he was an eminent leader, being an author of *The First Book of Discipline*'.

A couple of questions remain to be asked. If the Catholic Church was such a well-oiled operation, is it likely that they would allow their star turn to slip from their grasp and to blether freely, or under duress, so soon after the miracle? Protective custody seems the most logical option. And if someone threatened to strike your head off unless you came up with an explanation which fitted the Protestant scenario, I believe you might find your imagination working overtime on a creative answer.

November 11

1100   Henry I of England married Matilda, daughter of Malcolm III or Malcolm Canmore, King of Scots, who was killed with his son at Alnwick in 1093.

1598   Profiteering was rife in Scotland, with widespread food shortages resulting from summer storms; royal edicts were being widely ignored.

1723   Eighteen people drowned in the River Tweed near Abbotsford when a ferry-boat capsized as travellers headed from Gala to a fair at Melrose.

1896   First annual meeting in Edinburgh of Franco-Scottish Society which was set up to promote study of the historic links between the two countries.

1934   Wick harbour revenue was showing a substantial drop because of the failure of the herring fishing.

Gdansk for the Memory

As many as 30,000 Scots merchants and their employees are thought to have been resident in Poland during the reign of James VI (1566–1625). Eastern Europe was generally a target for Scots emigrants over the centuries, among them the grandfather of philosopher Immanuel Kant who settled at Klaipeda in Lithuania. Many important Scandinavian, German, Russian and Polish families can trace their roots back to Scotland.

November 12

1347   Scottish centre for trade with the Low Countries was established at Zeeland.

1572   Odd event reported from Montrose where the basin dried up for six hours, and folk were able to pick fish off the sand before the sea rushed in again.

1832   Former victualler Robert Andrew was sentenced to seven years transportation for stealing 13 bags of flour from the Old Mill in the Partick district of Glasgow.

1852   Duke of Sutherland offered to replace the whisky entitlement of crews fishing out of Helmsdale, with a supply of coffee and the equipment for making it.

1947   All records were broken by Scottish rose-hip collectors who gathered 144 tons during the season.

Witches' Brew

Traders in Edinburgh were under fire in 1659 for adulterating wine and beer. Ale was made strong and heady with hemp, coriander seed, Turkish pepper, soot and salt. When the Guild of Surgeons and Barbers split in 1772, the barbers were banned from performing surgery but, as a sweetener, were allowed to continue making whisky. Tremendous quantities of drink were consumed at funerals of the gentry in seventeenth- and eighteenth-century Scotland. So much so that there are a number of recorded instances of half-cut mourners forgetting to take along the corpse when time came for the burial!

November 13

1650   Palace of Holyrood House largely destroyed by fire while occupied by Cromwell's troops. However, the apartments of Mary Queen of Scots were saved.

1715   Battle of Sheriffmuir near Dunblane was a tactical defeat for the Jacobites under the Earl of Mar who failed to press home the advantage, and effectively signalled the end of the 1715 Uprising.

1854   The reputation of the Highland Brigade in the Crimea produced an 'almost unlimited supply of young men' wanting to join up during a recruiting drive in Aberdeen.

1935   James Maxton, leader of the ILP, was shouted down at an election meeting in Bridgeton, Glasgow, and a noisy audience sang 'Rule Britannia'.

1953   Smog masks were soon to be available in Scottish cities to protect people against the effects of smoke pollution.

Village Extraordinary

The clachan of Strontian in Argyll is said to be the only settlement in the world with a mineral element named after it.

November 14

1334   King Edward III entered Scotland in an effort to restore Edward Balliol's claim to the Scottish throne and quell rebellious nobles who were taking control of an increasing number of fortresses.

1770   Stirling-born explorer James Bruce, known as 'The Abyssinian', became the first white man to see the source of the Blue Nile.

1841   Thomas Bruce, Seventh Lord Elgin, who brought the Greek marbles to the British Museum despite criticism from Byron and others, died, aged 74.

1947   Government rejected a plea for a special petrol allowance for Highland shinty teams and their supporters who faced unusual travel problems.

1953   Conductress fined £2 at Dunfermline Sheriff Court for 'belling' her bus while a passenger, who suffered arm injuries, was boarding.

Les Parapluies de Glasgow

Umbrellas were introduced to Glasgow in 1782 by a Dr Jamieson who had come across the device – made of heavy, yellow cloth, cane ribs and a wooden handle – during a trip to Paris.

November 15

1585   Devastation wrought by the plague in Scotland was illustrated by James Melville's description of travelling across Edinburgh at midday and seeing only three people.

1715   *Glasgow Courant* – the city's first newspaper – appeared; the cover price was three halfpence.

1824   Edinburgh's 'Great Fire' burned out many buildings near Parliament House; up to 1,000 people were made homeless and eight were killed.

1884   Troops were sent to Skye after violence was threatened in documents circulating in the crofting communities; the Free Kirk ministers restored order.

1955   Glasgow magistrates said football clubs should be tougher with players who consistently fouled, as this was said to encourage rowdyism among spectators.

Sad Reflection

The talented Napier family of Merchiston, Edinburgh, worked to develop a mysterious weapon of defence against invasion in the sixteenth century. It was said to be a huge mirror designed to concentrate the sun's rays for the purpose of burning enemy ships, but the cloudy skies of Scotland seem to have put paid to the scheme.

November 16

1093   Margaret, wife of Malcolm Canmore, who introduced English influences into the Scottish Church, died. She was canonised in 1251.

1638   Kirk delegates gathered in Glasgow for an Assembly which outlawed bishops and set the Covenanters on the path to revolution.

1846   Scots railway companies considered making travel more comfortable for second-class passengers by imitating the French and introducing cushions, glass windows and lamps.

1857   Argyll and Sutherland Highlanders were awarded a clutch of Victoria Crosses at the Relief of Lucknow.

1951   Original Communion vessels of the old Barras Church in Lochmaben, Dumfriesshire, gifted to the Bantu Church in Africa.

Heads You Win

William Ewart Gladstone, Britain's Liberal leader through most of the nineteenth century, once declared that, from his personal observations, he was convinced that the largest heads in Britain were to be found in Aberdeen.

November 17

1292   John Balliol declared King of Scots after 18 months of deliberation chaired by Edward I of England who had schemed the appointment of this servant-sovereign.

1523   Parliament of Scotland witnessed a stand-up row between Regent Albany and the nobility over the conduct of the nation's affairs.

1771   Three hundred acres of Solway Moss, a thick, black mass, slid on to adjacent farmland, overturning houses and drowning cattle.

1826   Birth of John McArthur, a Renfrewshire boiler-maker who, after emigrating to America, distinguished himself in the Civil War. After being injured at Shiloh, he was created Major-General.

1952   First road-accident on the Hebridean isle of Great Bernera (population of 384) saw 52-year-old woman knocked down and fatally injured by a van.

Share and Share Alike

When a dispute arose between the East Lothian villages of Auldhame, Tynninghame and Preston as to which should have the privilege of enshrining the remains of St Baldred, the saint obligingly turned his corpse into three complete bodies, keeping everybody happy.

MORE A KICK THAN A PUNCH

The circumstances under which Glasgow gained, then lost, its title as punch-making capital of Europe make absorbing reading and constitute a salutary lesson on the influence of the medical profession in shaping our attitudes to healthy living.

Punch is said to have been 'discovered' (in that aggravatingly chauvinistic, European way – you see, it had always been there) in India in the late seventeenth century, one traveller describing it as an 'enervating liquor drunk on the Coromandel Coast'. It derived its name from the Hindustani word 'panch' meaning five, the number of required ingredients. Sailors brought it home and for a number of years it remained their speciality, the normal mix being spirit, water, sugar, lemon and spices.

However, once the landlubbers got a snifter of the magic brew it became a favourite with everyone, from grocer to major-general, and became particularly associated, so we're told, with the dominant Whig party.

But the general public should have been well warned of its explosive properties. Writing in the late 1600s the Revd Henry Teonge, a naval chaplain, recalled his first day as a padre on a warship when he innocently knocked back a few glasses of punch. This, he reported, had a very strange effect on him and it was only with considerable difficulty that he found his way to bed.

By the 1800s, it seems, a punch-bowl had become an indispensable vessel in every house above the humblest class. But it was the 'jolly topers of Scotland's western metropolis' who got the mixing of punch down to a fine art. The drink had been lauded in song and poem as a panacea, a cure-all of staggering success, and the Glaswegians took it on board with enthusiasm. The classic Glesca punch (more a kick than a punch, if we are to believe the stories of horrendous hangovers which followed a bout of punch-drinking) comprised lemon, rum, cold water, and sugar, the spices having been dropped somewhere along the line.

Such skill was required to get the precise proportions which would bring the elixir to life that a kind of secret society developed in the town, where initiates were introduced to the elusive mysteries of punch-mixing.

But the writing was already on the wall. Physicians in the late 1700s had begun to condemn the punch habit, describing the beverage as a 'heathenish liquor, nearest arsenic in its deleterious and poisonous qualities'.

And there is little doubt that the quantities which the Glaswegians consumed did dreadful damage to the system. Despite this, punch held sway in Glasgow until the 1830s when cholera was reported and doctors took the chance to warn people off the drink once and for all, saying it left the system open to illness. It quickly fell out of favour thereafter and punch-mixing was never to regain such popularity. A unique skill was lost to Glasgow.

Over the years, thousands of Glasgow holidaymakers must have passed through the square in the Costa Dorado port of Alicante in Spain where the most spectacular punch-drinking session in history took place. In 1694, Admiral Edward Russell, Commander of the Mediterranean Fleet, filled the marble fountain with gallons of wine, brandy and lime juice. A cabin-boy sailed around the fountain in a specially made dinghy serving punch to the partygoers. Admiral Ed sounds as if he had some Glasgow blood flowing in his veins.

November 18

1572	A very bright and clear star was observed by Scots in the constellation of Cassiopeia; brighter than Venus or Mercury, it vanished 16 months later.
1795	Clyde in spate flooded the centre of Glasgow and brought down a bridge which had been recently erected at the foot of the Saltmarket.
1854	Glasgow horse-cabbies planned a series of Sunday strikes but promised to help in life-or-death situations.
1928	Approximately 78 miles in length, the Great North Road between Inverness and Blair Atholl was completed at a cost of £630,000.
1932	A 19-year-old Scots girl who applied to join the Turkish Navy was refused because she did not have a Turkish education.

Shot in the Dark

Scottish graveyards were dangerous places in the days of the Resurrectionists or body-snatchers. Many families, anxious to protect the eternal slumber of their kinsfolk, set gun-traps operated by trip-wires along the dark paths. Several would-be body-snatchers were killed by this technique and many were injured.

November 19

1297	Rampaging Scots army under William Wallace arrived at the gates of Carlisle but, when faced with a lengthy siege, went off in search of softer targets.
1731	William Eadie, bellman of the Canongate, Edinburgh, died, aged 120. A Freeman of the city, he had married for a second time at the age of 100.
1820	Rioting in Edinburgh on the acquittal of Queen Caroline who had been accused by the Government of adultery, she had always retained the support of the ordinary people.
1905	Thirty-nine men suffocated during a fire at model lodging-house in Glasgow's Watson Street.
1927	Arran Banner, a new variety of seed-potato developed by Mr MacKelvie of Lamlash, was fetching £300 per ton.

Sounds of Silence

During the burial service in 1922 in Nova Scotia of Edinburgh-born Alexander Graham Bell, inventor of the telephone, it is said that every telephone in North America fell silent in tribute. A survey in 1986 showed that hospital wards in Dundee were ten times noisier than recommended. It was the famous Cromarty geologist Hugh Miller who first reported that the white, dry sand on the beaches of the island of Eigg produces a musical sound when walked upon.

November 20

1469   Parliament decreed that no one in Scotland under the rank of knight (except heralds and musicians) should wear clothes of silk.

1692   Arguments were heard in a bizarre legal dispute between the Earl of Tweed and Mr William Erskine over the ownership of a whale stranded near North Queensferry on the River Forth.

1725   Horse-post from Edinburgh to London vanished after passing through Berwick; both horse and rider were thought to have perished on tidal sands near Holy Island.

1845   Four men and three women faced Glasgow magistrates charged with desecrating the Sabbath by dancing, whistling and 'playing a trump' in the Back Wynd at 2 a.m.

1955   Plans completed for the improvement of the highway between Anniesland and Canniesburn, Glasgow, which was said to be Scotland's busiest motoring route.

Scandinavian Swot

A Swedish boy studying at Oban High set a remarkable record in 1982 by passing 13 'O' levels – all with 'A' grades.

November 21

1218   A papal bull issued by Honorius III affirmed the independence of the Scottish Church from English claims.

1591   The town council of Edinburgh agreed to help establish a small house for lepers at a sheltered spot at Greenside to the north of Calton Hill.

1835   About 40 people died late on a Saturday night when the dam on the Cartsburn Stream to the south of Greenock burst and flooded the Crawfordsdyke district.

1918   Seventy-four vessels of the German high seas fleet arrived off May Island in the Forth to offer themselves up for internment ten days after the Armistice; they were later scuttled in Scapa Flow, Orkney.

1949   Americans were snapping up tourist information on holidays in Scotland; supplies of brochures at a Texas holiday fair had to be replenished by a special air-delivery.

Foot Perfect

As early as 1688 the High Street and Cowgate in Edinburgh were laid with pavements when residents of other British cities were still plootering about in the mud.

November 22

1599   Kirk session in Stirling was dismayed to find that most of the money given to the poor in their district was in counterfeit coins called 'tinklars'.

1695   First recorded public concert in Edinburgh with the music of Bussoni and Correlli.

1773   Dr Johnson, having completed his famous tour of the Western Isles and visited James Boswell's father at Auchinleck, left Edinburgh for England.

1882   A collie dog which had been carrying the mail to and from Cardross station in Dunbartonshire, was to be sold after the post office gave orders that his services as a post-runner should be discontinued.

1949   Motor-vessel *Theron*, the most powerful sealer in the world, was launched at Port Glasgow; she was later to become an Antarctic exploration vessel.

Final Insult

Clansmen captured at Culloden were taken from prison hulks on the Thames to act as models for David Morier's well-known painting of the battle.

November 23

1200   William the Lion, King of Scots, left Lincoln for Scotland, after having paid homage to John, King of England, for lands held in the south.

1524   Edinburgh was in an uproar as an armed assault took place on the city by the Earls of Angus and Lennox – they were met by indiscriminate cannon fire from the Castle.

1665   Because of the good harvest many young fe'ed servants, from both the towns and rural areas, decided to marry at Martinmas.

1728   Church services in Glasgow were cancelled because of a particularly virulent outbreak of flu.

1851   Bay of Luce in Wigtownshire was reported to be producing large quantities of finely flavoured oysters.

Shades of the Yukon

In 1857 the Lomond Hills in Fife witnessed an amazing 'Fool's Gold' Rush with hundreds of tents being set up before prospectors could be convinced that they were digging up iron pyrites.

November 24

1440   William, teenage Sixth Earl of Douglas, was tricked into attending a dinner at Edinburgh Castle where he was seized and beheaded with his young brother, David, at the infamous 'Black Dinner'.

1542   Battle of Solway Moss saw defeat for the Scots under Oliver Sinclair, many of the Scots nobles surrendered after being overwhelmed by the English cavalry.

1601   Plague was reported to have broken out at Crail in Fife and in the Renfrewshire parishes of Eaglesham, Eastwood and Pollok.

1861   Thirty-five people killed when a jam-packed tenement building collapsed in Edinburgh's High Street. One of the injured cried, 'Heave awa' lads, I'm no deid yet!' from under the rubble and immortalised the event.

1924   Director of Roads at the Ministry of Transport said that the rapidly increasing number of cars meant that urgent reconstruction work was needed on Scottish roads, particularly on those in the Highlands.

Splendour in Miniature

The tiny Cathedral of the Isles on the Isle of Cumbrae, which seats just 100 worshippers, is thought to be the smallest in Europe.

LOST BENEATH THE SHIFTING SANDS

Stories of lost cities, abandoned villages – I'm a sucker for them. A few years back, when a drought in the Lake District saw the village of Mardale, flooded half a century earlier to slake the thirst of Manchester, emerge from the depths, it was all I could do to stop myself jumping into the car and joining the throngs who walked those once submerged streets. I suppose you could call it the Atlantis syndrome, the desire to explore somewhere hidden beneath the depths of the ocean, or in the middle of the desert, for hundreds, preferably thousands of years, hidden away from interference or 'improvement'.

On a variation of that theme, one of the saddest places I've visited is a national monument right in the heart of France. The village of Oradour, where occupying Germans massacred the entire population, has been preserved exactly as it was on the day of the catastrophe. The tramcar stands forlornly at the bend of the road, window shutters creek in the breeze, and a car still sits, jacked up in the workshop from which the mechanic was taken to his execution. It's one of the most unsettling places I know. If you're not French (and I saw French visitors cry openly), you feel something of an intruder.

However, we have our tragic locations in Scotland, Glencoe and Culloden to name but two. We also have many intriguing, mysterious sites. Perhaps one of the most remarkable is the unstable Morayshire coastline which was overtaken by sandstorms in the late 1600s and early 1700s.

Writing in the late 1940s, Alasdair Alpin MacGregor suggested that the Culbin Sands were the only region in Britain where sand dunes and shifting sandhills occupied an area sufficiently large enough to create the impression of an arid, lifeless desert. He went as far as to compare the fate of Culbin with that of the ash-covered Roman city of Pompeii.

In a few days during the autumn of 1694, the sands, carried forward by a westerly gale, began to move at an unprecedented rate, completing the work of a similar sandstorm almost 20 years previously. The sea-sand was driven over a flourishing agricultural community, and tradition in the area says that the storm broke so suddenly that harvesters were forced to abandon their scythes in the cornfields.

Since those days the 10,000-acres, which the Forestry Commission has tried to stabilise during this century, has occasionally offered up echoes of that remarkable event. The orchards and mansion-house of Culbin which belonged to the Kinnairds have reappeared and vanished again among the moving sand. A chimney-pot which temporarily appeared above the surface proved a big tourist attraction.

Prior to 1701, nearby Findhorn stood on a 'plessant plain' about a mile north-west of its present site. The original location is now at the bottom of the sea. The inhabitants, having foreseen the likely inundation, had gradually withdrawn inland. The drifting sands probably dammed the course of the river Findhorn, diverting it over the village site.

At that time a level moor stretched five miles east from Findhorn to Burghead, the sea encroaching in a crescent-shaped bay. The moor between the villages had supplied brush and firewood for the surrounding communities, and its removal almost certainly contributed to the flood. On the moor, near the shore, stood a conical mound, probably called Douffhillock by the locals, which gave fabulous views along the coast. Today it lies tantalisingly, mysteriously, just beneath the briny.

November 25

1034   Duncan I became King of Scots at the age of 33 on the death of Malcolm II.

1454   Floodwaters from the Clyde inundated the village of Govan forcing people on to the roofs of their houses.

1631   Lax observance of the Sabbath was causing anxiety to Scots Presbyterians, for example, travelling on a Sunday, once taboo, had become commonplace.

1835   The Church patronage of the Parish of Ochiltree in Ayrshire was bought by the Marquis of Bute for £240 at a public sale in Edinburgh.

1973   Scots drivers ignored a Government plea to conserve fuel during the current shortage by doing without their traditional Sunday run.

A Touch Ironic

After braving the remotest and most dangerous corners of Africa as a noted explorer, James Bruce died at the family home in Stirlingshire in 1794 after a dinner-party, when he fell down the stairs hurrying to escort an old lady to her carriage.

November 26

1601   A number of noblemen from the Dumfries area, including Lord Herries, were summoned to answer charges that they had disobeyed laws on entertaining papists and hearing masses.

1666   Plentiful supply of fish, including herring, was reported in the Forth although some believed it a 'very ominous sign'.

1805   Post-office opened for business in the Clydeside village of Dunoon.

1908   Passengers for Islay, Jura and Gigha were stormbound for two days on board the *Pioneer* in Ardpatrick Bay, Argyll.

| 1955 | Experiment connected with the manufacture of rayon sa~ acres of peatland in Galloway planted with bamboo. |

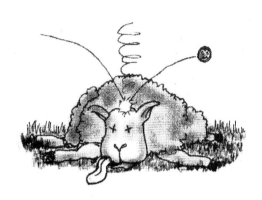

So Sheep May Safely Graze

One of Scotland's golfing pioneers in the New World, a M Lockhart, was arrested in New York for having a few practice strokes in Central Park's sheep-pasture in 1887.

November 27

1567	Ban on wearing 'culverins, dags, pistolets or other si firewerks' imposed in the streets of Edinburgh following bloody skirmish in the High Street between the Airth an Wemyss factions; many had been hurt.
1674	Exceptionally warm weather brought with it a seriou outbreak of influenza in both town and country; death were reported.
1830	Temperance movement in Arbroath took a knock whe one of its founders obtained a drinks licence for 'Th Sheep's Heid'.
1837	Mills on the Teviot, Nith and Clyde were halted by a lack of water following an exceptional frost in the Border hills headwaters.
1945	Any immediate hopes of a road bridge over the River Tay were dashed as the Government concluded that traffic flow did not justify such a link.

Power-Packed

Rob Roy MacGregor, outlaw cattle-rustler and certainly one of the larger than life characters of eighteenth-century Scotland, was in reality a wee man, possibly no taller than five foot, six inches.

November 28

1594   The Hamilton family of Livingston had been denounced as rebels for attacking and leaving for dead three messengers who delivered a court summons to their Linlithgowshire home.

1630   An Aberdeen woman was fined £5 by her kirk session for the superstitious practice of having her baby washed at St Fittich's Well at Nigg Bay in order to improve the child's health.

1831   Handkerchief theft was rife in Glasgow and Edinburgh and dangling hankies were said to be a great temptation to poor children.

1908   Glasgow University officers angrily denied that they had forbidden male and female students to speak to each other on the campus.

1945   Historic match between Rangers and the touring Moscow Dynamo side at Ibrox ends in a 2–2 draw.

Medieval Wine Lake

Scotland's consumption of claret in the 1300s was truly staggering for such a small nation. The historian Froissart reported on one occasion that he saw up to 200 vessels in Gascony, some as small as 50 tons, and most with a consignment of wine. Many were preparing to sail for Scotland. At Leith a hogshead of the new wine would be carted around town and everyone given a chance to buy a cut-price sample before proceeding to a bigger purchase.

November 29

1512   To mark the renewal of the ancient bond between Scotland and France, James IV was presented with a 35-gun warship by the French ambassador, de La Motte.

1658   This month's records showed that, in Scotland's small merchant-fleet, Glasgow boasted 12 vessels of up to 150 tons while Fife could muster 39 vessels between the various burghs.

1802   An increasing number of robbings and muggings in Edinburgh led to demands for a new police force for the city.

1927   A good season at the whelk gathering was reported along the Ayrshire coast.

1974   BBC apologised to the Scottish National Party over a political broadcast which was ruined by pop-music interference from Radio One.

Pilot of the Airwaves

Sir Compton Mackenzie, a founding figure in the Scottish National Party and author of *Whisky Galore*, could also have been the world's first disc-jockey. When the BBC offered him a record programme in 1927 he was off on his travels and his brother-in-law stood in.

November 30

1292 John Balliol, the selection of Edward I of England, was crowned King of Scots at Scone.

1623 About 9 p.m., with the moon shining brightly in the east, folk in Central Scotland noted a strange nocturnal rainbow which appeared in the western sky.

1662 Lobby grew for a greater recognition of St Andrew's Day. The national saint's day had been little recognised since the Reformation.

1710 A celebrated beauty, the Countess of Dundonald, who had been suffering from smallpox, died at Paisley Abbey.

1833 Glasgow had gained a nationwide reputation for the quality of its cured-beef hams – an order was even received from the royal kitchen at Windsor.

Impressive Second

Marischal College in Aberdeen, opened in 1906 on the site of the original educational establishment which was founded in 1593, is the second largest granite building in the world after Seville Cathedral.

December 1

1135 Henry of England died and David I, King of Scots, immediately went to war when his niece, Matilda, was bypassed for the throne in favour of Stephen, Count of Boulogne.

1602 Bomb-planting using 'petards' was common practice in Scotland in settling disputes. This led to a ban on all such explosive devices.

1833 Inmates of Cupar jail staged a mass breakout leaving behind one of their number who sprained an ankle in the breakout attempt.

1881 Farmers' Alliance founded at Aberdeen with delegations representing over 4,000 farmers attending.

1901 As a storm swept up the River Forth, the famous Bass Rock lighthouse was illuminated for the first time.

Home is Best

The importance of family life in late sixteenth-century Scotland is shown by an incident where head of the family, Thomson Lorn, was brought before the Provost of Aberdeen after being posted missing for seven weeks. He was warned that he would suffer the death penalty if he abandoned his family again without warning.

WHERE HAVE ALL THE AMAZONS GONE?

When I happened upon the legend of the 'bangster Amazons' of Burntisland, I really thought I'd cracked it. However, searching for an early spark, even a flicker of self-determination, among Scotland's ordinary womenfolk had proved a frustrating task. So, when I first came across this odd affair from 1615 it seemed to suggest, at least at first glance, that women's lib was hard at work under the Stuarts.

History has plenty of noble, high-bred women inclined to put the men in their place – Black Agnes, daughter of the Earl of Moray, who swept dust from the castle battlements in the faces of English attackers; the Countess of Carrick who threw Robert Bruce's father over her saddle when she took a sudden fancy to the young knight, and Mary Queen of Scots who, apart from being a woman who seemed to know what she wanted, was recognised as a smart operator in the sporting arena.

But where are the regiments of ordinary Scotswomen – the downtrodden, the unsung, the oppressed? Let's proceed to Burntisland where there had occurred 'an extraordinary riot' in the usually quiet, little burgh on the Forth.

The chamberlain of Queen Anne's estate in Dunfermline had been issuing 'warning of eviction' notices in the town. Nothing immediate was planned, but the people under their minister 'conceived a violent anger at the planned events' and, when an officer and his witness arrived at the Cross, 'a multitude of women, above ane hundred, of the bangster Amazon kind, maist uncourteously dung the officer and his witness off their feet. They were all hurt and bloodit and his letters and precepts reft frae him and cast away and sae stoned and chased out of town.'

But here we come to the crunch. The town magistrates had looked on without interfering, and a bailie's wife had been the leader of this 'tumultuous army'. Contemporary observers were in no doubt that the male inhabitants of the burgh had been the instigators. The women – downtrodden, unsung, oppressed and exploited!

Most other reports of the treatment of women around this time are equally depressing and distressing. The male of the species, who, of course, wrote the histories, seemed to assess their womenfolk in the same way that they might value a horse, a piece of land or some beautiful object to decorate their home. With such scant regard for the rights of women, abductions were commonplace.

Among the most heinous was the incident in 1591 when the young Duke of Lennox, cousin of James VI, had developed a 'violent attachment' for Lady Sophia Ruthven, daughter of the Earl of Gowrie. The king had the girl hidden away at Easter Wemyss in Fife, but the bold lad carried her off and forced her into marriage. Sadly, the young duchess died within the year.

When, in 1593, Lord Home, one of the king's chief courtiers, assisted James Gray to steal away violently the daughter of an Edinburgh merchant, the city magistrates went to Holyrood to complain. When the monarch asked them to name names, with Lord Home smirking in the background, the magistrates declined to point the finger 'because they expected for no justice'.

Pretty upsetting stuff. But I will not halt my quest until I find a woman who was able to stand up for her gender in those dark unenlightened days.

December 2

1584   A boy, who set fire to a heather-stack opposite the Tron in Edinburgh and endangered the whole town centre, was himself burned at the stake.

1689   William Mitchell, who had spoken against the government, was ordered to have his 'lug nailed upon the Tron' and to stand for an hour.

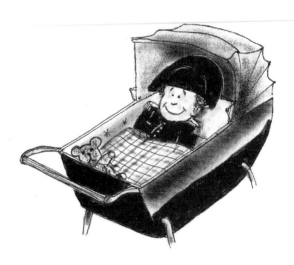

1805   A Glasgow baby whose father had served for nine years in the Royal Navy was baptised 'Nelson Trafalgar' in tribute to the fallen hero, killed in the sea-battle six weeks previously.

1848   Mary Slessor, the Dundee mill-girl turned African missionary, was born in Aberdeen.

1903   Efforts were under way to secure 500 Scottish fishermen for Nova Scotia's deep-sea fishing-fleet.

In Yersel

In 1916, Davie Kirkwood, the Red Clydesider, was the last political prisoner to be held in Edinburgh Castle.

December 3

1540   With the Reformation beginning to gain momentum, the Scots Parliament decreed that no one should question the authority of the Pope under pain of death.

1713   Article on the adventures of Fifer Alexander Selkirk in the Juan Fernandez Islands was published in a political magazine, and Defoe's *Robinson Crusoe* appeared six years later.

1789   Steamboat experiment on the Forth and Clyde Canal, organised by pioneer Patrick Miller, failed when the paddle-boards broke off.

1831   A woman was jailed for 60 days for stealing the clergyman's bible from the pulpit of the Methodist Chapel in Glasgow's John Street.

1978   Five conservationists arrested as they prepared to block a coaster docking at Glasgow with 1,000 tons of sperm-whale oil.

Chip off the Old Block

The Execution of Mary Queen of Scots, a motion-picture made in 1895 in New Jersey, was the first to use actors. The star of the costume drama was Mr R.L. Thomas, who played the tragic queen.

December 4

1214   Alexander II became King of Scots, aged about 16, on the death of his father, William the Lion, at Stirling.

1685   John Loudon, a Covenanting martyr, who had fought at Drumclog and Bothwell Brig, was executed in Edinburgh, having been captured by a member of his own family.

1745   The Highland army of Bonnie Prince Charlie entered Derby but minus the expected, crucial, Jacobite support from the North of England.

1928   St Andrews town council fixed the tariffs on the town golf-courses for the coming year – Old Course was 2/6d per round, Eden, 1/- and the Jubilee, 3d.

1981   Fifty-three East Kilbride schoolchildren were taken to hospital after a mass fainting in a local primary school; no fumes were found and experts classified it as a 'group reaction'.

Hold the Tonic

The phrase 'Dutch Courage' is said to originate from the habit of Scots mercenaries during the Hundred Years War (1337–1453) of drinking gin or Dutch spirit before going into battle. Juniper-berries from Scotland were the principal ingredient in the drink which was distilled in the Low Countries.

December 5

1189   Charter restored the castles of Berwick and Roxburgh to Scotland and ended, for a time at least, Scotland's feudal subjection to England dating from the Treaty of Falaise (1174).

1560   Francis II, boy-husband of Mary Queen of Scots, died from a brain abscess in Paris, leaving her a widow at the age of 17.

1845   Sweep fined half-a-crown for carrying his brushes and rods on the pavement in Glasgow's Saltmarket and endangering passers-by.

1952   The Ness district on the Isle of Lewis was selected as an area for influenza vaccine-trials.

1974   Fourteen-year-old Prince Andrew was in hospital in Elgin suffering headaches following a dormitory rag at Gordonstoun.

Fun day at Barlinnie Prison

Deil's Island

Both Rhum and the island of Stroma in the Pentland Firth were suggested in the 1950s as possible Alcatraz-style penal colonies for troublesome prisoners. Locals gave the idea the thumbs-down as they did to a proposal, made around the same time by the owner of Stroma, a Yorkshire umbrella-manufacturer, that the island should be offered as a prize in an American quiz show.

December 6

1593   Clan battle at Dryfe Sands in Dumfriesshire, in which Lord Maxwell was slain, was the last such conflict in Southern Scotland.

1664   A comet, the 'breadth of a reasonable man's hand', crossed Scotland from the south-east to north-west. It was seen in Edinburgh at about 3 a.m. and was very terrible in appearance.

1757   Sir David Baird of Newbyth, East Lothian, a general who fought with distinction in India, South Africa and Spain, was born.

1852   Savings Bank, recently established in Stornoway, was already doing a roaring trade.

1951   In a statement from Dalmeny House, Lord Rosebery offered a £1,000 reward for information on the doping of one of his racehorses.

Hook, Line and Sinker

The first and, some say, the greatest-ever Glasgow Charities Day stunt came in the early 1920s when a female swimmer was greeted at the Broomielaw having 'swum the Atlantic'. The stunt, which drew a vast, unwitting crowd of 40,000, was organised by Charles Oakley, who was to become an authority on the city of Glasgow.

December 7

521   Saint Columba of Iona, the apostle of the Scottish Highlands, was born. Missionaries from his island monastery travelled as far afield as Italy, Switzerland and Germany.

1599   New French wines had reached Scotland and profiteering was rife. The authorities ordered that no wine should be sold dearer than 5s a pint, under pain of confiscation.

1833   Police were searching for the father of a four-year-old Glasgow boy who had been sold to a chimney-sweep for 10/6d.

1922   Sir John Cargill, speaking at a Glasgow dinner, predicted that Labour's recent Parliamentary successes were just a passing phase.

1955   Patient villagers in Bridgefoot near Dundee, who had been using torches at night since their lamps were requisitioned during the First World War, petitioned for their return.

Flames of Revolt

Thomas Carlyle's classic history of the French Revolution might have been published much earlier than 1837 had not his friend and fellow Scot, the philosopher John Stuart Mill, accidentally thrown the manuscript of the first volume on the fire.

December 8

1331   David II, son of Robert the Bruce, was crowned and anointed at Scone by the Bishop of St Andrews.

1591   Ministers of the Kirk were calling at Holyrood to scold James VI about his personal religious habits and his 'defective kingcraft'.

1840   Blantyre missionary and explorer David Livingstone set out for Africa to begin a lifetime of work on the Dark Continent.

1848   Reports from Dumfries suggested that a cholera outbreak had already claimed up to 50 lives.

1984   Selkirk FC entered the record books after being beaten 20–0 by Stirling Albion in the Scottish Cup. It was the heaviest defeat for a senior British side this century.

Hall of Fame

When Sir James Hall, the East Lothian founder of experimental geology, studied military science at Brienne in France, he had the future Emperor Napoleon Bonaparte as one of his classmates.

BAPTISM – WITH A STING IN THE TAIL

Surely the bold Bastian was pushing his luck when he ordered the satyrs to flick their tails in the faces of the English gentry at the baptism feast of the future James VI in December 1566.

This was the last outrageous act (which almost caused a full-scale rammy) on an astonishing day during which Stirling Castle witnessed pomp and pageantry as well as scheming and animosity – an appropriate start to life – for a wee fellow who was to be the controversial ruler, not only of Scotland but the United Kingdom.

Certainly, the afternoon baptism was a splendid, glittering affair and was, according to the official histories, an event 'magnificent beyond compare'. However, you have to dig a little deeper behind the public relations picture to reach the real news of the day, and there was plenty of it.

First, the ceremony approved by Mary Queen of Scots, the proud mum, was 'according to the Popish ritual', and for this reason the Protestant lords refused to perform the usual offices. Only two of the 12 earls present took any part in the proceedings. The others, it is said, 'groaned at the waste and expenditure'.

Then we discover that Bothwell, now the Queen's favourite, presided, while the father, the discredited and unpopular Henry Darnley, although in the castle, failed to make an appearance. It is suggested that to prevent his attendance the 'dress, ornaments and servants' essential for such an occasion had been withheld from him.

Someone then put a right damper on the jollifications by informing the company that a poor man with a child on his knee was sitting at the castle gate. The child's head was so large (possibly from hydrocephalus) that its body could scarcely bear the weight. The Reformers nodded knowingly at this all-too-clear omen.

Then Bastian got to work. A French servant of Mary's, his job was to coach the team disguised as satyrs (lusty half-goat, half-men) who accompanied a procession into the banqueting hall. When the satyrs wagged their tails with their hands in the faces of the English guests, the visitors had what can only be described as a wee bad turn.

Indignantly, they retired behind their table, feeling insulted, and staged an impromptu sit-down strike, their backs to the entertainment. Hutton, one of Queen Elizabeth's squad, was all for giving Bastian a seeing-to, and sharp knives were mentioned. It was left to Queen Mary and the Earl of Bedford to calm things down. If there's a livelier baptism in Scottish history I want to hear about it.

A Question of Timing

Scotland's first alarm-clock is thought to have arrived by ship at Burntisland in the 1500s, the product of piracy. Wee Fea, a famous

Glasgow urchin of the early 1800s, performed an amazing sprint along Argyle Street to Jamaica Street in less than two minutes. Sadly, it is thought that he was kidnapped and killed by body-snatchers at the age of 14. The son of a Caithness farmer and one of 13 children, Alexander Bain (1810-1877) invented the grandfather-sized electric clock which in turn led to the adoption of Greenwich Mean Time across the country. After a particularly long, dry spell of weather in the 1700s, the Revd Russell, a well-known minister, was invited to preach in the Carse of Stirling. He prayed for the windows of heaven to open, and before he had completed his sermon a thunderplump had flattened crops as far as the eye could see. The farmers were not impressed.

December 9

1165   William the Lion became King of Scotland, aged about 22, on the death of the invalid Malcolm IV who had ruled for 12 years.

1575   The talk of sporting circles in Scotland was a speedy, little horse owned by Lord Hamilton which out-ran a number of larger steeds belonging to English gentleman on Solway Sands.

1664   Archbishop James Sharp made several land purchases in Fife; cynical Presbyterians suggested that the funds came from his abuse of office.

1835   The engine of Henry Bell's *Comet*, which had already been used at a distillery and a chemical works since being removed from the vessel, took on a new lease of life punching boiler-plates.

1947   Cupar Presbytery in Fife condemned whist drives because they offered 'money without sacrifice'.

Unkindest Cut of All

In the late 1600s, authorities in Scotland banned the export of hair to discourage the foreign-made periwigs which were flooding the home-market; a guinea for a set of golden locks was the going rate.

December 10

1577   In Perth, torchlit procession with piping and dancing, held to mark St Obert's Day, angered the austere leaders of the Reformation in the city.

1613   A warship exploded in the roads of Leith killing 24 men and injuring 60 others. Exploding munitions hindered rescue attempts and sabotage through the 'mad humour' of an Englishman was blamed.

1782   Alexander Spiers, one of the enterprising team of merchants who established Glasgow as a great commercial centre, and the largest tobacco port in Europe, died.

1833   Sir John Maxwell MP had set aside 100 acres of farmland on the south side of the Clyde where he hoped the new town of Pollokshields would rise, in a style similar to Regent's Park, London.

1952   Caithness education committee rejected a plan to supply pupils with a book called *ABC Guide to the Coronation* because it contained only English history.

Far-Fetched Tail

Eminent eighteenth-century High Court judge Lord Monboddo, who anticipated the science of anthropology, believed that children were born with tails, and nurses removed them at birth as part of some strange conspiracy. He was never able to prove his theory.

December 11

1673   Aberfoyle minister Robert Kirk, a firm believer in the world of fairies, was given permission to print a Gaelic translation of the final 100 Psalms.

1766   Alarm over the habit of the Glasgow citizenry storing gunpowder in their cellars, and people were asked to deposit their supplies in the city magazine.

1792   First National Convention of the Scottish Friends of the People, formed to demand parliamentary reform, met in Edinburgh.

1831   Nineteen couples, an unprecedented number, were proclaimed for marriage at the parish church of Arbroath.

1977   Nine-hundred-year-old Lanark racecourse ended racing after funds were withdrawn by the Betting Levy Board.

Sula Bassana

The solan goose, or gannet, found in enormous numbers on the Bass Rock was once sold in quantity to the citizens of Edinburgh where it graced many a dinner-table.

December 12

1580   George Auchinleck of Balmanno, a powerful figure in Edinburgh, was shot and left for dead in a passage near St Giles in a revenge attack by William Biccarton.

1691   James VII signed an order at St Germain allowing his loyal clans to sign an oath of allegiance to King William 'for their own safety'.

1804   Very generous public subscriptions were being made towards a proposed canal between Glasgow and the Bay of Ardrossan in Ayrshire.

1907   Two hundred and fifty emigrants refused to sail from Glasgow in the liner *Astoria* when they found she had only two funnels instead of the three-funnelled vessel illustrated on posters.

1955   Haircuts for men in Lanarkshire went up from to 2s to 2s 6d, with the boys paying 3d more for a short, back and sides.

Fearing the Worst

The only known Act of a Scots Parliament passed on English soil was approved at Twesilhaugh, Northumberland, just before the Battle of Flodden in 1513. It dispensed with the usual feudal death-duties of those who might be slain in the battle. This turned out, sadly, to be one of the most timely pieces of legislation on the statute book.

December 13

1635   Worst snowstorms experienced in Scotland in 60 years began; intense frost lasted four months, and the Tay was frozen over at Perth for four weeks and hundreds of thousands of sheep died.

1805   Six Edinburgh fleshers were convicted of bringing cattle into the city on a Sunday for slaughter and were fined by the sheriff.

1847   Two Glasgow cab-owners were fined 5s for having wet cushions in their vehicles.

1910   A letter from a minister on St Kilda stated that the 'natives' were all in good health with the spinning season in full swing.

1930   Work at Scottish shipyards was scaled down because of the lack of orders, with no improvement in prospect.

Hard-Boiled

In previous centuries Glasgow had a reputation for the wit and style of its signboards. Dr Strang, a noted observer of Glasgow goings-on, recorded one fine specimen which read, 'New Laid Eggs Every Morning – by me, Janet Stobie'.

December 14

1528   Five-year Peace of Berwick signed between Scotland and England with James V getting control of the strategic Douglas stronghold of Tantallon Castle in East Lothian.

1542   Death at Falkland Palace, some say from a broken heart over Scottish military failures, of James V, only six days after the birth of his daughter Mary Queen of Scots.

1765   John, 13th Lord Somerville, distinguished agriculturist, friend of Sir Walter Scott and the man who introduced the Merino breed of sheep to Great Britain, was born.

1886   Prison sentences were handed out to crofters who had been arrested earlier in the year during disturbances over evictions on Tiree.

1955   An order, designating 4,150 acres of the parish of Cumbernauld as a New Town, came into force.

Last on the Line

Dr Archie Cameron, brother of 'Gentle Lochiel' famed in the 1745 Uprisings, hanged at Tyburn in London, in June 1753. He was the last man in Britain to be executed for Jacobitism. He is thought to have returned from France in an attempt to recover Bonnie Prince Charlie's gold which is said to be buried along the shores of Loch Arkaig.

December 15

1558   James, Fourth Lord Fleming, who accompanied Mary Queen of Scots to her wedding in Paris, died with three other members of the Scottish Court at Dieppe. Poisoning was suspected.

1615   A national appeal was launched to raise cash for a group of Leith sailors who had been imprisoned in Algiers after a bloody skirmish with the 'merciless Turks'.

1788   People of Dysart in Fife were fearful that an underground fire currently raging would undermine the village which was said to be 'entirely supported by pillars of coal'.

1839   Captain Alexander Gerard, Aberdeen-born traveller who conducted one of the first surveys of the Himalayas for the East India Company, died.

1970   Burghead fishing boat *Rosebud II* was lost off Mull with her crew of seven.

King Billy's Secret

The tail of King William of Orange's horse on the equestrian statue in Glasgow's Cathedral square was originally designed to swish realistically. This enigma brought many late-night revellers to their senses.

THE RESURRECTION OF RICHARD II

Almost 600 years ago this week a funeral took place at the Church of the Preaching Friars in Stirling. Most believe it was the burial of an unnamed, half-daft individual, an unwitting pawn in a complex political manoeuvre. Others say, sensationally, that he was Richard II of England.

The 'official' version of Richard II's death tells how, after being usurped in 1399 by Henry IV, he was taken to Pontefract Castle where, intriguingly, one historian says that 'he seemed to have been murdered' on St Valentine's Day, 1400.

The corpse was exhibited at St Paul's Church, but contradictory reports about the manner of his death soon led to rumours. It was said that the body on show was not that of Richard but of his chaplain, Mandelain, who had been executed shortly before for treason and bore a striking resemblance to the king.

It is left to the Scots chroniclers Wyntoun and Bower to develop this tale. They suggested that Richard escaped to the Western Isles and worked in the kitchens of Donald, Lord of the Isles, until he was identified by a jester, according to one source, or a noble lady, according to another, as Richard of England.

Taken before Robert III he was put into the custody of the Duke of Albany and for 19 years, it is claimed, he spent a private life in Scotland. Many of his English supporters came north but failed to persuade him to try to regain his throne. After staying for a time in St Andrews, he died on 13 December 1419, in the Palace of Stirling and was buried on the north side of the altar at the Church of the Preaching Friars.

But who was the mystery man, if not the king? The widely held view now is that the 'resurrection' of Richard was a clever attempt by the Scots to undermine Henry IV's authority by creating a substitute, kept out of the public gaze. The story certainly convinced many of the English nobility who had an uncomfortable vision of Richard returning at the head of a Scots army to claim his throne.

For one 'poor, passive half-fool or madman' the plot meant a life of comfort and relative tranquillity, locked away from prying eyes, at a time when famine, murder and mayhem gripped the land and the weak normally fell by the wayside.

Don't Bank on It

Scottish bank-notes have never been legal tender, even here in Scotland. In theory you are supposed to take your notes, simply bills of promise, to the nearest bank headquarters and ask for legal tender, which can only be coinage. Without a banking system in medieval Scotland, most merchants converted their capital into beautiful gold and silver rings which were worn by the ladies of the family because, as one chronicler from the period suggests, 'there is no place as safe from robbery and violence as a woman's gentle hand'. Much of the bank-note paper produced for the Bank of England in the eighteenth and nineteenth centuries came from mills along the Water of Leith in Edinburgh.

December 16

1613   A ban was imposed on residents of Roxburgh, Selkirk, Liddesdale, and Annandale preventing them crossing into England to hunt and cut wood; it was an attempt to bring lasting Border harmony.

1821   James Sinclair, Earl of Caithness, who invented a road-going steam-locomotive, died.

1830   New five-arch bridge over the Don at Aberdeen – built with the accumulated interest of a 1605 gift of two pounds, five shillings and eight pence – had been completed.

1948   Edinburgh decided on a radical experiment by providing the city's refuse-men with gloves as protection against dermatitis.

1983   Scots nannie Carol Compton freed by an Italian court after being accused of starting a fire in a house on Elba. The sensational trial followed allegations of witchcraft.

Hooray Henrys

After his wedding to Mary Queen of Scots, Darnley, with a team of courtiers, strode up and down Edinburgh's High Street loudly bragging that he had returned Scotland to the Catholic faith.

December 17

1599   James VI decided that Scotland should come into line with other 'well governit commonwealths' like France, and have New Year's Day on 1 January instead of 25 March.

1685   Edinburgh's Isobel Cumming, distressed at an order quartering soldiers in her school for young ladies, successfully petitioned for exemption from this citizenly duty.

1851   Over 1,000 trees, some of great antiquity, were blown down in a gale at the Duke of Argyll's estate at Inveraray.

1910   Fishermen meeting at Buckie called for an end to trawling in the Moray Firth, and demanded more efficient sea-policing.

1969   Four hundred police-officers were on duty at Galashiels to cope with anti-apartheid demonstrators at a match between the South of Scotland and the South African Springboks.

Dangerous Slumber

Such was the paranoia within the Catholic Church as the first waves of the Reformation swept over Scotland that Richard Carmichael, a singer in the Royal Chapel at Stirling, was sentenced to be burned at the stake for mumbling in his sleep that the 'devil should take away the greedy priests'. He was reprieved at the last moment.

December 18

1661   Burntisland vessel *Elizabeth* was lost off the English coast with Scottish Records aboard; they were being returned from London where they had been taken by Cromwell.

1676   Extraordinarily low temperatures were experienced throughout Scotland; birds 'fell down frae the air deid', strong ales froze and old folk couldn't remember the like.

1805   Large cask of gin came ashore in Fife and soon, according to an eye-witness, 'numbers were lying around drunk'.

A little of what you fancy . . .

1892   Glasgow eccentric Alexander Petrie fined 7s 6d for loitering in Sauchiehall Street with copies of his newspaper *The Clincher*.

1902   Crew of the schooner *Lady Isabella*, which was wrecked on Little Cumbrae in the Clyde, owed their lives to a comrade who swam ashore with a lead-line.

Scuttle Coal

Scotland's strangest coalfield lies on the bed of Scapa Flow in Orkney, where hundreds of tons of what local people call 'sea coal' was dumped from the bunkers of German warships when they were being raised for salvage, having been scuttled by their crews while interned in 1919.

December 19

1655 Sir William Dick, a merchant reputed to be the richest man in Scotland in his day, died in London, aged 75.

1657 Poverty was on the increase throughout Scotland. Each day in Edinburgh a bell was rung to announce a roup or public auction of some 'poor, bankrupt soul's' household possessions.

1840 John Alston of Glasgow completed a Bible in raised type to allow the blind to read the Scriptures.

1854 Peter Mathieson, coachman to Sir Walter Scott for nearly 30 years, died.

1910 Glasgow School Board decided against a proposal to provide pupils at state-aided schools with free books, pens, pencils and stationery.

Pennies from Heaven

Gold coins from the coffers of Sir William Dick (see above), who was one of the biggest financial supporters of the Covenanters, were said on one occasion to have been poured from the window of his Edinburgh abode into carts waiting below, and carried to the army at Duns Law.

December 20

1555 Ships from Bordeaux, where the plague was raging, were refused permission to land cargo or crew at Leith unless guarantees that the vessels had no sickness aboard were given.

1560 First General Assembly of the Church of Scotland met in Edinburgh.

1745 Retreating Jacobite army forded the River Esk in the Borders which was in spate, then danced reels on the bank to dry their kilts.

1788 One man was killed and a second injured when a bucket, being lowered 100 feet down a Govan mineshaft, overturned.

1831 Woman robbed on the road from Paisley to Glasgow by a man with an English accent, moleskin trousers and a plush vest.

Elephant's Graveyard

Many Scots have gained their reputations with unusual aspects of scientific research. Nineteenth-century naturalist and palaeontologist Andrew Adams, who worked worldwide while serving as an army surgeon, made his name studying elephant fossils. In the early years of the Second World War an Aberdeen freighter lost a circus animal overboard in the North Sea. Less easy to verify is the story that a seine-netter later landed the carcass of an elephant in its nets.

December 21

1773   Birth at Montrose of botanist Robert Brown, an army surgeon who, during an Australian expedition, discovered 4,000 new plants.

1847   Crew of a Greenock ship were sentenced to 30 days in prison for refusing to sail on when one of their shipmates was lost overboard off Arran.

1908   War Office experiments with an aircraft at Blair Atholl declared a success as a 12-mile circular flight was completed.

1951   Shetland islanders furious over an Argentine plan to use the island's name on clothes and fabrics.

1988   Jumbo-jet blown apart by a terrorist bomb over Lockerbie while flying at 31,000 feet from London to New York – 279 passengers and crew and 11 townsfolk were killed.

Field of Battle

Warfare was a part of everyday life in sixteenth-century Scotland, but even soldiers had priorities. The siege of an English garrison at Haddington in 1548 was eased to allow the Scots foot-soldiers leave to bring in the harvest.

December 22

1596   James Carmichael, second son of the Laird of Carmichael, killed Stephen Bruntfield, Captain of Tantallon, in a duel at St Leonard's Craig in Edinburgh.

1666   After making an impassioned defence of the Covenant, Hugh McKail was executed at the Mercat Cross in Edinburgh; he had been captured during the Pentland Rising.

1794   After four years, the last edition of the Edinburgh-based literary magazine *Bee*, edited by James Anderson, was published.

1817   St Andrew's Roman Catholic Cathedral opened in Glasgow's Clyde Street.

1932   Fourteen plain-clothes police-officers injured during a meeting of the unemployed on Glasgow Green; demonstrators were furious at having been refused a hearing by Glasgow Corporation.

Choice of Critics

But for the children of Scots novelist George MacDonald, Lewis Carroll's classic – *Alice's Adventures in Wonderland* – might never have been published. Carroll tested the story on the children by reading it to them, and they immediately approved.

STARING INTO THE PIT OF DESPOND

Where were you in the wee sma' hours of Boxing Day, 1979. Speaking for myself, I was stoatin' off the headboard of my bed, convinced that the garden suburb of Jordanhill, Glasgow, was about to be swallowed by the Garscadden number three pit. This was the day of Britain's biggest earthquake this century (so far). Centred near Eskdalemuir in Dumfriesshire, it was felt over much of Britain.

The jolt experienced that morning was a special worry for folks west of Byres Road. Subsidence, caused by old mine workings, has always been a worry in this vicinity, not only for surveyors and insurance companies, but also to over-imaginative beings like myself who had this Dante-esque vision of the West End's smart-set disappearing *en masse* into the underworld. Good thing or a bad thing?

In Comrie, Perthshire, widely regarded as Scotland's earthquake epicentre, the community has a touch of the tremors so often that it's become hardly worth remarking on.

Glasgow and its surrounding area, however, has had its share of shakes in centuries past. The first detailed report of an earth tremor that I can uncover is dated very precisely. At 10 p.m. on 4 July 1570, 'their was ane quake in the cittie of Glagow and lastit bot ane schort space, but it causit the inhabitants of the said cittie to be in greit terrour and fear'.

On 8 November 1608, at nine o'clock in the evening, an earthquake was felt at St Andrews, Cupar, Edinburgh, Dundee and Glasgow. Dumbarton seems to have been particularly severely shaken on this occasion, with everyone running to the church 'for they looked presentlie for destructioun'. An extraordinary drouth (or drought) of the previous few months was blamed for the event, but, as we discovered earlier, salmon-fishing on Sundays in Aberdeen was also held to be responsible.

Glasgow reported further shocks in 1613, 1650, 1656, 1732. On 1 November 1755, the great Lisbon earthquake occurred. In the morning, during the space of an hour, the waters of Loch Lomond rose, and Loch Long, Loch Katrine and Loch Ness were reported as having been similarly disturbed.

In the *Scots Magazine* of the following year I was pleased to discover a graphic account, from an insomniac Kilmacolm correspondent, of a Renfrewshire rumble which echoes my 1979 experience. 'Being awake in bed, I felt about seven or eight shocks of an earthquake – the whole shocks were over in half a minute. The second was so great that it fairly lifted me off the bed, jolting me to the head of it. I believe that three or four such shocks would have laid this house, though a very strong one, in ruins.'

Other Glasgow tremors of special interest include one in 1786 with a rumbling noise which lasted three seconds, and was felt around Glasgow Cross in the early hours of the morning. Among other effects it got caged birds in the university just up the High Street into a tizzy. In January of the following year, in the Campsie Hills, some unusual effects of an earth tremor were reported. A burn ran dry, hedges were swept as if by a mysterious wind, and numerous farm-horses at the plough were said to have stood stock-still in the shafts through absolute fear.

December 23

1595   An array of Scots gentry had been summoned to appear before the king to settle disputes. James was said to be 'scandalised' that murder had become a daily occurrence.

1610   Licence granted for a public coach between Leith and Edinburgh at 2s a journey. It was probably the first documented public transport in Scotland.

1745   Lord Lewis Gordon won a skirmish for Bonnie Prince Charlie at Inverurie in Aberdeenshire.

1847   Because of unemployment, more than 5,000 Paisley 'Buddies' were dependent on soup-kitchens for their feeding.

1948   Councillors feared that a plan to sink a new pit at Menstrie would turn the fertile land of West Clackmannan into a great lake.

Shakin' All Over

Glasgow was one of several places shaken in 1984 by a powerful earth tremor. Students of coincidence noted that Radio Two was playing the Beach Boys' 'Good Vibrations' at the time.

December 24

1561   Leith resident William Balfour convicted of breaking laws to protect the Reformed Kirk by haranguing clergy at a service in St Giles.

1571   A Brechin innkeeper and his wife were arrested for the murder of numerous guests who had visited their hostelry over the years.

1610   A licence was granted for Scotland's first glass-factory which opened some years later at Wemyss in Fife, making high quality window glass. Drinking glasses were still being imported.

1724   General George Wade was appointed Commander-in-Chief in Scotland after his report on the need for military roads.

1828   Trial opened in Edinburgh of Burke the Body-snatcher, his partner, Hare, having escaped prosecution by turning king's evidence.

Up from the Depths

A set of five keys on a chain, thought to have been thrown into Loch Leven by George Douglas during Mary Queen of Scots' dramatic escape in 1568, were rediscovered in the 1830s during partial draining of the loch.

December 25

1319   A two-year truce between Scotland and England came into force; all intercourse between the nations was forbidden.

1609   James VI allowed Christmas to be celebrated for the first time since the Reformation, causing great anger among the stern ministers of the Kirk.

1680   School pupils in Edinburgh staged an anti-Papist demonstration in the High Street burning a wooden effigy of the Pope.

1851   Thieves, using a thick blanket of fog which covered Glasgow, had carried out many 'impudent and daring thefts'.

1950   A group of Scots students reclaimed the Stone of Scone, the Scots Coronation Stone, from Westminster Abbey. It had been carted off by Edward I in 1296.

Weighed Down by Guilt

Throughout his adult life James IV wore an iron chain round his waist as a penance for his part in his father's murder at Sauchieburn in 1488. Each year he added extra links to keep fresh the memory of his crime.

December 26

1251   Alexander III, King of Scots, was married at York to Margaret, daughter of the English King Henry. The bridegroom was only 10 and the bride was even younger.

1521   Failure of the Earl of Angus to appear before the Scots Parliament and explain recent disturbances saw him forfeit his estates.

1715   Episcopal clergy in Aberdeen presented a loyal address to the Auld Pretender, James Francis Stewart, as the Jacobite Uprising gained momentum.

1590   Trials began of the North Berwick witches, who were accused of trying to sink the king's ship in the Forth, and the principals were burned at the stake.

1904   J.M. Barrie's *Peter Pan* was performed for the first time at the Duke of York's Theatre in London.

Sam's Stars and Stripes

In 1961 Samuel Wilson, born in America of Greenock parents, was recognised by the American Congress as the original 'Uncle Sam', the personification of the United States.

December 27

1591　Earl of Bothwell staged a raid on Holyrood Palace in which he almost killed Chancellor Maitland and seized the king; eight conspirators were arrested and hanged the following day.

1698　'Man Stealing', or the removal of prisoners languishing in Scottish jails to work on the plantations, was prohibited by law.

1790　An increasing number of assaults and 'muggings' in Glasgow prompted calls for the setting up of a citizens' night-guard.

1805　Young man heavily fined for throwing stones on to a stage and orchestra pit during a show at the Theatre Royal, Queen Street, Glasgow.

1983　The Revd Donald Caskie, minister of the Scots Kirk in Paris for 25 years and dubbed the 'Tartan Pimpernel' because of his wartime exploits, died.

White-Slave Trade

In the seventeenth and eighteenth centuries Aberdeen was the centre of a highly organised and flourishing trade in kidnapped 'servants' for the American colonies. One ten-year-old slave, Peter Williamson, who was snatched at the harbour, later wrote a book on his experiences. The practice in Scotland of commuting a death sentence to one of lifetime slavery was recalled when fishermen at Alloa dragged a brass collar from the muddy bottom of the Forth inscribed: 'Alexander Stewart, found guilty of death for theft, at Perth, 5 December 1701, but gifted as perpetual servant to Sir John Erskine of Alva.'

December 28

1627　William Alexander, Earl of Stirling, granted a 31-year licence to print the king's version of the Psalms.

1734　Rob Roy MacGregor, outlaw, Highland gentleman, stuff of legend, died at Balquhidder in Perthshire, aged 74.

1879　First Tay rail bridge blown down in a gale while a train passed over; 78 passengers and crew died.

1906　Thirteen people were killed in a rail crash near Arbroath, said to have been caused by signals clogging with snow.

1934　Artist and writer Alasdair Gray was born in Glasgow.

Bute's Cotton Connection

Cotton was Scotland's single biggest industry in the 1800s right up until the American Civil War. Surprisingly, perhaps, the first cotton-mill, a very humble affair, was founded at Rothesay in 1778, followed by a similar operation soon after at Penicuik, Midlothian.

December 29

1455   Inverness slowly recovered from an assault by Donald, Earl of Ross, during which the town was almost burned to the ground.

1592   James Geddes of Glenhegden was gunned down outside a stable in Edinburgh's Cowgate, the latest killing in a long-running Borders feud.

1898   Plans for a harbour at Mallaig were set back by the discovery that the bay was underlaid by solid rock and not clay, as at first suspected.

1922   The windy corners of Scotland figured in Ministry of Agriculture research into the value of wind-power for generating electricity.

1975   Thirteen women entered the male bastion of Tennents Bar in Glasgow's Byres Road to put the new sex discrimination Act to the test; men cheered and offered their seats.

Judicial Jangling

One of the odd privileges of the door-keepers at the Court of Session in Edinburgh is to demand a five-shilling penalty from any noisy individual who appears at court wearing spurs.

December 30

1524   A fearful tempest which had lasted six days blew down many churches and houses.

1574   Kirk session in Aberdeen chastised a group of citizens for playing and singing 'filthy carols' on Christmas Day.

1627   Threat of foreign invasion saw plans afoot in Scotland to strengthen coastal defences. A major scheme was under way to fortify the port of Leith.

1930   Lord Mackay told an Educational Institute of Scotland conference in Aberdeen that the history of Scotland, as taught in Scottish schools, was unreal.

1969   Two detectives died from bullet wounds after a raid on a house in Allison Street, Glasgow, and a third was injured.

More than a Pest

Clan chieftains, not universally known for their sophistication, had, according to tradition, one particularly unspeakable form of torture. Victims were bound outdoors and left to the mercy of the clouds of midges which populated the Highland glens. Madness, it is said, was the normal outcome, with death not unheard of.

December 31

1567   Dundee merchant Robert Jack was hanged and quartered for bringing counterfeit coins called 'hardheads' into Scotland.

1808   Leith smacks, *Hope*, *Eliza* and *Queen Charlotte*, captured a large French privateer off the Yorkshire coast.

1811   A riotous and bloody New Year was seen in Edinburgh, with armed gangs roaming the streets. A police-officer and a civilian received fatal injuries.

1926   Sixty-nine children died in a fire panic at a Paisley cinema during a matinee showing of *The Desperate Desperado*.

1941   Manchester United football manager Alex Ferguson was born in Glasgow.

Guard Your Heritage

Most folk believe the term Scotch has always been reserved for the national drink. Not so. Up until 1918, when legislation was taken to change the name of the Scotch Education Department to Scottish, it was the common usage. Thereafter, we quickly lost the Flying Scotchman, the Scotch fiddle and the Scotch muffler. Surprisingly, the last bastion of the auld usage is in the Caledonian communities of the United States.

NINETEEN CENTURIES OF SCOTTISH HISTORY

A SELECTED CHRONOLOGY

AD 80 – AD 1000

80 Roman Governor of Britain Julius Agricola invaded Scotland, penetrating as far as Strathmore.

84 Picts and Britons under Calgacus heavily defeated by the Romans at Mons Graupius (possibly at Bennachie); up to 10,000 Caledonians may have died.

120 Work began on the construction of Hadrian's Wall to keep the hostile Highlanders in their own glens and straths.

139 Antonine Wall was built between the Clyde and Forth estuaries as a further safeguard against the woad-daubed tribes.

180 Antonine Wall finally abandoned.

211 Campaign by the Emperor Severus pushed back the rowdy Caledonians.

296 Pictish nation first gets a mention.

368 Scots first make their appearance joining forces with the Saxons and the Picts in an attack on Roman London.

400 St Ninian established the first Christian mission to Scotland, at Whithorn in Galloway.

407 Roman garrisons finally withdrawn from Britain.

500 Gaelic-speaking Scots crossed from Ireland to establish their kingdom of Dalriada, bringing with them the Stone of Destiny.

547 Angles founded the kingdom of Bernicia in Northumberland, which was strongly resisted at first by regional princes, including those from Dumbarton and Edinburgh.

563 St Columba came from Ireland to Iona. From his monastery he ventured into the Pictish heartland, converting them to Christianity.

573 St Kentigern (Mungo) called from Wales to episcopal sees, first at Hoddom in Dumfriesshire and then at Glasgow.

597 Death of St Columba.

603 Confederation of Scots and Britons defeated by the Angles at Dawston in Liddesdale.

635 Settlers from Northumbria began to move into areas north of the Tweed and into south-west Scotland.

637 Dalriada Scots staged an abortive attempt to conquer Ireland.

664 Synod of Whitby opted for the Roman rather than the Celtic church, with far-reaching consequences for Scotland.

685	Pictish victory at Nechtansmere in Forfarshire halted further expansionism by the Angles of Northumbria.
717	Nechtan, the Pictish ruler, finally rejected the Celtic church and expelled the Columban clergy.
731	Bishop of Hexham credited with bringing the relics of St Andrew to Fife.
750	Edbert of Northumbria added Kyle in Ayrshire to his kingdom which already included Cunningham, Galloway and Dumfriesshire.
756	Edbert and the Pictish king, MacFergus, subdued the Britons of Strathclyde.
794	Scandinavian emigration to Shetland, Orkney and the Hebrides began in earnest.
802	Danes plundered Iona – one of a series of raids which saw the headquarters of the Church in Scotland moved to Dunkeld.
843	Kenneth MacAlpin, King of Dalriada, succeeded to the throne of Pictland and united the Scots and the Picts in what was later to become Scotland.
870	After a four-month siege, Alcluid (Dumbarton Rock), capital of the Strathclyde Britons was taken by Danes and Norsemen from Ireland.
880	Norse and Gallgaels were settling in Dumfriesshire and Galloway, but within decades were under the sway of the kingdoms to the south.
937	Coalition of Scots, Strathclyde Britons and Norsemen were defeated at Brunanburgh (possibly in Dumfriesshire) by Athelstane, the Saxon King.
943	Malcolm I crowned when Constantine II, after six years as a vassal of Athelstane, abdicated and went into monastic retreat at Scone.
945	Malcolm accepted lease of lands on both sides of the Solway from the English King Edmund; Strathclyde chiefs dissented and their lands were laid waste, this area becoming part of Malcolm's domain.
960	Scots obtained possession of the fortress rock of Dun Eidin (Edinburgh).
990	Recorded date of the Battle of Luncarty, near Perth, when the Scots are said to have routed the Danes. This battle may have been pure myth.

AD 1001 – AD 1099

1005	Malcolm II – after struggling to contend with rivals for a decade – was finally crowned.
1014	Danes defeated by Malcolm's army at Mortlach in Banffshire.
1018	Malcolm II and Owen of Strathclyde united to defeat a Northumbrian army at Carham on the Tweed.
1034	Duncan, already ruler of Strathclyde, succeeded his

	grandfather Malcolm II as King of Scots, finally uniting Strathclyde with Scotland.
1040	Duncan is slain by Macbeth, who is quickly crowned.
1057	With the help of Siward, Earl of Northumbria, Malcolm III, Malcolm Canmore, son of Duncan, recovered his father's throne, killing Macbeth at Lumphanan in Aberdeenshire.
1069	Malcolm married Margaret, sister of the heir to the Saxon throne, whose family had fled north in the aftermath of the Norman conquest.
1092	For over 20 years Malcolm made war against the Normans in support of his brother-in-law Edgar.
1093	Malcolm Canmore fell in battle at Alnwick and Margaret died a few days later – from shock and grief, it's said.
1097	An English army put Edgar – son of Malcolm and Margaret – on the Scottish throne.
1098	Magnus Barelegs of Norway struck a deal with Edgar, giving him control of the Western Isles, and by dragging his longship across the isthmus at Tarbert, he also claimed Kintyre.

AD 1100 – AD 1199

1107	Alexander I became king on Edgar's death but his younger brother David ruled the southern part of the kingdom.
1111	The King of Scots assisted his son-in-law, Henry I of England, in a campaign against the Welsh.
1120	An uprising of Alexander's subjects in Moray and the Mearns was crushed but not before the royal residence at Invergowrie was attacked.
1124	David I, in reality a prosperous English knight, became king on Alexander's death, thus uniting the fragmented kingdom.
1130	An attempt by the Earl of Moray to gain the throne ended in defeat at Stracathro in Angus.
1135	Scots army marched into Durham to reinforce the claim of Matilda, only daughter of Henry I, to the English throne, as the Normans, under Stephen of Blois, pressed their claim.
1138	With civil strife in England on the accession of Stephen, David marched south again to advance his claims to Cumberland and Northumberland, but was defeated at Northallerton (Battle of the Standard).
1153	Malcolm IV succeeds to the throne but within a few years had given up his claims to the northern counties of England.
1158	Somerled emerged as a rebel leader in the Western Isles against Norse supremacy; and was finally recognised by Norway as King of the Isles.
1160	Galloway became officially subject to the Crown of

Scotland.

165   William the Lion became king.

174   Captured at Alnwick during a Northumberland raid, William obtained his freedom by acknowledging English overlordship in the Treaty of Falaise.

180   Inverness received an official visit from the king.

189   To obtain money for his crusade, Richard I of England sold back to King William the rights surrendered at Falaise. Scotland's independence was restored.

195   Norway annexed Shetland.

196   William the Lion attacked the Norse settlers in Caithness.

AD 1200 – AD 1299

214   Alexander II raised to the throne on the death of his father William at Stirling.

222   Argyll fell to Alexander's armies.

245   Continuing Border disputes between Scotland and England.

249   Alexander II died at Kerrera near Oban on an expedition to subdue the the clan chiefs of the Western Isles.

251   Ten-year-old Alexander III married Margaret, daughter of Henry III, at York.

263   A planned invasion of Central Scotland by Norwegians under King Haakon to consolidate their control of the Western Isles, collapsed after their defeat at the Battle of Largs.

266   Erik of Norway cedes the Hebrides to Scotland for a cash payment.

272   Edward I, known popularly as 'Hammer of the Scots', succeeded his father Henry III.

274   Robert the Bruce, future king and a leader of the independence struggle, born.

275   Work began on Sweetheart Abbey in Kirkcudbrightshire – founded by Devorguilla, mother of the future King John Balliol.

286   Alexander III thrown from his horse and killed on the Fife shore after a prosperous – and fairly peaceful – 37-year reign.

290   Treaty of Birgham confirmed that Scotland's chosen queen – the Maid of Norway – should marry Prince Edward of England. However, the Maid died in Orkney *en route* to Scotland.

291   Thirteen claimants to the throne – with strong Norman ancestry – put themselves forward.

292   Edward I, invited to arbitrate, forced acknowledgment of his supremacy, then appointed John Balliol.

295   Auld Alliance between Scotland and France was formalised by treaty.

296   King John renounced his allegiance and Edward stormed

into Scotland, defeating the Scots at Dunbar and marching as far as Elgin.

1297 Scotland was in arms again, and in September William Wallace and Andrew de Moray defeated Warrenne and Cressingham at Stirling Bridge.

1298 Scots resistance continued despite defeat at Falkirk; among the leaders were Robert the Bruce and Balliol's nephew, the Red Comyn.

AD **1300** – AD **1399**

1300 Pope Boniface VIII agreed with a Scots delegation that Scotland was a special daughter of Rome, and ordered an end to English harassment.

1304 Capture of Stirling Castle completed Edward of England's conquest of Scotland.

1305 Savage execution of patriot William Wallace hardened Scottish hearts against the English occupying forces.

1306 Bruce killed his rival the Red Comyn at Dumfries. Bruce was hurriedly crowned then defeated at Methven, forcing him to take to the hills.

1307 Landing in Ayrshire with a small force, King Robert won a victory at Loudoun Hill. On Edward I's death in Cumbria, English forces retired.

1308 In three campaigns Robert crushed the Comyns and their kinsmen in Buchan, Argyllshire and Galloway; then he began the capture of most English-held castles.

1314 Battle of Bannockburn resulted in an unexpected Scottish victory.

1315 Scots began cross-Border raids into England, and campaigns against the English in Ireland.

1319 Berwick – held by English forces for over 20 years – fell.

1320 Declaration written and signed at Arbroath asserts Scottish independence.

1322 Scots victory at Byland Abbey in Yorkshire.

1326 By summoning burgesses as well as tenants-in-chief Robert established the Scottish parliament as a representative assembly, The Treaty of Corbeil renewed the Auld Alliance.

1328 By the Treaty of Northampton England at last acknowledged Scottish independence.

1329 King of Scots died at Cardross from leprosy, leaving Randolph to act as Regent.

1332 The death of Randolph, Earl of Moray, left the way open for Edward Balliol, son of King John, to invade and secure victory at Dupplin Moor; a vassal of England, he was crowned at Scone.

1333 Balliol fled south. David Bruce, aged nine, was in Paris and Edward III invaded Scotland, besieged Berwick and inflicted a crushing defeat on the Scots at Halidon Hill.

1337	Scots struggle to maintain independence continued under Robert the Steward until Edward's attention was diverted by the outbreak of the Hundred Years War.
1346	Encouraged by his French allies, David II invaded England but was defeated at Neville's Cross.
1349	Plague was first reported in Scotland – outbreaks were to occur over the next 300 years.
1355	Battle of Nesbit – a Scots victory including capture of Sir Thomas Gray.
1356	Edward's III's forces devastated large parts of Southern Scotland – later known as 'Burnt Candlemas'.
1357	David II – in English custody since Neville's Cross – was released on payment of a large ransom.
1364	A proposal by David, anxious to clear the ransom payment, that his heir be a son of Edward III, was thrown out by the Scots Parliament.
1371	Robert II, the first of the Stuart kings came to the throne.
1382	Battle of Benrig – the Scots, under the Earl of Dunbar, defeated an English force which was *en route* to occupy Roxburgh Castle.
1383	A truce between England and Scotland's ally, France, failed to prevent an English raid which reached as far as Edinburgh.
1388	Invading England, the Earl of Douglas captured Sir Henry Percy at Otterburn but was himself killed.
1390	Robert II died and was replaced by his crippled son, also Robert.
1396	Formal clan-battle at Perth in the presence of the king and invited dignitaries.
1398	Dukedom of Albany created; last holder was the Duke of Saxe-Coburg, grandson of Queen Victoria.

AD 1400 – AD 1499

1400	An English invasion-force reached Leith unopposed before retiring south.
1402	Battle of Homildon in Northumbria was a heavy defeat for the Scots. Duke of Rothesay died in custody at Falkland.
1406	Future James I captured by English on a sea journey to France.
1411	Lord of the Isles pressed his claims to the Earldom of Ross but was defeated at the Battle of Harlaw.
1413	A papal bull confirmed the founding of St Andrews University – the first in Scotland.
1420	Murdoch succeeded his father as Duke of Albany and Regent of Scotland.
1421	Albany's brother, John, Earl of Buchan, helped secure a famous victory with his French allies over the English at Baugé.
1423	Treaty of London provided for the release of James I from

	captivity.
1424	Earls of Buchan and Douglas were among the Scots killed at the Battle of Verneuil.
1425	Execution of Albany, two of his sons and his father-in-law, the Earl of Lennox.
1427	During a parliament at Inverness, James I ordered the imprisonment of 50 Highland chiefs.
1437	James I stabbed to death in the Dominican monastery at Perth.
1440	Young Earl of Douglas and his brother seized and executed at the infamous 'Black Dinner'; an attempt by the aristocracy to curb the power of the Douglases.
1448	Douglases defeated the Percys at Sark, near Gretna.
1451	Glasgow University founded by Bishop William Turnbull, also its first chancellor.
1452	William, Eighth Earl of Douglas, murdered at Stirling Castle by James II.
1455	Defeat of the Black Douglases at Arkinholm (Langholm) finally broke the family's power.
1457	Famous Act ordering that 'futeball and golf be utterly cryit doune'.
1460	James II killed by an exploding cannon at the siege of Roxburgh Castle. Birth of William Dunbar, poet and priest. James III crowned.
1467	Lords of the Articles – a sort of working committee which prepared business for the full Scots parliament – came into existence.
1471	The See of St Andrews was made into an archbishopric – a powerful new force in Scottish politics.
1472	Orkney and Shetland, having been given in unredeemed pledge in payment of the dowry of James III's Danish bride, Margaret, was annexed to the Scottish Crown.
1476	Rebelling in conjunction with the exiled Earl of Douglas, John, Lord of the Isles, forfeited the Earldom of Ross.
1482	King James's preference for men of humble origins backfired – his favourites were hanged over Lauder Bridge by nobles led by the Earl of Angus.
1484	Albany renewed his pact with Edward IV and invaded Scotland with the exiled Douglas. Albany was forced to flee to France and Douglas was captured.
1488	Battle of Sauchieburn: amid accusations that he was responsible for the 'inbringing of Englishmen', the king was killed in the aftermath of the battle.
1489	Sir Andrew Wood defeated the English in a naval battle off Dunbar.
1493	Regular revolts indicated that the national security was threatened by the power of the Lord of the Isles. James IV compelled John Macdonald to surrender the Lordship to the Crown.

1495	James IV visited the Western Highlands. Foundation of King's College, Aberdeen.
1496	An important education Act was passed, compelling wealthy Scots to have their sons educated.
1498	James IV was back in the West Highlands giving charge of the southern isles to the Earl of Argyll and the northern territories to the Earl of Huntly.

AD 1500 – AD 1599

1500	Historian and scholar Hector Boece arrived in Aberdeen to become principal of the five-year-old university.
1503	James IV married Margaret, daughter of Henry VII of England. Through this marriage Mary Queen of Scots and then James VI claimed succession to the throne of England.
1504	Naval victory for Sir Andrew Wood over the English off Dundee.
1507	Printing was introduced by Walter Chapman, a servant in the royal household.
1512	Compilation of the Book of Lismore, a collection of Gaelic verse, some dating from the early fourteenth century, began.
1513	Having invaded England in support of his French allies, James IV and most of his nobility were slain at Flodden.
1515	Duke of Albany, heir-presumptive became leader of a pro-French party which was opposed by an English faction led by the Earl of Angus.
1520	'Cleanse the Causeway': an Edinburgh street-fight between the Douglas and the Hamilton families.
1522	John Knox became a student at Glasgow and the poet Gavin Douglas died.
1525	Angus obtained control of the government and guardianship of the young king.
1528	James V escaped from the Douglases, Angus' lands were confiscated and, having returned from Germany, Reformer Patrick Hamilton was burned at St Andrews.
1529	Border-reiver Johnny Armstrong and his followers hanged by royal command.
1532	Court of Session established. Royal expedition to the Highlands.
1535	Henry VIII proposed that James confiscate church property and marry Henry's daughter Mary Tudor.
1537	By marrying Madeleine, daughter of Francis I of France, James confirmed the Auld Alliance and opposition to the Reformation.
1538	On Madeleine's death, James married Mary of Guise, another Frenchwoman.
1540	Hostility among the Scots nobility reached new heights, forcing increasing royal dependence on the clergy. Act

	permitted the use of scriptures in the vernacular.
1542	Death of James V, shortly after the Battle of Solway Moss. Mary, a week-old child, was heir, but Arran became Regent. Scots victory at Hadden Rig in Roxburghshire.
1543	Treaties of Greenwich – abandoned by the Scots within a few months – promised peace between the old enemies and marriage of Mary to Prince Edward.
1544	Hertford's invasion of Scotland (the Rough Wooing) united most Scots against England.
1545	Angus defeated an English force at Ancrum Moor in the Borders.
1546	Cardinal Beaten executed Reformer George Wishart at St Andrews; in turn, reformers murdered Beaton and seized the castle.
1547	St Andrews Castle was retaken with French help. The Duke of Somerset (Hertford) defeated the Scots at Pinkie, near Musselburgh.
1548	Mary Queen of Scots sent to France and was betrothed to the Dauphin Francis under the Treaty of Haddington.
1550	Death of Mackinnon, the last abbot of Iona.
1554	Mary of Guise succeeded Arran as Regent and placed the French in a position of power in Scotland.
1555	Sir David Lindsay, poet and tutor to James V, died.
1556	Craftsmen of the Scottish burghs given the right to regulate their industries.
1557	'Lords of the Congregation', Reformation leaders, signed a covenant to protect the Reformed religion.
1558	Mary married the Dauphin Francis and conferred on him the title of 'King of Scotland'; French influence in Scotland was at its height.
1559	The Reformation, with Knox back in Scotland after a term as galley-slave, began in earnest with wrecking of churches and monasteries.
1560	Treaty of Edinburgh between France and England saw all foreign troops leave Scotland. Scots parliament abolished papal jurisdiction.
1561	Following the death of the Dauphin, Mary arrived at Leith to take the reins of government. Almost immediately, she celebrated mass, infuriating Knox and the fathers of the Reformation.
1562	Earl of Moray ended Huntly's rebellion – by defeating him at Corrichie near Aberdeen.
1565	Mary married her Catholic cousin, Henry, Lord Darnley.
1566	Riccio, who had become Mary's favourite, stabbed to death at Holyrood. James VI born.
1567	Mary, it is thought, plotted with the Earl of Bothwell in the murder of Darnley. Bothwell and Mary were married and prompted a revolt which secured her surrender at Carberry hill. The Reformed church was legalised.

1568	Having escaped from Lochleven Castle, Mary was finally defeated at Langside and the queen fled to England.
1570	Regent Moray was assassinated at Linlithgow by Hamilton of Bothwellhaugh.
1571	Another Regent, Lennox, was shot at Stirling and replaced by the Earl of Mar. Execution of James Hamilton, Archbishop of St Andrews.
1572	On Mar's death, Morton became Regent. John Knox died at Edinburgh.
1573	Edinburgh Castle fell with the help of English artillery. The cause of Mary was finally lost with her party agreeing at 'The Pacification of Perth' to acknowledge James VI.
1577	'Novo Erectio' of Glasgow University.
1578	Second Book of Discipline. Temporary overthrow of Morton. First yearly meeting of the Convention of Royal Burghs.
1579	Bible printed in Scotland for the first time.
1581	Execution of Regent Morton. James VI 'kidnapped' in Raid of Ruthven.
1582	Poet and royal tutor George Buchanan died.
1583	Foundation of Edinburgh University – a year after its Royal Charter from James VI.
1584	'Black Acts' declared the king head of the Kirk and authorised the appointments of bishops; it became treason for ministers to preach on public affairs. Protestant nobles fled to England.
1585	Religious league formed between England and Scotland.
1587	Mary was executed at Fotheringay Castle. Crown annexe ecclesiastical property.
1588	Preparations were being made to defend Scotland against the Spanish Armada.
1589	James VI married Anne of Denmark at Uppsala in Sweden. A rebellion by Catholic nobles was easily overcome.
1590	Beginning of the North Berwick witch-trials.
1592	Presbyterian church became more powerful force after the Estates, unhappy with the King, passed an Act abolishing bishoprics and giving government of the Kirk to the sessions, presbyteries and synods.
1593	Marischal College in Aberdeen founded.
1594	Forced to take action again Huntly and Errol, James crushed the Catholic cause in the north.
1596	James, threatening to deprive Edinburgh of its title as capital after rioting, forced its citizens into submission, depriving the Kirk of the city's support.
1598	Dundee Assembly attended mainly by northern clergy, where Presbyterianism had little hold, decided that their 'commissioners' should sit in parliament.

1600   Gowrie Conspiracy: James VI escaped a kidnap or assassination attempt and the plotters were executed with great barbarity. Prince Charles born Dunfermline. Bishops appointed to the sees of Aberdeen, Ross and Caithness.

1603   Death of Elizabeth I of England. James VI succeeded to her throne uniting the Crowns, although the parliaments functioned separately.

1605   Failed gunpowder-plot at Westminster. Renewed attempt to colonise Lewis by Lowland adventurers. Border Commission established to put down disorder.

1607   Union of Crowns led to Border laws being abolished. MacKenzie of Kintail acquired Lewis.

1609   Statutes of Iona – a plan to bring peace to the Western Highlands – included suppression of bards and setting up of wayside inns.

1612   Scots parliament confirmed Acts allowing bishops to be grafted on to the Presbyterian system.

1614   John Napier of Merchiston invented logarithms. Islay granted to Campbell of Cawdor.

1615   Jesuit John Ogilvie executed in Glasgow as persecution of Catholics grew apace.

1617   James VI visited Scotland on a round of official visits and participated in parliamentary business.

1618   A bribed and threatened Perth Assembly passed Five Articles which included kneeling at communion. They were approved by parliament three years later.

1622   Colony of Nova Scotia founded with baronetcies on offer for Scots entrepreneurs.

1625   James VI died and his son, Charles, became king. Act of Revocation reclaiming church lands for the Crown.

1633   Anglican ceremonial at the King's Edinburgh coronation caused great anxiety among the Presbyterians.

1635   Appointment of Archbishop Spottiswoode as Chancellor offended the nobility and alarmed the Kirk.

1636   Book of Canons – an attempt to force English-style worship on the people of Scotland – was rejected by Presbyterians.

1637   Attempted introduction of the book led to the infamous St Giles riot and the creation of 'the Tables', virtually a provisional government.

1638   National Covenant signed at Greyfriars in Edinburgh. A Glasgow Assembly excluded bishops, admitted laymen and turned previous legislation on its head.

1639   Covenanters soon had control of the country and Charles was forced to accept the Pacification of Berwick. Charles won the Marquis of Montrose over to his cause.

1640   Hostilities resumed in the 'Second Bishop's War', with a Scots force occupying Newcastle.

1641	Treaty of Ripon brought peace, but within a year the Covenanters were siding with the Long Parliament as a mercenary army against the king.
1644	Scots played an important part in the Parliamentary victory at Marston Moor, but Montrose secured a victory for the king, routing Lord Elcho at Tippermuir.
1645	A series of victories for Montrose made him temporarily master of Scotland before being defeated at Philiphaugh by Covenanting cavalry.
1646	Charles I walked into the Scots lines at Newark but they held on to the king for eight months until the issue of backpay was settled.
1648	Scots defeated by Cromwell at Preston.
1649	Execution of Charles I. On hearing of his death the Scots immediately declared his son Charles II king, appealing to him to embrace the Covenant.
1650	Huntly and Montrose executed. Scots defeated by Cromwell at Dunbar.
1651	Scots did not yield, crowning Charles at Scone and invading England. Cromwell turned in pursuit, and destroyed them at Worcester. Monk completed the conquest of Scotland.
1652	Scotland was united with England in the Commonwealth; administration in Scotland was predominantly English.
1653	Quakers first reported in Scotland.
1654	Royalists under the Earl of Glencairn defeated at Dalnaspidal.
1658	Death of Cromwell.
1660	Charles II's restoration as acclaimed by Royalists, while Presbyterians hoped the king would establish their religious system in England.
1661	Full episcopacy superseded presbytery. Argyll was beheaded for treason and other Covenanters were executed. Acts against swearing, to encourage industry and to protect Scots trade, were passed.
1662	No Covenanter could hold public office, 350 ministers were expelled from their parishes as a result and field conventicles were reported.
1666	'Pentland Rising' ended with the rout of Covenanters from South-west Scotland at Rullion Green in the Pentland Hills.
1670	Despite some indulgences the conventicles and the Covenanters came under greater pressure.
1676	Severe laws were passed making it a crime to give sustenance to the Covenanters.
1678	Hoping to provoke revolt in order to deal a crushing blow, Lauderdale quartered 8,000 Highlanders – the so-called Highland Host – for six weeks in the West of Scotland.
1679	Archbishop Sharp was murdered on Magus Muir near St

Andrews. Rebellion by Covenanters saw victory at Drumclog, then defeat by the Duke of Monmouth at Bothwell Bridge.

1680 Declaration of Sanquhar repudiating Charles as king left the 'Cameronians' as rebels. West of Scotland put under martial law. The 'Killing Times' begin.

1685 Charles II died. Covenanters sorely oppressed and atrocities reported. James VII & II became king.

1687 New indulgence strengthened the Presbyterian cause by allowing exiled ministers back to Scotland.

1688 William of Orange was invited to protect the liberties of the people after the birth of the Catholic Prince of Wales. James escaped to France and the English parliament claimed he had abdicated.

1689 William and Mary accepted the Crown of Scotland. Highland army disintegrated after victory at Killiecrankie, Viscount Dundee having been killed.

1690 James VII concedes Ireland after his defeat by William of Orange at the Battle of the Boyne. The present Presbyterian system of government in the Church of Scotland was established by parliament.

1692 MacEion of Glencoe failed to sign an oath of allegiance to William in sufficient time, leading to the infamous Massacre of Glencoe.

1695 Bank of Scotland and the Company Trading to Africa and the Indies, which eventually sent out the Darien expedition, founded.

1696 English support withdrawn for the Darien scheme – seen as competition. Estates declared that every parish should have a school – claimed as the first system of national education in the world.

1697 Barrier Act: any measure approved by the General Assembly of the Church of Scotland had to be remitted and approved by a majority of presbyteries before being finally passed.

1698 Three expeditions sailed from Scotland to Darien, each in turn being forced to abandon the colony in the jungle of Central America.

AD 1700 – AD 1799

1702 Anne, daughter of James VII, succeeded to the thrones of Scotland and England. English choice of her successor, Sophia, Electress of Hanover, rejected by the Scots.

1703 Act Anent Peace and War in which Scotland asserted its right (after Anne's death) to an independent foreign policy, free of English control.

1704 Negotiation for Union began – feelings had become so bitter in both countries that union or war seemed the only alternatives.

1706	By the Treaty of Union Scottish Commissioners agreed to an incorporating union (English representatives would not consider a federal solution). Safeguards to maintain Scottish identity were included.
1707	The Treaty of Union was passed by both parliaments and received royal assent.
1708	Scots dissatisfaction expressed on the new 'partnership' and their loss of influence. French fleet with the Auld Pretender, James VIII, aboard appeared off Montrose, but fled.
1709	Parliament's application to Scotland of the English law on treason was seen by the Scots as a violation of the Act of Union.
1712	A motion in the House of Commons to repeal the Union was lost by three proxy votes. The reimposition of lay patronage in the Kirk was seen as running contrary to the spirit of the Union.
1714	George I became king on the death of Queen Anne.
1715	Jacobite uprising of 'the Fifteen' failed, mainly due to lack of French support. Twenty people were executed for their part in the 'rebellion'.
1719	Spanish support for the Jacobites saw a landing at Loch Duich, but the main expedition was dispersed by storms and the invaders were defeated at the Battle of Glenshiel.
1724	Levellers' Rising in Galloway: new enclosures were demolished by tenants thrown off their land to make way for 'improvements'.
1725	Malt-tax riots saw the abolition of the office of Secretary for Scotland. Military road-building was under way in the Highlands.
1727	Royal Bank of Scotland formed. George I died.
1737	Bitter animosity aroused against the government by penalties imposed on Edinburgh after the Porteous Riot.
1739	The Black Watch, otherwise known as the 42nd Regiment, was formed, the first Highland regiment added to the British army. *Scots Magazine* first published.
1745	Jacobite army, smaller than its 'Fifteen' predecessor and again with only token French support, occupied Edinburgh, defeated Cope at Prestonpans and advanced towards London as far as Derby.
1746	Retreating to Scotland, Bonnie Prince Charlie secured a victory at Falkirk, and made for the Highlands and final defeat at Culloden. Disarming Act passed.
1747	Heritable jurisdictions – which allowed local dignitaries to try even capital offences – were abolished.
1751	Turnpike Act made for cheaper and speedier carriage of goods to market.
1752	Highland estates forfeited after the 'Forty-Five' were taken over by the Crown and rental used to build schools

	and churches, and encourage economic growth.
1757	During the Seven Years War, the government began to recruit regiments from the Jacobite clans.
1760	George II died. Scots industry began to expand. Carron Ironworks commenced smelting of ironstone; Scottish banks opened branches in country towns.
1765	James Watt's invention of a separate condenser made possible the adaptation of steam-engines to drive all sorts of machinery,
1768	*Encyclopaedia Britannica* founded in Edinburgh.
1769	Patriarchal relationship between Highland chiefs and their clanspeople had ended, rents were raised and tenants evicted, and overseas emigration as a result of these 'Clearances' began in earnest.
1770	Work was well under way on Edinburgh's New Town – the vision of architect James Craig. Short leases which had held back land-improvement for centuries were ended.
1771	Excavation and dredging had made the Clyde one of the great maritime rivers of Europe.
1772	Collapse of the Ayr Bank.
1776	American War of Independence ruined Virginia trade of Glasgow's tobacco lords but heralded the development of the cotton industry. Adam Smith published his *Wealth of Nations*.
1782	Repeal of the post-Culloden Act which prohibited the use of Highland dress.
1783	Scottish affairs were dominated for the following two decades by Henry Dundas, exercising patronage. He influenced elections and was able to suppress most opposition.
1784	Highland estates forfeited after the 'Forty-Five' restored to their legal heirs. Highland and Agricultural Society formed, as was the Scottish Fishery Board.
1786	After the first cotton-mill at Rothesay (1779), mills were springing up widely, most notably at New Lanark, and Glasgow was soon to follow. Andrew Meikle was working in East Lothian on his steam-driven threshing-machine.
1788	Bonnie Prince Charlie died in Rome. Jacobite heroine Flora Macdonald died two years later, having spent a number of years in North America.
1790	The first carding-machine in Scotland was erected at Galashiels, and mills sprang up for the woollen industry.
1792	Convention in Edinburgh to discuss parliamentary reform in the aftermath of the French Revolution.
1793	Radicals – including advocate Thomas Muir – transported for sedition. The following year Thomas Downie and Robert Watt, leaders in a plot to seize Edinburgh Castle, were sentenced to death for treason.
1796	Formation of a Whig party in Edinburgh with a

programme of parliamentary and burgh reform.

1797 Riots, over raising of the militia in expectation of a French invasion, saw 11 deaths in skirmish with soldiers at Tranent, East Lothian.

AD 1800 – AD 1899

1800 Bad harvests meant widespread food shortages; it was the era of the 'Meal Mobs'.

1801 Heavy engineering in the Clyde Valley received another boost with David Mushet's discovery of smelting the local blackband ironstone. Crinan Canal opened.

1802 A flurry of new periodicals – including the *Edinburgh Review* – was noted around this time.

1803 Boost for parish schools, as houses were to be provided for teachers and salaries slightly increased.

1804 Work began on the Caledonian Canal and the upgrading of Highland roads.

1807 The Sutherland Clearances – the high-handed removal of tenants to the coast to make way for sheep – began.

1810 Kilmarnock and Troon railway opened. Bell Rock lighthouse was completed, and Scotland led the way in the Savings Bank movement.

1812 The world's first steamboat on a navigable river – Henry Bell's *Comet* – was launched at Port Glasgow and quickly transformed seafaring.

1817 A Whig weekly newspaper – *The Scotsman* – published in Edinburgh; and the *Edinburgh Magazine* appeared as a Tory rival to the *Edinburgh Review*.

1819 Development of charitable relief influenced by Dr Thomas Chalmers, whose principle was that charity should keep alive mutual help and social ties.

1820 So-called Radical War: yeomanry occupied Glasgow when 60,000 went on strike. After minor skirmishes, including the Battle of Bonnymuir, three leaders were executed.

1822 George IV's spectacular Tartan Tour of Scotland. Caledonian Canal opened to traffic.

1823 Charles Mackintosh patented waterproof fabric and an improved system of land-drainage was introduced by James Smith, of Deanston, Perthshire.

1827 Small, local railways were in use for the coal and iron industries but were not fully mechanised until the 1840s. First practical reaping-machine invented in Forfarshire.

1829 J.B. Neilson's discovery of the hot-blast smelting process first applied at the Clyde Ironworks in Glasgow. Kirk sent Dr Alexander Duff to India as her first missionary.

1832 Scottish Reform Act extended right to vote and increased the number of MPs to 53; followed by further Acts in

1868, 1885, and 1918.

1833   Burgh Reform Act gave voters the right to elect their own councils.

1834   The Kirk – worried about the drift away from Christianity – collected money to build 220 churches.

1842   Queen Victoria's first visit to Scotland.

1843   Long-running disputes on patronage led to the 'Disruption' when 474 ministers constituted themselves as the Free Church of Scotland.

1845   Scottish Poor Law introduced compulsory assessment for relief of the poor, again encouraging Highland landlords to favour emigration and lessen the numbers in receipt of relief.

1846   East coast rail route, connecting Scotland and England, opened, followed two years later by the Carlisle-Carstairs western link. United Presbyterian Church formed.

1848   Last Chartist demonstrations. Scotland plagued by a serious cholera outbreak.

1849   First of the annual Caledonian Balls in London to raise funds for Scottish charities.

1850   Young's works for the distillation of oil from shale opened at Bathgate.

1852   Highland Emigration Society founded.

1855   Victorian fascination with Scotland culminated in the construction of Balmoral Castle.

1857   Police forces were instituted in every Scottish burgh and county. A series of Improvement Acts were introduced for Scotland's urban areas

1859   Loch Katrine Waterworks opened by Queen Victoria.

1860   Coal Mines Regulation Act introduced and Willie Park won the world's first professional golf tournament at Prestwick.

1868   Scottish Reform Art increased the number of Scottish MPs to 60. Scottish Co-operative Wholesale Society was up and running.

1869   Wallace Monument at Stirling was completed.

1872   Parish school system abolished and replaced by the administration of school boards elected by ratepayers. Education became compulsory for all children between 5 and 14.

1874   By the Patronage Act the right of electing parish ministers in the Church of Scotland was given to congregations.

1877   First linoleum factory in Scotland was opened at Kirkcaldy. Giant Singer sewing-machine factory at Clydebank celebrated its tenth year of operation.

1878   Roman Catholic hierarchy in Scotland was restored, Roman Catholics having been given civil and religious liberty in 1829. City of Glasgow Bank collapsed.

1879   Tay Bridge collapsed. The cost of mining illustrated by two disasters in as many years at Blantyre, which claimed 246 lives.

1880   Caledonian Railway reached Oban; six years earlier the Highland railway reached its most northerly point at Thurso on the Pentland Firth.

1881   Householders' Act gave some Scotswomen a local vote.

1882   'Crofters War': land-raids and riots over lack of tenure in the Highlands, including Battle of the Braes in Skye, led to the creation of Napier Commission, the Crofters Act (1886) and the Crofters Commission.

1883   Sir William Smith founded the Boys' Brigade movement in Glasgow. University College, Dundee, founded.

1885   Reform Act: the number of Scottish MPs increased to 72 and the office of Secretary of State for Scotland was reconstituted. Within a couple of years a Scottish Office had been established at Whitehall.

1886   Scottish Home Rule Association formed. Crofters' riot in Tiree.

1888   Two great Scottish institutions established – the Scottish Labour Party, founded by Keir Hardie, and Celtic Football Club, which took to the field for the first time.

1889   Local Government (Scotland) Act set up county councils and set compulsory standards in education,

1891   An Commun Gaidhealach was founded for the cultivation of the Gaelic language and culture, and the following year the first National Mod was held at Oban.

1894   Scottish Grand Committee came into existence and parochial boards were replaced by elected parish councils to deal with poor relief and other local affairs.

1897   Scottish Trades Union Congress founded. Congested Districts Act looked to improve the urban areas of Scotland.

AD 1900 – AD 1980

1900   Free Church and the United Presbyterian Church came together as the United Free Church of Scotland.

1901   Education (Scotland) Act became law. The Glasgow International Exhibition was staged.

1907   Clydebank-built *Lusitania* regained the Atlantic-crossing record for Britain – held by Germany for the previous decade.

1908   Scottish Education Act extended the power of School Boards.

1911   Series of strikes began throughout Scotland including a dockers' riot at Dundee. Board of Agriculture set up.

1914   Housing of Working Classes Act came into force seeking improved living conditions. War was declared (4 August).

1915   Unrest among so-called Red Clydesiders. Gretna troop-train disaster – 215 people killed.

1918	County or large burgh became the administrative area for education in Scotland; number of parliamentary voters in Scotland raised from 800,000 (1910) to 2,211,000 (1918), including women over 30.
1919	Forty-hour strike and the famous George Square workers' demonstration.
1920	The Labour Party made significant gains on Glasgow Corporation.
1921	Scottish railway companies absorbed by the LNER or LMS companies. Kirk given liberty to adjudicate on matters of doctrine, worship, government and discipline.
1922	BBC's first radio broadcast from Glasgow.
1924	Lossiemouth-born Ramsay MacDonald became Britain's first Labour Prime Minister. Gold medal in Paris Olympics 400 metres for Eric Liddell.
1926	General Strike in May saw many Scots down tools; disturbances reported as blackleg labour operated trams and buses; troops sent into most large Scots towns and cities.
1928	Women got the vote for parliamentary and local elections on the same terms as men. The Grampian Hydro-electric power scheme was launched.
1929	Church of Scotland and United Free Church of Scotland amalgamated.
1930	Formation of the National Scottish Development Council announced.
1931	National Government formed. National Trust for Scotland and the Scottish Youth Hostel Association established. *Dictionary of the Older Scottish Tongue* first published.
1934	Scottish National Party was founded. The Cunard White Star liner, *Queen Mary*, was launched at John Brown's yard in Clydebank.
1936	Scottish Economic Committee established. London-based journalist charged after an attempt to shoot Edward VIII. Saltire Society formed.
1937	Hydro-electric stations of the Galloway Water-Power Company commenced operation.
1938	Empire Exhibition – a £10m pioneering international fair – was opened in Glasgow's Bellahouston Park. Iona Community founded by Revd George MacLeod.
1939	Commencement of the Second World War. Transfer of Scottish Office to Edinburgh.
1941	United States commitment to join the war emerged at a dinner in Glasgow; Hess parachuted into a Renfrewshire field; Clydebank blitz.
1943	North of Scotland Hydro-Electric Board formed.
1945	Scottish National Party won the Motherwell by-election.
1947	First Edinburgh International Festival. Lord Boyd-Orr, world-renowned Scots nutritionist, won the Nobel Prize.

	National Coal Board established.
1948	National Health Service established.
1949	Scottish Covenant arguing for Home Rule got 2.5m signatures.
1953	Royal Commission on Scottish Affairs reported.
1954	Work began on the Dounreay Fast Reactor in Caithness.
1955	Scottish Television began transmission.
1961	Steel strip mill at Ravenscraig and Linwood car-plant established.
1962	Scottish Development Department set up.
1964	University of Strathclyde – formerly the Royal College of Science and Technology – was founded.
1965	Establishment of the Highlands and Islands Development Board.
1967	Scottish National Party victory in the Hamilton by-election. First research instigated for North Sea oil.
1969	Wheatley Report on local government suggested reorganisation of regions and districts.
1971	Workers took over the shipyards on the Clyde as the famous UCS work-in was launched.
1973	Britain joined the European Economic Community. Kilbrandon Report recommended setting up of a separate Scottish legislature.
1974	Scottish National Party captured 11 seats at Westminster.
1975	Scottish Development Agency was established with clear signs of a run-down of heavy engineering in Central Scotland.
1979	Referendum on Scotland and Wales Act proposing devolution proved inconclusive and a campaign for a Scottish Assembly started.

abattoirs, 40, 76
Abercromby, Sir Ralph
  (soldier), 54–55
Aberdeen (shire), *see under
  more specific entry*
Aberfoyle, 275
abscesses, 190, 270
accents, 123
accidents, 11, 13, 37, 41, 48,
  55, 59, 65, 70, 74, 76, 78,
  81,111, 121, 149, 150, 165,
  167, 168, 171, 173, 178,
  194, 218, 227, 244–45, 253,
  256, 263, 272
acoustics, 11
acrobats, 154
adultery, *see* sexual behaviour
adventure/exploration, 91,
  117, 122, 126, 144, 186,
  211, 254
Aeronautical Society of Great
  Britain, 18
agriculture, *see* farming
Aidan (monk), 194
'Aiken Drum', 111
Airdrie, 73, 140
air-raids, 31, 65, 71, 75, 93,
  108, 162, 196, 198, 210,
  231, 248
airships, 150
Albany, Dukes of, 24, 39, 57,
  69, 109, 111, 165
Albion Rovers, 172
alcohol, *see* drink/drinking
Alexander I, 96
Alexander II, 153, 269
Alexander III, 19, 24, 36,
  122, 153, 189, 199, 210,
  216, 286
Alexander, Sir William
  (colonist), 218, 287
Allan, David (painter), 41, 50,
  175
allegiance, 173
Alloa, 41, 175, 182, 207, 287
Alloway, 27, 217
All-the-World (siege engine),
  30
ambassadors, 71, 95, 197
ambition, 107
Americans, *see* United States
  of America
anatomy, 16, 200, 238
An Commun Gaidhealach,
  100, 230
Anderson, John, 18, 33
Andrew, Prince, 270
*Ane Satyre of the Thrie
  Estaites*, 13
anger, 58, 85, 109, 137, 205,
  245, 256
Angus, 26, 52, 64, 177, 187,
  286
Angus, David (minister), 116
Annan (dale), 101, 102, 131
anthrax, 157
Anti-Monarchists, 148, 208
antiquities, 44
Anti-Saloon League, *see*
  drink/drinking
Antonine Wall, 61
appearances, 22, 62, 114, 119
Arbroath, 48, 81, 177, 239,
  251, 275, 287

archaeology, 44, 127, 237,
  255
archery, 18, 40, 117, 181, 190
Archimedes (steamship), 132
architecture, 89, 106, 125,
  184
Ardrossan, 233, 276
Argentina, 282
Argyll (shire), 13, 18, 57, 79,
  101, 102, 141, 171, 177, 210,
  212, 226, 230, 250, 263
Argyll and Sutherland Highlanders, 256
Aristotle, 10
Armada, *see* Spain
Armadale, 88
Armstrong, Archy (jester), 78
Armstrong, John (poet),
  52–53
Arran, 31, 74, 117, 141, 204,
  245, 258, 282
arrests, 69, 110
arrivals, 55, 137, 154, 178
Arrochar, 139
art, 41, 42, 50, 66, 69, 132,
  139, 178, 186, 260
Arthur, Sir John (priest), 113
astrology, *see* fortune-telling
astronomy, 60, 99, 216, 238
athletics, 68, 78, 167, 273
Athole, Earl of, 98
Atlantis, 35, 262
atrocities, 187, 200
Auchinleck, 260
Auchtermuchty, 117
auctions, 192
audiences, 55, 158, 210, 287
Auld Alliance, 47, 55, 122,
  183, 225, 237, 265
Auld Nick (Satan), 16, 115,
  165, 166, 167, 169
Auld Pretender (James VIII),
  60, 105, 198, 230, 286
Auld Reekie (Edinburgh), 44
Auldcorne, Steven (Sabbath-
  breaker), 100
Aurora Borealis, *see* northern
  lights
Australia, 18, 32, 43, 184,
  217, 222
Austria, 116
aviation, 13, 17, 18, 79, 108,
  116, 160, 168, 171, 184,
  191, 194, 195, 198, 202,
  242, 282
Ayr (shire), *see under more
  specific entry*

bagpipes, 48, 106, 131, 140,
  178, 201, 202, 222, 223, 249
Baillie, William (Covenanter),
  182
Bain, Alexander (clock-
  maker), 274
Baird, Sir David (soldier), 271
Baird, Janet (criminal), 55
Baird, John Logie (inventor),
  28, 181
bakers, 16, 83, 145, 162
balance, 10, 23
baldness, 179
Balfour, John (witchfinder),
  11
Balliol family, 23, 30, 38, 73,

96, 99, 148, 175, 215, 256,
  266
balloons, 33, 191
Balquhidder, 287
bamboo, 264
Banchory, 94
Bane, Donald (swordsman),
  140
Banff (shire), 83, 99, 228, 23■
banishment and transportation
  12, 26, 27, 28, 55, 58,
  79, 89, 101–2, 110, 122,
  142, 144, 156, 172, 182,
  188, 202, 209, 210, 216,
  235, 245, 253
Bankfoot, 11
banking/finance, 50, 60, 94,
  95, 108, 112, 122, 123, 127,
  140, 154, 157, 171, 204,
  228, 237, 271, 278, 279, 28■
bannocks, 173
baptism, 41, 113, 197, 273
Barassie, 19
bards, 33
Barra, 117
Barrhead, 223
Barrie, Sir James (writer),
  122, 286
barometers, 186
Barton, Sir Andrew (salty
  dog), 217
Bass Conqueror, 28
Bass Rock, 82, 266, 275
Bastian, 273
battles, 21, 190
  Ancrum Moor (1545), 52
  Arkinholm (1455), 129
  Auldearn (1645), 107
  Bannockburn (1314), 95,
    136, 139, 142
  Baugé (1421), 69
  The Butts (1544), 117
  Carberry Hill (1567), 134
  Corrichie (1562), 242
  Culloden (1746), 18, 20, 85,
    88, 117, 137, 181, 206,
    249, 260
  Dunbar (1296 and 1650),
    96, 136, 198, 235
  Dupplin Moor (1332), 175,
    215
  Falkirk (1298 and 1746),
    165, 167, 247
  Flodden (1513), 21, 38, 70,
    109, 150, 174–75, 193,
    212, 238, 276
  Glenshiel (1719), 131
  Halidon Hill (1333), 161
  Homildon (1402), 206
  Killicrankie (1689), 77, 140,
    167, 192
  Langside (1568), 18
  Largs (1263), 221
  Loudoun Hill (1307), 107
  Methven (1306), 138
  Nesbit Moor (1305 and
    1402), 140, 219
  Neville's Cross (1346), 22,
    231
  Otterburn (1388), 67
  Philiphaugh (1645), 206
  Pinkie (1547), 204, 210
  Prestonpans (1745), 18, 28,
    188, 212

Sauchieburn (1488), 42, 286
Sheriffmuir (1715), 247, 254
Solway Moss (1542), 261
Standard (1138), 188
Stirling Bridge (1297), 205
Verneuil (1424), 183
bayonets, *see* warfare
Beach Boys, 285
beards, 108, 238
bears, 60, 186
beasts of burden, 28, 29, 140, 246
Beaton, Cardinal David, 27, 94
Beattock, 42, 84, 130
Beaumont, Comyns (journalist), 23
beds, *see* sleep
Beeching, Dr Richard (rail-closer), 74
bees/beekeeping, 157, 215
Beggars' Summons, 10
begging, 21, 57, 65, 76, 102, 112, 244, 248, 252
belching, 25, 209
Belgium, 157, 177
Bell, Alexander Graham (inventor), 139, 259
Bell, 'Professor' Charlie (prize-fighter), 90
Bell, Henry (engineer), 23, 117
Bell, Dr Joseph (surgeon), 223
bells, 54, 101, 162, 242, 258
Bengal, 37
berrypicking, 167
Berwick (shire), 16, 58, 80, 89, 92, 103, 105, 121, 130, 132, 134, 137, 161, 178, 188, 201, 207, 222, 251, 259, 270, 277
betrayal/treachery, 48, 173, 264
betting, *see* gambling
bibles, 65, 91, 195, 251, 269, 281
bicycles, 131
big people, 84
billiards/snooker, 43
birds, 18, 27, 36, 38, 39, 45, 50, 59, 119, 157, 171, 179, 186, 192, 201, 275
Bisset, Habbakuk (lawyer), 42
bizarre events, 45, 66, 121, 138
Black Agnes, 267
Black Dinner, 261
Black Isle, 39
Black, Joseph (chemist), 88
Black Rood, 231
Black Watch, 42
blackmail, 249
Blaikie, John (slicer), 85
Blair Atholl, 11, 42, 258, 282
Blair, Robert (astronomer), 60
Blairgowrie, 16, 38, 167
Blantyre, 68
Bleary Bob, *see* Robert II, 67
Blind Harry (minstrel), 97, 247
blindness, 252
blood/bleeding, 71, 91, 121, 218
Blundell, Dom Odo (diver), 127

body parts, 16, 81, 184, 189, 200, 221, 222, 238
bodysnatchers, 27, 44, 258
Boece, Hector (chronicler), 164, 186
Bonawe, 250
Bonnie Dundee (John Graham of Claverhouse), 167
Bonnie Prince Charlie (Prince Charles Edward Stuart), 11, 42, 72, 94, 137, 138, 156, 166, 198, 200, 206, 207
Bo'ness, 47, 110
books, 16, 47, 64, 79, 81, 108, 111, 211, 212, 251
booty/plunder, 136, 188
Border Country, 27, 46, 48, 52, 63, 74, 80, 85, 90, 98, 110, 125, 127, 129, 130, 151, 178, 182, 208, 249, 251, 279
Borulawski, Count (musician), 65
Boswell, James (biographer), 111, 181, 205, 242, 260
botany, 13, 34, 282
Bothwell, 33, 46, 58, 125, 148, 166, 184, 216, 287
boundaries, 200
Bowes-Lyon, Elizabeth (Queen Mother), 95, 182
bowls, 231
boxing, 90, 138, 155
Boy Scouts, 91
Boyd, Janet (witch), 244
Boyd, Robert (reformer), 81
Boyd Orr, Lord (nutritionist), 228
bracken, 74
Braemar, 192, 239
Branks, 110
brass neck, 57–58, 63, 68, 69, 139, 189, 215
Braxfield, Lord (judge), 204
Brazil, 79, 131
breast-feeding, 41
Brechin, 30, 42, 137, 285
brewing, *see* drink/drinking
bridge, 55
bridges, 13, 24, 101, 111, 143, 146, 156, 159, 168, 250, 258, 264, 279, 287
Britannia, 50
British Medical Association, 9
broadcasting, *see* television and radio
Brora, 110
Brotherhood of Horse Whisperers, 165
Brown, James (adventurer), 58
Brown, Robert (botanist), 282
Brown, Thomas (fisherman), 229
Broxburn, 238
Bruce, Edward (patriot), 32, 95, 145, 223
Bruce, James (explorer), 255, 263
Bruce, Robert (king), 34, 38, 44, 57, 74, 75, 107, 138, 154, 156, 159, 161, 175, 189
Buccleuch family, 52, 121, 131

Buchan, 24, 74
Buchanan Charity Society, 57
Buchanan, George (tutor), 79, 218
Buchanan, Thomas (church-man), 45
Buckhaven, 102
Buckie, 279
Budd, Mrs (large lady), 123
Buffalo Bill's Wild West Show, 113, 163
building trade, 63, 74, 122, 131, 132
Burghead, 263, 277
Burke and Hare (medical suppliers), 200, 285
Burns, Sir Alexander (traveller), 245
Burns, Gilbert (poet's brother), 217
Burns, Robert (poet), 24, 27, 83, 97, 143, 153, 171, 190
Burns, Thomas (missionary/pioneer), 71
Burntisland, 37, 100, 229, 267, 280
Butcher Cumberland (general), 20, 85, 88
butchers, 81, 177, 207, 276
Bute, 178, 288

cabbages, 106, 215
Cadder, 54
Cadie, Janet (transvestite), 186
Caithness, 127, 138, 164, 175, 187, 194, 198, 274, 275
Calderwood, David (chronicler), 45
Caledonian Canal, 143, 201, 209
Caledonian Forest, 102
Caledonian Railway, 42, 101, 134, 228
calendar, 279
Calgacus, 228
Callander, 64
camels, 18, 116
Camerons, 37, 242, 277
Campania, 227
Campbells, 73, 183, 233
Campbeltown, 184, 226
Campsie, 84, 106
Canada, 12, 35, 69, 91, 123, 125, 155, 160, 200, 203, 218, 223, 242, 268
canals, 143, 201, 209, 222, 276
Canna, 178
Cannich, 242
capture/captivity, 155, 162, 170, 173, 187, 206, 239
Cardross, 260
carelessness, 75, 156
Carey, Sir Robert, 73
Carfine (taxidermist), 210
Cargill, Donald (Covenanter), 215
Carlyle, Alexander (minister), 28
Carlyle, Thomas (historian), 227, 272
Carmichael, Sir John (victim), 101
Carmichael, Robert (teacher), 12

Carnegie, Andrew (multi-millionaire), 143, 208, 233
Carrick, 83, 195
Carse of Gowrie, 157
Carson, Willie (jockey), 181
Carstairs, 182
Carstairs, William (diplomat), 160
Caskie, Donald (minister), 287
Cassilis, Earls of, 195, 245
castaways, 86
castles, 98, 220
  Balmoral, 149, 188, 200, 227, 239, 266
  Borthwick, 48
  Craigmillar, 123
  Dumbarton, 11, 125
  Edinburgh, 31, 33, 37, 60, 66, 198, 230, 269
  Eilean Donan, 131
  Falkland, 26, 111, 140, 154, 181, 277
  Fast, 127, 161
  Hume, 228
  Lewis,
  Roxburgh, 52, 173
  Stirling, 21, 30, 33, 40, 48, 165, 195, 197
  Tantallon, 277
cats, 184, 211, 242
cattle, 16, 29, 102, 117, 118, 121, 156, 205, 220, 245
celebrations, 182
Celtic FC, 118
Ceres, 162
Chalmers, Thomas (theologian), 149–50
Charles I (king), 31, 81, 139, 140, 144, 153, 154, 158, 231
Charles II (king), 10, 26, 34, 88, 101, 244
Charlotte Dundas, 12, 74
charms, 55, 234
Chaseabout Raid, 192
Chaucer, William (writer), 79
cheats, 192
cheerfulness, 239
chemistry, 88
childbirth/pregnancy, 88, 186, 252
children, 43, 44, 60, 67, 70, 75, 80, 88, 95, 121, 123, 142, 155, 162, 163, 164, 177, 192, 198, 199, 205, 209, 213, 216, 223, 271, 283, 286, 289
Chile, 71, 94
chimneysweeps, 207, 270, 271
chivalry, 150
chocolate, see food
cholera, see health
Chopin, Frederick, 217
Christmas, 16, 27, 85, 149, 286
church affairs, see religion
cinemas, 13, 89, 195, 212, 223, 239, 269, 289
circuses, 18, 35, 55, 90, 232, 251
Clackmannan (shire), 11, 54, 188
Claim of Right, 84
clairvoyance, see fortune-telling

clans, 217, 221, 226, 271, 276, 288
Clark, Jim (racing-driver), 81, 172
Clark and Ramsay (poisoners), 51
Clark, William (old stager), 85
Clayson Committee, 172
clearances, 132, 155
Clerk, Sir John (unionist), 19, 51
clocks/clockwatchers, see time
close calls, 64, 74
clothing, 63, 80, 83, 95, 117, 149–50, 214, 259
clouds, 180
clowns, 35
Cluny's Cage, 206
Cluthas, 19
Clydebank, 16, 34, 40, 65, 70, 73, 79, 99, 107, 169, 211, 217, 233, 248
Clyde FC, 110
Clydesdale FC, 64
coal, see mining
cobblers, 83
Cochrane, William (bagpiper), 140
Cockburn Association, 103
Cockburn, Lord, 104
Cockburnspath, 103
Cockenzie, 18
cocking, 27, 173
cod war, 127
Coldingham, 75, 160, 189
Coldstream, 177
Cole, Blanche (singer), 105
colours, 73, 89, 112, 145, 147, 175, 220
comedy, see entertainment
Comet (horse), 90
Comet (steamship), 23, 274
commerce, see trade
communication, 33, 53, 245
companionship, 59
compensation, 52
competition, 66, 123, 150, 161
Compton, Carol (nanny), 279
con-artists, 20, 129, 184
Concorde, 198
conspiracy, 175, 205
contests, 152, 222
Cook, Thomas (travel agent), 142
cool head, 171
Cope, Sir John (soldier), 188
coronations, 67, 73, 74, 85, 110, 177, 212, 272
cosmic events, see sky events
courage, 171
Court of Session, 110
Covenanters, 71, 85, 105, 107, 111, 162, 182, 206, 207, 235, 237, 269
Crab, John (engineer), 30
Craig, J. (hero), 200
Craig, James (architect), 125
Craig, Mungo (bagpiper), 106
Crail, 28, 261
Cramond, 33
Crathie, 204
Crawford, John (lawyer), 66
Crawford, Captain Thomas

(soldier), 11
crawlers, 182
'Creeping Parliament', 182
Crichton, the 'Admirable' (adventurer), 149
cricket, 26, 113
crime, 11, 29, 142
Crimea, 200, 254
crofters, 34, 66, 73, 117, 143, 167, 206, 227, 250, 255
Cromarty, 81, 259
Cromwell, Oliver (soldier), 76, 116, 142, 162, 198, 214
cross-dressing, see sexual behaviour
crowds, 17, 24, 75, 107, 111, 124, 154, 167, 178, 192, 194, 199, 205, 250
cruelty, 78, 220
Crusoe, Robinson, see Selkirk, Alexander
Culbin Sands, 269
Culloden, see battles
Culross, 165
Cumbernauld, 11, 102, 277
Cumbrae, 261
Cumin, William (litigant), 54
Cupar, 43, 58, 75, 99, 266, 274
Currie, 204
curry/hot dishes, 210
Curry (jester), 188
cursing, see swearing
Customs and Excise, 31, 161, 232
Cuthbertson, William (thief), 209
Cutty Sark, 134
cycling, 73, 131

Dalkeith, 131, 199
dancing, 25, 76, 79, 86, 166, 182, 186, 212, 244, 251, 259
Danzig, 159, 194, 211
Darien Expedition, 63, 75, 143, 167
darkness, 45–46
Darnley, Lord, 26, 62, 152, 279
Dasher, 74
Dauphin Francis, 176, 270
David I, 83, 92, 94, 116, 188, 248, 266
David II, 22, 57, 58, 74, 156, 222, 231, 249, 272
Davidson, John (virginal maker), 36
deafness, 209
death, 24, 38, 166, 178
debt, 227
debutantes, 149
decapitation, see executions
decorating, 198, 220
dedication, 91
deer, 79
defiance, 73
deformation, 62, 222
demolition, 73, 86
Demon Dwarves, 138
Dempster, John (rustler), 58
Denmark, 117, 154, 156, 194
Denny, 168
dentistry, 75, 108, 115, 182, 190, 205
despair, 84, 117
Detector of Robberies, 80

development aid, 161
Devil, *see* Auld Nick
Devil Dogs, *see*
  witches/witchcraft
Devorguilla (benefactress),
  188
Diana (whaler), 246
Dick, Sir William (merchant),
  281
Dickson, John, 173
Dickson of Kilbucko (cheery
  neb), 215
Dinely, Sir John (eccentric),
  89
Dingwall, 37, 202
diplomacy, 39
disappearances, 34, 39, 83,
  125
disasters, 111, 216, 221, 223,
  230, 23
  287, 289
discoveries, 107, 262
disguises, 108, 116, 158, 247
disinterest, 47, 49
disputes, 52, 188
'Disruption'(1843), 12, 104,
  241
dissection, 27
distance, 47, 61, 148
disturbances, 70, 73, 97, 126,
  155, 161, 166, 195, 255
divorce, 210
Docherty, John (volunteer),
  42
dogs, 9, 19, 69, 72, 81, 112,
  138, 139, 177, 233, 244, 260
Don, *see* rivers
Donibristle, 229
Dornoch, 113, 168, 181, 227
Douglas, David (explorer),
  117
Douglas, Earls of, 48, 128,
  162, 166, 223
Douglas, Sir James (knight),
  189
Douglas, Mary (house-
  breaker), 216
Dowding, Lord Hugh (flier),
  223
Doyle, Sir Arthur Conan
  (writer), 90
'Dragon Hole', 101
draughts, 205
dreams, 51, 180
drinking/drinks, 40, 52, 63,
  65, 103, 110, 117, 121, 122,
  134, 138, 168, 172, 177,
  215, 237, 269, 280
  ale, 13, 134, 221, 254
  barmaids, 26
  drunkenness, 11, 12, 16, 23,
  66, 68, 89, 90, 94, 95, 96,
  139, 159, 160, 209, 226,
  227, 230, 254
  measures, 132, 170
  punch, 257–58
  whisky, 9, 13, 16, 22, 34,
  135, 144, 171, 232, 253,
  254
  wine, 10, 48, 82, 89, 166,
  265
driving, *see* motor racing/
  motoring
drought, 127, 145, 167, 177,
  178, 222, 230
drownings, 17, 26, 31, 39, 41,

107, 110, 112, 118, 154,
  181, 183, 201, 206, 215,
  218, 226, 227, 253
drugs/drug abuse, 38, 271
Drummond, Robert (public
  suicide), 84
Duchess of Hamilton, 154
Duchess of Montrose, 94
ducks, *see* birds
Duds, Doctor (quack
  physician), 212
duelling, 12, 44, 85, 140, 282
Duly, David (tailor), 212
Dumbarton, 11, 134, 139,
  142, 196, 199, 233, 244, 250
Dumbreck FC, 64
Dumfries (shire), 38, 70, 71,
  78, 79, 101, 102, 111, 126,
  132, 192, 209, 225, 263,
  271, 272
Dunbar, 119, 183
Dunbar, William (poet), 182
Dunbartonshire, 61, 239
Dunblane, 74, 178, 254
Duncan I (king), 181, 263
Dundee, 16, 33, 36, 39, 42,
  48, 53, 54, 75, 78, 122, 140,
  150, 172, 195, 207, 213,
  227, 236, 246, 251, 268,
  271, 289
Dundee United FC, 173
Dundrennan Abbey, 111
Dunfermline, 19, 44, 66, 122,
  140, 181, 200, 204, 208,
  236, 255, 267
dung, 179, 191, 192
Dunkeld, 200
Dunoon, 102, 263
Duns, 105, 140, 166, 177
Duntocher, 12, 152
Durham, James (soldier), 19
Durness, 210
Dyce, 53
Dysart, 89, 277
dysentery, 235
dyspepsia, *see* indigestion

Eadie, William (old-timer),
  258
eagles, 16, 216
Eaglesham, 107
earache, 268
early closing, 113, 196
earthquakes, 27, 37, 53, 54,
  121, 145, 149, 165, 239,
  244, 250, 284–85
East Kilbride, 269
East Linton, 33, 205
East Lothian, 28, 33, 68, 82,
  83, 108, 113, 121, 146, 160,
  205
East Wemyss, 29
Eastern FC, 64
eccentricity, 23, 59, 86, 89,
  280
eclipses, 45
economics, 61, 67, 127, 136,
  245, 251
Ecurie Ecosse, 170
Edinburgh, *see* under more
  specific entry
education, 11, 12, 19, 21, 23,
  27, 43, 47, 57, 74, 78, 105,
  106, 107, 132, 142, 167,
  184, 198, 202, 207, 210,
  218, 225, 239, 248, 258,

259, 266, 281, 286, 288
eels, 32, 237
efficiency, 66
Egfrith (king), 115
eggs, 66, 78, 95, 136, 146,
  276
Eglinton, Earls of, 238
Egypt, 55, 226
Eigg, 89, 175, 178, 259
electricity, 34, 57, 121, 221,
  288
elephants, 55, 128, 142, 143,
  182
Elgin (shire), 17, 37, 81, 137,
  181
Elphinstone, Sir George
  (provost), 165, 189
Elphinstone, Sir Keith
  (designer), 172
Elphinstone, Bishop William,
  238
embarrassment, 20, 166, 178,
  206
emergency services, 13, 85
emigration, 12, 43, 71, 81, 91,
  103, 155, 208, 222, 233,
  276,
employment, 28, 39, 58, 68,
  79, 101, 118, 145, 208, 223,
  285
Encyclopedia Britannica,
  191, 194
England and the English, 12,
  14, 19, 20, 42, 46, 48, 49,
  54, 60, 72 – 73, 89, 100,
  102, 108, 111, 150, 192,
  207, 244
entertainment, 13, 20, 22, 25,
  36, 50, 55, 80, 82, 89, 105,
  116, 146, 154, 158, 168,
  193, 195, 212, 226, 287
enthusiasm, 204, 220, 230
environment, 57, 181, 269
'Equivalent Money', 175
Eriskay, 34
Erskine, Lord Thomas
  (chancellor), 24
escalades, 11
escapades, 33
escapes, 41, 48, 101, 114,
  142, 154, 192, 202, 206,
  212, 215, 216, 223, 230,
  266, 286
Eskdalemuir, 284
espionage, 62, 68, 85, 137,
  183
ethnic groups, 113, 200, 238,
  244
evacuation, 194, 198
evaporation, 171
evictions, 167, 210, 267, 277
executions, 21, 28, 34, 37, 40,
  42, 48, 51–52, 53, 54, 57,
  59, 66, 71, 82, 84, 89, 97,
  98, 107, 115, 116, 122, 126,
  132, 168, 173, 182, 184,
  189, 194, 202, 219, 233,
  236, 249, 250, 251, 268,
  283, 287, 289
exhibitions, 112, 168
expense accounts, 92–93, 123
experiments, 86, 114
exploitation, 139, 267
exploration, *see* adventure
explosions/explosives, 44, 65,
  74, 100, 149, 213, 216, 223,

237, 266, 275, 282
extinct animals, 143
extra-terrestrials, 223
extroverts, 73
Eyemouth, 89, 177
eyesight, 67, 159, 200, 252

'Facetious Bailie Hood', 31
fair holidays, 28, 95, 160
Fair Isle, 217
fairs, 28, 178, 188
faith, 57–58
falconry, 193
Falkirk, 13, 80, 127, 154, 216
Falkland Palace, see castles
fall guys, 195
false alarms, 94, 228
fame, 52
family life, 80, 102, 266
famine, 37, 42, 46, 52, 55, 66,
    68, 81, 88, 95, 118, 133,
    138, 161, 171, 177
fantasies, 98, 143
farming, 13, 14, 29, 32, 34,
    37, 40, 42, 44, 46, 52, 53,
    64, 66, 74, 79, 86, 115, 122,
    127, 131, 140, 143, 149,
    177, 192, 205, 218, 238,
    253, 256, 266
farting, 25, 209
fashion, 48, 49, 73, 84, 109,
    136, 144, 145, 212, 228
fasting, 37, 163
Faulds, Henry (doctor), 142
Faw, Johnny (gipsy), 43
Fawkes, Guy (terrorist), 100
fear, 46, 53, 133, 143, 166,
    222
feet, 50, 115, 127
femininity, 68, 183
feminism, 24, 33, 46, 56, 63,
    68, 81, 83, 84, 106, 126, 152,
    221, 228, 231, 267, 288
Fenwick, 251
Fergus Mor mac Erc (king),
    67
Ferguson, Alex (football
    manager), 289
Ferguson, David (churchman),
    45
Ferguson, James (stargazer),
    99
Ferguson, Patrick (inventor),
    225
Fergusson, Arthur (con man),
    184
Fergusson, John
    (entrepreneur), 23
Fergusson, Robert (poet), 231
ferries, 37, 44, 159, 253
fertiliser, 179, 191, 192
festivities, 101, 183, 185
Fettercairn, 231
feuds/vendettas, 48, 89, 125,
    171
Fife, 18, 19, 26, 27, 28, 29,
    32, 38, 43, 44, 46, 58, 66,
    69, 82, 85, 102, 110, 148,
    154, 157, 162, 165, 175,
    193, 215, 221, 229, 265,
    268, 274
finance, see banking/finance
Findhorn, 263
Findlay (whaler), 150
fingerprints, 142
fires, 16, 31, 32, 33, 57, 61,

63, 79, 82, 88, 90, 95, 98,
    99, 106, 116, 117, 121, 123,
    134, 137, 140, 142, 150,
    175, 178, 184, 188, 207,
    209, 217, 225, 228, 242,
    243, 245, 255, 258, 268,
    277
firsts, 28, 31, 55, 60, 83, 91,
    112, 115, 122, 128, 134,
    166, 182, 184, 196, 218,
    231, 238, 251, 256, 260,
    281, 285
fish/fishing, 17, 25, 34, 36,
    41, 53, 65, 71, 79, 84, 91,
    96, 99, 102, 105, 116, 118,
    125, 127, 131, 140, 141,
    150, 156, 161, 162, 173,
    175, 177, 183, 193, 194,
    227, 229, 233, 239, 253,
    254, 263, 268
flags and banners, 73, 161,
    168, 186, 207
flagstones, 210
Flanders, 31, 32, 42, 128
Fleming, Alexander
    (scientist), 139
Fleming, Lord, 150
Fleming, Rhoda (suffragette),
    154
Fletcher, Madame
    (revolutionary), 115
Fletcher of Saltoun
    (nationalist), 249
flies, 83, 168
flitting, 121
Flodden, see battles
floods, see weather
'Flowers o' the Forest', 175
flowers, 94, 166, 203
flu, 261, 264, 270
fluoride, 206
folk remedies, 11, 22, 121,
    128, 209, 233
folklore, 69, 91
food/feasting, 15, 18, 25, 29,
    49, 82, 83, 90, 92, 98, 106,
    107, 118, 119, 129, 137,
    138, 149, 159, 162, 165,
    177, 181, 188, 192, 201,
    212, 216, 223, 228, 244,
    261, 265
football, 14, 16, 17, 29, 40,
    47, 63, 68, 76, 79, 89, 97,
    101, 106, 108, 110, 117,
    118,138, 150, 154, 157, 172,
    182, 204, 205, 220, 222,
    226, 232, 245, 255, 265, 289
Forbes, Duncan of Culloden,
    135
forests, see trees
Forfar (shire), 32, 79, 95, 115,
    191
forgiveness, 97
fornication, see sexual
    behaviour
Fort Augustus, 127
Fort William, 110, 248
Forteviot, 36
Forth and Clyde Canal, 12,
    73, 74, 168, 269
Forth bridges, 24, 55, 141,
    200, 218
Fortingall, 227
Fortrose, 116
fortune-telling, 52, 59, 74, 83,
    127, 216, 244

Foula, 55
foxes, 94
France and the French, 9, 11,
    12, 16, 18, 21, 24, 26, 27,
    32, 33, 35, 37, 42, 46, 47,
    55, 62, 65, 69, 70, 71, 74,
    75, 77, 78, 82, 85, 89, 112,
    115, 120, 121, 123, 126,
    136, 139, 143, 150, 154,
    156, 157, 176, 182, 183,
    186, 187, 198, 201, 206,
    219, 225, 228, 231, 242,
    244, 262, 271, 272, 277,
    281, 287
Fraserburgh, 41, 110, 227,
    248
fraud/forgery, 37, 126, 143,
    159, 260, 289
Free Church of Scotland, see
    religion
fresh air, 142, 204
Freuchie, 26
Friends of Liberty, 157
friendship, 186
Friskin, James (Jacobite
    negro), 162
frogs, 11, 45, 114, 179
fruit, 37, 63, 134, 143, 167,
    189, 237
fuel, 71, 73, 119, 126, 144,
    255, 263
funerals, 17, 21, 24, 38, 43,
    63, 90, 123, 131, 133, 148,
    172, 188, 225, 245, 253,
    259, 270
Fyfe, Will (comedian), 168

Gaelic, 21, 74, 83, 86, 91,
    100, 154, 224
Galashiels, 253, 279
gales, see weather
gambling/betting, 23, 68, 94,
    106, 152, 175, 205
Garde Ecossaise, see France
gardening, 39, 89, 110
Gardenstone, Lord
    (eccentric), 59
Gardiner, James (soldier), 212
Gardner, John (minister), 17
Gareloch, 31
Garscadden, Kathleen (broad-
    caster), 44
gas, 16, 31, 166, 188, 200
Geddes, Jenny (rioter), 158
Geddie, John (beekeeper),
    215
Gemmel, Andrew (beggar),
    76
generosity, 42
Gentles, Thomas (thief), 122
geology, 46, 178
George IV (king), 76, 182
Gerard, Captain Alexander
    (voyager), 277
Germany and the Germans, 9,
    33, 37, 41, 66, 81, 96, 126,
    138, 139, 140, 157, 163,
    172, 173, 182, 183, 192
ghosts and ghoulies, 161,
    167, 174, 196
giants and dwarves, 22, 37,
    65, 80, 83, 138, 264
Gibbon, Margaret (thief), 250
Gibson, Walter (merchant),
    65
gifts, 256, 279

Gillies, David (pretender), 69
gipsies, 43, 59, 79, 117, 192, 251
giraffes, 187
Girdleness Lighthouse, 216
Girvan, 112
Gladstone, William (prime minister), 81, 256
Glasgow, *see under more specific entry*
glassmaking, 44, 58, 107, 227, 285
Glenbervie, 24
Glencairn, Earls of, 142
Glencorse, 180
glens
  Artney, 34
  Coe, 13, 15, 22, 139, 142
  Finnan, 168, 186
  Great, 244
  Isla, 187
  Loth, 9
  Roy, 32
gluttony, 18, 90, 166, 181
gold/gold-diggers, 57, 118, 154, 188, 222, 236, 261, 277
golf, 19, 33, 40, 41, 43, 48, 79, 110, 120, 126, 135, 152–53, 155, 200, 217, 264, 269
Golspie, 9
'Gondolier', 208
Gordon family, 43, 52
Gordon, Lady Jean (coal-miner), 110
Gordonstoun School, 134, 142, 248, 270
gossip, 110
Gourock, 96, 111
gout, 11, 168
Graham, Billy (evangelist), 69
Graham, Dougal (storyteller), 162
Graham, James (quack doctor), 87
Graham, Richard (wizard), 53
Grange, Lord (Jacobite), 27
Grangemouth, 52, 212
Granger, James (minister), 76
granite, 266
Grant, James (bandit), 230
Grant, J.A. (explorer), 64
Granton, 37
Granville, Kilmarnock FC, 64
gratitude, 242
graveyards, 38, 44, 63, 148, 161, 186
Gray, Alasdair (writer), 287
Gray, Andrew (prodigal son), 81
Great Bernera, 256
Great Michael, 154, 230
Great Train Robbery, 177
Greece, 48, 66, 122, 180
greed, 51
Greenland, 147, 150, 165, 191
Greenock, 23, 60, 89, 90, 94, 103, 110, 113, 143, 147, 167, 176, 177, 183, 189, 200, 227, 259, 282
Gregory, David (inventor), 186
Greig, Sir Samuel (admiral), 239
Greyfriars Bobby, 19
Greysteil, 89

Grieve, Robert (adminis-trator), 85
Griffin's Egg, 136
Gruinard, 157
guillotine, 115
guilt, 169
Gulf Stream, 116
guns, *see* warfare
Guthrie, James (helmsman), 58
Guthrie, James (minister), 71
Guthrie, Jane (spirit dealer), 121

Ha', Rab (glutton), 181
habit, 135, 149, 155, 171
Haddington, 24, 75, 95, 103, 121, 140, 206, 208, 231, 251
Hadrian's Wall, 34
haggis, 48, 92
Haig, Earl (soldier), 138
hailstones, *see* weather
hair, 108, 192, 198, 274, 276
Hair, Sandy (footballer), 110
Hall, Sir James (geologist), 272
Hallowe'en, 27, 244
Hamilton, 11, 75, 79, 87, 160, 164, 202, 220, 223
Hamilton, Patrick (martyr), 53
Hamilton, Thomas (hat-maker), 156
Hamilton, Willie (MP), 148
Hammer of the Scots (Edward I), 21, 30, 73, 96, 133, 149, 157, 177
handfasting, *see* marriage
Hanley, Cliff (writer), 242
hares, 230
Harthill, 54
harvests, *see* farming
hats/headgear, 38, 63, 93, 109, 151, 156
hauntings, *see* ghosts and ghoulies
Hawaii, 117
Hawick, 52, 131, 213, 227, 230
Hay, Sir George (glassmaker), 44
Head, William (entrepreneur), 23
heads/headaches, 80, 128, 156, 166, 207, 217, 256
health, 22, 142, 149, 186, 216
  cholera, 36, 53, 245, 272
  doctors, 11, 52
  hospitals, 192, 228
  leprosy, 154, 259
  plague, 28, 63, 66, 81, 106, 107, 127, 140, 150, 159, 164, 172, 175, 188, 201, 211, 222, 239, 255, 261
  quack medicine, 87
  smallpox, 33, 86, 100, 216, 266
Heart of Midlothian, 222
heatwaves, 112, 139
Hedderwick, James (journa-list), 23
Helensburgh, 117, 164, 181, 184
Hellfire Clubs, 107
Helmsdale, 253
Henderson, Robert (miracle-

worker), 159
Henryson, Robert (poet), 204
hens, 115, 146, 192
Hepburn, Thomas, 64
herbal remedies, *see* folk remedies
Herd Laddie (draughts champion), 205
heresy, 96
heroes/heroines, 91, 268
Heron, Lady (beauty), 174
Hertsyde, Margaret (thief), 122
Hess, Rudolf (fugitive), 107
hiding-places, 31, 76, 187, 206, 208, 213
High Blantyre, 237
High Court of Justiciary, 17
Highland and Agricultural Society of Scotland, 38
Highland Brigade, 254
Highland Dress, 181
Highland Games, 57, 231
Highland Railway, 33
highwaymen, *see* robbery
Hill, David Octavius (painter), 104
hoarding, 86, 131
hoaxes, 20, 21, 82, 114, 271
hobbies, 146
Hog family (serfs), 75
Hogg, James (poet), 22, 27
Hogmanay, 10, 11, 289
hold-ups, 181
holidays, 28, 58, 157, 206, 259
Holinshed, Ralph (historian), 9
Holland, 39, 57, 65, 66, 68, 100, 118, 131, 152, 207, 253
Holyrood, 16, 19, 31, 46, 52, 62, 66, 72, 73, 121, 138, 149, 166, 185, 197, 200, 254, 287
homage, 92, 157, 176
home comforts, 63
homecoming, 212
homes/dwellings, *see* housing
Hong Kong, 16
hooped skirts, 74, 187
horses/horse-racing, 16, 18, 28, 31, 32, 37, 40–41, 55, 58, 59, 72, 73, 77–78, 85, 88, 90, 96, 101, 109, 119, 140, 143, 155, 157, 170, 175, 177, 181, 201, 207, 215, 218, 220, 225, 227, 258, 271, 274, 275, 277
hospitality, 98
hostages, 11, 222
hotheads, 46, 109
Houdini, Harry (escapologist), 206
housebreaking/burglary, 23, 59, 63, 216
housing, 49, 63, 81, 86, 106, 119, 178, 204, 210, 223, 275
Hudson's Bay Company, 250
humiliation, 23, 92, 148, 170, 221
hunger, 124–25, 126, 170, 221
hunting/hawking, 15, 38, 40, 42, 53, 74, 157, 186, 192, 210, 237, 244

huntly, 21, 24, 48, 126, 225, 242

Hurorian, 39

hurricanes, *see* weather

hustlers, 123

hygiene, 57, 86, 91, 94, 184

hypnotism, 245

hypocrits, 170

hypothermia, 9, 79

ice, *see* weather

Iceland, 127

idolatry, *see* religion

illnesses, *see* health

image, 61

impatience, 255

import/export, *see* trade/ commerce

imposters, 48, 70

improvisation, 241

Inchkeith, 86

Inchkenneth, 225

India, 128, 148, 183, 210

indigestion, 88

industry, 52, 61, 69, 74, 78, 113, 132, 133, 142, 147, 171, 181, 245, 288

influenza, *see* health

Innes the Lion Tamer, 197

insects, 48, 124, 188

insurance, 94, 113

invasion, 60, 70, 72, 75, 91, 102, 124, 132, 189, 210, 251, 255, 288

inventions, 28, 39, 85, 137, 140, 150, 151, 172, 181, 186

Inveraray, 13, 102, 153, 226, 241, 279

Inverbervie, 213

Inverclyde, Lord, 41

Inveresk, 28, 81

Inverkeithing, 53, 229

Inverness (shire), 16, 29, 32, 33, 83, 116, 162, 166, 167, 186, 199, 223, 250, 258, 288

Inverurie, 285

invincibility, 205

Iolaire, 10

Iona, Isle of, 37, 129, 148, 194, 215

Iran, 48

Iraq, 237

Ireland, 9, 16, 27, 29, 32, 88, 95, 137, 141, 142, 145, 171, 186, 205, 209, 223, 237, 244

Irvine, 116, 161

Irvine, Robert (murderer), 100

Isabel, 105

islands, 31, 35, 55, 82, 86, 116, 141, 148, 155, 157, 177 (*see also under individual name*)

Islay, 18, 210, 263

Isle of Man, 116

Italy and the Italians, 11, 51, 62, 75, 87, 149, 200, 216

Jack, Robert (forger), 289

Jacobites, 11, 18, 20, 48, 59, 60, 68, 71, 72, 82, 88, 94, 131, 184, 186, 187, 192, 198, 207, 210, 221, 269, 281

jailbreaks, *see* prisons

James I, 57, 63, 75, 110, 118, 137, 139, 150, 165

James II, 13, 24, 48, 58, 73,

100, 173, 182, 231

James III, 28, 33, 42, 154, 212, 239

James IV, 27, 33, 42, 89, 140, 150, 174, 182, 188, 193, 195, 223, 286

James V, 21, 25, 40, 43, 98, 109, 112, 120, 198, 212, 277

James VI & I, 16, 31, 46, 48, 49, 52, 53, 58, 70, 73, 78, 79, 80, 88, 107, 110, 111, 117, 123, 131, 139, 144, 149, 166, 172, 173, 178, 194, 197, 207, 215, 218, 230, 244, 249, 272, 279

Janet the Windbreaker, 209

Japan, 142, 203

jealousy, 31, 215

Jedburgh, 24, 130, 149, 170, 206

Jersey, 203

Jesuits, 94

jesters, 13, 78, 188, 245

Jew's Harp, 244

jewellery, 66, 122

jiggin', *see* dancing

Jinglin' Geordie Heriot (philanthropist), 41

jobs, 12, 68

Jocelin (bishop), 117, 149

Jock the Tup, 220

Johnston, Alexander (map-maker), 144

Johnston, Tom (Secretary of State), 211

Johnstone, 218

Jolson, Al, 13

Jones, John Paul (mariner), 93, 150, 161

jousting, 78, 102

judges, *see* law

Jura, 28, 263

justice, 24, 27, 43, 59, 63, 65, 79, 95, 102, 126, 128, 134, 139, 146, 150, 198, 204, 207, 208

Justice, James Robertson (actor), 193

jute, 33

Kate the Witch, 204

Kays, 217

Keith, Marshall (soldier), 116

Kello, Revd John (murderer), 219

Kelly, Earl of, 16

Kelso, 26, 58, 75, 83, 122, 128, 149, 193, 200, 232

Kelvin, Lord (physicist), 227

Kenmure, 228

Kennedy, John (grocer), 41

Kennedy, Sir John (prisoner), 165

Kerr, Kenneth (adventurer), 28

Kerr, Lord, 16

Kerrera, 153

kidnapping, 102, 200, 287

Kilbirnie, 11

Killiecrankie, *see* battles

Killin, 64

Kilmacolm, 284 – 85

Kilmarnock, 114, 116, 120, 184, 209

Kilmun, 142

Kilpatrick, William (rustler),

156

Kilsyth, 11, 182, 184

Kiltearn, 192, 215

kilts, 48, 128, 148, 181, 194, 217, 281

Kincaid, John (witch-pricker), 83

Kincardine (shire), 24, 90, 148, 216

'King of the Bean', 12

King's Own Scottish Borderers, 68

Kinghorn, 43, 53, 54, 175

kings and queens, 23, 36, 48, 58, 63, 66, 67, 73, 78, 97, 121, 123, 130, 156, 200

Kingussie, 31, 143, 206

Kinloss, 116

Kinnoull, Earls of, 90

Kinross (shire), 44, 157, 192

Kintyre, 9

Kirk, Robert (minister), 275

Kirkcaldy, 70, 89, 95, 198, 238

Kirkconnel, 70

Kirkcudbright (shire), 27, 111, 150, 161, 162

Kirkintilloch, 37, 97, 209

Kirkliston, 143

Kirkwall, 21, 33, 127, 153, 163

Kirkwood, Davie (revolutionary), 269

Kirriemuir, 47, 122

Kitchener, Lord (general), 186

knackeries, *see* abbatoirs

knights, 91, 102, 130, 201

Knox, John (reformer), 42, 61, 107, 251

Knox, Robert (anatomist), 200

Knox, Ronald (priest), 21

Kyle of Lochalsh, 115

'La Milo' (poseuse), 36

Lady Jane, 66

Laird o' Cockpen, 244

Lanark (shire), 11, 37, 54, 58, 73, 95, 125, 132, 182, 198, 211, 220, 228, 242, 244, 245, 275

landslips, 13, 256

Langside, *see* battles

language, 11, 19, 37, 86, 112, 122, 123, 126, 155, 166

Largo, 19, 32

Lauder (dale), 24

laughter, 86

Laurel, Stan (comedian), 159

law/lawyers, 17, 18, 24, 37, 66, 72, 89, 107, 110, 116, 123, 126, 150, 165, 172, 259

Law, Denis (footballer), 232

Law, John (gambler), 123

laziness, 225

Learmonth, Prof. J.R. (surgeon), 63

Lee, J.P. (inventor), 85

leeches, *see* myths/legends

legends, 94

Leighton, Bishop Robert, 242

Leith, 31, 33, 47, 58, 77, 80, 84, 89, 91, 96, 100, 102, 105, 109, 118, 121, 132, 142, 149, 150, 154, 155,

167, 177, 178, 186, 196, 207, 210, 220, 227, 238, 242, 265, 274, 277, 281, 285, 289
Lennox, Earls of, 162, 178, 267
Lennoxtown, 112
leprosy, *see* health
Lerwick, 21, 105, 140
Leslie, David (general), 198, 206
Leslie, George, 106
Lesmahagow, 147
letters, *see* postal service
Leven, 158
Leviathan, 37
Lewis, 140, 270
liars, 69
libraries, *see* books
Liddell, Andrew (drunk), 160
Life Assurance Act (1774), 94
lifeboats, 66
light, 16, 48, 102, 140, 161, 177, 200, 221, 237, 271
lighthouses, 177, 216
lightning, *see* weather
Lincoln, Abraham (president), 12
Lindores Abbey, 42
Lindsay, Sir David (playwright), 13, 55, 98, 174
Lindsay, Sir David (jouster), 91, 102
Lindsay, J.B. (communications pioneer), 207
Linlithgow, 16, 58, 121, 139, 142, 174, 184, 228, 265
lions, 55, 232
Lipton, Sir Thomas (merchant), 15
Lister, Joseph (surgeon), 137
'Little Egypt', 43, 192
little people, 275
Livingston, 64, 265
Livingstone, David (missionary/explorer), 68, 251, 272
Loch Ness Monster, 10, 75, 141
loch(s), 17, 127
  Arkaig, 277
  Awe, 91
  Eriboll, 160
  Fyne, 91, 216
  Holy, 137, 142
  Katrine, 52, 139, 284
  Laggan, 167
  Laxford, 250
  Leven, 101, 286
  Linlithgow, 10, 154
  Lomond, 139, 144, 244
  Long, 284
  Ness, 284
  Rannoch, 121
  Sunart, 241
  Tay, 121
Lochcarron, 15
Locherbie, 282
Lochgelly, 236
Lochgoilhead, 57
Lochhart, Lady Euphemia (transvestite spy), 68
Lochmaben, 165, 173, 256
Lochwinnoch, 118
locusts, 124, 171

Logan of Restalrig, 127, 161
loneliness, 132
long-jump, 192
Lord Lyon, King of Arms, 156, 182
'Lords of the Soil', 103
losers, 23
Lossiemouth, 29
Lost Tribe of Israel, 189
loudmouths, 279
love/lovers, 80
luck, 55
Luftwaffe, 162
Lulach, 79
Lusitania, 70
Lyte, Henry F. (songwriter), 193

MacAlpin, Kenneth (king), 36
McArthur, John (soldier), 256
Macbeth, 34, 181
Macbeth, 158, 207
MacCalvean, Eupham (witch), 129
McCaskill, Ian (weatherman), 220
McClean, Tom (adventurer), 35
McCulloch, Horatio (artist), 186
McCulloch, Jimmy (guitarist), 217
MacDonald, Flora (Jacobite), 137, 167, 205
MacDonald, George (novelist), 283
Macdonald, Sir John (soothsayer), 28
MacDonald, R. (athlete), 167
MacDonald, Ramsay (prime minister), 10, 29, 120
Macdonalds, 74
MacDonnell, Col. Alex (chieftain), 226
MacEion, 13
MacEwan, Sir William (surgeon), 218
MacFarlanes, 139, 222
McGill, James (fur trader), 223
McGilter, John (drunk), 78
MacGregor, Alasdair Alpin (writer), 262
McGregor, John (piper), 137
MacGregor, Rob Roy (bandit), 61, 247, 264, 287
MacGregors, 34, 193, 247
McIntyre, Dr Robert (nationalist), 85
McKail, Hugh, (covenanter), 283
McKairter, Hugh (tobacco spinner), 68
McKellar, Andrew (golfer), 152
Mackenzie, Alexander (explorer), 125
Mackenzie, Charles (adventurer), 150
Mackenzie, Sir Compton (author), 265
McKie, Gilbert (goalkeeper), 110
Mackintosh, Charles Rennie (architect), 245
MacLauchlan, Margaret

(martyr), 108
MacLean, John (revolutionary), 37, 107
MacLeods, 248
MacMillan, Kilpatrick (cyclist), 132
MacMurray, Margaret (Gaelic-speaker), 83
Macphee, Alexander (crofter), 241
Macpherson, James (hoaxer), 41, 178
MacPhersons, 85
MacQuarie, Lachlan (pioneer), 32
McQueen, John (underwear thief), 234
magic/conjuring, 110
'Maid of Norway', 36, 216
mail, *see* postal services
Maitland family, 38
Malcolm III (Canmore), 79, 96, 189, 253
Mallaig, 288
Malpas, Maurice (footballer), 173
Manuel, Peter (murderer), 122
Maple Hill clan, 15
Mar, Earls of, 192, 254
March, Earls of, 33, 59
Margaret of Denmark, 46, 154
Mariner, 160
markets, 28, 83, 86, 131
marmalade, 122
Marocco (horse), 77
marriage, 27, 46, 48, 54, 58, 59, 63, 79, 85, 117, 154, 156, 248, 275, 286
Martin, Marion (brothel-keeper), 181
martyrs, 53, 96
Mary Queen of Scots, 11, 18, 25, 26, 42, 48, 62, 63, 66, 77, 78, 81, 95, 101, 111, 112, 134, 150, 152, 176, 186, 192, 218, 228, 242, 269, 286
mass murders, 165
massacres, 13, 15, 142, 195, 204
Masson, Francis (botanist), 203
Mathieson, Peter (coachman), 281
Mathieson, Wilson (umbrella manufacturer), 118
Maxton, James (MP), 42, 254
Maxwell, James Clark (scientist), 139
Maxwell, Lord (fugitive), 116
May, Henry (hero), 237
May Island, 141, 259
Maybole, 149
Mayne, William (golf club manufacturer), 79
measurement, 47
Mechin the Ratcatcher, 209
media, 68, 243, 248
medicine, 16, 18, 27, 34, 63, 148, 158, 165, 172, 182, 202, 212, 218, 226, 230, 250, 257
meetings, 28, 38, 42, 56, 63, 64, 73, 80, 111, 116, 122, 127, 130, 162

Meikle, Andrew (inventor), 83

Melrose, 48, 75, 77, 116, 253

Melville, Andrew (theologian), 137

Melville, James (scholar), 45

memory, 227, 251, 254

Mendelssohn, Felix (composer), 183

Menteith, Sir John (betrayer), 173

Menteith, Robert (angling minister), 156

Mercer, Hugh (soldier), 18

mermaids, 198

messengers/messages, 73, 91, 170

mice, 149

midges, 211, 288

Midlothian, 123

Miller, Bessie (witch), 81

Miller, Hugh (geologist), 259

Miller, Patrick (steamship pioneer), 127, 269

mining, 26, 37, 54, 65, 70, 102, 110, 114, 118, 126, 132, 133, 188, 198, 199, 216, 230, 281, 285

'Mirk' Monday, 45

missionaries, 48, 89, 178, 251

mistaken identity, 129, 158, 216

Mitchell, Alexander (postmaster), 16

Moffat, 12

moles, 59

Mollison, Jim (aviator), 184

moments of glory, 110, 126, 172

Monboddo, Lord (anthropologist), 275

money, see banking/finance

monkeys, 275

Monkland Canal, 222

'Mons Meg' (cannon), 31

monsters, 10, 140

Montgomerie family, 78

Montgomery's Highlanders, 12

Montrose, 23, 52, 53, 54, 95, 108, 121, 194, 233, 245, 253, 282

Montrose, Marquis of, 57, 85, 107, 182, 205

Moore, Sir John (soldier), 21

morals, 25, 85, 101, 204

Moray, 26, 37, 43, 48, 80, 142, 151, 173, 184, 227, 242, 262

Morison, Madge (transvestite), 38

Morocco, 81

Morris, Chris (footballer), 157

Morris, Tom (golfer), 152, 217

Morrison, Agnes (fortuneteller), 59

Morton, Regent, 22

Motherwell, 85, 221, 228

motor racing/motoring, 28, 81, 84, 108, 111, 126, 160, 170, 220, 263

mountaineering, 11, 50, 84

mountains and hills
  Ben Alder, 206

Ben Ledi, 141

Ben Nevis, 180

Ben Wyvis, 37, 192

Eildon Hills, 237

Gargunnock Hills, 154

Lammermuirs, 69, 219

Lomond Hills, 261

Ochils, 40

Schiehallion, 238

Traprain Law, 108

'Muck Andrew', 192

muggings, 29, 69, 102, 129, 287

Muir, Thomas, (radical advocate), 11, 173

Mull, Isle of, 31, 32, 212, 222, 226, 277

multiple personality, 256

mummies, 226

Munro, Sir Henry (tenant), 37

Murchison, Sir Roderick (geologist), 46

murder, 21, 23, 34, 38, 42, 43, 46, 50, 62, 64, 69, 89, 94, 100, 101, 122, 142, 165, 168, 200, 207, 219, 223, 245, 261, 285, 288

Murdoch, William (inventor), 151

Murray, Lilian (pioneer dentist), 115

museums and art galleries, 182

music/musicians, 10, 11, 23, 29, 36, 47, 62, 65, 89, 105, 106, 111, 117, 131, 183, 193, 199, 208, 217, 225, 237, 244, 259, 260

Musselburgh, 63, 68, 81, 152, 204, 252

mutiny, 91, 156, 248, 282

Mylne, Walter (martyr), 96

mysteries/miracles, 21, 24, 27, 31, 39, 102, 114–15, 119, 121, 141, 159, 166, 184, 252

mythical kingdoms, 141, 275

myths and legends, 16

Nairn, 107

names/nicknames, 21, 39, 42, 44, 94, 128, 129, 156, 166, 219, 224–25, 228, 254, 268

Napier, John (landowner), 63

Napoleon Bonaparte, 41, 128, 167, 272

Nasmyth, Sir James (botanist), 34

National Gallery of Scotland, 69

National Party of Scotland, 176

natural wonders, 27, 32, 102, 105

naturism, 68, 90, 139

Naughton, Muriel (jockey), 31

Nautilus, 41

necromancy, see witches/witchcraft

negotiations, 82

Nelson, Horatio (admiral), 87

Nessie, see Loch Ness Monster

New Galloway, 228

New Lanark, 134

new year, see Hogmanay

New Zealand, 18, 23, 71, 167

Newbattle Abbey, 121, 199, 206, 244

Newhaven, 70, 84, 91, 231

Newhouse, 54

Newmilns, 12

newspapers, 15, 243
  Bee, 283
  Caledonian Mercury, 12
  Evening Citizen, 23
  Forward, 228
  Glasgow Advertiser, 28
  (Glasgow) Herald, 28, 245
  Illustrated London News, 124
  Inverness Courier, 15
  John o' Groats Journal, 215
  Kelso Mail, 230
  North Briton, 126
  Old England, 20
  Scots Magazine, 239, 284
  Scotsman, 12
  Scottish Daily Express, 28, 68
  State Journal (Kansas), 14
  Times, 17

Newton Stewart, 228

Nicholson, Willie (packman poet), 111

Nicolle David (pacemaker), 165

noise/noise pollution, 112, 192, 198, 259

North Berwick, 53, 54, 82, 128, 169, 244, 286

North British Railway, 137

North Sea, 132

North Uist, 116

Northern Isles, see Orkney or Shetland

northern lights, see sky events

Norway, 28, 131, 148, 154, 242

noses/nosebleeds, 71, 214–15

nuclear industry, 101, 113, 180

nudity, see naturism

Oakley, Charles (Glaswegian), 271

oatcakes, 165

Oban, 13, 64, 100, 148, 153, 198, 259

obesity, 121, 123, 142

obsession, 152

Ochiltree, 263

odd behaviour, 77, 119

oddities, 17, 53, 121, 133, 155, 171, 182, 205, 245, 253

off limits, 143

Ogilvie, John (scientist), 47

Ogilvie, John (martyr), 181

Ogilvie, Sir John ('known Papist'), 213

Old King Cole, 248

Old Nelly (worthy), 177

old timers, 11, 33, 38, 69, 72, 76, 85, 90, 139, 142, 150, 153, 162, 168, 177, 210, 215, 248, 258

Oliphant, James (minister), 242

Oliphant, Sir William (soldier), 30

omens, 27, 42, 51, 52, 60, 66,

86, 105, 134, 138, 171, 172, 263
openings, 76, 122, 171
opera, *see* entertainment
optimism, 68, 128
Ord of Caithness, 175
Orkney, 16, 21, 27, 33, 36, 46, 66, 75, 88, 122, 124, 127, 138, 139, 141, 148, 163, 167, 187, 194, 205, 214, 215, 216, 218, 230, 231, 256
Ossian, *see* Macpherson, James
outdoor activities, 106, 111, 160, 167
overcrowding, 108, 121, 143
over-enthusiasm, 76
over-optimism, 162, 255
over-reaction, 108, 143
Owen, Robert (social reformer), 134
oysters, *see* food

pageantry, 76, 79
Paisley, 53, 81, 95, 101, 106, 116, 118, 122, 163, 187, 222, 281, 285, 289
palmistry, *see* fortune-telling
panics, 21, 33, 45, 237
Pankhurst, Emily (suffragette), 56
parachutists, 107, 140
parrot, Dr Delphine (bacteriologist), 83
Partick Thistle FC, 110
partying, 18, 23, 26, 31, 38, 40, 41, 42, 46, 49, 94, 117, 118, 131, 182, 244
patience, 271
patronage, 263
peacemakers, 150
Peacock, the, 26
peat, 144
pedestrians, 72, 101, 120, 138, 139, 225, 227, 260, 270
Peebles (shire), 34, 96, 209
Peirson, Alison (witch), 121
Pencaitland, 121
penguins, 47
Penicuik, 19, 178, 288
pensions, 153
Pentland Firth, 66, 172
Perseverance (whaler), 165
Persia, 4
Perth (shire), 11, 12, 16, 17, 19, 21, 23, 28, 33, 34, 41, 47, 48, 53, 63, 64, 69, 71, 73, 74, 75, 80, 85, 86, 88, 90, 95, 98, 101, 106, 107, 112, 117, 118, 138, 141, 143, 144, 148, 149, 153, 154, 163, 172, 175, 193, 198, 200, 212, 216, 220, 227, 228, 238, 250, 274, 287
Peterhead, 96, 126, 165
Petrie, Alexander (eccentric), 280
Philip of France (king), 47
photography, 66, 104
Physics, 180, 227
Picasso, Pablo, 42
picnics, 188
Picts, 34, 36, 115
Pied Pipers, 41

piers/jetties, 117
pigeons, 15, 150, 245
pigs, 43, 59, 172, 189, 218, 249
Pinkerton, Alan (detective), 208
pirates/piracy, 81, 84, 116, 118, 167, 217, 273
Pitscottie, John (sportsman), 47
plague/pestilence, *see* health
plants, *see* botany
plots, 51, 94, 248
poaching, 12, 140, 226, 231, 238
poisoning, 51, 83, 94, 145, 153, 209, 277
Poland, 214, 253
police, 27, 34, 56, 63, 78, 93, 102, 111, 123, 126, 150, 154, 157, 167, 200, 204, 213
politeness, 184
Politician, 34
politics, 29, 46, 52, 120, 148, 157, 165, 182, 232, 237, 240, 243, 254, 256, 271
pollution, 17, 44, 57, 220, 254
Pomeranian, 123
Pontius Pilate, 227
popes and the papacy, 42, 63, 71, 81, 119, 122, 138, 259
popularity, 52, 90
population, 44, 85, 95, 99, 106, 155, 160, 171, 255
porpoises, 33
Port Glasgow, 112, 260
Porteous Riot, 88, 201
Portobello, 53, 128
Portpatrick, 27, 184
Portugal, 118
postal services, 21, 24, 29, 32, 50, 71, 75, 94, 103, 156, 166, 175, 183, 184, 220, 225, 227, 259, 260, 263
potions, 51, 199
poverty, 10, 15, 29, 42, 53, 63, 64, 75, 78, 101, 106, 123, 153, 223, 232, 233, 249, 281
Prat, John (tenant), 36
prehistory, 112, 134
premonitions, *see* fortune-telling
preservatives, 122
Prestongrange, Lord, 117
Prestonpans, 63, 91, 106
Prestwick, 152, 217
pretenders, 69, 70, 252, 278
Prince of Asturias, 189
priorities, 16
prisons, 34, 41, 48, 79, 80, 81, 83, 88, 96, 106, 107, 113, 118, 128, 165, 174, 199, 201, 216, 223, 269, 271
Pritchard, Dr Edward (murderer), 168
procrastination, 57–58
profiteering, 249, 253, 271
propaganda, 247, 253
prostitution, *see* sexual behaviour
Provost Kerr of Peebles, 209
Prussia, 11, 83
public-speaking, 52
publishing, 52, 171, 272, 283

punishment, 44, 57, 75, 79, 84, 102, 106, 110, 118, 126, 127, 144, 150, 156, 204
punctuality, 42

QEII, 73
quack medicine, 80, 172, 212
Queen Elizabeth (liner), 16, 55, 89, 217
Queen Mary (liner), 34, 55, 111, 217, 221
Queen's Park FC, 64, 138, 154
Queensferry (north and south) 66, 211, 229, 259
quizzes, 66, 271

rabbits, 16, 74
radicals, 80, 104
railways, 12, 13, 18, 24, 33, 37, 41, 42, 64, 74, 78, 101, 106, 111, 120, 126, 128, 131, 133, 137, 148, 150, 159, 161, 172, 177, 178, 188, 200, 256, 287
rain/rainbows, *see* weather
'Rajah Boys', the, 248
'Rambler', 242
Ramsay, Allan (poet), 45
Ramsay, Andrew (teacher), 105
Rangers FC, 31, 110, 117
Rannoch Moor, 13
rats, 41, 149, 164, 209, 211, 250–51
real estate, 189, 274
Reay, 160
Red Comyn (competitor), 38
reform, 11, 52, 73, 115, 126, 157, 173, 191
Reformation, *see* religion
refugees, 127
regalia, 73, 76, 79
Reid, Alexander (art dealer), 132
Reidswire Raid, 151
relics, 66, 79, 156, 207, 256
religion, 42, 45, 47, 63, 204, 261
   churches, 12, 28, 30, 71, 76, 102, 204, 207, 283
   clergy, 22, 69, 157, 195, 210
   disputes, 52, 68, 104, 204, 216, 231
   hymns, 26, 47
   idolatry, 28, 107, 233, 250
   personalities, 16, 23, 53, 57, 79, 120, 132
   Reformation, 10, 66, 74, 96, 143, 145, 204, 252, 269, 288
   services, 15, 69, 72, 79, 102, 163, 189, 213, 230, 242, 261
remoteness, 68, 116, 153, 255
Renfrew (shire), 107, 125, 139, 239
repentance, 181
reprieves, 106, 121, 181, 202
rescues, 66, 140, 173, 228
'Restoration' (1660–61), 10, 86, 158
resurrectionists, *see* body-snatchers
revolution, 42, 115, 157, 189, 272

Rhum, 155, 178, 271
Riccio, Davie (musician), 62
Richardson, Sir John
  (explorer), 126
Riding of the Three Estates,
  16
riots, 20, 34, 36, 37, 44, 56,
  69, 70, 89, 115, 134, 158,
  189, 201, 207, 210, 216,
  245, 258
Ritchie, Meg (athlete), 222
rivers
  Carron, 168
  Clyde, 26, 32, 39, 46, 74,
    91, 96, 123, 125, 151, 175,
    183, 223, 236, 264
  Don and Dee, 46, 53, 140
  Eden, 198
  Ericht, 17
  Esk, 150, 281
  Findhorn, 173
  Forth, 33, 37, 41, 66, 84, 86,
    91, 100, 105, 132, 137,
    154, 159, 165, 182, 183,
    211
  Garry, 192
  Leven, 122
  Nith, 264
  Spey, 21, 85, 230
  Tay, 38, 69, 111, 153, 228,
    264, 276, 287
  Teviot, 264
  Tweed, 130, 193, 206, 253
  Tyne, 24, 209
roads, 12, 22, 48, 54, 220,
  258, 259, 261
robbery/banditry, 11, 26, 28,
  37, 42, 59, 60, 61, 80, 96,
  101, 122, 127, 157, 160,
  175, 177, 181, 186, 209,
  221, 233, 265, 269, 281,
  286
Robert III (king), 59, 85, 176,
  182, 217, 224–25
Robert Lindsay (lifeboat), 239
Robertson of Struan
  (Jacobite), 188
Robertson, George (apothe-
  cary), 149
Robin Hood Riot (1561), 158
Robinson Crusoe, *see*
  Alexander Selkirk
Robson, James (teacher), 210
Roche, Eustachius (miner),
  188
Rockall, 35
rodents, *see* rats
Roger Stewart, 103
Rolling Stones, 134
Rollock, Robert (churchman),
  45
romance, 96, 189
Romans, 26, 34, 48, 61, 64,
  81, 95, 105, 108, 152, 181,
  225, 227, 228, 243
Rosneath, 164
Ross and Cromarty, 17, 46,
  95, 128, 148, 178, 181, 232
Ross, Donald (old-timer), 215
Ross, John (minister), 16
Rosyth, 231
Rothes, 24, 81
Rothesay, 21, 24, 28, 59, 111,
  153, 216, 221
'Rough Wooing', 91
Row, John (reformer), 252

Rowdiness, 96, 166
Roxburgh (shire), 12, 16, 26,
  52–53, 58, 76, 92, 95, 199,
  279
Roxburgh, William (botanist),
  145
Royal and Ancient Golf Club,
  110
Royal Bank of Scotland, 122
Royal Botanic Gardens
  (Edinburgh), 94
Royal Oak (battleship), 230
royal visits, 76, 111
Ruadh, Mairi (bard), 33
rugby, 18, 23, 43, 61, 90, 138,
  232, 279
Rule, Elspeth (witch), 101
rum, 103, 177
rumours, 222, 233
Runciman, Alexander
  (painter), 178
Runrig, 44
Russia, 37, 52, 71, 79, 107,
  134, 137, 147, 151, 194, 239
rustling, 58, 156
Rutherglen, 19, 83, 100

sabbath-breaking, 15, 41, 47,
  79, 91, 100, 106, 111, 170,
  202, 217, 259, 263, 276
saints and saintly dedications
  St Adamnan, 215
  St Blane, 178
  St Boisil, 48
  St Brendan, 35
  St Colm's Isle, 211
  St Columba, 129, 215, 271
  St Cuthbert, 69
  St Donan, 89
  St Ebba, 189
  St Fillan, 212
  St Fittich's Well, 265
  St Giles, 23, 54
  St Magnus, 16, 88
  St Margaret, 156, 207, 256
  St Michael's Well, 83
  St Obert, 274
  St Patrick, 9
Salmon, the (dance), 25
sanctuaries, 127, 187, 191,
  233
Sanday, 33, 205
Sanderson and Flockhart
  (racing team), 170
Sandilands, Sir James, 23
Sandrazol, 107
Sanquhar, 71, 193
satan, *see* Auld Nick
Scapa Flow, 139, 281
Scone, 17, 27, 38, 47, 57, 67,
  74, 177, 182, 215, 266
scorpions, 123
Scotch and Scottish, 289
Scotch Mail, 12
Scotichronicon, 250
'Scotland the Brave', 140
Scotlandwell, 44
Scots Guards, 101
Scott, Sir Walter (novelist),
  40, 70, 151, 277
Scottish Development
  Agency, 94
Scottish Friends of the
  People, 275
Scottish National Party, 91,
  140, 265

Scottish Tourist Board, 178
Scottish Trades Union
  Congress, 73, 89
Scottish Vegetarian Society,
  238
Scottishness, 15, 19, 27, 31,
  36, 46, 54, 58, 68, 70, 81,
  83, 97, 116, 130, 144, 148,
  176, 259, 266, 275, 288
Scotus, John Duns
  (philosopher), 207
screwballs, *see* eccentrics
scurvy, 60
seafaring, 28, 37, 54, 60, 66,
  81, 84, 93, 108, 116, 118,
  151, 183, 186, 227
Seaforth Highlanders, 128
seals, 198, 231, 250, 260
seaweed, 138
secret societies, 107, 165, 257
sedan chairs, *see* taxis
Selkirk, 54, 69, 93, 121, 206,
  272, 279
Selkirk, Alexander
  (adventurer), 32, 269
Semple, Robert (playwright),
  22
servants, 71, 116, 126, 146,
  165, 213, 261
sewage/sanitation, 57, 86, 91,
  94, 113, 230, 279
sexism, 123, 246, 265
sexual behaviour, 25, 29, 38,
  48, 52, 62, 67, 68, 84, 87,
  108, 119–120, 150, 157,
  174, 186, 191, 204, 243,
  245, 258
Shakespeare, William (playwright), 34, 77, 158, 198,
  207, 226
Shand, Jimmy (bandleader),
  29
Shaw, Sir John (whaler), 147
sheep, 11, 18, 46, 52, 59, 64,
  102, 132, 155, 171, 176,
  205, 220, 238, 264, 277
Sheshader, 73
Shetland, 21, 46, 49, 57, 68,
  71, 80, 105, 127, 148, 162,
  171, 198, 213, 218, 282
Shillinglaw, Joseph (minister),
  80
shinty, 70, 255
shipbuilding/shipping, 12, 23,
  33, 38, 39, 46, 52, 58, 70,
  74, 89, 91, 105, 113, 116,
  126, 132, 134, 154, 159,
  162, 165, 171, 172, 176,
  189, 198, 205, 211, 231,
  233, 236, 241, 265, 276
shipwrecks, 34, 74, 139, 154,
  203, 217, 226, 233, 242, 280
shoemakers/cobblers, 127
shops/shopping, 60, 66, 90,
  239
sieges/blockades, *see* warfare
silkworms, 145
Sinclair family, 127, 148, 279
Sirius, 196
Six Foot Club, 37
skiing, 90, 144, 184
Skirmischur, Walter
  (standard-bearer), 75
sky events, 21, 28, 31, 42,
  45–46, 60, 64, 66, 86, 114,
  134, 141, 154, 171, 178,

209, 223, 258, 266, 271

Skye, 86, 117, 137, 177, 195, 248, 250, 255

slavery/servitude, 132, 148, 249, 287

sleep, 9, 41, 54, 60, 99, 126, 147, 156, 167, 192, 280

Slessor, Mary (missionary), 268

smallpox, *see* health

Smellie, Richard (sewage engineer), 113

smells, 57, 249

Smith, Adam (economist), 139

Smith, Madeleine (alleged poisoner), 145, 153

Smith, Sir William (Boys Brigade founder), 222

Smith the Hen-stealer, 192

smog/fog, 44, 155, 220, 254, 286

smoking/smokers, 34, 68, 90, 106, 111, 134, 138, 151, 171, 176, 249, 274

Smollett, George (rebel), 139

smuggling, 31, 74, 89, 171, 230

snakes, 108

Snizort, 195

snow, *see* weather

'Soaperie', 147

soapmaking, 147 – 48

Society for the Propagation of Christian Knowledge, 23, 241

Solway, 93, 101, 256

Somerled, 248

sorcery, *see* witches/witchcraft

South Africa, 203, 279

South Uist, 78

souvenirs, 153

Spain and the Spaniards, 25–26, 60, 66, 75, 77, 112, 117, 118, 131, 149, 172, 189, 211, 217, 243

speed, 66, 172, 177, 188, 217

spiders, 107

Spiers, Alexander (tobacco merchant), 274

Spittal, Robert (bridge-builder), 159

spitting/hacking, 222

sponsorship, 122

sport, 14, 16, 18, 27, 31, 33, 37, 40, 43, 68, 70, 138, 173, 231

Spott, 219

spurs, 50, 288

spying, *see* espionage

St Andrews, 30, 33, 43, 53, 66, 110, 120, 121, 137, 157, 167, 182, 186, 198, 213, 233, 236, 269

St Kilda, 27, 35, 50, 123, 170, 194, 201, 276

Staffa, 183

stage-coaches, 143, 150, 151, 163, 285

Stair, Earl of (politician), 15, 142

stamina, 55

stars, *see* astronomy/sky events

starvation, *see* famine

statues, 28, 68, 81, 88, 167, 188, 233

steamships/steam engines, 39, 74, 117, 127, 132, 196, 205, 269, 274, 279

Stein, Jock (football manager), 204

Stercovius, John (fancy-dresser), 214

Stevenson, Allan (ploughing pioneer), 218

Stewart, Frances (model), 50

Stewart, Henry (cardinal), 156

Steyne, Margaret (adultress), 84

Stirling (shire), 13, 16, 21, 30, 57, 61, 89, 93, 95, 96, 112, 140, 154, 160, 167, 168, 172, 181, 198, 212, 217, 228, 245, 255, 260, 269, 278

Stone of Destiny, 27, 85, 132, 177

Stonehaven, 11, 76

stones/rocks, 105, 145, 178, 210

'Stonewall' Jackson (foot-baller), 14

storms, *see* weather

Stornoway, 10, 13, 34, 36, 73, 91, 102, 125, 134, 271

storytelling, 162

strange illnesses, 133

strange locations, 11, 98, 142, 187

Strange, Robert (fugitive), 187

Strath Oykell, 232

Strathaven, 194

Strathearn, 26

Strathfillan, 212

Strathmore, 23

Strathnaver, 132

streaking, 90, 171

street fighting, 23, 99, 149, 154, 161, 165, 264

strikes, 13, 32, 54, 79, 145, 208, 227, 245, 258

Stroma, 271

Stromness, 66, 163

Strontian, 241, 254

stubborness, 16, 146

students, 46, 73, 86, 128, 137, 157, 228, 238, 244, 251, 286

submarines, 31, 115, 137, 140, 230

suffragettes, 24, 46, 56, 154, 162, 188, 200

suicide, 84

sunbathing, 68, 139

sunshine, *see* weather

superstars, 139

superstition, *see* tradition

Sutherland, 9, 113, 128, 160, 164, 176, 210, 227, 250, 253

swans, 10, 38, 139

swearing, 204

Sweden, 71, 108, 136, 259

'Sweet Singers', 47

sweets, *see* food

swimming/diving, 84, 127, 177, 181, 271

Switzerland, 61

swords, *see* warfare

Symington, 146

Symington, William (steam

pioneer), 12

'Tailor and Cutter', 48

Tain, 88

tall people, *see* giants and dwarves

Tarbert, 177

tartan, 48, 76, 96, 117, 172, 181

tattie-howkers, 209

taxation, 53, 133, 159, 199, 213

taxidermy, 210

taxis, 18, 33, 75, 187, 258, 269

tea/coffee, 15, 69, 101, 134, 135, 227, 253

teaching, *see* education

teetotalism/temperance, 13, 84, 106, 264

telephones, 90, 245, 259

television and radio, 21, 22, 28, 44, 120, 170, 181, 201, 220, 265

Telford, Thomas (engineer), 32

Templeton and Hair (cowherds), 76

theatre, *see* entertainment

theft, *see* robbery

Third Lanark FC, 64

Thom, William (poet), 54

Three Estates, 55, 63

thumbscrews, *see* torture

Thurso, 172, 201, 242

tidal forces, 24, 117, 155, 253

Tighnabruich, 225

'Tim' (speaking clock), 90

time, 28, 42, 90, 151, 159, 273–74

tinkers, 173

Tiree, 167, 277

Titanic, 193

titles, 37, 166

Toad in the Hole, 114 – 15

tobacco, *see* smoking/smokers

Tobermory, 222

tombs, 11

Tomintoul, 69

toothache, *see* dentistry

'Tornado', 43

Torphichen, 75

torture, 110, 160, 195, 288

tourism, *see* travellers

trade/commerce, 16, 36, 39, 46, 53, 54, 58, 61, 64, 65, 66, 68, 95, 103, 112, 113, 126, 132, 159, 166, 175, 227, 237, 243, 253, 265, 274

trades/crafts, 46, 85

traditions, 28, 33, 48, 55, 74, 98–99, 106, 115, 265

tramcars, 24, 111, 146, 196

Tranent, 18, 194

transport, 18, 24, 28, 44, 48, 54, 63, 70, 74, 89, 91, 132, 143, 188, 193, 246, 249, 255, 258, 285

travellers, 13, 44, 48, 58, 83, 119, 142, 148, 182, 189, 199, 200, 211, 263

treachery, *see* betrayal

treason, 54, 173, 184

treasure, 108, 136, 154, 161

treaties/pacts, 54, 55, 58, 83,

92, 95, 100, 134, 148, 173, 222, 270, 286

trees, 11, 13, 34, 64, 71, 98, 117, 119, 127, 128, 154, 188, 223, 227, 279

trial delays, *see* justice

troglodytes, 108

trolley buses, 50

Troon, 94, 120, 165

Tullibardine, Marquis of (Jacobite), 168

tunnels, 211

Turkey, 39, 116, 149, 258

Turnberry, 233

Turnbull, Bishop William, 13

turtles, 193

Tytler, James (balloonist), 191

U-Boats, 115

UFOs, *see* sky events

Ullapool, 156

umbrellas, 101, 118, 255, 271

underwear, 234

Union Canal, 239

Union, Treaty of (1707), 15, 21, 54, 68, 73, 93, 101, 175

United States of America and Americans, 12, 14, 18, 21, 22, 23, 27, 54, 55, 57, 61, 65, 81, 93, 103, 110, 117, 123, 137, 139, 147, 156, 158, 165, 176, 178, 188, 191, 200, 206, 208, 225, 259, 264, 287

universities, 13, 18, 63, 73, 79, 83, 88, 96, 110, 173, 204, 210, 223, 227, 228, 237, 238, 265

Unst, 57

unusual drinks, 51

unusual jobs, 106

uprisings, 172, 186, 254

Urquhart, David (adventurer), 39

Urquhart, Sir Thomas (historian), 81, 86

Vale of Leven FC, 64

Vallam, James and George (bandits), 42

valuation, 31, 206

vampires, 205

vandalism, 31, 63, 64, 78, 86, 89, 132, 158, 236

Vanguard, 233

vegetables, 88, 106, 235, 249, 250, 258

venereal disease, *see* sexual behaviour

Vestina (goddess of health), 87

Victoria, Queen, and the Victorians, 25, 63, 68, 96, 103, 110, 114, 124, 144, 185, 188, 204, 208, 210, 227, 237, 239

vikings, 50, 148, 221

violence, 156, 161,162, 178, 189

volcanoes, 28, 82, 87

Vulcan, 73

vultures, 11

Wade, General George (road builder), 220, 285

wages/salaries, 28, 31, 54, 122, 220, 230

Wales, 204, 232

Wales, Prince and Princess of, 44, 55, 69, 134, 192

Wallace, Lady (fashion queen), 109

Wallace, William (patriot), 75, 97, 131, 132, 165, 173, 205, 219, 227, 247, 258

wallpaper, 149, 198

Wanlockhead, 26

War-Wolf (siege engine), 30

Wardlaw, Henry (bishop), 96

Wardlaw, Walter (bishop), 71

warfare (*see also* battles *and* World Wars), 18, 50, 60
    air-raids, 31, 65, 71
    awards, 31, 200
    border raids, 33, 54, 92, 131, 233
    civilians, 38, 46, 89, 105, 177, 183, 189, 209, 213
    guerillas, 34, 251
    recruiting, 71, 156, 186, 189, 194, 200, 204
    sieges, 30, 68, 82, 94, 132, 134, 154, 201, 258
    soldiers, 19, 21, 38, 44, 111, 125, 128, 143, 177, 194, 204, 226, 233, 282
    war games, 12, 117, 167, 201, 255
    weapons, 20, 27, 28, 31, 58, 76, 85, 165, 193, 223
    warnings, 52, 66, 174–75

Warwick Vase, 105

water, 52, 90, 139, 145, 150, 159, 206, 219–20

Watson, William (drunk), 120

Watson-Watt, Robert (inventor), 137

Watt, A.P. (literary agent), 251

Watt, James (engineer), 39, 139

Watt, Jim (boxer), 90

Waverley (paddle-steamer), 121

weapons, *see* warfare

weather, 78, 122, 186, 220
    drought, 127
    floods, 24, 156, 168, 173, 195, 199, 209, 216, 228, 258, 259, 263
    frost, 9, 13, 24, 38, 186, 280
    hail, 17, 110, 171, 187
    ice, 17, 32, 48, 156, 238
    rain, 18, 106, 121, 185, 274
    sandstorms, 112
    snow, 9, 27, 37, 41, 176, 192, 276
    storms and wind, 12, 21, 26, 27, 32, 33, 46, 55, 57, 69, 75, 183, 187, 212, 221, 222, 228, 233, 238, 248, 253, 263, 288
    sunshine, 139, 192, 242, 255
    thunder and lightning, 16, 17, 104, 149, 171
    waterspouts, 184

weavers, 54, 80, 93, 194, 209

weddings, *see* marriages

Wells, Alan (sprinter), 222

Wembley Wizards, 76

Wemyss, Countess of (drinker), 90

West Highland Railway, 13

West Indies, 164, 189

Western Isles, 13, 50, 91, 116, 148, 153, 166, 182, 199, 223, 233, 251, 278

whales/whaling, 47, 49, 66, 95, 147, 150, 161, 165, 168, 213, 220, 246, 250, 259

'Whilliwas', 160

whipping/lashing, 44, 50, 55, 58, 89, 216, 251

whisky, *see* drink/drinking

Whiteford, Col. Walter (coffee-shop owner), 227

Wick, 153, 253

Wigton (shire), 108, 261

Wilcox, Al (kiltie comedian), 217

wild west, 14

Wilkie, Prof. William (academic), 186

William the Lion (king), 36, 43, 75, 83, 92, 155, 160, 170, 177, 206, 227, 260, 274, 277

William of Orange (king), 13, 59, 68, 116, 160

Williamson, George (swimming instructor), 181

Williamson, William (baker), 16

wills, 95

Wilson, Charles (physicist), 180

Wilson, Daniel (antiquarian), 112

Wilson, James (immigrant), 193

Wilson, James (radical), 194

wind, *see* weather

wine, *see* drink/drinking

Wishart, Robert (bishop), 30

witches/witchcraft, 11, 26, 45, 53, 81, 83, 101, 110, 113, 121, 129, 166, 167, 169–70, 177, 186, 202, 207, 216, 219, 244, 286

Witt, Jacob de (artist), 66

'Wolf of Badenoch' (Alexander Stewart), 137

wolves, 225, 243

Wood, Dr Alexander (eccentric), 59

Wood, Sir Andrew (swashbuckler), 143, 178

Woodcock, Willie (coach operator), 217

woodcutters, 81

Woodward, Val (chairperson), 166

wool, *see* sheep

work, *see* employment

World Wars, First and Second, 22, 31, 42, 65, 71, 85, 103, 107, 108, 111, 121, 138, 139, 143, 148, 173, 196, 230, 244, 247–48, 259, 271, 287

wrecking, 205, 251

writing/poetry, 27, 28, 33, 54, 97, 111, 120, 122, 163, 171, 182, 210

young people, 12, 18, 42, 70, 101, 193

'Young Pretender', *see* Bonnie Prince Charlie

Young, James (gambler), 23

youth organisations, 28, 91, 222

Yuill, James, (minister), 12

Zeppelins, 31

zoos, 47, 60, 187